Using QuarkXPress 4.0

Online Services

Delmar Online
To access a wide variety of Delmar products and services on the World Wide Web, point your browser to:

http://www.delmar.com
or email: info@delmar.com

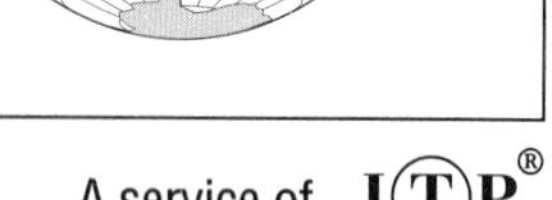

thomson.com
To access International Thomson Publishing's home site for information on more than 34 publishers and 20,000 products, point your browser to:

http://www.thomson.com
or email: findit@kiosk.thomson.com

A service of I(T)P®

Using QuarkXPress 4.0

Suzanne Sayegh Thomas

an International Thomson Publishing company I(T)P®

Albany • Bonn • Boston • Cincinnati • Detroit • London • Madrid
Melbourne • Mexico City • New York • Pacific Grove • Paris •
San Francisco • Singapore • Tokyo • Toronto • Washington

NOTICE TO THE READER

Publisher does not warrant or guarantee any of the products described herein or perform any independent analysis in connection with any of the product information contained herein. Publisher does not assume, and expressly disclaims, any obligation to obtain and include information other than that provided to it by the manufacturer.

The reader is expressly warned to consider and adopt all safety precautions that might be indicated by the activities herein and to avoid all potential hazards. By following the instructions contained herein, the reader willingly assumes all risks in connection with such instructions.

The publisher makes no representation or warranties of any kind, including but not limited to, the warranties of fitness for particular purpose or merchantability, nor are any such representations implied with respect to the material set forth herein, and the publisher takes no responsibility with respect to such material. The publisher shall not be liable for any special, consequential, or exemplary damages resulting, in whole or part, from the readers' use of, or reliance upon, this material.

Cover design and art by Nicole Reamer

Delmar Staff:

Publisher, Alar Elken

Production Manager, Larry Main

Art Director, Nicole Reamer

Printed in Canada

For more information, contact:
Delmar Publishers
3 Columbia Circle, Box 15015
Albany, New York 12212-5015

International Thomson Publishing Europe
Berkshire House 168-173 • High Holborn
London, WC1V7AA

International Thomson Editores
Campos Eliseos 385, Piso 7 • Col Polanco 11560 Mexico
D F Mexico

International Thomson Publishing GmbH
Königswinterer Strasse 418 • 53227
Bonn • Germany

Thomas Nelson Australia
102 Dodds Street • 221 Henderson Road
South Melbourne, 3205 • Victoria, Australia

International Thomson Publishing Asia
#05-10 Henderson Building • Singapore 0315

Nelson Canada
1120 Birchmont Road • Scarborough, Ontario
Canada M1K 5G4

International Thomson Publishing - Japan
Hirakawacho Kyowa Building, 3F
2-2-1 Hirakawacho
Chiyoda-ku, Tokyo 102 • Japan

4 5 6 7 8 9 10 XXX 01 00 99

Library of Congress Cataloging-in-Publication Data
Thomas, Suzanne Sayegh
QuarkXPress 4.0 / Suzanne Sayegh Thomas.
p. cm.
ISBN 0-8273-7815-7
1. QuarkXPress (Computer file) 2. Desktop publishing. I. Title.
Z253.532.Q37T47 1998 98-12996
686.2 ' 2544536--dc21 CIP

DEDICATION

For my daughters, Elizabeth and Katherine,
who have brought me more joy than any success or achievement.
Their love is worth a billion books.

Preface

Image from *Business Characters*
by Susan LeVan, for Artville

Perhaps more than any earlier release of QuarkXPress, version 4.0 arrived with a reputation for being a tough program to learn. The suite of Bézier graphics tools and long document functions, along with a revamped interface, made many experienced XPress users wary of upgrading to a program they had learned, often with difficulty and at considerable expense. But like earlier versions, this new and dramatic release has something for everyone. Designers will enjoy the ease of creating PostScript artwork within QuarkXPress; publishers will appreciate the ability to create a table of contents and index within a series of documents, as well as come to rely on the Book function which ensures uniformity of styles throughout multiple documents; and writers, especially technical writers who have long understood that QuarkXPress is the easiest and most powerful word processor available, will enjoy the new tabbed interface that allows them to make multiple text and graphics selections with one command. So, even though there is much to learn with this new version, users will find the same intuitive interface, the same (if expanded) menu options, and the same speed and efficiency with which QuarkXPress has always dealt with text and graphics.

One of the challenges in writing a textbook on QuarkXPress 4.0 was to translate the 900-page manual that ships with the program into step-by-step, keystroke-by-keystroke lessons that cover the program's functions. In meeting this challenge, I have begun with functions that relate to familiar word processing commands, such as selecting and formatting text, and then moved on to the more complex functions in XPress. Although the lessons are presented sequentially, once you have mastered the material in the first few lessons, feel free to move around the book. You can work with any lesson without having done the exercises in the previous lessons, because all the necessary commands are explained in each exercise.

In the process of writing and typesetting this book, I have come to appreciate not only the new features in QuarkXPress 4.0, but also the assistance of many people who helped to make it possible. Among those to whom I am most grateful are:

- ❍ Amy Sneltzer, head of the Quark 4.0 Beta team, who was enormously supportive of the project, supplying me with beta versions *and* manuals!
- ❍ Elizabeth Jones, Associate Product Manager at Quark, who generously allowed me to include both Macintosh and Windows demo versions of QuarkXPress 4.0 on the CD-ROM. Thanks also to Kay Christian, Product Manager at Quark, for all her help with the demo versions.
- ❍ Tech support at Quark who were especially diligent and knowledgeable in responding to my many questions about how the new features worked. One of the advantages of writing a Quark book is that you get to work with the remarkably talented people who make up the Quark team.
- ❍ Kathryn Leide, Acquisitions Manager of Artville, who allowed me to reproduce the Artville images in the unit folders. These are high-resolution images created by some of the most talented digital artists in the industry, and using them in the exercises will give you a good feel for how great art can embellish pages.
- ❍ Mark Niemann-Ross, Product Manager of Extensis, for the demo versions of their powerful XTensions. Most of the chapter openers were created using various QX-Effects, and with the demo versions readers will also have the opportunity to work with the unlimited design opportunities they provide.
- ❍ Helen Kornblum, Marketing Director of TESOL (Teachers of English to Speakers of Other Languages), who graciously allowed me to use some of the TESOL Program Book files for the Index review.
- ❍ Joseph Dai of Dai Data, whose photographs provided exciting opportunities for graphics manipulation in QuarkXPress.
- ❍ John Cacchione at Delmar who reviewed the manuscript for Macintosh/Windows terminology and keystrokes.
- ❍ Charles Dickens for *Great Expectations* and for dying within the requirements of copyright law.

Image from *Business Characters* by Susan LeVan, for Artville

Introduction to QuarkXPress 4.0

WELCOME TO QUARKXPRESS 4.0!

QuarkXPress 4.0 represents a radical departure from earlier versions of XPress and from other page layout programs. Before version 4.0, XPress contained powerful tools for styling text and manipulating graphics. Strong typographical functions combined with flexible layout commands have made QuarkXPress the choice of professional typesetters, page layout designers, and graphic artists who learned very early that you can print almost any image from XPress.

With version 4.0 a powerful graphics suite has been added to the typography and layout functions. The ability to draw Bézier lines, paths, and boxes and to create clipping paths around images lets XPress users perform many graphic functions directly in XPress without recourse to dedicated graphic programs. QuarkXPress 4.0 will not replace graphics applications, but will give users wider flexibility within XPress.

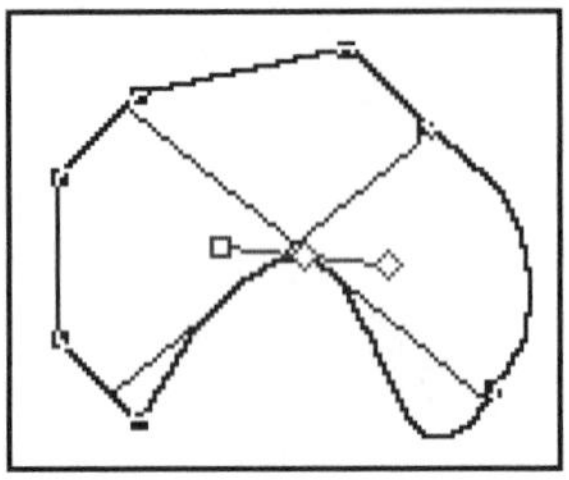

A Bézier shape contains anchor points that display direction handles. Use these points and handles to reshape the item.

Among other new features in version 4.0 are the Book, List, and Index functions, which make the production of long documents far more efficient and error-proof than was possible in earlier versions. Anyone working in the journalism, publishing, or advertising industry will welcome the ability to synchronize multiple project documents and create a table of contents and index within XPress.

If, at first, you feel that there is too much in version 4.0 to learn in this lifetime, relax! You will be learning one function at a time. If you have used earlier versions of XPress, much of the material will be familiar to you. Dialog boxes have changed a little, but it's easier to get to them. Once you're there, you'll not only find that it's easier to navigate to other dialog boxes, but also that the same options are waiting to be selected and modified once you arrive.

USING THIS BOOK

This book is divided into units covering the major functions in QuarkXPress 4.0. It's a good idea to start with the first few chapters to get a feel for how the program works. Once you're comfortable with creating items (boxes and lines) and styling text, you can learn pretty much anything else.

Each unit is divided into lessons that include exercises on the particular function covered in the lesson. Since "perfect practice makes perfect," doing these exercises a few times but changing the values and dimensions of text and objects is a good way to become comfortable with a function. Keep in mind that there is more than one way to accomplish many of the functions in XPress. Some ways may be more elegant than others, but they're not wrong. There are very few wrong things you can do in XPress and breaking the program is not one of them.

At the beginning of each unit is a list of terms covered in the unit. The terms are explained in the text and are defined in the glossary at the end of the book. Learning the meaning of these terms will make you more comfortable with QuarkXPress terminology as it relates to the printing and publishing industries.

Who's in charge here?

The tool you select determines which QuarkXPress commands are available from the Menu. The Style menu, for example, is available only when the Content tool is active and a text box is selected.

MACINTOSH/WINDOWS ISSUES

QuarkXPress 4.0 for Macintosh and Windows behave seamlessly across both platforms. Each platform reads a few different types of graphic formats and installs and accesses printers differently, but the functionality is exactly the same. Even most of the keystrokes are the same—with two exceptions. The Command key on the Macintosh is the Ctrl key in Windows; the Option key on the Macintosh is the Alt key in Windows. That's just about it! Master those two differences and you can work in any shop.

In this book, when you see Alt/Option, Windows users should press the Alt key and Macintosh users should press the Option key. Command/Ctrl works the same way, with Macintosh users pressing the Command key and any other key, while Windows users should press the Ctrl key and any other key. For example Command/Ctrl-M translates as Macintosh users pressing the Command and M keys simultaneously and Windows users pressing the Ctrl and M keys simultaneously. Where keystrokes become more complicated, the full keystroke is given, such as Command-Option-Shift-F (Macintosh) or Ctrl-Alt-Shift-F (Windows). Where Windows users press the Enter key on the keyboard to end a paragraph or select a bordered option in a dialog box, Macintosh users can press the Return and Enter keys interchangeably.

WARNING!

Some fonts may differ in character spacing and sizes between the two platforms; this can cause text reflow, usually in text runarounds. Always check your output from a printed copy. Also, some character sets may differ between platforms, causing characters like bullets and dashes to appear differently in cross-platform documents.

FONT CHOICES

The only two fonts referred to in this text are Times and Helvetica. Windows users can substitute Arial and Times New Roman. Feel free to substitute *any* font installed in your system. It rarely makes any difference which typeface you use, although point size might make a difference in some of the exercises.

Although QuarkXPress for Macintosh OS and QuarkXPress for Windows can read each other's files, font selection for each platform is a significant issue. To avoid conflicts, use the same version of each font from the same font vendor on both platforms.

Hide Tools	F8
Hide Measurements	F9
Show Document Layout	F10
Show Style Sheets	F11
Show Colors	F12
Show Trap Information	⌥F12
Show Lists	⌥F11
Show Index	

The last panel on the View menu lets you show and hide tools and palettes.

MENU BAR CONVENTIONS

Rather than clutter up the text with arrows to direct you to the correct sequence of accessing functions, I've chosen to use the / mark. When you're told, "Choose Style/Font/Helvetica," you should pull down the Style menu at the top of the screen, drag down to select Font, and drag to the right to select Helvetica. Windows users can just click the underlined character to navigate the menus.

TOUGH STUFF

Two areas that can appear complex are printing documents and specifying color. Rather than leave these functions to units at the back of the book so you can spend the whole time living in fear, these functions are covered at various times throughout the unit. The more esoteric color commands are left to a later unit, but methods for creating, editing, and applying color from different color models appear early in the text so you can enjoy using color in your exercises. All the printing functions, however, are covered individually throughout the book, so you can see what your documents look like in the real world.

EXERCISES

Many of the exercises involve working with one or two functions. Unless you're specifically told to save a file, you can close it without saving your changes. However, if the next exercise asks you to open a file without any specific attributes like facing pages or an automatic text box, you can use the same document you created for the previous exercise. Delete the previous items or add a new page to the original document. Otherwise, you're going to get a lot of practice creating new documents.

Tool Preferences

Double-click on any of the item creation tools (such as a box or line tool) to display the Tool Preferences dialog box. Click the Modify button, make your selections, and click on Save. Every item you draw from that point on will reflect the modifications. Items drawn before you made the modifications are not affected.

ACTIVE DOCUMENTS

You can have as many documents open on the desktop as your computer memory allows. However, only one document can be the active document, that is, the document that can be edited, saved, or closed. When an exercise tells you to "Activate the Newsletter document," for example, click on the title bar at the top of the page that displays the document's name to activate the document. Any editing now occurs in that (selected) document.

PROJECTS FOLDER

Before you begin working with this book, create a file called something like Projects or My Work on your hard drive or on an external drive. When you save working files from the exercises, save them to this folder, because you won't be able to save them to the CD-ROM.

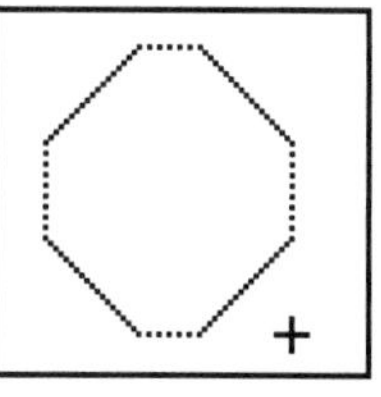

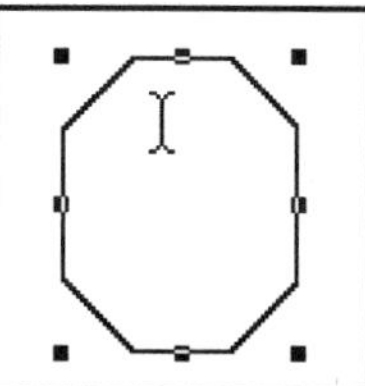

Select any standard-shape text box tool and drag the crosshair pointer to create the text box. When you release the mouse button, the blinking I-beam text cursor appears inside the text box, indicating that you can type in that box. You can only type in a text box, not on the blank page.

LAUNCHING QUARKXPRESS 4.0

If you have installed QuarkXPress properly, the QuarkXPress 4.0 folder should be on your hard drive. Double-click on that folder and scroll to locate the QuarkXPress application icon. Double-click on that icon to launch the program. Only two things appear on the screen, a menu bar and a tool palette.

THINKING IN BOXES

Before using any tools in QuarkXPress, you have to understand how text and graphics live in a document. Every text character must be typed in or imported into a text box—any kind of text box—or typed on a text path. You can't have text flowing on the pasteboard or on a blank page. You must first create and select the text box or text path, then type or import the text.

Pictures must be imported into picture boxes. You don't have to have a border around the box, and you can apply a color or no color to the background of the box, but you must have a picture box selected before you can bring a graphic into an XPress document.

OPENING AND SAVING FILES

The data and graphics files on the CD-ROM cannot be saved to the CD-ROM. If you open a file from the CD-ROM, you won't be able to save it to the CD-ROM. Before beginning work on a unit, drag the unit folder to your hard drive. Open the file in QuarkXPress or import a graphic or text file from the folder on your hard drive and save it to your Projects folder, also on the hard drive or on an external drive. If you inadvertently overwrite the file, you can always get the original from the CD-ROM.

FYI

The Type menu (Macintosh) and Version menu (Windows) in the Save as dialog box lets you save 4.0 documents in 3.3 format so they can be opened in earlier versions of QuarkXPress. If you plan to open files in QuarkXPress for Windows version 3.3 or 3.31 running on Windows 3.11, limit the file name to eight characters and use the appropriate file name extension for documents (*.qxd) or templates (*.qxt).

Windows info

If you find that file extensions are not displaying, check your Windows Explorer settings. The Windows documentation provides instructions for displaying file extensions if they are not visible.

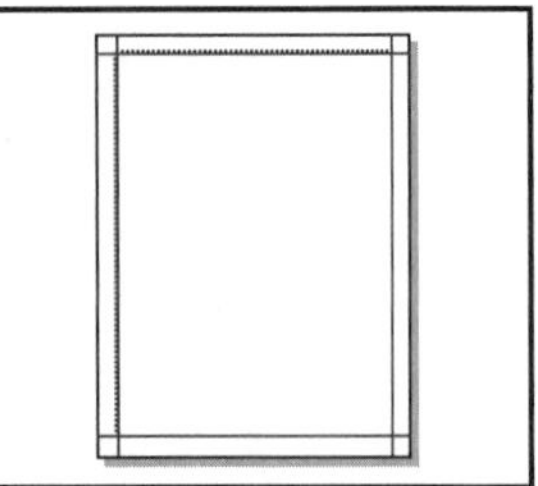

The area inside the page area, including the margin guides, is the printable area. The white area beyond the page is the pasteboard. Items on the pasteboard do not print.

MENU COMMANDS

Menu commands like Ctrl-O (File/Open) or Command-S (File/Save) are printed at the top of most pages where exercises reference those commands. Macintosh and Windows commands appear in separate areas, making it easier for you to practice using them.

FILE EXTENSIONS

When saving files, always use the correct file extension. For example, when saving a QuarkXPress document, add the .qxd extension to label it as a QuarkXPress document or .txt to indicate that the file is a text file. Graphic files should also be saved with identifying extensions such as .tiff or .jpeg for TIFF and JPEG files. This makes it easier for you and for anyone accessing your files to know what they are, as well as labeling your files according to usual industry practice. You do want to make money using QuarkXPress, don't you?

KEYBOARD SHORTCUTS

QuarkXPress contains hundreds of commands, most of which can be accessed from the function keys at the top of the keyboard or by typing keyboard shortcuts. For example, pressing Command/Ctrl-N to create a new document, saves you the work of moving the mouse to the top of the page, dragging down on the File menu, dragging down to select New, and dragging over to select Document. Instead, with one keystroke you can display the New Document dialog box. Likewise, pressing F9 on the function keypad displays or hides the Measurements palette without requiring you to do so from the View menu. Learning and using the keyboard and function key shortcuts will have you working more easily and efficiently in XPress. You will find most of them in the sidebar of the lessons when they occur in an exercise.

PASTEBOARD

Two areas constitute a QuarkXPress page, the printable area that exists between the page guides and the pasteboard. The pasteboard is the white, non-printing area that surrounds a page or page spread. Nothing entirely on the pasteboard will print, so you can use it to store items (boxes, lines, groups, and text paths) while you're working on a page. If you're creating a bleed (text or graphics that run off the page), the bleed area will print, but nothing that is entirely on the pasteboard will print.

VIEWING PAGES

There are three ways to view your pages at different levels of magnification. Click with the Zoom tool to enlarge or reduce the document view. Or, enter a custom percentage in the View Percent field in the lower left corner of the document page. And you can always select a specified viewing percentage from the View menu.

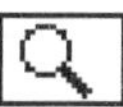

Zoom tool

ZOOM TOOL

Using the Zoom tool does not change the size of text or items, just the view of those elements. The Zoom tool defaults to increasing the magnification level in 25% increments, but you can change this value in the Tool Preferences dialog box. You can access the Zoom tool when another tool is active by pressing the Control key (Macintosh) or Ctrl-Spacebar (Windows). Keep it pressed while zooming in on the page. Each time you click, you increase the view percentage by the Increment amount specified in the Tool Preferences dialog box (Edit/Preferences/Document/Tool). Pressing the Option key (Macintosh) or the Ctrl-Alt-Spacebar keys (Windows) while clicking with the Zoom tool reduces the view percentages.

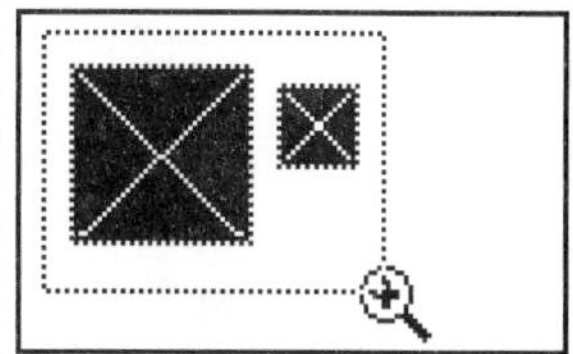

Click and drag with the Zoom tool to select all items within the zoom marquee.

VIEW PERCENT FIELD

Either drag to select the value in the View Percent field in the lower left corner of the document window or press Control-V (Macintosh) or Ctrl-Alt-V (Windows) to highlight the current value. Type any value between 10 and 800 and press the Return key to change the view percentage. You don't have to type the % sign.

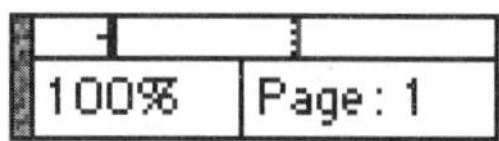

View Percent field in the lower left corner of the document window.

VIEW MENU

Use the View menu to select specified viewing percentages. Select Fit in Window to scale the view to center and fit the entire page in the document window, regardless of the size of your screen. To fit the largest spread and its pasteboard in the document window, press the Alt/Option key before selecting Fit in Window.

Hide Guides	F7
Show Baseline Grid	⌥F7
✓Snap to Guides	⇧F7
Hide Rulers	⌘R
Show Invisibles	⌘I

These·are→ invisibles.¶

Use these options under the View menu to hide and display guides and rulers and to show and hide Invisibles, the invisible text codes XPress inserts when you type. The dot between the words indicates that the Spacebar was pressed; the arrow, that the Tab key was pressed, and the ¶ mark that the Return key was pressed at the end of a paragraph.

DOCUMENT WINDOWS

On the Macintosh, select Windows under the View menu and choose either Stack Documents or Tile Documents when you have more than one document open. Stack Documents layers multiple documents, displaying only a portion of each document. Tile Documents resizes all open document windows so that equal portions of each document are displayed on the screen. Below these options are listed the names of all the open documents. In Windows '95, you can use the Windows menu to select Cascade, Tile Horizontally, or Tile Vertically.

View Style Item Page
Fit in Window Ctrl+0
50%
75%
✔ Actual Size Ctrl+1
200%
Thumbnails
Hide Guides
Show Baseline Grid
✔ Snap to Guides
Hide Rulers Ctrl+R
Show Invisibles Ctrl+I
Hide Tools
Show Measurements
Show Document Layout
Show Style Sheets
Show Colors
Show Trap Information

Most viewing options under the View menu can be accessed with keyboard shortcuts. Thumbnails view is a non-editing view; you can move pages within a document or to and from documents, but you cannot edit anything on the pages.

Tools missing?

If the Tool palette doesn't appear, choose View/Show Tools to display it or press F8.

Big tip

To temporarily change the Content tool—or any item-creation tool—to the Item tool, press the Command/Ctrl key until you have finished moving the item.

TOOL PALETTE

The QuarkXPress 4.0 tool palette (Figure 0.1) contains tools for creating and editing items (boxes, lines, text paths) and contents (text and graphics). Display the default Tool palette by choosing View/Show Tools (F8). Select a tool by clicking on it. The tool remains active while you use it. Only the Item tool and Content tool remain active (selected) after use.

TOOLS

The QuarkXPress 4.0 default tool palette contains fourteen visible tools and fourteen pop-out tools. An arrow next to a tool indicates that there are pop-out tools associated with the displayed tool. Click on the arrow to see the other available tools.

DEFAULT TOOL PALETTE

The **Item tool** is used to select, move, resize, and reshape items—boxes, lines, text paths, and groups are items.

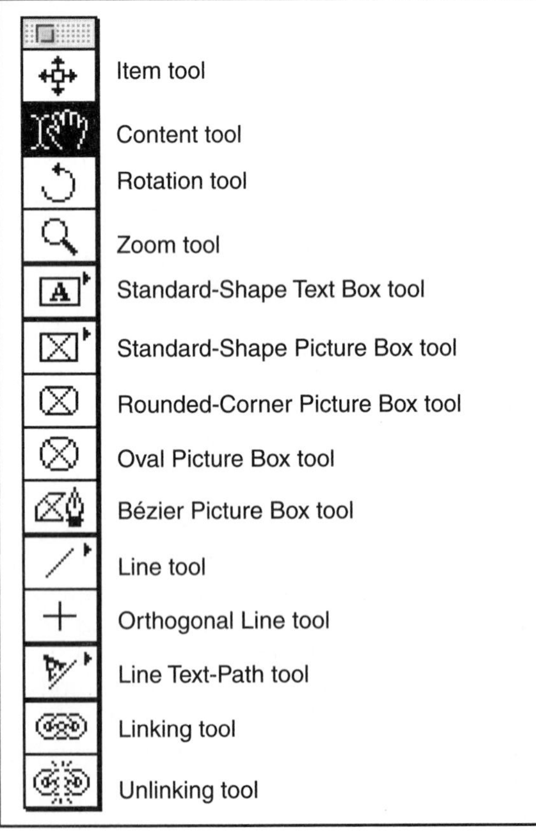

Figure 0.1. The QuarkXPress 4.0 default Tool palette.

Content tool imports and edits text and graphics.

Rotation tool rotates items visually.

Zoom tool enlarges or reduces the document view.

Text Box tool (standard-shape) creates a rectangular text box. It also provides access to other text box tools.

Picture Box tool (standard-shape) creates a rectangular picture box. It also provides access to other picture box tools.

Line tool draws lines at any angle. It also provides access to other line tools.

Orthogonal Line tool draws only horizontal or vertical lines.

Line Text-Path tool creates a straight line at any angle that contains text. It also provides access to other text-path tools.

Linking tool links text chains to flow text among text boxes.

Unlinking tool breaks links among linked text boxes.

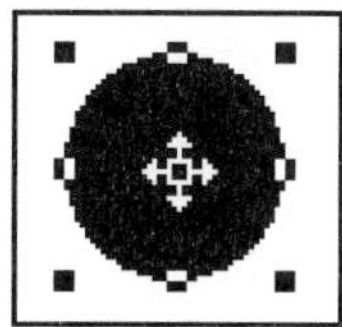

The Item tool, the first tool in the Tool palette, displays the Move pointer when placed on a selected item. The Item tool is also used to select items such as boxes and lines.

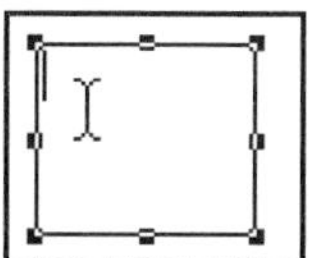

When the Content tool is active, you can type in any kind of text box.

ITEM TOOL

In QuarkXPress, *items* are boxes, lines, text paths, and groups. Select the Item tool to move, cut, copy, and paste items. Clicking on an item with the Item tool selects it. An item must be selected before it can modified by any tool or command. Once an item is selected, it can be moved with the Item tool without resizing or reshaping it.

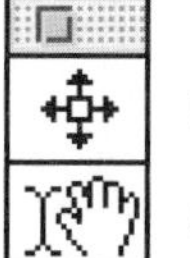

Item tool

Content tool

Before you can delete an item such as a box, line, group, or text path, you must select the item. If you use the Item tool, you can delete the item with the Delete key (Macintosh) or either the Delete or Backspace keys (Windows). Otherwise, when an item is selected with another tool, you must use the Item/Delete command.

CONTENT TOOL

When the Content tool is active (selected), you can cut, copy, paste, clear, and edit text and pictures. The Content tool must be active before you can type in a text box or import text into any text box.

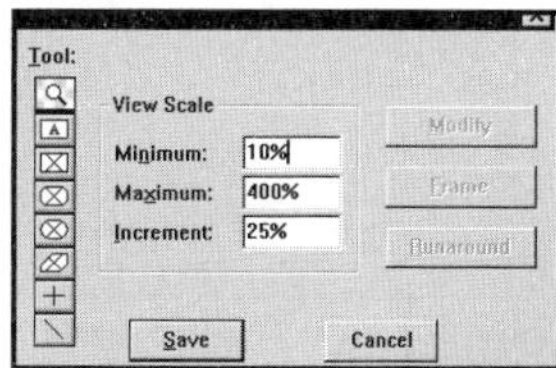

Clicking the Tool tab in the General Document Preferences dialog box lets you customize the viewing scale for the document. If you display this dialog box when no documents are open, your changes will apply to every document you work with in XPress.

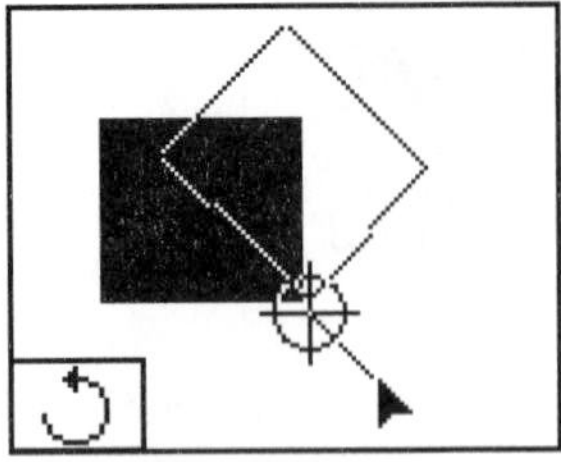

Clicking on a resizing handle with the Rotation tool specifies that point as the point of rotation.

ROTATION TOOL

When you select this tool, the pointer changes to the Rotation pointer. Click on any resizing handle of a selected item and drag to rotate the item visually. Once you start dragging, the Rotation pointer changes to the Arrowhead pointer. The longer the handle you drag out, the easier it is to rotate the item. Once you release the mouse button, the cursor reverts to the Item tool or to the Content tool.

The Freehand Text Box tool creates text boxes in any shape by dragging the crosshair pointer.

STANDARD-SHAPE VS. BÉZIER TOOLS

The standard-shape tools are the conventional drawing tools used to create items with resizing handles. You can't arbitrarily reshape these items, only resize them. Any reshaping is limited to the options under the Shape menu (Item/Shape) if the Shape command is selected (Item/Edit/Shape).

Bézier items, however, contain Bézier points—what the rest of the world calls anchor points—that can be edited and deleted. Anchor points can also be added to an item, making it possible to shape it any way you want.

Any standard-shape item can be converted to a Bézier item via the Shape menu. Once you do that, the item displays the Bézier points and allows you to reshape the item by dragging the points and the direction handles that the points display.

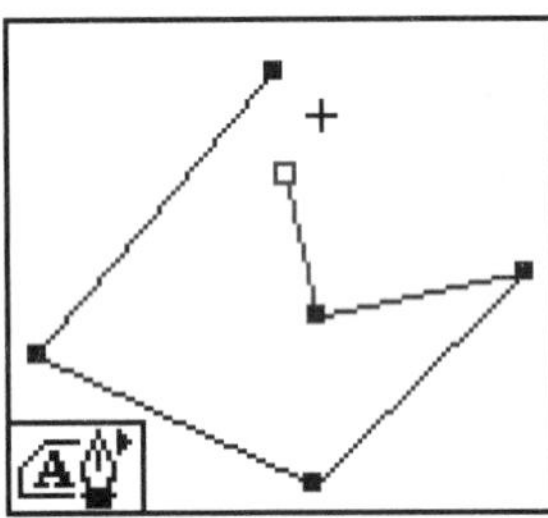

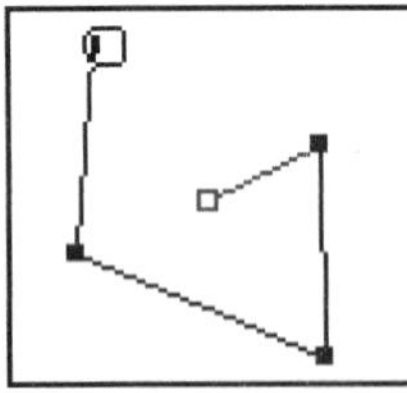

Click with the Bézier Text Box tool to create text boxes of any shape. Click on top of the first Bézier point to close the shape.

TEXT BOX POP-OUT TOOLS

The first three Text Box pop-out tools are also standard-shape text box tools (Figure 0.2). The Rounded-Corner Text Box tool creates rectangular boxes with curved corners. The Concave-Corner Text Box tool creates rectangular text boxes with corners rounded inward. The Beveled-Corner Text Box tool creates rectangular text boxes with beveled corners. The Oval Text Box tool creates oval or circular text boxes. To use these tools, click on the tool to select it.

Icon	Tool
A	Standard-Shape Text Box tool
A	Freehand Text Box tool
A	Bézier Text Box tool
A	Oval Text Box tool
A	Concave-Corner text box tool
A	Beveled-Corner text box tool
A	Rounded-Corner text box tool

Figure 0.2. The standard-shape and Bézier Text Box tools.

The Bézier Text Box tool creates a text box of any desired shape. Unlike the standard-shape tools, you don't click and drag with this tool. Click to set the first Bézier point, release the mouse button and move to another area, click to create a second Bézier point and a line between those two Bézier points. Click on top of the first Bézier point to close the box. Figure 0.2 displays the standard-shape and Bézier Text Box tools.

The Freehand Text Box tool works like a pencil. Click and drag to draw any shape. When you close the shape, the I-beam cursor appears, allowing you to type inside the text box.

PICTURE BOX POP-OUT TOOLS

Picture boxes are used to hold graphics that you import into XPress. The first two Picture Box pop-out tools, the Concave-Corner and Beveled-Corner picture box tools, draw picture boxes with corners rounded inward and outward, respectively. The Freehand Picture Box tool draws picture boxes in any shape. Unlike dragging with the other Picture Box tools to create a picture box, use the Freehand Picture Box tool as a pencil to draw irregularly shaped picture boxes. Figure 0.3 displays the standard-shape and Bézier Picture Box tools.

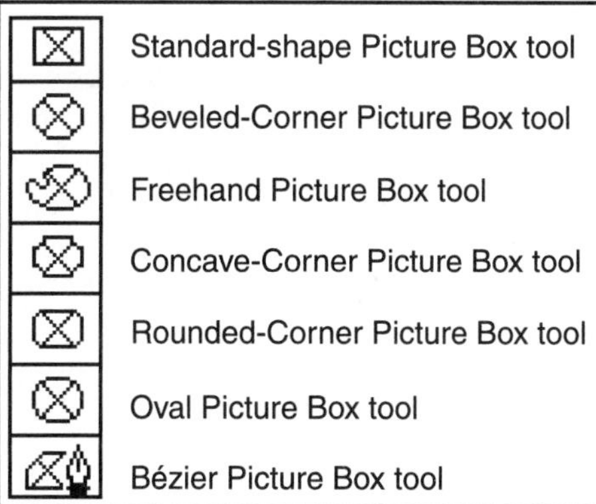

Figure 0.3. The Standard-Shape and Bézier Picture Box tools. The Freehand Picture Box tool creates Bézier picture boxes in any shape.

LINE TOOL POP-OUT TOOLS

Line tools create lines, or open items. Any open item in XPress is called a *line*. Any closed item such as a box is called a *shape*. Use the Orthogonal Line tool to draw only horizontal or vertical lines. The Line tool, however, can draw straight lines at any angle. Figure 0.4 displays the standard-shape and Bézier Line tools.

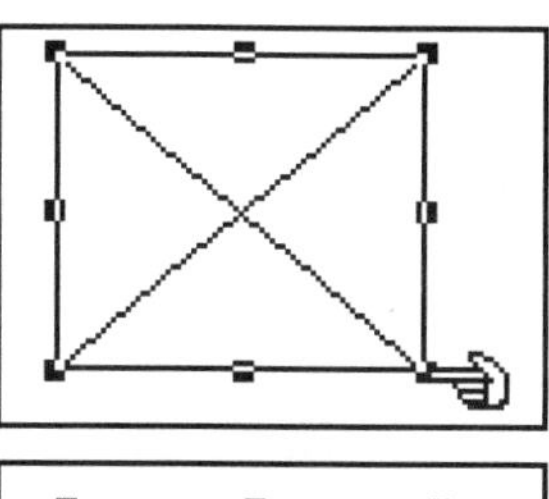

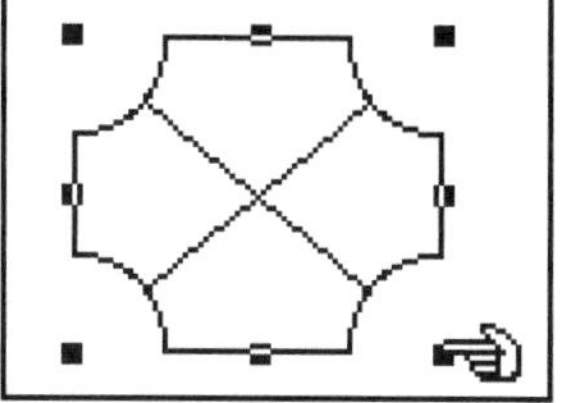

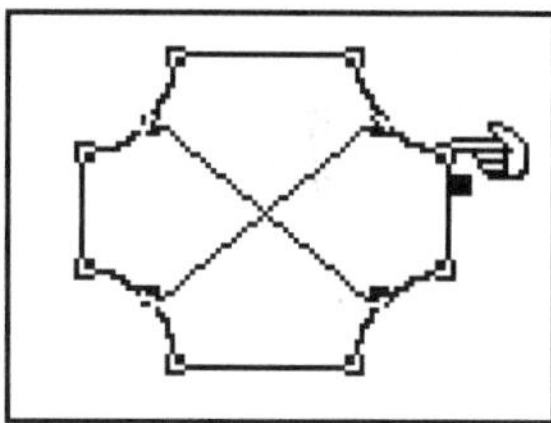

The standard-shape picture box (top) contains only eight resizing handles. Changing its shape from the Item menu (center) still limits the shaping to what you can do with the eight resizing handles. Converting the standard-shape box to a Bézier box (bottom) replaces the eight resizing handles with Bézier points that can be reshaped in any direction.

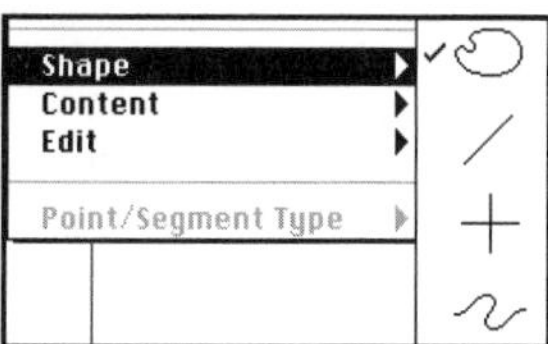

Selecting the Bézier shape from the Shape menu converts the selected item to a Bézier item.

Use the Freehand Picture Box tool to draw irregularly shaped picture boxes around graphics.

The Bézier Line tool draws lines with Bézier points that can be manipulated to change the shape of the line. Like the Bézier Text Box tool and Bézier Picture Box tool, you click with the Bézier Line tool to create the first Bézier point, move to another area, and click to create the second point and the line between the two points. When you have finished dragging the line, click on any other tool to deselect the Bézier Line tool.

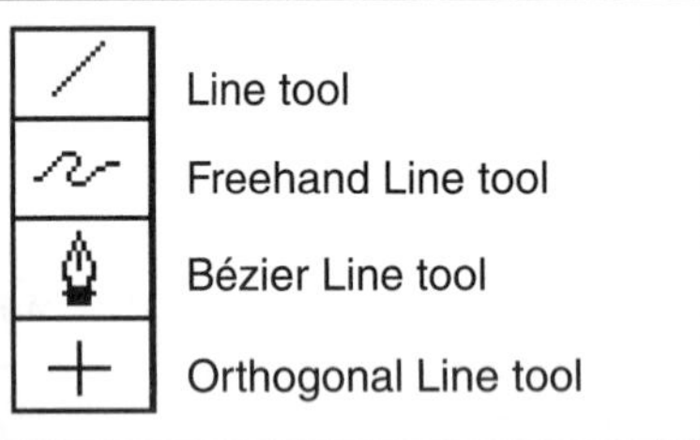

Figure 0.4. The Standard-Shape and Bézier Line tools.

The Freehand Line tool works like a pencil. Click and drag once and draw the line. Click on any other tool to deselect the Bézier Freehand Line tool. Select the Item tool or Content tool and click and drag on any of the Bézier points or direction handles to reshape the line.

Sticky tool

Press the Alt/Option key before selecting a tool to keep it active until you select another tool.

TEXT-PATH POP-OUT TOOLS

All text must be typed in or imported into some kind of text box or typed on a text path. The four Text-Path tools (Figure 0.5) include the Freehand Text-Path tool, which works like a pencil and creates an irregularly shaped text path; the Line Text-Path tool, used to create text on a line at any angle; the Orthogonal Text-Path tool, used to create horizontal or vertical text paths; and the Bézier Text-Path tool, for creating Bézier text paths that can be reshaped by dragging the Bézier points and control handles. After drawing with any of these tools, click on any other tool in the Tool palette to display the I-beam text cursor on the path you just drew.

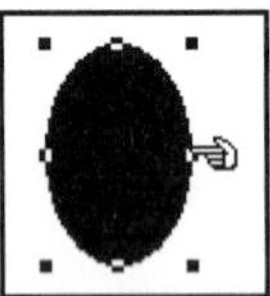

Clicking on a resizing handle with either the Content tool or the Item tool changes the cursor to the Resizing pointer.

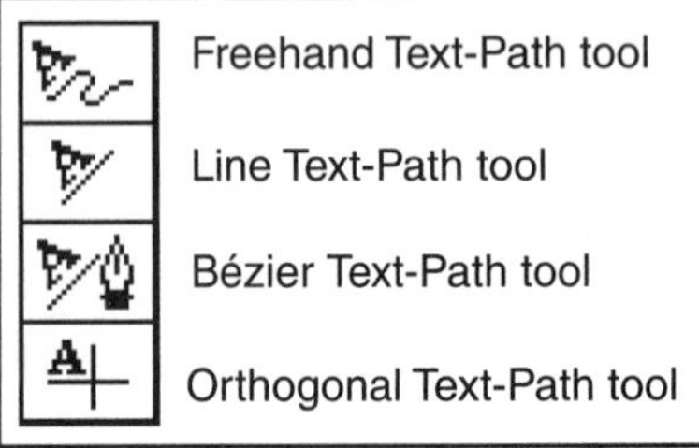

Figure 0.5. The Text-Path tools.

LINKING AND UNLINKING TOOLS

Because all text in XPress must be typed in a text box, typed on a text path, or imported into a text box, you may need more than one text box to hold all the text. In this case, you want the text to flow properly from one text box to another. In other words, you want the text boxes linked. If you create a new document with the Automatic Text Box options selected, XPress will automatically flow the text from the text box on one page to the text box on the subsequent pages. The text is automatically linked because the text boxes are linked. If you don't select the Automatic Text Box option in the New Document dialog box, or if you want the text in an automatic text box to flow somewhere other than to the text box on the next page, you will have to link those text boxes manually with the Linking tool. To unlink any text box from its text chain, use the Unlinking tool.

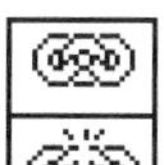

Linking tool

Unlinking tool

The Linking tool (top) is used to link text from one text box to another. The Unlinking tool (bottom) breaks the link between linked text boxes.

PLAY TIME

QuarkXPress is basically an electronic playground filled with dozens of toys like text, graphics, design, and layout functions. Use these tools (Figure 0.6) and commands to create spectacular pages that communicate information in an orderly, intelligent, and exciting manner. Take your time in learning how to use these functions; some are amazingly simple, but even the more complex ones can be mastered with a little practice. The important thing is to take each function step-by-step. Repeat an exercise that you found difficult and soon you'll find yourself doing things automatically while concentrating on learning something new. Enjoy experimenting with different text and graphics commands. You can't break the program and you'll be surprised at what you will learn. Like thousands of students before you, you'll find yourself becoming a devoted—and talented—"Quarkie."

Square off!

Pressing the Shift key while drawing with any of the standard-shape rectangle box tools creates a square. Pressing the Shift key while drawing with any of the oval box tools creates a circle.

FYI

To add any pop-out tool to the Tool palette, press the Control key (Macintosh) or Ctrl key (Windows) while you click and drag to select a tool from the pop-out tools.

FYI

Press Command-Tab (Macintosh) or Ctrl-Alt-Tab (Windows) to select the tool below the selected tool; press Command-Shift-Tab (Macintosh) or Ctrl-Alt-Shift-Tab (Windows) to select the tool above the currently selected tool.

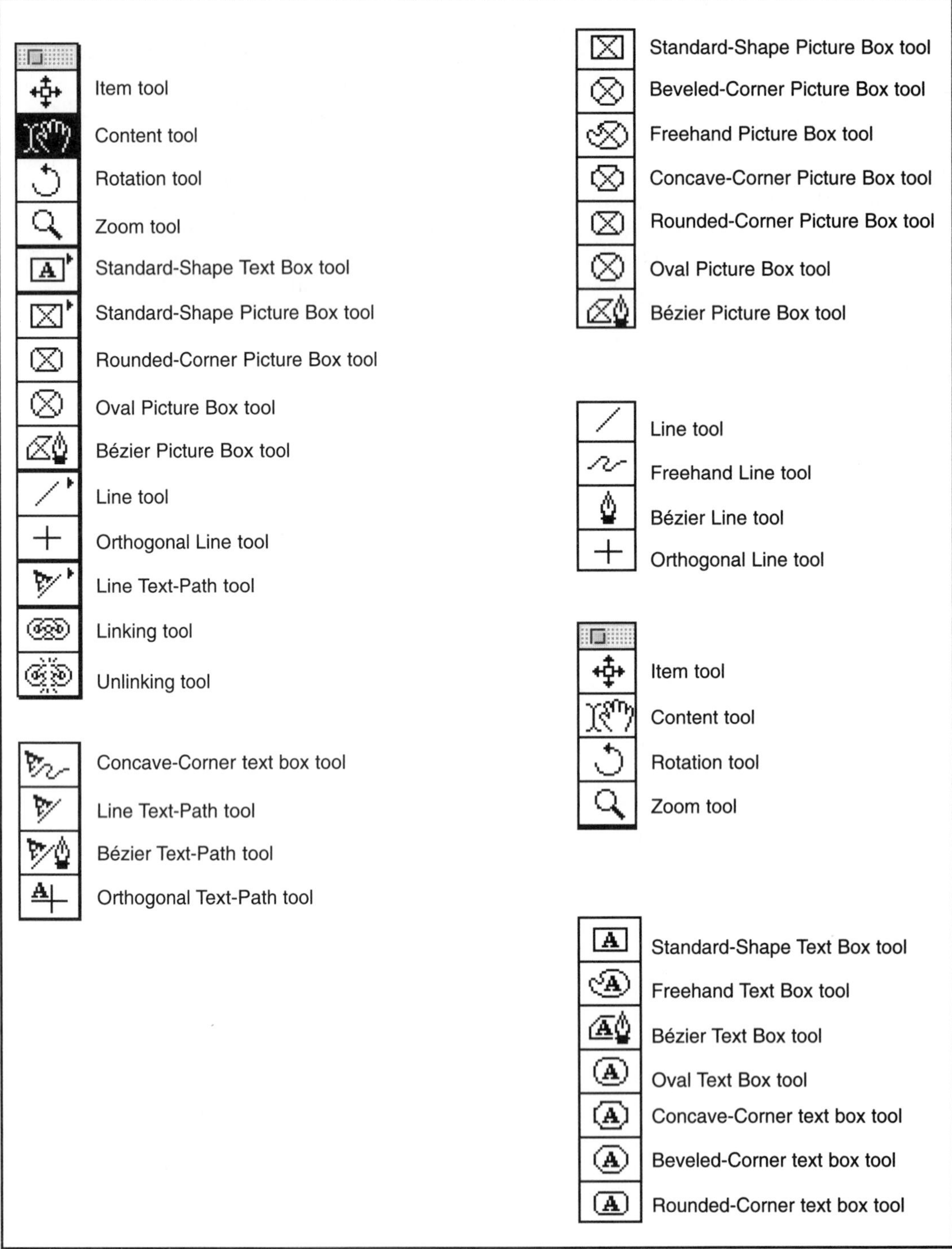

Figure 0.6. The QuarkXPress 4.0 Tool palette.

UNIT 1 Working with QuarkXPress Files

Image from *Business Characters* by Susan LeVan, for Artville

OVERVIEW

In this unit you will learn how to:
Create a new document
Specify margins and columns
Import text
Style text
Open, close, and save documents
Edit text
Set application preferences

TERMS

automatic text box
Clear
Clipboard
Copy
Cut
Document Layout palette
facing pages
greek
master page
non-facing pages
Open
orientation
Paste
preview
Revert to Saved
Save
Save as

HOW IT WORKS:

In Photoshop, change the mode of the image from RGB to Grayscale, reduce it to the size of the QuarkXPress picture box, and save it as a JPEG file. Use the Bézier Text-Path tool to draw a text box around the "artwork" inside the frame. Set the type inside the Bézier text box, color it white, and center it in the irregularly shaped text box. Give the box a background of None to make it transparent against the image. Set the Unit type in a standard-shape text box with a background of None.

Orientation: 

Portrait orientation (selected) prints from the top to the bottom of the page. Landscape orientation prints from the left to right sides of the page.

Column Guides
Columns: 1
Gutter Width: 0.167"

Specify the number of columns for a new document in the Column Guides field. You can always change the number of columns on any document page or on a master page later on.

FYI

No matter which unit of measure you specify in the Measurements palette or in any of the dialog boxes, XPress always displays the Width and Height values of a page in inches in the New Document dialog box.

Tip

If you are saddle-stitching or hole-punching your pages in a facing pages document, make the inside margin a little larger to accommodate the binding or holes.

LESSON 1
CREATING A NEW DOCUMENT

A new document is created from the File menu (File/New/Document) or by pressing the keyboard shortcut keys, Command-N (Macintosh) or Ctrl-N (Windows). When you choose File/New/Document, the New Document dialog box appears (Figure 1.1). It contains four areas: the Page area where you specify page size and orientation; the Margin Guides area where you specify the margin sizes and whether this will be a facing pages document with printing on both sides of the page (as in a book or newsletter); the Column Guides area where you specify the number of columns in the document and the distance between multiple columns; and the Automatic Text Box option where you can tell XPress to create a text box automatically on the first page of the document and on all subsequent pages based on that master page.

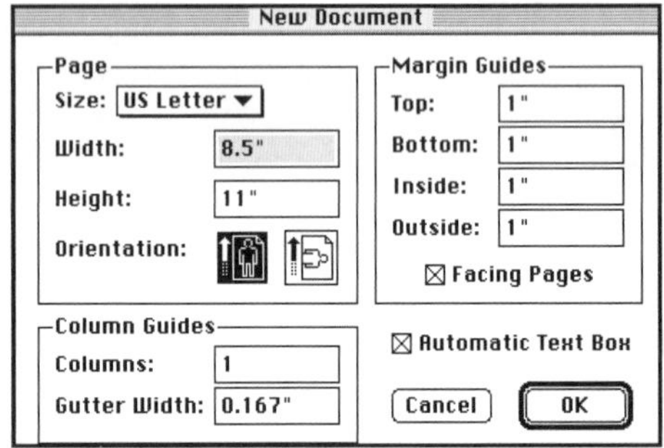

Figure 1.1. The New Document dialog box is where you specify the size and type of pages in the document, margin width, and number of columns. If the document is to be printed on both sides of the paper, select the Facing Pages option. If you will be importing text into the document, select the Automatic Text Box option.

PAGE SIZE

The Page Size option refers to the size of the paper you will be printing on. If you create a document with a specific page size in the New Document dialog box, you can change the page size later as long as the new page size is large enough to accommodate all the text and graphics elements you have already created. To change the page size, select Document Setup from the File menu and select a new size from the Size pull-down menu. You can also change the Width and Height dimensions for any page size.

IMPORTING TEXT

Because QuarkXPress is primarily a page layout program, one that marries text to graphics, getting the text into XPress is an important task. All text in XPress, whether it's imported from a text file, copied and pasted from another document, or typed directly into an XPress document, must be typed in a text box, imported into a text box, or typed on a text path. You can't have text floating around a page as you do in an illustration program. Text can only live in XPress in a text box or on a text path. To import text into a selected text box, choose File/Get Text and navigate to a text file or to a word processor file. XPress ships with filters for the most popular word processors. Drag the appropriate filters to the XTension folder before launching XPress and you will be able to import files from those word processors. You can import ASCII text files directly into a selected picture box.

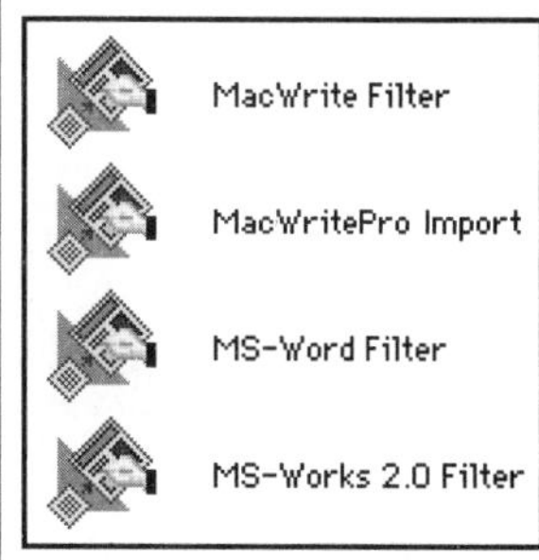

Some of the Macintosh word processor filters that ship with QuarkXPress 4.0. Similar filters ship with the Windows version.

AUTOMATIC TEXT BOX OPTION

When you create a new document, two things happen automatically: A single master page called Master Page A is created and a single document page based on that master page is also created. This means that every newly created QuarkXPress document comes into this world with one master page and one document page. If you're creating a text-intensive document like a book chapter or magazine article, select the Automatic Text Box option. When you select the Automatic Text Box option in the New Document dialog box, you tell XPress to create a text box automatically on that default Master Page A. And because the default document page 1 is based on Master Page A, it will also have a text box. It's a genetic thing. If both parents have black eyes and black hair, the offspring will have black eyes and black hair. Any default document page takes on the characteristics of the default master page.

Where text comes from

Text can be typed directly into a text box or imported from another application like a word processor, provided the filter for that word processor is present in the XTensions folder in the QuarkXPress folder.

Furthermore, if you select the Automatic Text Box option, not only will the default document page 1 display a text box, but every new page you insert in the document that is based on that default Master Page A will have an automatic text box. For example, if you want page numbers and a logo to appear on every page in the document, you would create a smaller text box and enter the command for consecutive page numbers. Then create or import the logo onto Master Page A. With Automatic Text Box selected, if you import or type more text than will fit into the text box on the first page, any pages that XPress adds will automatically contain a text box into which the additional text will flow, as well as any other items like the page number box and the logo (Figure 1.2).

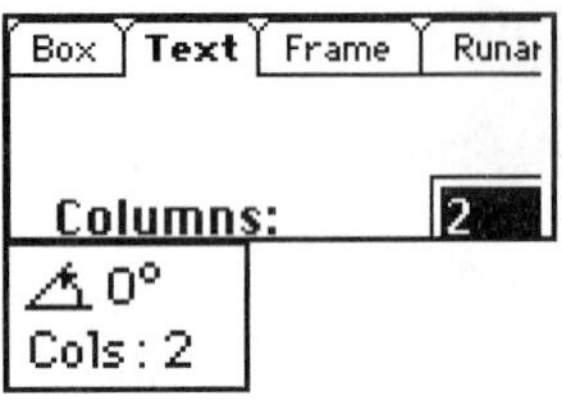

Type a number in the Cols field of the Measurements palette (F10), or in the Columns field of the Text Modify tab of the Item/ Modify box to change the number of columns on any selected text box.

Think like XPress

Don't forget that all text in XPress must be positioned inside a text box. You can't create type anywhere on the page unless you create a text box to hold the text.

FYI

Unless you trash the XPress Preferences file in the QuarkXPress 4.0 folder, the default values in the New Document dialog box reflect the last options you selected.

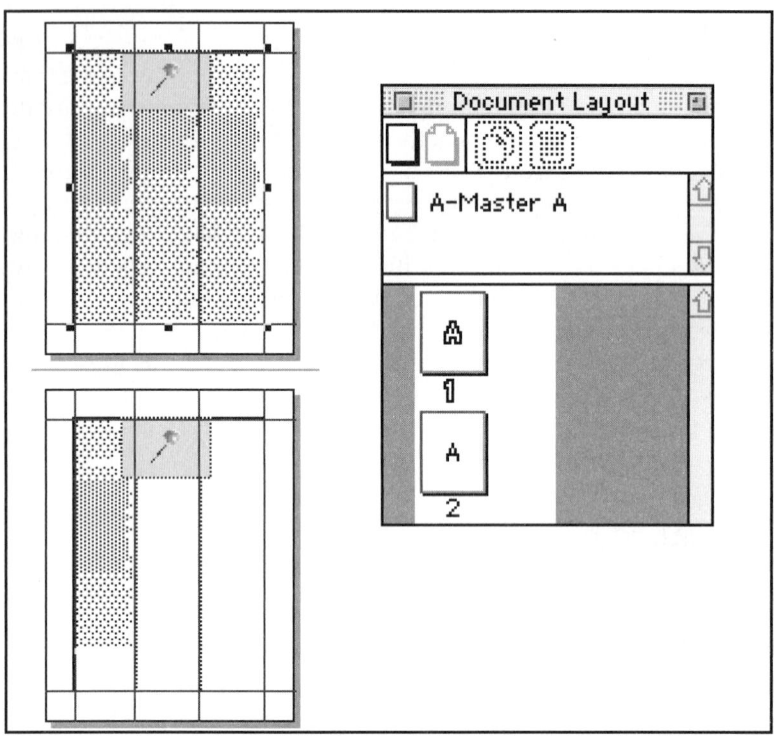

Figure 1.2. Because Master Page A was created with an automatic 3-column text box and a picture box containing a graphic, a 3-column text box and the graphic appear on document page 1. When a new page was needed to hold the imported text, a second document page based on Master Page A with its 3-column text box and graphic was added.

If, for example, your document is a four-page newsletter, it is a text-intensive document and you would choose the Automatic Text Box option. If, in contrast, your new document is a poster, you would not need to select the Automatic Text Box option because most of the items in the document will be graphics and any text boxes you need can be created manually.

COLUMNS

The New Document dialog box defaults to creating the new document with just one column. You can type any number in the Columns field in the Column Guides area of the dialog box to set the number of columns for the automatic text box that appears on Master Page A and on document page 1. If you don't choose the Automatic Text Box option in the New Document dialog box, the column guides will display, but they will not be part of any text box. Silly!

You can change the number of columns of any text box on any page of the document at any time. For example, if you type 4 in the Columns field of the New Document dialog box and you want the text box on page 10 of the document to have only one column, display the Measurements palette (View/Show Measurements). Then select the text box on page 10 and type the new number in the Cols field of the Measurements palette. You can also select the text box and choose Item/Modify. Click the Text tab and change the number in the Columns field of the Text Modify dialog box. Whenever you change the number of columns of a selected text box (a text box must be selected before you can do anything with it), that new column number is displayed in both the Text Modify dialog box and the Measurements palette.

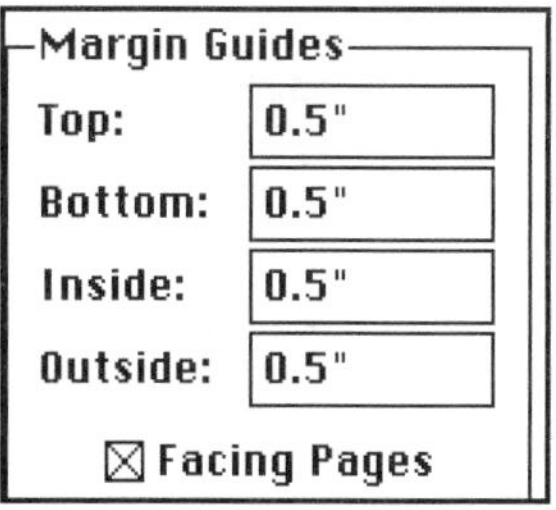

Selecting the Facing Pages option changes the Left and Right margin guides to Inside and Outside. When you are printing a book, you want the inside margins to be a little wider so that when the book is bound, the text on the inside margins doesn't run into the binding and become difficult, if not impossible, to read.

FACING PAGES

The Facing Pages option is selected when you will be printing the document on both sides of the paper, such as for a book or magazine. Deselect this option if you will be printing on only one side of the paper, such as for a flyer or product label, etc. You can change a document from non-facing pages to facing pages in the Document Setup dialog box (File/Document Setup), but you cannot change a facing pages document to a non-facing pages document.

EXERCISE A

The QuarkXPress for Windows icon in the QuarkXPress folder on the hard drive.

1. Begin by creating a new folder named Projects on your hard drive or on an external drive. Launch QuarkXPress by double-clicking on the QuarkXPress icon in the QuarkXPress 4.0 folder on your hard drive. Choose File/New/Document to display the New Document dialog box.
2. Choose US Letter, Portrait orientation, 1 column, and half-inch margins (0.5"). Deselect Facing Pages so that its option box is empty. If there is an X in it (Macintosh) or a check mark (Windows), click inside the box to remove the X or check mark and deselect the option. Make sure that Automatic Text Box is selected. If its option box is empty, click inside the box to display the X and select the option. Click on OK.
3. Choose View/Show Document Layout (F10/Macintosh; F4/Windows) to display the Document Layout palette. The palette for this new document displays only two page icons, one for Master Page A in the center panel and another icon for document page 1 in the lower panel (Figure 1.3).

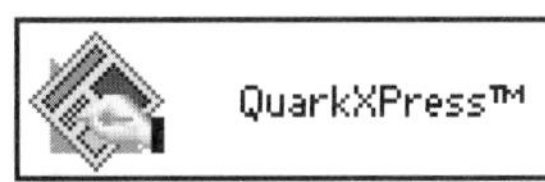

The QuarkXPress for Macintosh icon in the QuarkXPress folder on the hard drive.

Macintosh Commands

⌘-E File/Get Text/Picture

Windows Commands

Ctrl-E File/Get Text/Picture

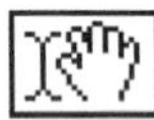

Content tool

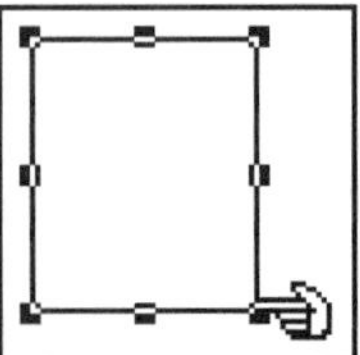

When a standard-shape item is selected, it displays eight handles. Click on any handle to display the Pointer and drag to resize the item.

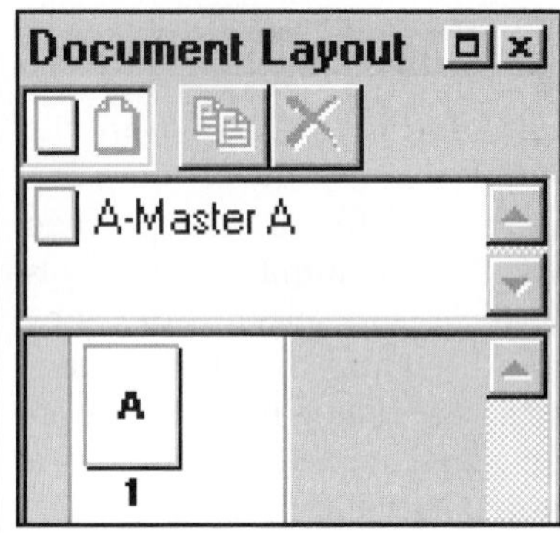

Figure 1.3. The Document Layout palette for a new document.

4. Click on the page and notice that the automatic text box appears selected and the I-beam cursor is displayed at the top of the box. The Content tool is also selected. Whenever the I-beam cursor appears, you know you are in a selected text box and anything you type will appear inside the box. Type *Headline* and press the Return/Enter key.

5. With the text box still selected (the eight handles appear around the four sides of the box), and the Content tool selected, choose File/Get Text. Navigate to the Unit 01 folder on the CD-ROM. Open this folder and locate the file named *Atext.txt.* Click on it to highlight it and click on Open. (Or just double-click on the file's name to open the file.) It flows into the selected text box beneath the Headline text (Figure 1.4).

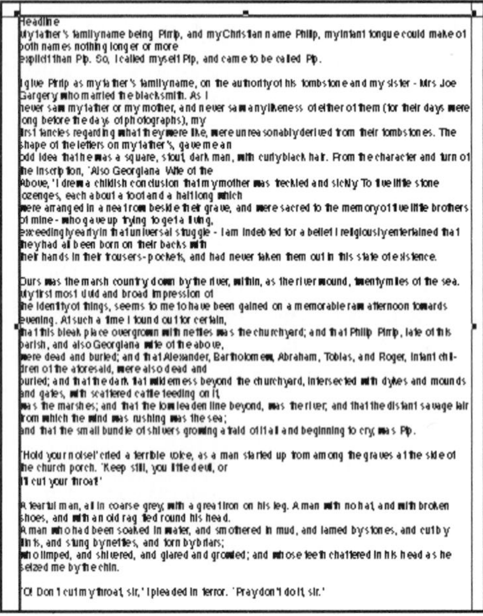

Figure 1.4. Text is imported into the selected text box.

6. Double-click on the word *Headline* to select it. Choose Style/Font/Helvetica. If you have the entire Helvetica font family installed, choose Helvetica Bold. If not, choose Helvetica, then choose Style/Type Style/Bold. Choose Style/Size/48. Choose Style/Alignment/Centered to center the word in the middle of the text box at the top of the page. If your system displays only TrueType fonts, select any font.

7. Click before the first word under the headline and drag to select the rest of the text on the page. Choose Style/Font/Times. Choose Style/Size/12. Your screen should resemble Figure 1.5. Because you reduced the type size, not all the text on the page may be formatted in Times.

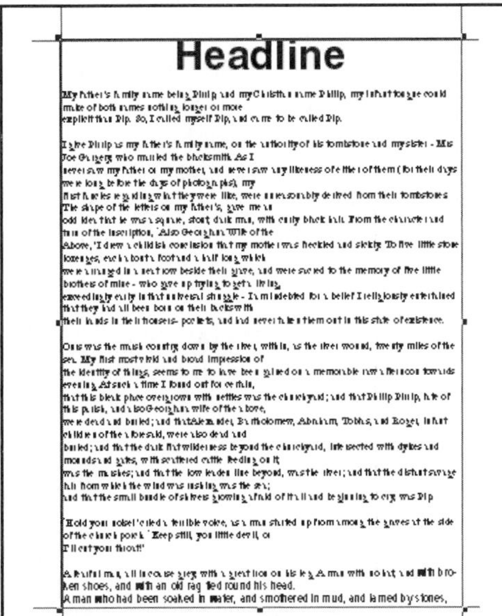

Figure 1.5. Both the headline and body text are formatted.

8. With the text box still selected, choose View/Show Measurements (F9) to display the Measurements palette. Type 3 in the Cols field and press the Return/Enter key. The text flows into the three columns on that page only.

9. With the text box still selected, choose Item/Modify. Click on the Text tab to display the Text Modify dialog box. Notice that the Columns field displays 3 because you changed the number of columns in the Measurements palette. Type 1 in the Columns field and click on OK. The text now flows in only one column.

10. Leave this file open. You will need it for the next exercise.

Macintosh Commands

⌘-Shift-B Style/Type Style/Bold
⌘-M Item/Modify

Windows Commands

Ctrl-Shift-B Style/Type Style/Bold
Ctrl-M Item/Modify

The Palatino font family includes every character in the Roman, italic, bold, and bold italic typefaces.

Easy selecting

To select a range of text, click at the start of the selection, press the Shift key, then click at the end of the selection.

Macintosh Commands

⌘-S File/Save

Windows Commands

Ctrl-S File/Save

LESSON 2 SAVING FILES

Until you have saved the file to disk, it lives only in the computer's memory bank, which isn't very stable. A power surge, an accidental shutdown, or a system crash means you could lose any documents stored in memory. To avoid losing your work, choose one of several options for saving files in QuarkXPress.

☒ Auto Library Save
☒ Save Document Position

Check these options to automatically save a Library whenever you add a Library entry and to remember the size and position of your document window when you save the document.

SAVE AS

If you have not already saved a file, choosing File/Save always displays the Save as dialog box. Once the Save as dialog box appears, you can rename your file and save it at another location. For example, if you think File#1 is what you want, but you want to try a few more formatting options, choose File/Save as and name the file File#2. File #1 remains untouched where you last saved it. Once you have named a file, every time you choose File/Save, XPress will save the file under its current name at its current location on the drive without prompting you with a dialog box. The Save as command is particularly useful for backing up an active file to another location.

SAVE

Choosing the Save command from the File menu saves the file under its current name to the last saved location. If, in the process of saving the file, it encounters an earlier file saved with that name to that location, it overwrites the earlier file and replaces it with the newer one. Use the keyboard commands for saving a file frequently. You will weep less.

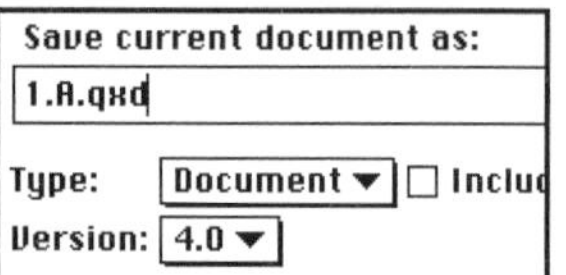

Type a name for the file, select the document or preview format and a file version. The .qxd extension specifies that this file is a QuarkXPress document, as opposed to a QuarkXPress library or QuarkXPress template.

EXERCISE B

1. With the *Headline* file still open, choose File/Save to display the Save as dialog box. The Save command overwrites any existing file with the same name but is not functional until the file has been saved once.
2. Navigate to your Projects folder and open it. Type *File.qxd* in the text field. Use the Save as Type pull-down menu or select Document and the Version pull-down menu to select the version of QuarkXPress you are working in. On the Macintosh only, click to select the Include Preview check box to display a thumbnail of the first page of the file when you open the file at a later date. Click on Save.

3. Choose File/Close to close the file without quitting QuarkXPress.

Macintosh Commands

⌘-W File/Close

Windows Commands

Ctrl-F4 File/Close

LESSON 3 OPENING FILES

Once you have created and saved a QuarkXPress document (file), you can open that same file later using the Open command. Whenever you save a file, you save the XPress preferences data with it and that data is recorded in the XPress Preferences file in the QuarkXPress folder on the hard drive. Changes made to font kerning tables and hyphenation exceptions are some of the information stored in the XPress Preferences file. If you take the file from one computer to another, XPress will know that it is opening a file on a new system and will ask you if you want to keep the document settings or use the XPress Preferences file on the new machine. Unless you have changed font kerning and hyphenation exceptions, it's usually safe to use XPress Preferences.

XPress Preferences

The XPress Preferences file records your document preferences in a file created in the QuarkXPress 4.0 folder. Trashing the XPress Preferences file causes QuarkXPress to create a new XPress Preferences file with the default settings the next time you launch XPress.

LESSON 4 CLOSING FILES

When you close a file, you remove it from the desktop. That's all you do. You don't quit QuarkXPress, you simply close the file just as you would close a file drawer. If you have saved the file before choosing the File/Close command, the file will simply close. If, however, you didn't save the file after doing anything with it, an alert will appear giving you three options. You can click Cancel to cancel the save and return to the document. You can click No, in which case, XPress will simply close the file without including any of the changes you made to that file since the last time you saved it. Or you can click the Yes button. XPress will then save the file with all the changes you made to it since the last time you saved it and then close the document.

There are three ways to close a document: Choose the Close command from the File menu; click in the Close box in the upper left corner of the document (Macintosh) or upper right corner (Windows); or press Command-W (Macintosh).

Windows info

Windows users can close all open files from an option under the Windows menu.

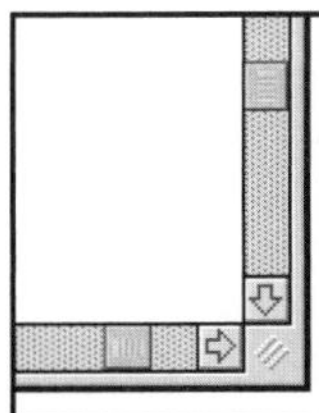

Drag the scroll bars or click on the arrows on the right and lower sides of the document page to move around the page.

Macintosh Commands

⌘-O File/Open
⌘-Option-S File/Save as
⌘-W File/Close

Windows Commands

Ctrl-O File/Open
Ctrl-Alt-S File/Save as
Ctrl-F4 File/Close

The Content tool (left) appears highlighted when selected (right).

☒ Include Preview

Selecting Include Preview (Macintosh only) displays a thumbnail of the first page of the document in the Open dialog box.

LESSON 5
REVERT TO SAVED

Sometimes you open a file, make changes, and realize that you've done things that are just too much trouble to edit or delete. If you haven't saved the file since you opened it, you can use the Revert to Saved command under the File menu to close the file and automatically open the original file, the one you last saved. When you choose the Revert to Saved command, an alert appears telling you that any changes made to the file since you opened it will be lost. Click OK to close the file and revert to the last saved version of the file. If you click the Cancel button, the Revert to Saved command is canceled and you're returned to the document.

EXERCISE C

1. Choose File/Open. Navigate to the Projects folder where you stored the *File.qxd* file or open the *File.qxd* file in the Unit 1 folder on the CD-ROM. Highlight the name of the file and click on Open. You can always open a file by double-clicking on the file name. If you get the message "Uses fonts not installed in your system," click on OK to ignore the message. The file appears on the screen and is available for editing.
2. Choose File/Save as. In the Save as dialog box, click to select the Preview box (Macintosh only). This will display a thumbnail view of the first document page when you next open the file. Click on Save. Don't change the name of the file. Click Replace to overwrite the existing file when asked if you want to replace the existing file. Choose File/Close to close the file.
3. Choose File/Open and highlight the *File.qxd* file. Click to select the Preview check box in the Open dialog box to display a thumbnail of the first page of the file (Macintosh only). Click on Open to open the file (Figure 1.6).

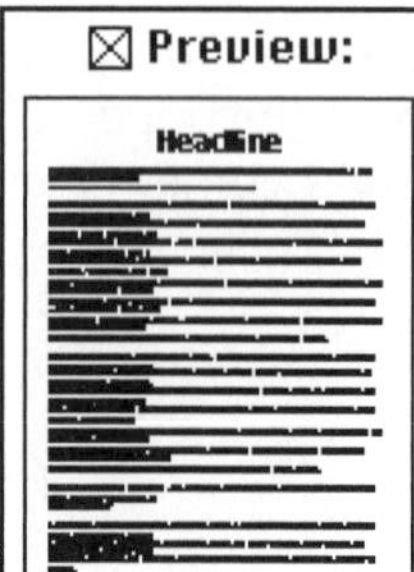

Figure 1.6. Clicking Preview (Macintosh only) in the Open dialog box displays a thumbnail of the document's first page if that document was saved with the Preview option selected.

4. Type a few words anywhere in the file. Drag to select them and format them in 48 pt type so you'll be able to see them easily. Choose File/Close. The alert tells you that you have made changes since you last saved the file. Click on the Cancel button to return to the document.
5. Choose File/Revert to Saved. At the alert, click OK to close the current document without saving the changes and open (revert to) the original *File.qxd* document. Choose File/Close.

Macintosh Commands

⌘-W File/Close
⌘-O File/Open
⌘-1 View/Actual Size
⌘-W File/Close

Windows Commands

Ctrl-O File/Open
Ctrl-F4 File/Close
Ctrl-1 View/Actual Size
Ctrl-F4 File/Close

LESSON 6
EDITING TEXT

You can edit text as you create it by making selections from the Style menu before you begin to type or as you are typing. You can also edit text by selecting it and applying format commands to it. It's important to remember that you must select text characters before you can edit them. If, for example, you want to change the font or size of a word, that word must be highlighted (selected). If you find nothing is happening when you're making selections from the Style menu, that's because you haven't selected any text. If you find yourself typing away and no text appears, that's because you're not typing in a text box.

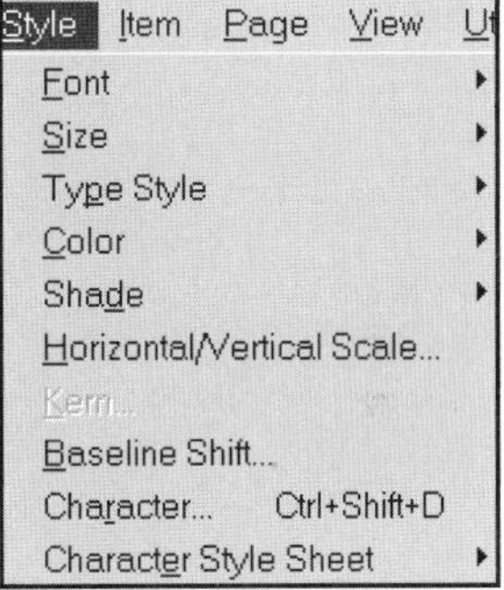

Use the Style menu to access all the text formatting options. A triangle to the right of any menu item indicates another menu associated with the main selection.

COPY AND PASTE SELECTIONS

When you copy selected text or items (boxes and lines), they are copied to the Clipboard. The Clipboard is a special area of memory designed to hold anything copied with the Copy command. When you select text or items and choose Edit/Copy, that selection is placed on the Clipboard and remains there until you copy something else with the Copy command. Copying does not remove the selection, it just copies it to the Clipboard.

Once a selection is on the Clipboard, it can be pasted anywhere in the document by choosing the Paste command and the appropriate tool. The selection remains on the Clipboard after it has been pasted, allowing you to paste it again until something else is copied and overrides the first selection on the Clipboard.

EXERCISE D

1. Choose File/Open. Navigate to the *File.qxd* file in the Unit 01 folder on the CD-ROM. Double-click on it to open it. Choose View/Actual Size to display the document at 100% magnifica-

tion. You have already used the Style menu to edit the Headline text. Now you will edit the body of the text.

2. Triple-click anywhere in the first line of the body of the text (below *Headline*) to select just that line. Just as double-clicking selects one word, triple-clicking selects one line. Choose Style/Color and drag to select red. The black text becomes red. Choose Edit/Copy to copy that first line of red text to the Clipboard.
3. Choose Edit/Show Clipboard and notice that the selected red text you copied appears in the Clipboard window. Click in the document's Close box to close it.
4. Click at the beginning of the next paragraph, just before the words *I give Pirrip* and choose Edit/Paste. The red text appears at the beginning of the paragraph.
5. Choose Edit/Undo to undo the Paste command. The red text is removed from the paragraph, but it still remains on the Clipboard available for pasting. Choose Edit/Paste again to paste the red text back in the paragraph or anywhere else you click. Close the file (File/Close). Don't save your changes.

Macintosh Commands

⌘-C Edit/Copy
⌘-V Edit/Paste
⌘-X Edit/Cut
⌘-Z Edit/Undo
⌘-W File/Close

Windows Commands

Ctrl-C Edit/Copy
Ctrl-X Edit Cut
Ctrl-V Edit Paste
Ctrl-Z Edit/Undo
Ctrl-F4 File/Close

Your undoing

To undo almost any action, choose Edit/Undo before performing another action like typing or choosing a command from the Main Menu.

LESSON 7
CUT AND CLEAR/DELETE TEXT SELECTIONS

When you cut a text selection, that text is not only placed on the Clipboard, but is also removed from the document. Because it's on the Clipboard, it can be pasted back into the document as long as nothing else was copied to the Clipboard.

Clearing a selection (Macintosh) or deleting a selection (Windows), although it removes selected text from the document, does not place that material on the Clipboard. The Clear/Delete command is useful when you want to remove text from the document without overriding what you have on the Clipboard. For example, you may have used the Copy command to copy a name to the Clipboard so you could paste it in different locations in the document. While doing this, you may want to remove a word from a paragraph. If you used the Cut command to remove the word, that word would override the name on the Clipboard. However, if you use the Edit/Clear (Macintosh) or Edit/Delete (Windows) command, the word is removed without touching anything on the Clipboard.

Easy viewing

To enlarge your view of the document (not the document itself), choose a higher magnification from the View menu. You could also type any magnification level in the View Percent field in the lower left corner of the page. Type your magnification value and press Return or Enter to execute the command. If you don't want to bother scrolling down to the bottom of the page, press Control-V, type your value (up to 800%) in the View Percent field, and press Return or Enter. You don't have to type the percent sign.

EXERCISE E

1. Create a new file (File/New/Document) with an automatic text box. Type your name in the text box. Press the Return/Enter key, type the first line of your address, and press the Return/Enter key.
2. Drag to select all the words in your name. Choose Edit/Copy. Click in the line after your address and choose Edit/Paste. Press the Return/Enter key and choose Edit/Paste again.
3. Triple-click in the address line to select the entire line of text. Choose Edit/Cut. Click after the last line of text and choose Edit/Paste. The address line appears because the Cut command places the selection on the Clipboard.
4. Triple-click to select any line of your name. Choose Edit/Clear (Macintosh) or Edit/Delete (Windows). Choose Edit/Show Clipboard and notice that the address line is still available on the Clipboard, but your name line is not. The Clear/Delete command removes a selection without placing it on the Clipboard.
5. Continue to use the Copy, Paste, Cut, and Clear/Delete commands until you are comfortable with them. Close this file. Don't save your changes.

Macintosh Commands

⌘-N File/New/Document
⌘-X Edit/Cut
⌘-V Edit/Paste

Windows Commands

Ctrl-N File/New/Document
Ctrl-X Edit Cut
Ctrl-V Edit Paste

LESSON 8
APPLICATION PREFERENCES

QuarkXPress lets you set preferences that affect how the application behaves regardless of what document you have open. By making selections in the Application Preferences dialog box, you can personalize your version of QuarkXPress for the way you work. When you choose Edit/Preferences/Application, four tabbed areas appear.

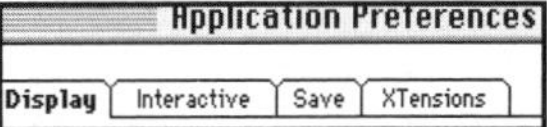

The Application Preferences dialog box displays four tabbed dialog boxes where you can customize different functions of QuarkXPress.

DISPLAY TAB

Click on the Display tab to select colors for margin and grid guides. Checking Full-screen Documents (Macintosh only) maximizes the display of new documents on-screen when you create, tile, or stack documents. Select Off-screen Draw to specify that XPress redraw the entire screen at once rather than piece by piece. Deselect this option if you don't have a lot of memory and computer horsepower.

INTERACTIVE TAB

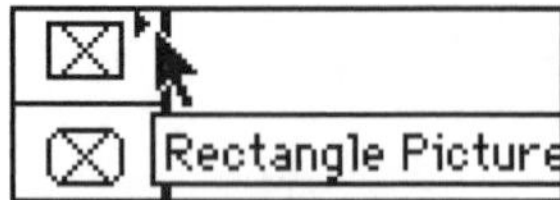

When Show Tool Tips is checked, tool names appear when you move the cursor onto the tool.

The options in the Interactive dialog box determine how quickly you can scroll documents and how the documents update. Use the slider to reduce or increase scrolling. Check Speed Scroll to temporarily greek (display as gray bars) pictures and blends for faster scrolling. If you check Live Scroll, the document updates as you click on the horizontal and vertical scroll bars. Always check Smart Quotes to prevent quotation marks from appearing as feet and inches marks (a typographical mortal sin). Select a style for quotes from the Format menu; the default option is the most widely used.

Avoid selecting the Drag and Drop text box, because when you cut, copy, and paste text with the mouse instead of using the menu or keyboard shortcuts, you can mistakenly move or delete text. With the option selected, you can highlight the text and drag it to a new location. Pressing the Shift key while dragging the highlighted text copies and pastes the text.

Select the Show Tool Tips box to display the names of tools or palette icons when you place your pointer on them.

The XTensions tab provides options for displaying the XTensions Manager at startup. XTensions are add-ons or plug-ins such as text and graphics filters that increase the functionality of QuarkXPress.

SAVE TAB

When Auto Save is selected in the Save dialog box, XPress will automatically save your changes to a temporary file in your document folder at a specified time, every five minutes, for example. Checking Auto Backup lets you specify the number of document revisions XPress will save every time you choose the Save command.

XTENSIONS TAB

XTensions are mini applications that extend the power and functionality of QuarkXPress. Some of them are import filters such as word processing filters and graphics filters; others affect the way you use color or create type. The hundreds of XTensions now available from vendors can make QuarkXPress do just about anything. To manage all these XTensions, use the XTensions Manager available from the Utilities menu. You can tell the XTensions manager which XTensions to load at startup, and you can create sets of XTensions to use with different projects. The options you select in the XTensions tab of the Application Preferences dialog box determine if and when the XTensions Manager appears when you launch QuarkXPress.

Use the XTensions tab in the Application Preferences dialog box to specify if and when the XTensions Manager appears at startup.

Image from *Roundhead Executives* by Barton Stabler, for Artville

OVERVIEW

In this unit you will learn how to:

Add and delete document pages

Use the Document Layout palette

Number pages and use the Section command

Print documents

TERMS

absolute page number
Consecutive Page Number symbol
default
folio
Page Number box
Section
spread (page)

HOW IT WORKS:

Import the image and resize it to fit the picture box. Use the Bézier Text-Path tool to draw a path around the edge of the walkway in the image. Enter the text, format it, and track it. With the text path selected, use the Text Path Modify dialog box and select the 3-D effect in the upper right corner of the Text Orientation field. Align the text from the top to the baseline of the text path to make it appear to be "standing up" on the path.

LESSON 1
THE DOCUMENT LAYOUT PALETTE

As soon as you create a new XPress document, two things happen: a single document page appears and a master page, Master Page A, is created. You can access document pages and master pages from the Menu or from the Document Layout palette (Figure 2.1).

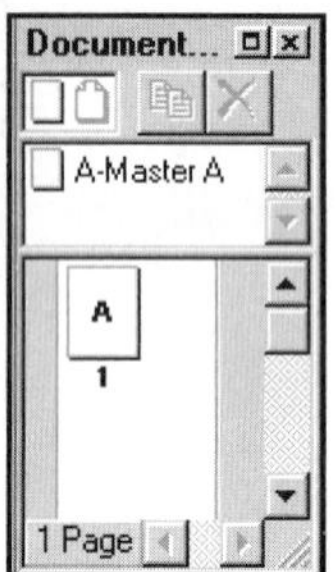

Figure 2.1. When a new document is created, one master page, Master Page A, and one document page based on Master Page A are automatically created. This document was created without selecting the Facing Pages option.

The Document Layout palette is divided into three panels: the Icon panel, the Master Page panel, and the Document Page panel. The Icon panel displays a thumbnail of the current master page, which in Figure 2.1 is a non-facing page. The dimmed icons to the right of the thumbnail are used to duplicate and to delete master pages and document pages.

The Master Page panel also displays an icon and name for the master page that is automatically created when you create a new document. In Figure 2.1 there is only the default master page, Master Page A. When you add new master pages, their icons and names will also appear in this second panel. You can highlight the master page name (Macintosh) or double-click on it (Windows) and change it, but the original letter will remain. In Figure 2.2 the name of the master page has been changed to Introduction, but the letter A remains, indicating that this is the first (default) master page created in the document. The Document Layout palette was also resized to fully display the new master page name.

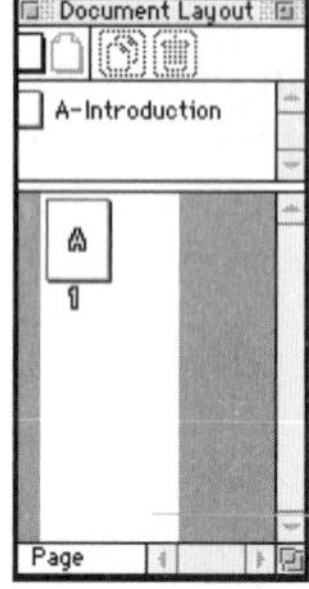

Figure 2.2. Click on the name of a master page to highlight it and type a new name for the master page. Here, the name of Master Page A is changed to Introduction. You can resize the Document Layout panel to view pages and page names more clearly.

The third panel is the Document Page panel. This panel displays an icon of every document page in the file. Double-clicking on any document page icon takes you to that page and centers it on the screen. If that document page is based on a master page, the master page letter appears on the icon and the page position in the document—not necessarily the page number (folio)—is displayed beneath the icon.

ADDING DOCUMENT PAGES

The easiest way to add document pages is to select a Master Page icon and drag it down onto the Document Page panel in the Document Layout palette. In Figure 2.1, there is only one document page, and it is the first page in the file. Figure 2.3 displays the Document Layout palette for a two-page document and the Page Number box in the lower left corner of the palette displays 2 Pages, indicating that there are two document pages in this file. If you click once on any page icon, the Page Number box will display the actual page number for that document page.

TIP

Keep the Document Layout palette open when navigating a document. It's the easiest way to see page numbers and get to specific pages.

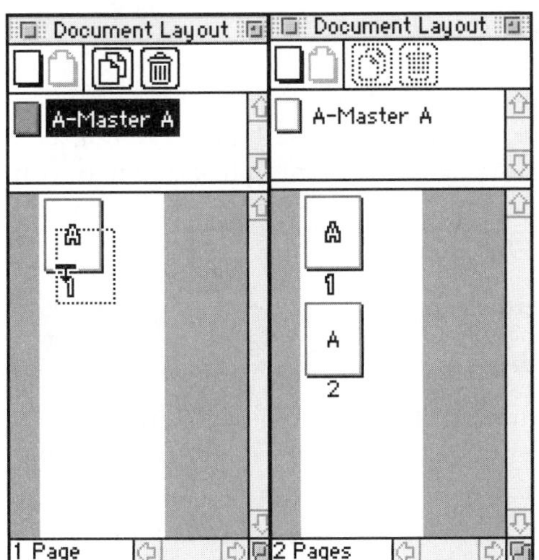

Figure 2.3. The Master A icon was dragged down onto the page panel of the Document Layout palette (left). The Document Layout palette now displays one master page and two document pages. The number of pages in a document appears in the Page Number box in the lower left corner of the palette.

FYI

You can't type in the automatic text box on a master page. Always create a separate text box for page numbers on the master page.

Figure 2.4 displays the Document Layout palette with the second document page highlighted (selected) and Page 2 displayed in the Page Number box. When Page 2 was assigned a folio number of 10, highlighting that page displays page 10 in the Page Number box (Figure 2.5). The asterisk after Page 10 indicates that a new section, starting with page 10, was created on that document page.

Macintosh Commands

⌘-N File/New/Document

Windows Commands

Ctrl-N File/New/Document

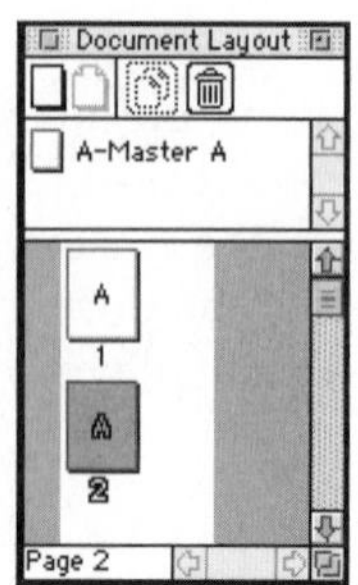

Figure 2.4. Double-clicking on document page 2 highlights the icon for that page and displays its page number in the Page Number box on the Document Layout palette.

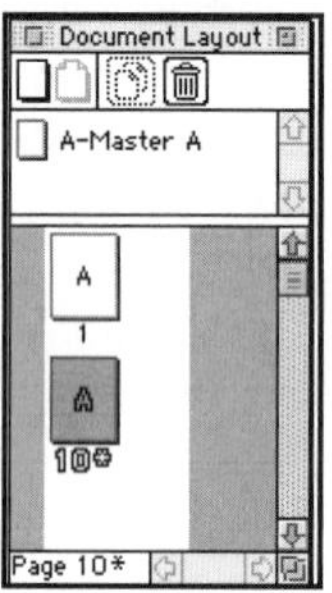

Figure 2.5. The asterisk after page 10 indicates that the page begins a new section starting with page number 10. However, the document page is still the second page in the document.

You can also add document pages from the Page menu. Choosing Insert from the Page menu displays the Insert Pages dialog box where you specify how many pages you want to insert, where you want them inserted in the document, and what master page you want those new pages based on.

EXERCISE A

1. Choose File/New/Document and create a new document without facing pages but with an automatic text box. When the document page appears, choose View/Show Document Layout (F10/Macintosh; F4/Windows) to display the Document Layout palette (Figure 2.1). This palette displays icons for the two default pages, master page A and document page 1 based on Master Page A.
2. Click on the Master Page A icon and drag it down onto the Document Page panel below page 1. Release the mouse button (Figure 2.3). You now have two document pages based on Master Page A.

3. Choose View/Fit in Window to fit the document to the screen. Click in the pasteboard area outside of the document area to deselect everything. Choose Page/Insert to display the Insert Pages dialog box (Figure 2.6). Type 2 in the Insert field and click on the at end of document button to insert two pages after page 2. Leave the Master Page pull-down menu set to A-Master A. Click on OK. The Document Layout palette now displays four document pages (Figure 2.7). You might have to use the resize box in the lower right corner of the palette to see all four page icons.

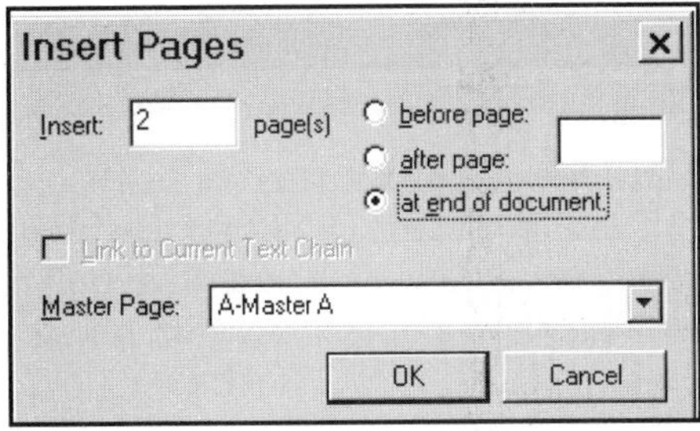

Figure 2.6. Use the Insert command to insert pages at a specific position in the document.

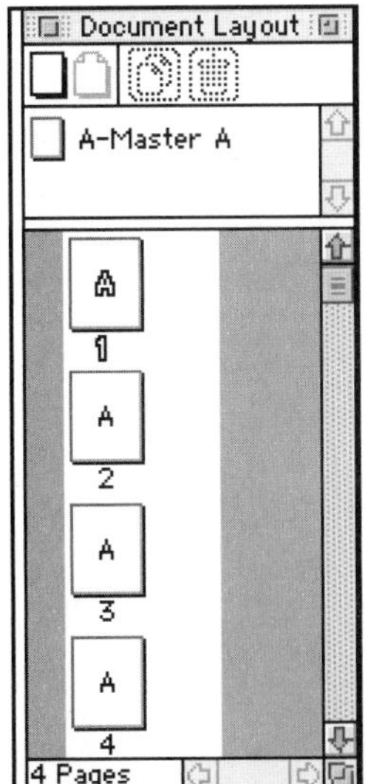

Figure 2.7. Two pages are added to the document.

4. Choose File/Save and save this file as *Pages.qxd* in your Projects folder. You will be using it in the next exercise.

Macintosh Commands

⌘-0 [zero] View/Fit in Window
⌘-S File/Save

Windows Commands

Ctrl-0 [zero] View/Fit in Window
Ctrl-S File/Save

Macintosh Commands

⌘-O File/Open
F10 View/Show Document Layout

Windows Commands

Ctrl-O File/Open
F4 View/Show Document Layout

FYI

Deletion of pages in the Document Layout palette cannot be undone. Always save your document before deleting document pages or master pages.

Tip

You can Shift-select a range of pages in the Document Layout palette and then click the Trash icon (Macintosh) or ✗ icon (Windows) to delete those pages.

LESSON 2
DELETING DOCUMENT PAGES

QuarkXPress requires that you have at least one document page in a file. You can, however, delete any other document pages you inserted in the document and you can delete the default document page as long as you leave one document page in the file. Pages can be deleted from the Document Layout palette and from the Menu Bar.

EXERCISE B

1. If necessary, open the *Pages.qxd* file you just created or open the *Pages.qxd* file in the Unit 02 folder on the CD-ROM. Display the Document Layout palette (View/Show Document Layout). The Document Layout palette displays a document with one master page and four document pages.
2. Click once on the Page 1 icon in the Document Layout palette to select it. Then click once on the Trash icon (Macintosh) or on the ✗ icon (Windows) in the Icon panel of the palette (Figure 2.8). At the alert, click OK. Page 1 is removed, leaving three pages in the document.

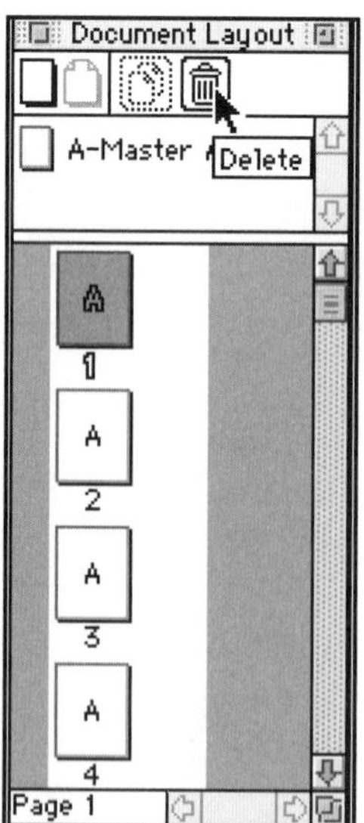

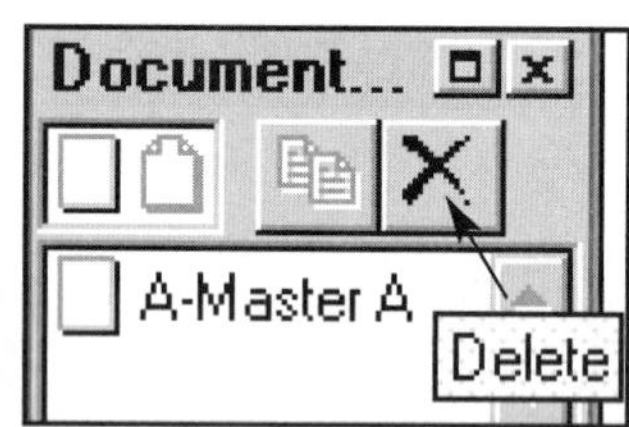

Figure 2.8. Click on a page to select it and click on the Trash icon (Macintosh) or ✗ icon (Windows) in the Document Layout palette to delete the page.

3. Double-click on the Page 2 icon in the palette to select it and to go to that page. Choose Page/Delete from the Menu Bar to display the Delete Pages dialog box (Figure 2.9). Because Page 2 was selected in the palette, the Delete page(s) field displays 2. Click on OK. There are now two document pages left.

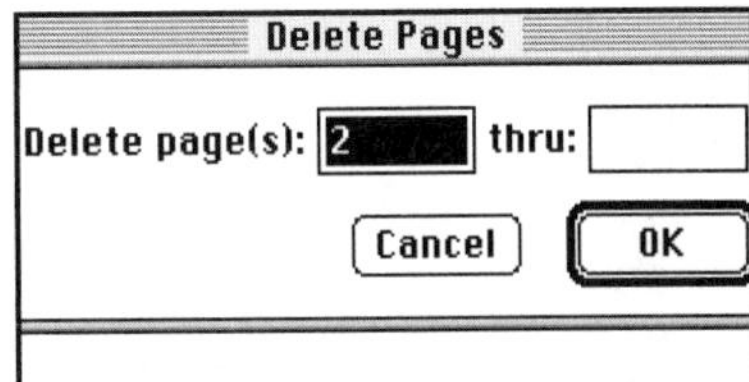

Figure 2.9. You can delete a single page or a range of pages in the Delete Pages dialog box. Typing end in the thru field will delete every page from the selected page (2) to the end of the document.

4. Click in the pasteboard area to deselect everything. Choose Page/Insert. Type 4 in the Insert field and click on the at end of document button. Click on OK to add four pages based on Master Page A. You now have six document pages.
5. Double-click on document page 3 in the Document Layout palette. Choose Page/Delete to display the Delete Pages dialog box. Leave 3 in the Delete page(s) field, press the Tab key and type 5 in the thru field to delete pages 3, 4, and 5. Click on OK. The Document Layout palette now displays only three document pages. (Figure 2.10).
6. Close this file (File/Close). Don't save your changes.

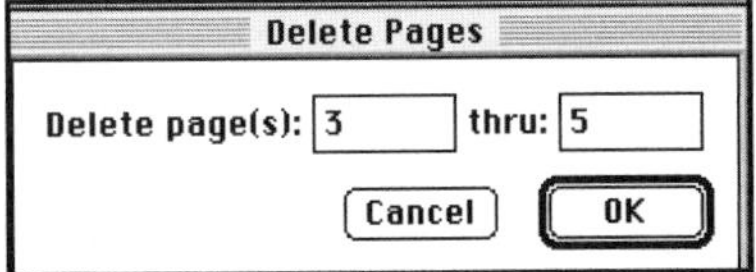

Figure 2.10. Use the Delete Pages dialog box to delete a range of pages.

LESSON 3 NUMBERING PAGES

Until you apply the Consecutive Page Number command, all pages in the document are numbered sequentially as they appear in the Document Layout palette. They do not display these numbers on the printed page because XPress does not consider them numbered pages. To give a page a page number or folio, you must apply the Consecutive Page Number command.

Macintosh Commands

⌘-W File/Close

Windows Commands

Ctrl-F4 File/Close

FYI

You must double-click on a page to get to that page and have its page number appear in the Delete Pages dialog box.

Folio

Folio is another name for page number. The term *folio* also includes any other identifying material that appears with the page number at the top or bottom of every document page.

Macintosh Commands

⌘-O File/Open
⌘-3 Consecutive Page Number command
⌘-Option-S File/Save as

Windows Commands

Ctrl-3 Consecutive Page Number command
Ctrl-Alt-S File/Save as

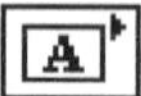

Rectangle Text Box tool

FYI

The Consecutive Page Number symbol <#> appears only on the master page. The document pages display the actual page number, not the symbol.

EXERCISE C

1. Open the *Pages.qxd* file and display the Document Layout palette (View/Show Document Layout). The palette displays four document pages. Double-click on the Master Page A icon in the Document Layout palette to get to Master Page A.
2. Click on the standard-shape Rectangle Text Box tool in the Tool palette and click and drag on the page to draw a text box on top of the automatic text box. As soon as you release the mouse, the Content tool becomes selected, allowing you to type inside that new text box. Press Command-3 (Macintosh) or Ctrl-3 (Windows). Be sure to keep the modifier key pressed while you press 3. Command/Ctrl-3 is the Consecutive Page Number command. When you release the key the Consecutive Page Number symbol (<#>) appears.
3. Double-click on the symbol and use the Style menu to give it a bold typeface, a large size, and a color.
4. Double-click on the first document page icon in the Document Layout palette and notice that the number 1 appears. Double-click on the other three pages and notice that they are consecutively numbered (Figure 2.11).

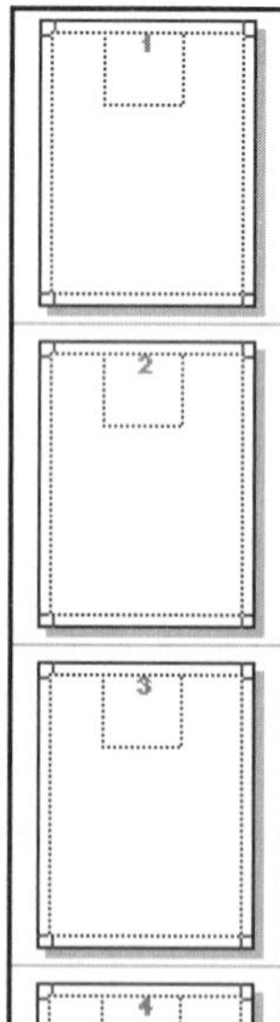

Figure 2.11. The Command-3 (Macintosh) or Ctrl-3 (Windows) command is the Consecutive Page Number command. Because it was applied to Master Page A, all document pages display consecutive page numbers.

5. Choose File/Save as and save this file as *Numbers.qxd* in your Projects folder.

LESSON 4
USING THE SECTION COMMAND

In a long document like a book, the first few pages (called front matter) that include copyright information, a preface, and table of contents are usually numbered with Roman numerals. The first chapter of the book then begins with Arabic number 1. To display these two numbering styles in XPress, use the Section command.

Macintosh Commands

⌘-O File/Open
F10 View/Show Document Layout

Windows Commands

Ctrl-O File/Open
F4 View/Show Document Layout

EXERCISE D

1. If necessary, open the *Numbers.qxd* file you just saved or open the *Numbers.qxd* file (File/Open) in the Unit 02 folder on the CD-ROM. It displays four pages numbered consecutively. Display the Document Layout palette (F10/Macintosh; F4/Windows).
2. Click (Macintosh) on the *title bar* of Master Page A to highlight it, or double-click on the title bar (Windows). Type *Introduction* and press Return/Enter. The master page is named *Introduction* but still retains the letter A.
3. Click on the Master Page A icon and click on the Duplicate Page icon in the Icon panel of the Document Layout palette to duplicate Master Page A. The duplicate is labeled Master Page B (Figure 2.12) and contains the text box with the Consecutive Page Number command. Click (Macintosh) or double-click (Windows) on the title of Master Page B and type *Body* and press Return/Enter. The master page is named Body but still retains the letter B.

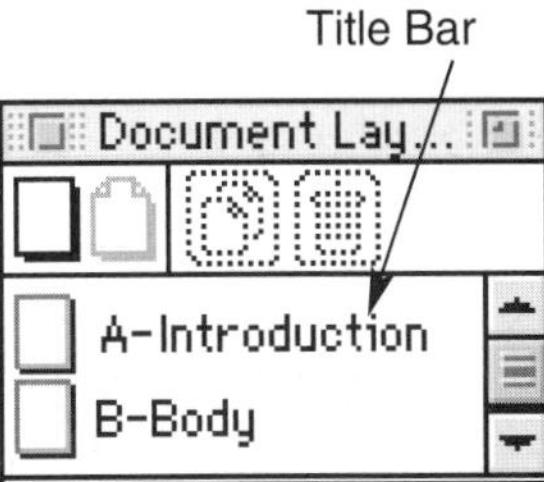

When you assign a name to a master page, it still retains its alphabetical listing.

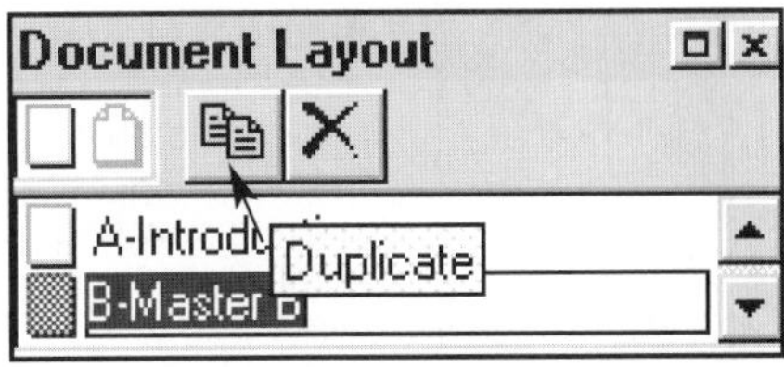

Figure 2.12. Select a master page and click on the Duplicate icon in the icon panel to duplicate a master page.

4. Drag Master Page B down onto document page 2 to apply it to page 2. Repeat to apply Master Page B to document pages 3 and 4. Your Document Layout palette should resemble Figure 2.13.

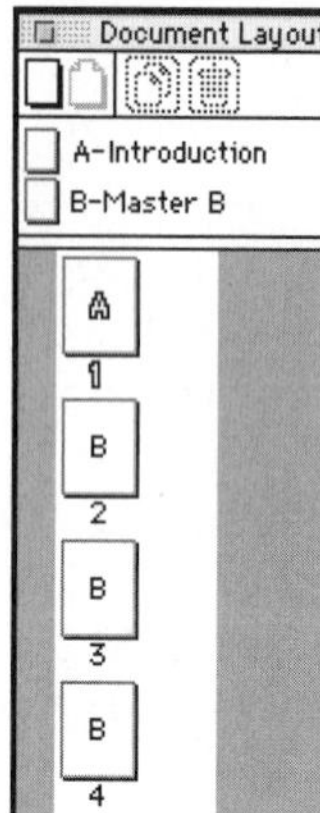

Figure 2.13. Master Page B has been applied to document pages 2, 3, and 4.

Type a comma between noncontinuous pages to print noncontinuous pages. Don't press the Spacebar after the comma.

5. Double-click on page 1 to go to page 1. Choose Page/Section to display the Section dialog box. Click in the Section Start check box to specify the start of a new page numbering section. Leave the Prefix field empty and type 5 in the Number field. Use the Format pull-down menu to select small Roman numerals (Figure 2.14) and click on OK. Page 1 now displays v in the text box you created for the page number and the three subsequent pages also display their page numbers in Roman numerals.

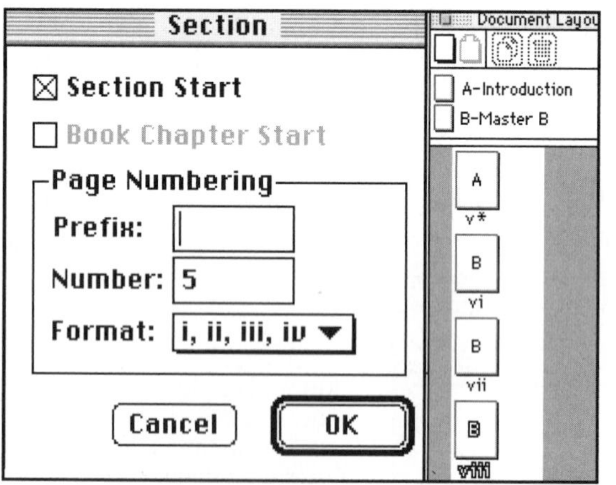

Figure 2.14. The asterisk next to page v indicates that the page starts a new section beginning with page v.

Document page 2 has an absolute page number of 2 and a folio number of vi.

6. Double-click on document page 2 (page number vi) to get to page 2. Choose Page/Section and click in the Section Start box to select it. Type 3 in the Number field and use the Format pull-down menu to select the Arabic numbers, the first option. Click on OK. Now document pages 3, 4, and 5 display Arabic numbers consecutively from number 3 (Figure 2.15).

Figure 2.15. The second document page is sectioned to begin at page number 3.

7. Close this file (File/Close). Don't save your changes.

Macintosh Commands

⌘-W File/Close

Windows Commands

Ctrl-F4 File/Close

LESSON 5
NAVIGATING A DOCUMENT

There are four ways of getting around an XPress document. You can double-click on the page icon for any page in the Document Layout palette, as you did in the previous exercise, to display that page on the screen. You can use the Go to command from the Page menu and type the absolute page number in the dialog box to display that page. The absolute page number is the page's actual position in the document regardless of any page numbers assigned to that page with the Section command. For example, if you use the Section command to apply consecutive page numbers to a document and the third page of the document is 107, the absolute page number for that page is 3. You must type a plus sign before the absolute page number to get to the third page of the document (Figure 2.16). Otherwise, type 107 in the Go to dialog box to get to page 107, the third page in the document.

The second page in this document is absolute page number 2 even though it has been given the folio 64 via the Section command. The first page in this document is both absolute page number 1 and folio page 1.

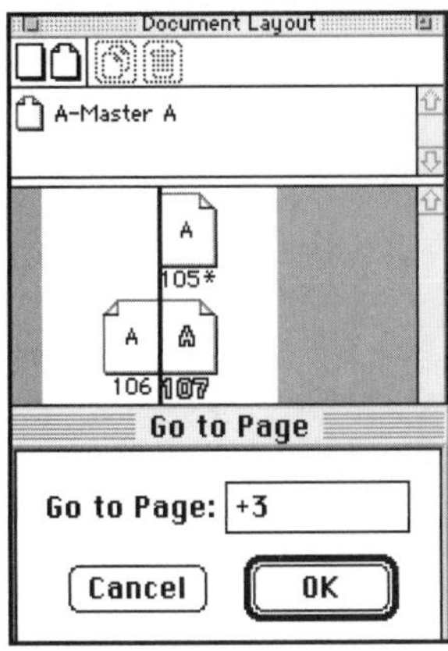

Figure 2.16. Type a + sign before the absolute page number (3) to get to sectioned page number 107, the third page in the document.

Macintosh Commands

⌘-O File/Open

⌘-3 Consecutive Page Number command

Windows Commands

Ctrl-O File/Open

Ctrl-3 Consecutive Page Number command

You can also type a page number in the Page Number field on the Document Layout palette (Figure 2.17). Again, you must type either the correct page number (like 107) or the absolute page number with the + sign (like +3) to get to the third page of the document which is page number 107.

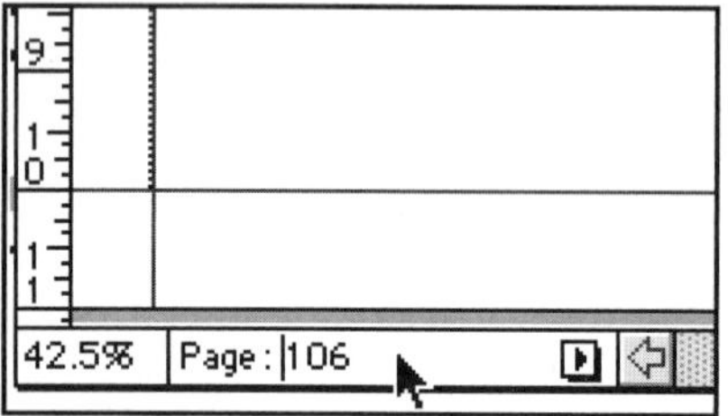

Figure 2.17. Highlight the current page number in the Page Number field and type another number to display that page.

Another way to navigate a document is to use the Go-To-Page icons at the bottom of the document page (Figure 2.18). The pages display the actual page number, but the position of the icon tells you whether it's the first, second, third, etc. page in the document.

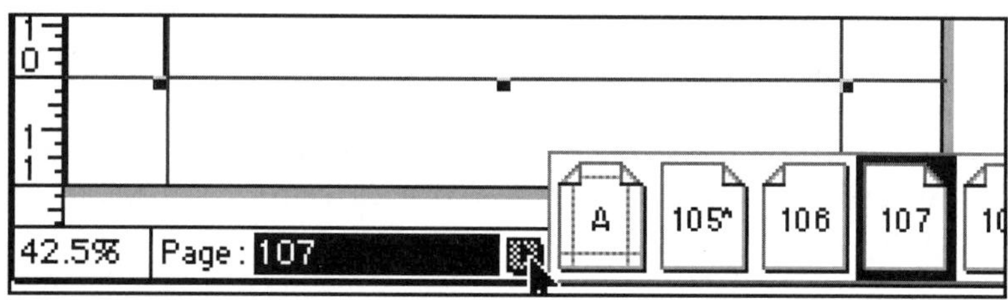

Figure 2.18. Click on the page arrow to display all the document pages. Then drag to select a page to navigate to that page. Page A is Master Page A.

EXERCISE E

1. Open the *Pages.qxd* file in your Projects folder or in the Unit 02 folder on the CD-ROM. Display the Document Layout palette (F10/Macintosh; F4/Windows). Double-click on Master Page A to get to the master page.

Rectangle Text Box tool

2. Use the Rectangle Text Box tool to draw a rectangle on the page. Choose Item/Modify and choose red from the Color pull-down menu in the Box field on the right side of the dialog box. Click on OK. Type *Page*, press the Spacebar, and press Command-3 (Macintosh) or Ctrl-3 (Windows) to create the Consecutive Page Number command. Choose Edit/Select All to select all the type and the <#> symbol in the text box. Use

the Style menu to format it in a large type. Choose Style/Color and drag to select yellow. Choose Style/Alignment/Centered to center the type horizontally in the box.

3. With the text box still selected, choose Item/Modify. Click on the Text tab and use the Vertical Alignment pull-down menu to select Centered. Click on OK (Figure 2.19).

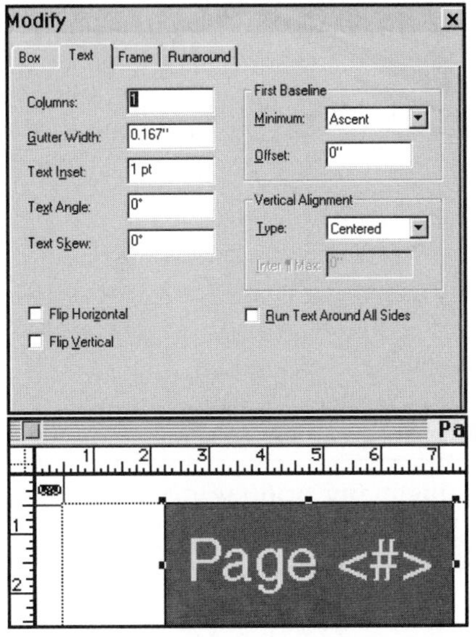

Figure 2.19. The Consecutive Page Number command is sectioned, styled, and centered in the text box on Master Page A.

4. Double-click on page 1 in the document panel of the Document Layout palette to get to page 1.

5. Choose Page/Go to. Type 3 in the Go to Page field and click on OK. Page 3 appears centered on the screen and its document page number is outlined in the Document Layout palette (Macintosh) or boldfaced (Windows), indicating that it is the selected page. Anything you type or create now will appear on that page.

6. Double-click on document page 1 to get to that page. Choose Page/Section. Click on Section Start. Type 10 in the Number field to make document page 1 page number 10. Click on OK (Figure 2.20).

Macintosh Commands

⌘-Shift-C Style/Alignment/Centered

⌘-J Page/Go to Page

Windows Commands

Ctrl-Shift-C Style/Alignment/Centered

Ctrl-J Page/Go to Page

Standard-Shape Rectangle Text Box tool

Macintosh Commands

⌘-C File/Close
⌘-O File/Open
⌘-A Edit/Select All

Windows Commands

Ctrl-O File/Open
Ctrl-A Edit/Select All
Ctrl F4 File/Close

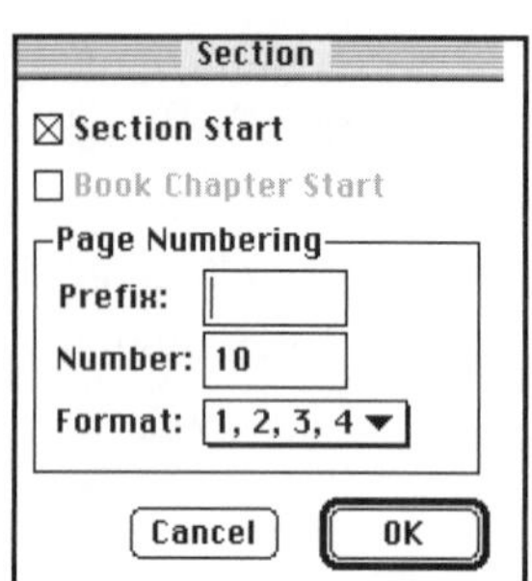

Figure 2.20. The Section command is used to create page numbers starting from page 10. The asterisk next to page 10 on the Document Layout palette indicates that the page is the start of a new section.

7. Click on the arrow in the Page Number field at the bottom of any document page and drag to get to that page (Figure 2.18).
8. Close this file (File/Close). Don't save your changes.

Page Positioning

If a selected output device such as an image-setter allows for repositioning the document, this menu in the Setup tab lets you specify where the page is printed on the medium relative to the edges or center of the print medium.

LESSON 6
PRINTING LESSON 1
PRINT DOCUMENT DIALOG BOX

Although QuarkXPress 4.0 contains many printing options, most documents require only a few selections to print a document that accurately reflects your text, graphics, and design specifications. You must first specify a printer, then tell XPress which pages you want to print to that printer, in what order, at what size, and how you want the color images printed. You make all these selections from the Print Document dialog box.

EXERCISE F

☐ Fit in Print Area

Fit in Print Area

Select this option in the Setup tab to reduce or enlarge pages in the document to fit the imageable area of the selected printer.

1. Turn on the printer. Open the *Numbers.qxd* file in your Projects folder or in the Unit 02 folder on the CD-ROM. Display the Document Layout palette (F10/Macintosh; F4/Windows). Double-click on Master Page A to get to the master page. Click inside the text box with the Consecutive Page Number command and choose Edit/Select All. Use the Style menu to change its color from red to black.
2. Because a master page is displayed, if you choose the Print command now, only the master page will print. To print the document, double-click on any document page in the document page panel of the Document Layout palette.

3. Choose File/Print to display the Print Document dialog box (Figure 2.21). Leave the Print Style menu at Document and the Separations check box deselected because you are not printing color separations (the four process color plates, cyan, magenta, yellow, and black).

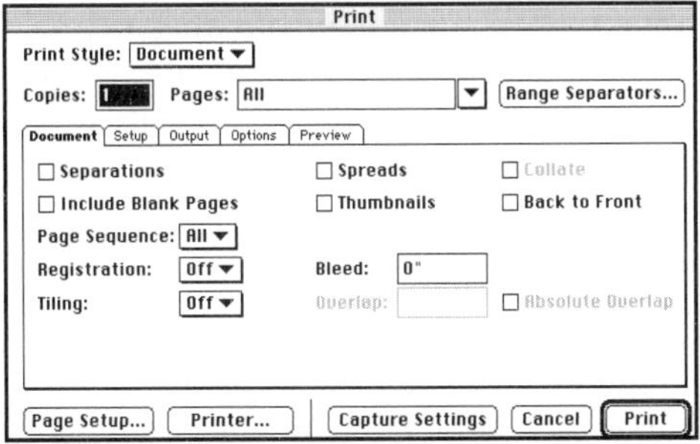

Figure 2.21. The Print Document dialog box (Macintosh above; Windows below) is where you make selections about how a document prints.

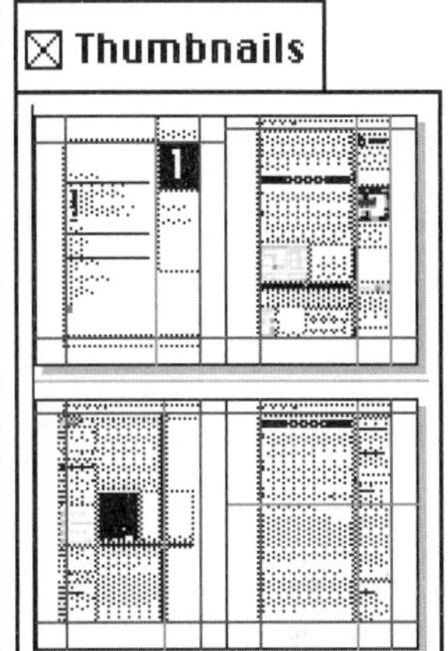

Select the Thumbnails check box in the Print dialog box to print many document pages on one sheet of paper as thumbnails, or icons of the page.

4. The Copies field defaults to 1, but you can change this value to print any number of copies. Leave it set to print one copy. If you leave the default All in the Pages field, every page in the document will print. For this exercise, you will print only pages 1 and 4. Because these are discontinuous pages, you must use a range separator. Click the Range Separators button in the upper right corner of the Print dialog box (Figure 2.22). It displays a comma as the separator for discontinuous pages. Click on OK. Select All in the Pages field and type 1,4 (1 comma 4).

Paper Offset: 0"
Page Gap: 0"

The Paper Offset and Page Gap fields are available only when an imagesetter is selected from the list of PPDs.

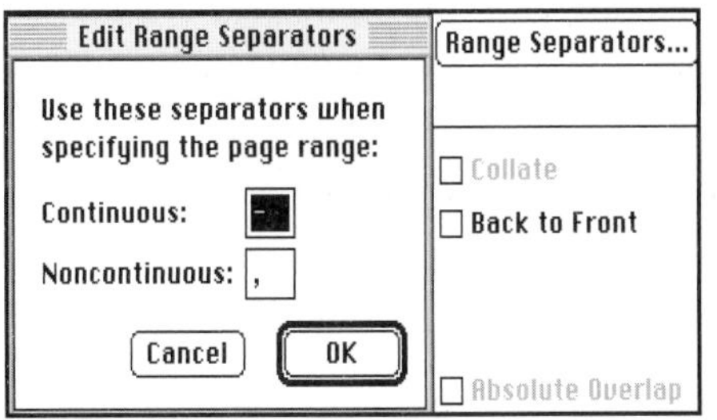

Figure 2.22. Click the Range Separators button in the Print Document dialog box to select a separator when printing continuous pages (like 1–5) and noncontinuous pages (like 1,3,6).

5. Leave the Spreads check box deselected because this document does not contain a *spread*, pages arranged in a horizontal row in the Document Layout palette. Make sure that Include Blank Pages, Thumbnails, and Back to Front are also deselected.

6. If you make complicated print selections, you can click the Capture Settings button to save the current output specifications with the document. The next time you choose File/Print these settings will appear automatically. Don't click on this button.

7. When your Print dialog box resembles Figure 2.23, click on the Setup tab in the Print dialog box. Use the Printer Description pull-down menu to select your printer. If the name of your printer doesn't appear in the list, select a generic printer description. Leave the Paper Size set to US Letter. If you were printing to a larger size paper, you would use this menu to select a different Paper Size option, including a Custom option. Typing a number greater than 100% in the Reduce or Enlarge field will print your pages larger than the actual size; reducing the value in this field prints the pages at the smaller size. For example, typing 50% in the Reduce or Enlarge field prints pages at half their actual size.

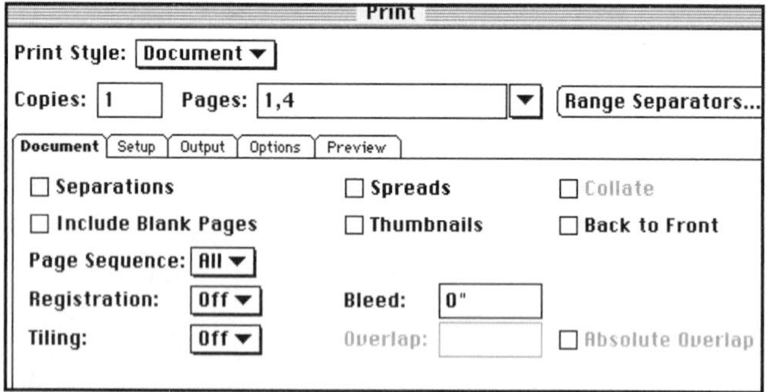

Figure 2.23. The Print dialog box is where you access dialog boxes to specify how your document will print and which pages will print. Here, pages 1 and 4 will print.

8. When you have finished making your selections, click on the Print button in the lower right corner of the dialog box. Pages 1 and 4 should print.

9. Close this file (File/Close). Don't save your changes.

If your continuous pages are all odd or even pages, you can select Odd or Even from the Page Sequence pull-down menu.

Paper Size: US Letter
Paper Width: 8.5"
Paper Height: 11"

The Paper Width and Paper Height values change to reflect the selected Paper Size option.

PPDs

PPDs are PostScript Printer Description files. Select the appropriate PPD for your printer to ensure that the default information in the Print dialog box matches your output device. You can customize this list of PPDs by selecting PPD Manager from the Utilities menu and clicking on the check mark for any unneeded devices to remove them from the Include field. Click the Update button to execute the command.

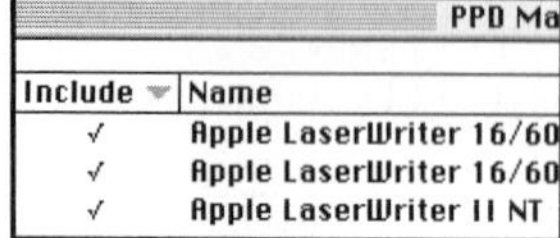

OVERVIEW

In this unit you will learn how to:

Create and edit master pages
Insert and delete document pages
Apply master pages to document pages
Duplicate and delete master pages
Copy pages and items between documents
Move document pages

TERMS

Keep Changes/Delete Changes
master page items
Thumbnails

Image from *Business Characters* by Susan LeVan, for Artville

---

HOW IT WORKS:

In Photoshop, change the mode of the color image from RGB to Grayscale. Then crop the image so the imagesetter will not have to process more of the image than is necessary. Import the image into a standard-shape oval picture box. Use the Bézier Text-Path tool to draw a text path to the right of the picture box. Type the unit information on the path with the Content tool and format it. Manipulate the anchor points and direction handles on the text path to reshape the path so it follows the outline of the picture box.

LESSON 1
CREATING MASTER PAGES

Icon panel

The Icon panel displays blank icons for master pages. The Duplicate icon is used to duplicate a selected master page. The Delete icon is used to delete selected master and document pages.

Look at any book or magazine and you will notice that most pages share common elements like page numbers (folios) and page headers. Some publications, such as corporate newsletters, have a logo that appears on every page of the newsletter. If a publication has a three-column format, then that format applies to every page in the publication except where artwork overrides the columnar format. These repeating text and graphic elements are called *master page items.* In QuarkXPress, you create these master page items on the master pages. These master page items will then appear on every document page based on that master page. You can have many master pages in one document and you can have blank pages that display no master page items. Master pages give a document consistency of format and should be the first thing you set up when you create a document of more than one page.

When you click OK in the New Document dialog box, two things happen: one document page is created and Master Page A is created. Both pages are blank, and unless you specified an automatic text box in the New Document dialog box, no items appear on the master page or on the document page.

When you place text or graphic elements on that default master page, Master Page A, those items appear automatically on document page 1 because that first document page is always based on Master Page A. Any pages you insert in the document, either from the Document Layout palette or from the Page menu, that are based on Master Page A will display any elements you created on that master page.

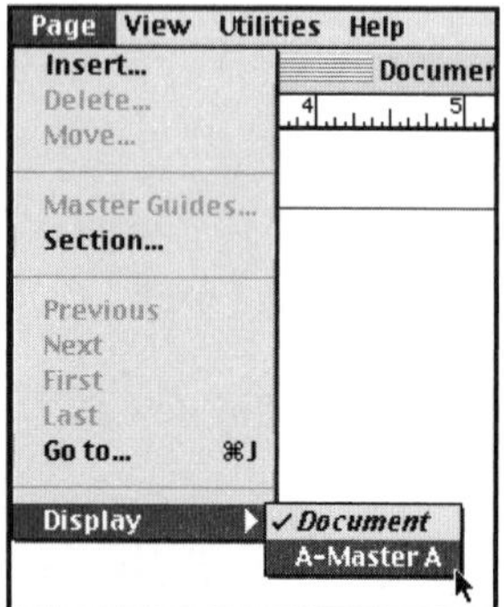

Use the Page menu to get to any document page or master page.

DOCUMENT LAYOUT PALETTE

The Document Layout palette displays three panels. The Icon panel at the top is where icons for blank master pages and for duplicating and deleting master pages appear. The Delete icon can also be used to delete document pages. The Master Page panel, the center panel, displays icons for all the master pages in the document. The lowest panel, the Document Page panel, displays icons for all the document pages in the file. The Document Layout palette makes it easy to navigate a document. Just double-click on any master page or on any document page and you will be on that page.

CHANGING MASTER GUIDES

When you create a new document, you specify the margin widths in the New Document dialog box. These values are applied to every document page based on the default master page, Master Page A. To change those master guides, you must be on the master page and use the Master Guides command from the Page menu.

INSERTING DOCUMENT PAGES BASED ON MASTER PAGES

Once a master page is created, dragging its icon down onto the document panel of the Page Layout palette adds another document page based on that master page. If you are on a document page, choose Page/Insert to insert additional document pages based on a master page selected from the Master Page pull-down menu in the Insert Pages dialog box.

Macintosh Commands

⌘-N File/New/Document
⌘-0 [zero] View/Fit in Window
⌘-Y Edit/Preferences/Document

Windows Commands

Ctrl-N File/New
Ctrl-0 [zero] View/Fit in Window
Ctrl-Y Edit/Preferences/Document

EXERCISE A

1. Create a new, non-facing pages document with an automatic text box, one-inch margins, and one column (File/New/Document). Display the Document Layout palette (F10/Macintosh; F4 Windows). The Document Layout palette displays Master Page A and one document page that is based on Master Page A (Figure 3.1).

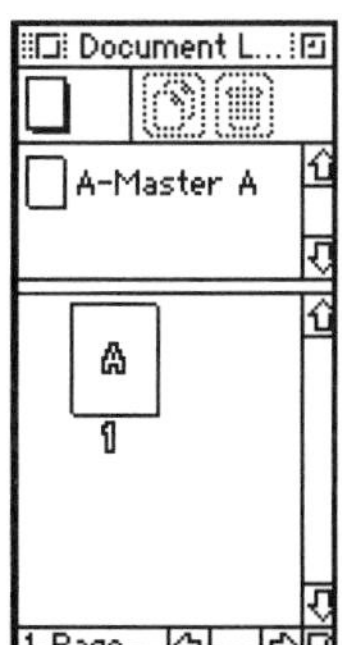

Figure 3.1. When a new document is created, Master Page A and document page 1 are created automatically. The letter A on the document page icon indicates that the page is based on Master Page A.

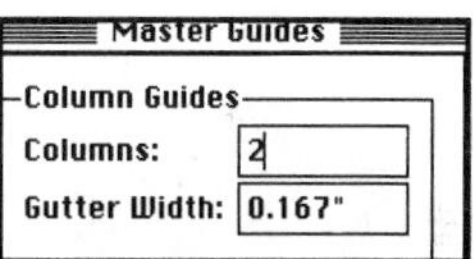

The only way to globally change the number of columns in a document is to use the Master Guides dialog box. This box appears only when you are actually on the master page.

2. Double-click on Master Page A to get to the master page. Choose Page/Master Guides. Change the Top and Bottom margins to two inches. Click on OK.

3. Choose Edit/Preferences/Document, click on the General tab, and select inches as the Horizontal and Vertical unit of measure. Click on OK.

4. Still on Master Page A, choose View/Fit in Window. Use the standard-shape Rectangle Picture Box tool to draw a picture box at the top of the page. Use the Measurements palette

Rectangle Picture Box tool

Macintosh Commands

⌘-E File/Get Text/Picture
⌘-Option-Shift-F Fit a picture proportionally in the box
⌘-M Item/Modify

Windows Commands

Ctrl-E File/Get Text/Picture
Ctrl-Alt-Shift-F Fit a picture proportionally in the box
Ctrl-M Item/Modify

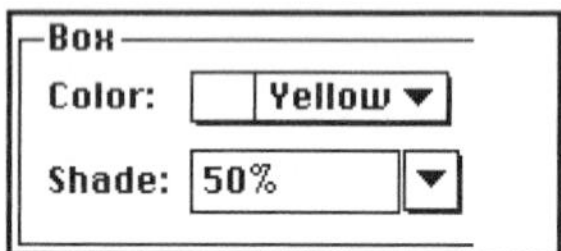

The Box tab in the Modify box contains the Box field where you apply color and a percentage (screen) of that color to any selected box.

Picture Mover pointer

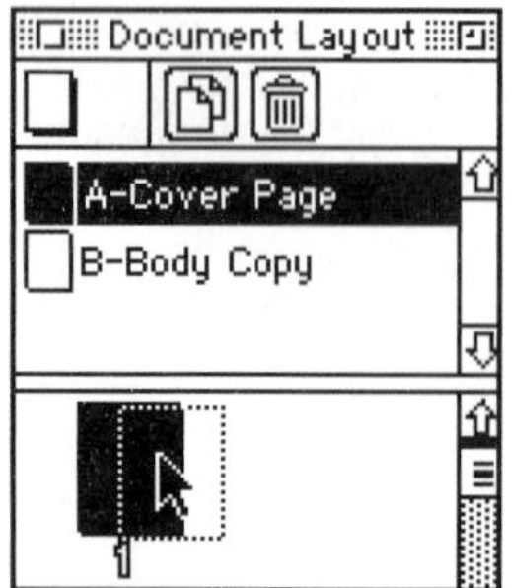

Drag a master page icon on top of a document page to apply the master page formatting.

(View/Show Measurements or F9) or the Modify Box dialog box (Item/Modify) to make the box six and a half inches wide and two inches high.

5. With the picture box still selected, choose File/Get Picture. Navigate to the Unit 03 folder on the CD-ROM and double-click on the file named *Gator.eps* to open the graphic file in the selected picture box.
6. Click inside the picture box to display the Picture Mover pointer. Press Command-Option-Shift-< [less than symbol] (Macintosh) or Ctrl-Alt-Shift-< (Windows) twice to proportionally reduce the graphic in 5% increments. Pressing those keys twice reduces the image to 90% of its original size. Use the Picture Mover pointer to position the image in the box.
7. With the picture box still selected, choose Item/Modify. Click on the Box tab and use the Box field to select Yellow as the box color. Use the Shade pull-down menu to select 50%. Click OK.
8. Double-click on document page 1 in the Document Layout palette and notice that the graphic you created on Master Page A appears on document page 1, because that document page is based on Master Page A.
9. Click on the Master Page A icon in the Document Layout palette and drag the icon down until it appears beneath document page 1. Double-click on the document page 2 icon in the Document Layout palette to get to page 2. Because you created a second document page based on Master Page A, it too displays the alligator image.
10. Choose Page/Insert to display the Insert Pages dialog box (Figure 3.2). Leave 1 as the number of pages to insert, but click on the at end of document button to insert the page after page 2. Make sure that the Master Page pull-down menu displays A-Master A. Click on OK to insert the third page in the document (Figure 3.3).

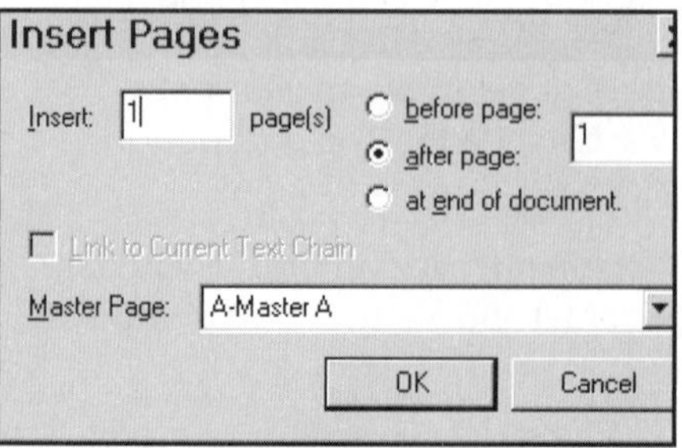

Figure 3.2. The Insert Pages dialog box lets you insert pages based on a master page or on a blank page. Because this is a non-facing page document, the Blank Facing Page option is dimmed and not available.

11. Save this file as *Gator.qxd* in your Projects folder (File/Save). You will need it for the next exercise.

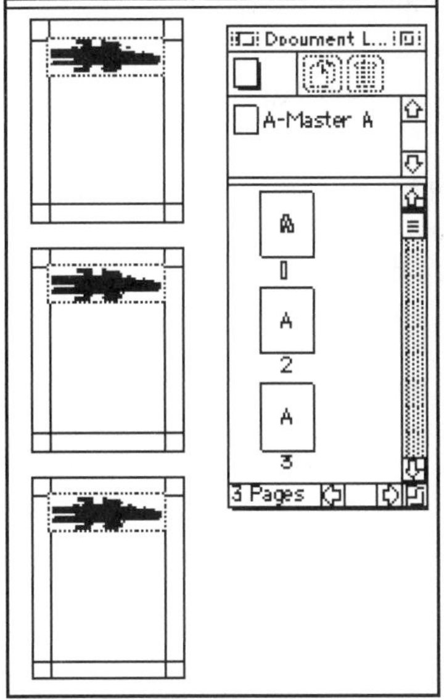

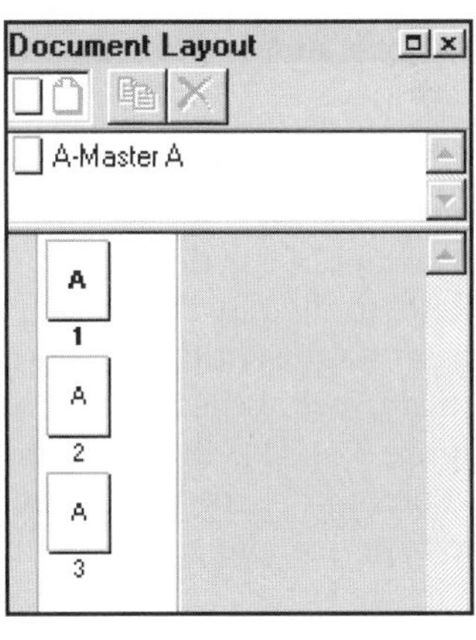

Figure 3.3. Because the three document pages are based on Master Page A, they all display the master page element, the alligator graphic.

Macintosh Commands

⌘-S File/Save
⌘-O File/Open
⌘-M Item/Modify

Windows Commands

Ctrl-S File/Save
Ctrl-O File/Open
Ctrl-M Item/Modify

Sorry!

You cannot undo actions performed in the Document Layout palette.

LESSON 2 MODIFYING MASTER PAGES

The power of master pages lies in their ability to be modified and to apply that modification to every document page based on that master page. In working with long documents, this can be a critical function if, for example, you have to change the typeface of the page number on a 300-page book.

FYI

Any master pages created after the default Master Page A appears will display the margin values specified originally in the New Document dialog box. These margins can also be changed with the Master Guides command if you are on the master page.

EXERCISE B

1. If necessary, open the *Gator.qxd* file you just created or open the *Gator.qxd* file in the Unit 03 folder on the CD-ROM (File/Open). Display the Measurements palette (F9) and the Document Layout palette (F10/Macintosh; F4/Windows).
2. Double-click on the Master Page A icon in the Document Layout palette to display Master Page A. Click on the picture box to select it and choose Item/Modify. In the Box tab, use the Box fields to change the box color from 50% yellow to 50% Cyan. Click on OK. Double-click on document page 1 and notice that the picture box reflects the change you just made on the master page. Scroll through the document and notice that all three pages display the blue box.

When you double-click on any master page or document page, its name appears in the Page Number field in the lower left corner of the document. Highlight that number, type another page number, and press Return/Enter to get to the new page.

Text Box tool

FYI

Don't forget to press the Return/Enter key after typing information in the Measurements palette to execute the command.

Content tool

Zoom tool

Watch your ps and ps

Typing a p after a value applies the value in picas. Typing a p before the value applies the value in points. 7p2p applies a value of 7 picas and 2 points. Pica values are not case-sensitive.

3. Click once (Macintosh) or double-click (Windows) on the name bar of Master Page A to highlight its name. Type *Cover Page* and press Return/Enter to rename Master Page A as Cover Page.
4. Double-click on Cover Page to get to the master page. Notice that Cover Page appears in the Page Number field in the lower left corner of the document. Resize the Document Layout palette to display the entire name. Notice that the name of the master page is outlined (Macintosh) or boldfaced (Windows), indicating that the master page is the active (selected) page (Figure 3.4). Use the standard-shape Text Box tool to draw a text box under the picture box. Use the Measurements palette and type 1 in the X field, 3 in the Y field, 6.5 in the W field, and 1.5 in the H field. Press Return/Enter.

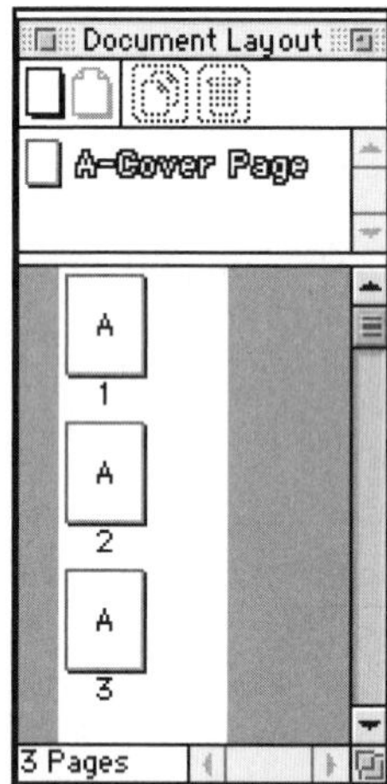

Figure 3.4. Use the resize box to expand the Document Layout palette. The Cover Page master page name is outlined because the master page is active. Anything you create or edit on this page will be reflected on the document pages based on Master Page A.

5. With the text box still selected and the Content tool active, choose File/Get Text. Locate the *Gator.txt* file in the Unit 03 folder on the CD-ROM, and double-click on it to import it into the selected text box.
6. Use the Zoom tool to enlarge the display magnification so you can see the type. Quadruple-click to select the first paragraph. Use the Measurements palette or the Style menu to format it in Helvetica bold at 24 points. Choose Style/Color/Magenta to apply the color to the selected type. Click on the center align icon in the Measurements palette to center the line in the box.
7. With the type still selected, choose Style/Formats. Type p6 in the Space After field to add 6 points of space after the paragraph. Click on OK.
8. Quadruple-click to select the second line of type. Format it in

Times italic at 14 points. Center it in the text box (Style/Alignment/Centered).

9. With the text box still selected, choose Item/Modify. Click on the Text tab. In the First Baseline area, type .5 in the Offset field to offset the first line of text one half inch from the top of the text box. Click on OK.
10. Double-click on the first document page in the Document Layout palette and notice that the formatted text box appears on that page and on every document page in the file.
11. Choose Page/Display/A-Cover A as another way to get to the Cover Page master page. Choose Page/Master Guides. Type 2 in the Columns field and click on OK.
12. Scroll through the document pages and notice that all three pages display the text box and two columns. Save this file as *Gator1.qxd* in your Projects folder (File/Save As).

Macintosh Commands

⌘-Shift-C Style/Alignment/Centered
⌘-Shift-F Style/Formats
⌘-M Item/Modify
⌘-O File/Open

Windows Commands

Ctrl-Shift-C Style/Alignment/Centered
Ctrl-M Item/Modify
Ctrl-F Style/Formats
Ctrl-O File/Open

First Baseline	
Minimum:	Ascent ▼
Offset:	0.5"

Use the Text Modify dialog box to drop the first line of text one half inch from the top of the text box.

LESSON 3
MULTIPLE MASTER PAGES

A document such as a magazine uses multiple master pages. One master page controls the text flow, another the advertising artwork, and another the front matter. Each master page is formatted separately and then applied to the appropriate document pages.

EXERCISE C

1. If necessary, open the *Gator1.qxd* file you just saved or open the *Gator1.qxd* file in the Unit 03 folder on the CD-ROM. Display the Document Layout palette (F9/Macintosh; F4 /Windows).
2. Click on the blank master page icon in the top panel of the Document Layout palette and drag it down beneath the Cover Page master page icon to create another master page, Master Page B (Figure 3.5).

Pick a tool, any tool!

Although you must select the Content tool to import text into a text box, in Version 4.0 you can use either the Content tool or the Item tool to import a graphic into a picture box.

Macintosh Commands

⌘-3 Consecutive Page Number command

Windows Commands

Ctrl-3 Consecutive Page Number command

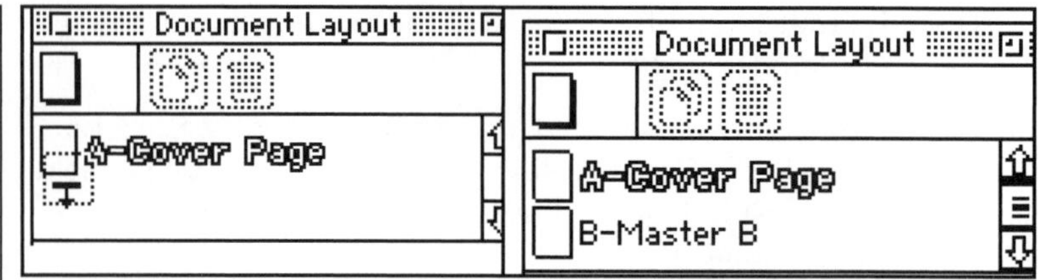

Figure 3.5. Drag the blank master page icon down beneath the Cover Page master page icon (left) to create a new master page, Master Page B (right).

3. Click once (Macintosh) or double-click (Windows) on the name bar for Master Page B and type *Body Copy*. Press Return/Enter to rename the master page.
4. Double-click on the Body Copy master page to get to it. Use the standard-shape Text Box tool to draw a text box at the bottom of the page. With the text box selected, apply the values in Figure 3.6.

Text Box tool

X: 1"	W: 6.5"
Y: 9.5"	H: 0.5"

Figure 3.6. Position and size dimensions for the text box that will contain the page number information.

5. Click inside the text box and press Command-3 (Macintosh) or Ctrl-3 (Windows) to insert the Consecutive Page Number symbol. Select the symbol and format it in Helvetica bold at 18 points. Center it in the box.
6. With the text box still selected, choose Item/Modify, click on the Text tab, and choose Centered from the Vertical Alignment pull-down menu. Click on OK.

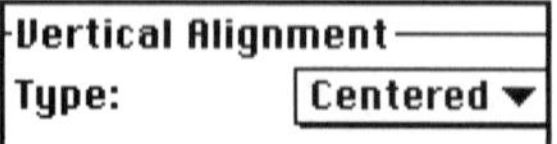

The Vertical Alignment field in the Text Modify dialog box is used to center the text in vertically in the text box.

7. Double-click on any document page to get to the document pages and choose Page/Insert. Insert three pages at the end of the document based on the Body Copy master page (Figure 3.7).

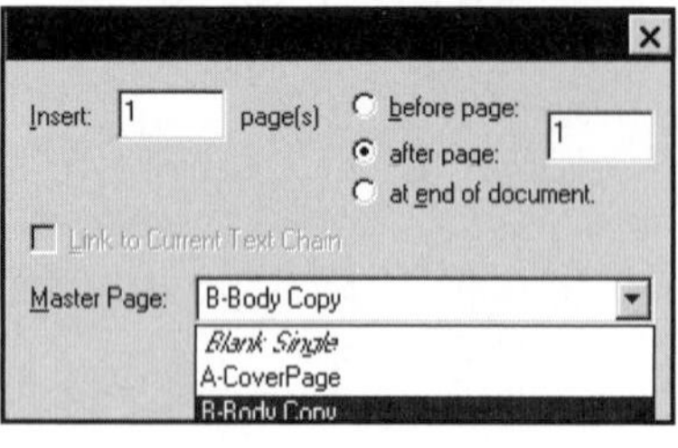

Figure 3.7. Insert three pages at the end of the document. Use the Master Page pull-down menu to select B-Body Copy.

8. Scroll through the last three pages in the document and notice that they display only the page numbers 4, 5, and 6 because they are the fourth, fifth, and sixth pages in the document. Because they are based on the Body Copy master page, they do not display any of the elements from the Cover Page master page.

9. Double-click on page 4 to get to it. Choose Page/Section to display the Section dialog box. Click to select the Section Start check box. Type 1 in the Number field and click OK to renumber the pages consecutively from number one.

10. Double-click on document page 1, the fourth page in the document, to select it. Because you selected it, its page number appears outlined in the Document Layout palette. And because you applied the Section Start command to that page, an asterisk appears after its name, indicating that a page number command was applied to the page. Notice that the last three pages in the document are numbered consecutively from page 1 to page 3 (Figure 3.8).

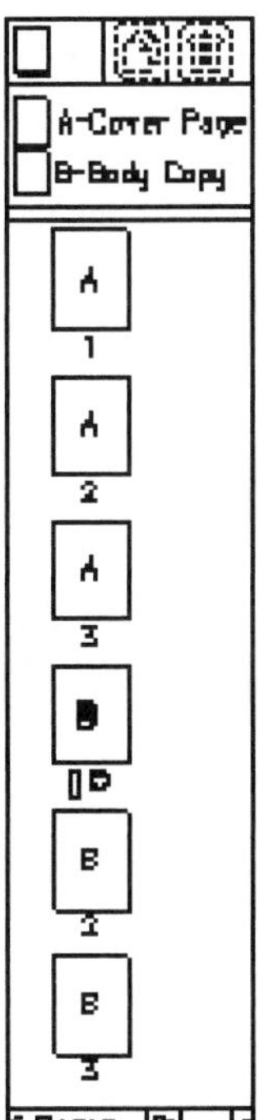

Figure 3.8. The last three document pages are based on Master Page B. Page 1 is highlighted because it is selected. The asterisk indicates that the Section Start command was applied to that page.

11. Save this file as *Master.qxd* in your Projects folder (File/Save As).

Macintosh Commands

⌘-Option-S File/Save as

Windows Commands

Ctrl-Alt-S File/Save as

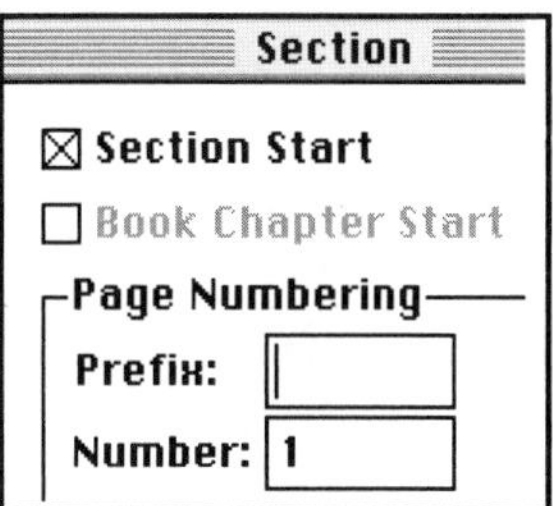

You must select the Section Start check box to apply a new page number sequence.

Macintosh Commands

⌘-O File/Open
⌘-M Item/Modify

Windows Commands

Ctrl-O File/Open
Ctrl-M Item/Modify

Tabbed Dialog Boxes

Tabbed dialog boxes let you enter different kinds of information about a selection by clicking on the appropriate tab. You click on OK only after you have entered all the values in the different tabs.

LESSON 4
APPLYING MASTER PAGES

There are two ways of creating document pages that contain master page items: *create* the master page and then insert document pages based on that master page; or *apply* a master page to an existing document page. To do this, just drag the master page icon down onto the document page area of the Document Layout palette and cover the document page.

What happens at this point depends on an option you select in the General Preferences Document dialog box (Figure 3.9). The Keep Changes option should really read, "Keep changes made to master page items on this document page when I reapply the same master page or a different master page to this document page." The Delete Changes option tells XPress to delete any master page items that you have edited on the document page when you reapply the same master page or a different master page.

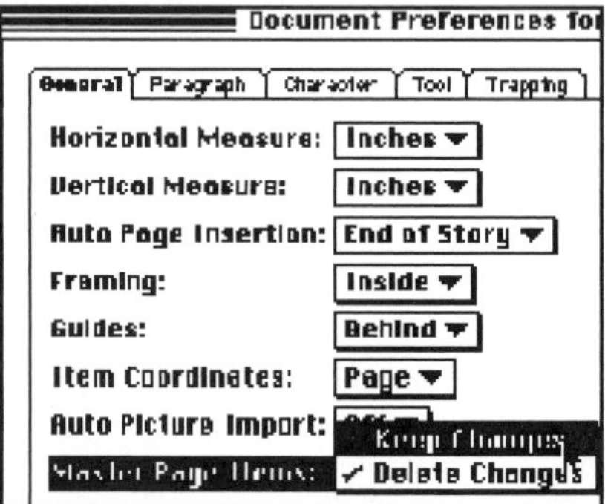

Figure 3.9. Select Keep Changes or Delete Changes to specify what happens to edited master page items on a document page when you reapply the same master page or apply a different master page to the document page.

EXERCISE D

1. If necessary, open the *Master.qxd* file you created in the last exercise or open the *Master.qxd* file in the Unit 03 folder on the CD-ROM (File/Open). Display the Document Layout palette (F9/Macintosh; F4/Windows).

2. This file contains six document pages based on two master pages. Double-click on document page 1, which is based on the Cover Page master page. It displays a picture box and a text box. Select the picture box and choose Item/Modify. Change the box color to 100% Red and click on OK. You have now edited a master page item.

3. Double-click on page 2, which is also based on the Cover Page master page. Its box is still cyan because you did not make the color change on the master page, only on a document page.
4. Choose Edit/Preferences/Document. Click on the General tab and choose Keep Changes from the Master Pages Items pull-down menu at the bottom of the dialog box. Click on OK.
5. Click on the Cover Page master page icon in the Document Layout palette and drag it over document page 1, the page you just edited. Nothing appears to be different, but if you select the Item tool and drag the red picture box down, you'll see the blue picture box behind it (Figure 3.10). Because the red picture box is an edited (changed) master page item and you told XPress to keep any changed master page item when you reapplied the master page, the red box remains on the page.

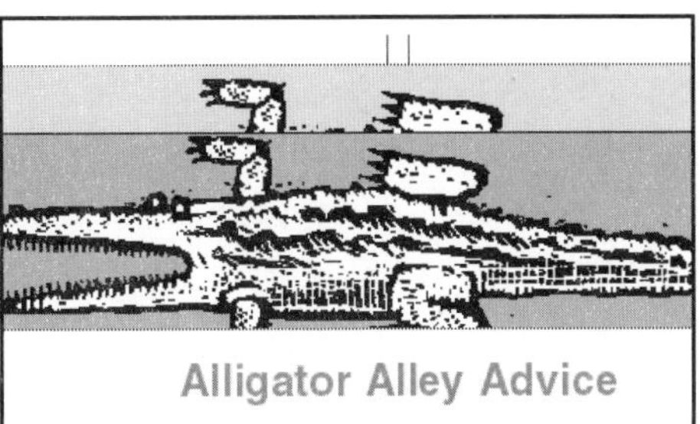

Figure 3.10. Because Keep Changes was selected in the General Document Preferences dialog box, the edited picture box was kept when the Cover Page master page was reapplied to the document page.

6. Drag the Cover Page master page icon down on top of document page 4, which is based on the Body Copy master page. The page number box disappears and only the two master page elements from Master Page A (Cover Page) appear on the fourth document page. Because you did not make any changes to any master page item on that document page, there was nothing to keep and the entire page was replaced by the elements on Master Page A (Cover Page) when you applied the new master page.
7. Choose File/Revert to Saved. Click on OK to revert to the last saved version of the file. Choose Edit/Preferences/Document. Click on the General tab and this time choose Delete Changes from the Master Pages Items pull-down menu at the bottom of the dialog box. Click on OK.
8. Double-click on the first document page and select the blue picture box. Choose Item/Modify. Change the box color to 50% Green and click on OK. You have edited a master page item.

Macintosh Commands

⌘-Y Edit/Preferences/Document
⌘-M Item/Modify

Windows Commands

Ctrl-Y Edit/Preferences/Document
Ctrl-M Item/Modify

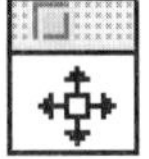

item tool

Macintosh Commands

⌘-W File/Close

Windows Commands

Ctrl-F4 File/Close

9. Drag the Cover Page master page icon down on top of the first document page to reapply the Cover Page master page items to that page. Double-click on document page 1 and notice that the green box has been replaced by the blue box, the master page item. Although you edited a master page item on page 1, because you told XPress to delete any edited master page items, only the master page items from the Cover Page master page appear.
10. Drag the Body Copy master page on top of document page 1. Notice that the picture box and text box are replaced by the single text box which is the only master page item on Master Page B, the Body Copy master page. Document page 1 now displays a B, indicating that it is based on Master Page B and not on master page A (Figure 3.11).

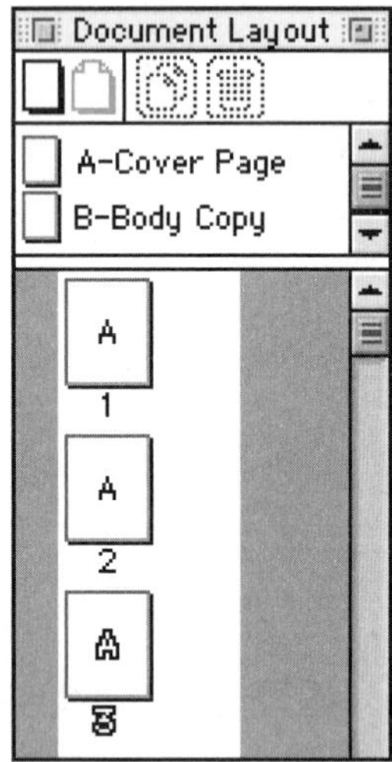

Figure 3.11. The first document page displays a B, indicating that it is based on Master Page B, the Body Copy master page.

11. Close this file. Don't save your changes.

LESSON 5
DUPLICATING AND DELETING MASTER PAGES

When you want some master page items to appear on another master page, the easiest thing to do is to duplicate the master page and then edit it. Regardless of what you name master pages, they always appear in the Document Layout palette in alphabetical order as A, B, C, etc.

To delete a master page, click on the master page icon and click on the Delete icon in the top panel of the Document Layout palette. Deleting a master page deletes any of its master page items applied to the document pages based on the deleted master page.

EXERCISE E

1. Open the *Master.qxd* file you created in an earlier exercise or open the *Master.qxd* file in the Unit 03 folder on the CD-ROM (File/Open). Display the Document Layout palette (F9/Macintosh; F4/Windows).
2. Click once on Master Page B, the Body Copy master page, to select it. Then click on the Duplicate icon in the first panel of the Document Layout palette (Figure 3.12) to create Master Page C. Double-click on Master Page C to get to it. It displays only the page number text box.

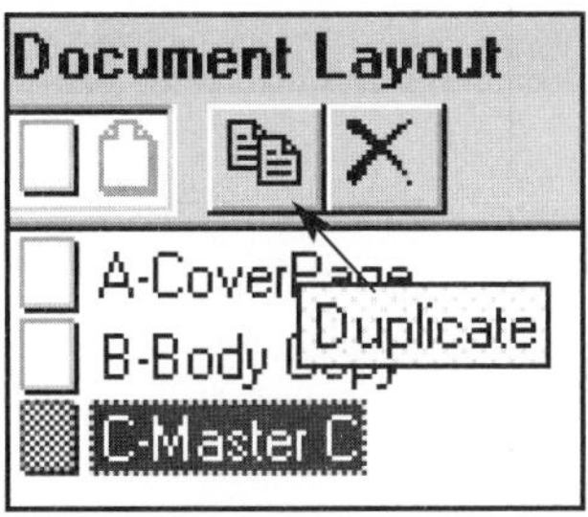

Figure 3.12. Click once on a master page to select it, and click on the Duplicate icon to duplicate that master page. The duplicate is automatically named in alphabetical order.

3. Choose Edit/Preferences/Document. Click on the General tab and make sure that Master Page Items displays Keep Changes. Click on OK.
4. Use the Oval Picture Box tool to draw an oval on the page. Choose File/Get Picture. Navigate to the Unit 03 folder on the CD-ROM and double-click on the file named *CD.eps* to import it into the selected Picture box.
5. Drag the handles on the picture box to resize it so that it fits around the CD-ROM image. Master Page C now displays both the picture box and the page number text box. Drag the Master Page C icon on top of document page 1, where it replaces all the elements on that page.

Macintosh Commands

⌘-O File/Open
⌘-Y Edit/Preferences/Document
⌘-E File/Get Text/Picture

Windows Commands

Ctrl-O File/Open
Ctrl-Y Edit/Preferences/Document
Ctrl-E File/Get Text/Picture

FYI

The Delete icon on the Macintosh Document Layout palette is a trash icon; the Windows Delete icon is a large ***X***.

Tip

Pressing Command-Option-Shift-< (Macintosh) or Ctrl-Alt-Shift-< (Windows) reduces the size of the image proportionately. Substitute the > [greater than symbol] to proportionately increase the size of the image in 5% increments.

Oval Picture Box tool

Macintosh Commands

⌘-W File/Close

Macintosh Commands

Ctrl-F4 File/Close

6. Click once on the Master Page B icon, Body Copy, to select it, and click on the Delete icon in the top panel of the Document Layout panel. At the alert, click on OK to delete the master page. The text box with the page number disappears from every document page formerly based on Master Page B. No document pages display B, indicating that Master Page B is no longer available.
7. Click on document page 2 and drag it up next to document page 1 to create a two-page spread.
8. Click on document page 4 and drag it up next to document page 3 to create another spread.
9. Click on document page 6 and drag it up next to document page 5 to create the last spread. Your screen should resemble Figure 3.13 with the last three pages not based on any master page and only two master pages in the document, Master Page A (Cover Page) and Master Page C (Figure 3.13). Close this file (File/Close). Don't save your changes.

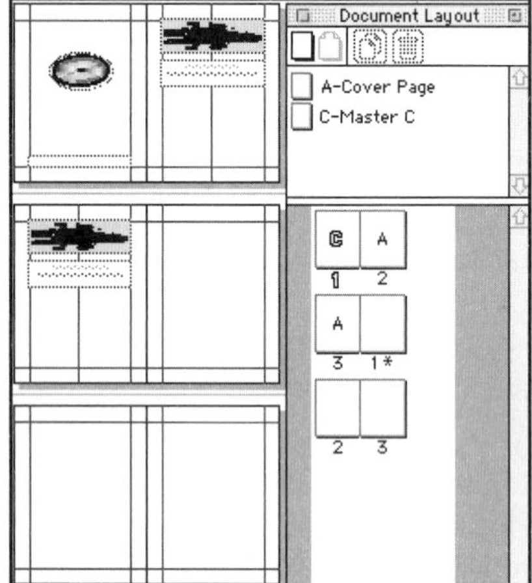

Figure 3.13. When Master Page B was deleted, its master page items were removed from any document page based on Master Page B.

LESSON 6
WORKING WITH LEFT AND RIGHT MASTER PAGES

When you create a facing pages document, Master Page A that is automatically created with the document has two pages, a left and right page (Figure 3.14). You must place master page elements on both the left and right master pages if you want them to appear on the corresponding left and right document pages.

Figure 3.14. A facing pages document has two pages for Master Page A, a left and right page. These two pages must be formatted separately to apply master page items to all the document pages.

EXERCISE F

1. Create a new file with an automatic text box, facing pages, two columns, and one-inch margins. Display the Measurements palette (F9). Choose Page/Insert and insert three more pages at the end of the document based on Master Page A.
2. Double-click on Master Page A to get to it. Choose View/Fit in Window (Command/Ctrl-0 [zero] or press Control-V (Macintosh) or Ctrl-Alt-V (Windows) and type 30 in the View Box. Press Return/Enter. You want to display both the left and right master pages on the screen.
3. Use the standard-shape Text Box tool to draw a text box about one half inch high (.5) at the bottom of the left master page and position it directly below the bottom margin guide.
4. Click inside the text box with the Content tool and press Command-3 (Macintosh) or Ctrl-3 (Windows) to insert the Consecutive Page Number Symbol. Double-click to select the symbol and format it from the Style menu or from the Measurements palette.
5. Keep the text box selected and choose Item/Duplicate. Use the Item tool to drag the duplicate to the same position on the right master page.
6. Scroll to the top of the left master page, draw a one-inch high text box across the page and position it directly above the top margin guide. Type Left Page Header in the box, triple-click to select the line, and format it. Make sure it is left aligned.

Macintosh Commands

⌘-0 [zero] View/Fit in Window
⌘-3 Consecutive Page Number

Windows Commands

Ctrl-0 [zero] View/Fit in Window
Ctrl-3 Consecutive Page Number

Text Box tool

Content tool

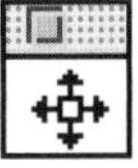

Item tool

Macintosh Commands

⌘-D Item/Duplicate
⌘-W File/Close

Windows Commands

Ctrl-D Item/Duplicate
Ctrl-F4 File/Close

7. With the header box still selected, choose Item/Duplicate and use the Item tool to drag the duplicate box to the same position on the right master page. Select the Content tool and change Left to Right in the header box on the right master page. Click on the right align icon in the Measurements palette to align the header text with the right side of the text box. Your screen should resemble Figure 3.15.

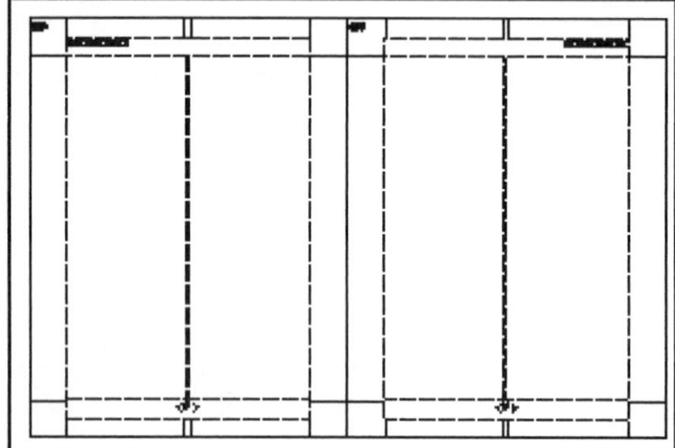

Figure 3.15. Both the left and right master pages for Master Page A are formatted with header and footer text boxes.

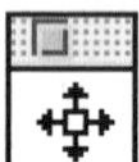

Item tool

8. Close this file (File/Close). Don't save your changes.

LESSON 7 MASTER PAGES AND DOCUMENT PAGES

Content tool

Master pages live to serve document pages. The only reason to have any master page in a document is to achieve consistency across multiple document pages. Each time you drag down a master page icon onto the document area or select a master page from the Insert Pages dialog box, you are ensuring that consistency. If you drag any document page from Document 1 to Document 2, not only does that page move to Document 2, but the master page on which that page is based also moves to Document 2.

When document pages are copied between documents—you can't copy master pages between documents—they are drag-copied. This means that as you drag a page from one document (source document) to another (target document), you create a copy of that page in the new document.

COPYING PAGES BETWEEN DOCUMENTS

There are a few rules of engagement for copying pages between documents. (1) First, both documents must be open, although only one file can be selected (active). This isn't like the Append command that lets you navigate to a file. (2) The target document must have the same or larger page size as the source document. You cannot drag-copy a page from the source document that is larger than the page size in the target document. (3) You can drag-copy a non-facing page to a facing page document, but not the other way around. (4) Both documents must be in Thumbnails view.

COPYING ITEMS BETWEEN DOCUMENTS

It's a lot easier to copy an item between documents because you can drag-copy any selected item—box, line, group, or text path—with the Item tool to another document without having to be in Thumbnails view.

MOVING DOCUMENT PAGES

Although you can move document pages around in the Document Layout palette, you can also use the Move command to move those pages to a new location in the document. Like the Insert Pages and Delete Pages dialog boxes, the Move Page dialog box allows you to specify a range of pages to be moved and a new position in the document for those moved pages.

EXERCISE G

1. Create a document (File/New) without an automatic text box; use portrait (vertical) orientation, non-facing pages, and one-inch margins. Double-click on the Master Page A icon to get to the master page. Use any of the picture box tools to draw a picture box on the master page. Display the Colors palette (F12), click the Background icon, and fill the selected picture box with a color. Double-click on document page 1 to get to the document page. Choose View/Thumbnails. Resize the window so that only the document page is visible.
2. Repeat to create another new document with facing pages. Draw another picture box on the master page in the second document. Display the Document Layout palette (View/Show Document Layout). Choose View/Thumbnails (Shift F6).
3. Click on Document1 to activate it. With either the Content tool or the Item tool, click on document page 1 in the Document Layout palette and drag it onto Document2, next to page 1 to create a two-page spread. Click on Document2 to activate it and notice that the Document Layout palette for Document2 displays a new master page, Master Page B (Figure 3.16). Double-click on Master Page B and notice that it is a copy of Master Page A from Document 1.

Macintosh Commands

⌘-N File/New/Document
Shift-F6 View/Thumbnails

Windows Commands

Ctrl-N File/New/Document
Shift-F6 View/Thumbnails

Thumbnails

Thumbnails view is a non-editable view. All you can do in this view is add pages, apply master pages, and move pages around on the Document Layout palette. You can't edit any of the text or items on the master or document pages.

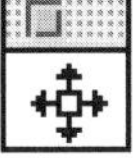

Item tool

Cheat sheet

If you reduce the magnification value to 12%, you approximate Thumbnails view and can edit text and items.

Content tool

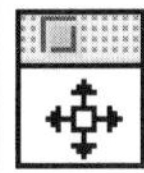

Item tool

Macintosh Commands

⌘-W File/Close

Windows Commands

Ctrl-F4 File/Close

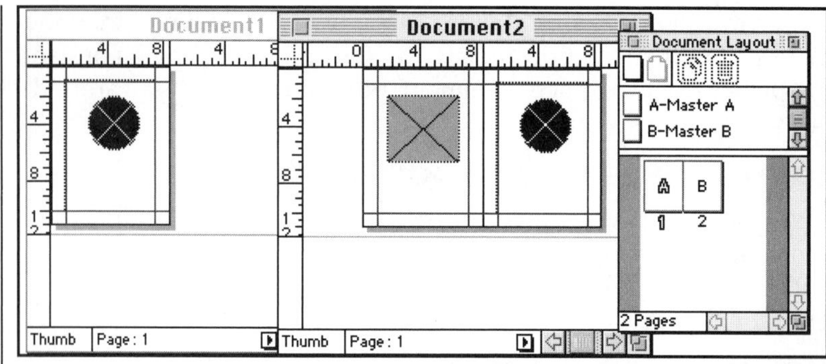

Figure 3.16. When a document page was drag-copied from Document1 to Document2, the master page was also copied to Document2 and named Master Page B.

4. Still in Document2, choose View/50% to get out of Thumbnails view. Click on Document1 to activate it and change the view. You can't drag copy *items* in Thumbnails view.
5. With both documents in an editable view, click on the picture box in one document and drag it to the other document. Repeat for the second document. You can drag-copy items from one document page or from one master page to another document's master page or document page.
6. Double-click on document page 2 in Document2, the second page in the spread that's based on Master Page B. Choose Page/Move to display the Move Pages dialog box. Type 2 in the Move page(s) field. Click to select the before page option and type 1 in the field to move page 2 before page 1. Click on OK. Your Document Layout palette should resemble Figure 3.17.

Drag-copying linked text boxes

If you drag-copy a linked text box (a text box that has text flowing from one manually linked or from one automatic text box to another in the document) from one document page to any document page in a target document, all the linked text will come with that copied text box. However, that text box will display the Overflow Indicator, telling you that there is more text than can be displayed in just that one text box.

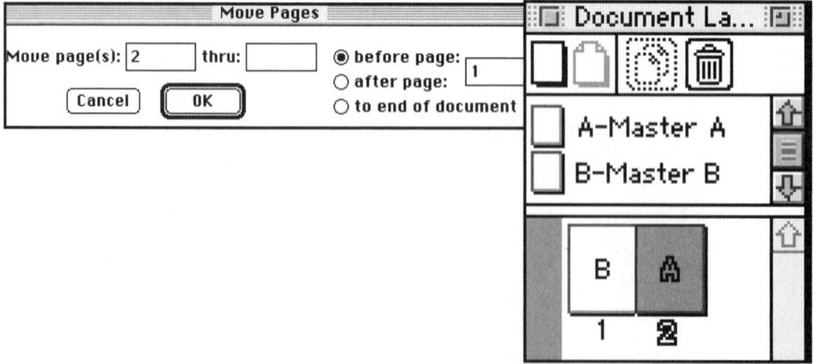

Figure 3.17. Move a single page or range of pages to a new location in the document using the Move Pages dialog box.

7. Close both files (File/Close). Don't save your changes.

UNIT 4

TEXT BOXES

Image from *Business Characters* by Susan LeVan, for Artville

OVERVIEW

In this unit you will learn how to:
Set document preferences
Import text
Modify text boxes
Use the Measurements palette
Specify leading
Change text box shapes
Specify spot colors

TERMS

Auto Page Insertion
Auto Picture Import
filters
guides
jump lines
link
paragraph alignment
spot color
Undo
unit of measure
unlink

HOW IT WORKS:

In Photoshop, change the mode of the image from RGB to Grayscale, crop it to the size of an XPress picture box, and save it as a JPEG file. Import the image into a picture box. Create the text in a standard-shape text box and format it. With the text box selected, choose Create Effect from the QX-Effects menu that appears when the QX-Effects XTension is loaded. Select Emboss from the Contents field, change the Color Mode to Grayscale, select Cutout from the Emboss Type menu, and adjust the Highlight and Shadow Intensity values to create the effect. QX-Effects creates a TIFF file for the effect called *Emboss 1* which is saved in the same folder as the XPress file and is needed for printing the effect.

LESSON 1
SETTING DOCUMENT PREFERENCES

Because many of the options you select in the Preferences dialog boxes affect how text is displayed, you should set those preferences before importing and creating text. You can always go back into any Preferences dialog boxes and make changes at any time in the document construction process. The Document Preferences dialog box is where you make choices about how your document will appear and how it behaves. When you choose Edit/Preferences/Document (Figure 4.1), the Document Preferences dialog box appears (Figure 4.2).

Preferences ▶ | Application... ⌘⌥⇧Y
Style Sheets... ⇧F11 | Document... ⌘Y
Colors... ⇧F12 | Index...

Figure 4.1. Select Document preferences from the Preferences pull-out menu under the Edit menu.

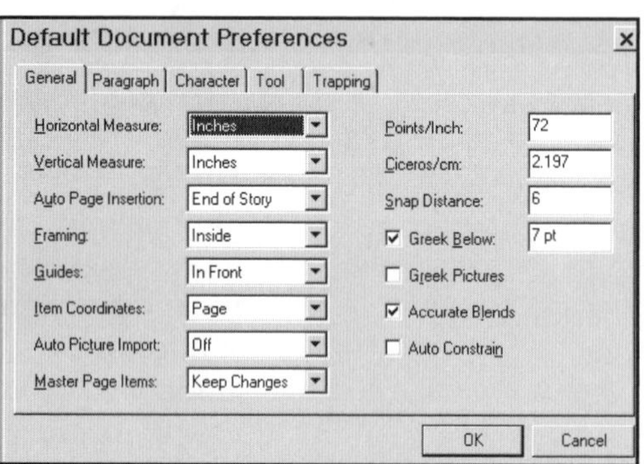

Figure 4.2. The General Preferences dialog box.

Quark does math!

To increase or decrease a value in the Measurements palette, type the symbol and value next to the existing value and press the Return/Enter key. For example, if the height of a box reads 4p on the Measurements palette, and you want to increase its width by 7 picas, type + 7p after the 4p value.

W: 8p5
H: 4p + 7p

HORIZONTAL AND VERTICAL MEASURE

Horizontal and Vertical Measure specify the unit of measure reflected in the rulers and in all the dialog boxes and palettes. You can always override a unit of measure by typing the appropriate symbol for that format. For example, if you specify picas as the unit of measure in the General Preferences dialog box and want to resize a box to 4 inches, just type 4" in the appropriate field.

AUTO PAGE INSERTION

The Auto Page Insertion option tells XPress to add or not to add pages when you import or type more text than can fit into the available text boxes. However, you must have selected the Automatic Text Box option in the New Document dialog box for this option to work. Selecting End of Story or End of Document will not automatically add needed pages unless the document was created with an automatic text box. For example, if you are producing a four-page newsletter, you do not want more than four pages in the document. Select the Automatic Text Box option when you first create the document and then use the Document Preferences dialog box to set Auto Page Insertion to Off. Now, if you import or type more text than can fit into those four pages, you will have to edit the text to make it fit in the four-page document.

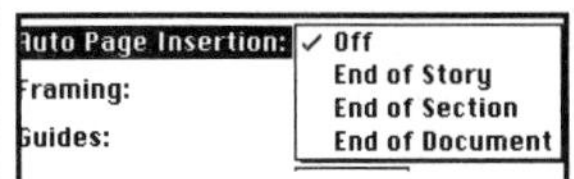

Selecting an auto page insertion option will automatically add pages to the document should you flow more text than can fit into the available pages—if you selected the Automatic Text Box option in the New Document dialog box.

FRAMING

Framing refers to the frames (borders) placed around a box. If the size of the box is critical, select the Outside option, which does not apply the frame to the area inside the box.

GUIDES

Guides are non-printing lines that you pull down and out from the horizontal and vertical rulers. They are used to align items on a page, and are generally useless unless they are in front of the item. In version 4.0 this is the default setting (finally!).

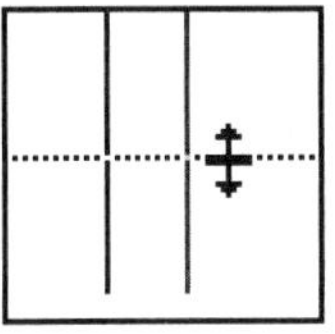

Click on a guide and use the Guide cursor to move the guide around the page.

ITEM COORDINATES

Item Coordinates specifies how the rulers appear. If you have a two-page (or more) spread and select Page from the Item Coordinates pull-down menu, the ruler will begin at zero at the top of the right page of the spread. Selecting Spread continues the ruler measurements across the multiple-page spread.

AUTO PICTURE IMPORT

Auto Picture Import tells XPress to notify you if an image originally used in a document is missing or has been modified since you last saved the document. When Off is selected from the Auto Picture Import pull-down menu, XPress does not notify you that an image has been modified and does not display the modified image. Selecting On tells XPress to automatically load the modified image. On (verify) displays a dialog box telling you that the image has been modified and allows you either to display the original image or to update the original to the modified version.

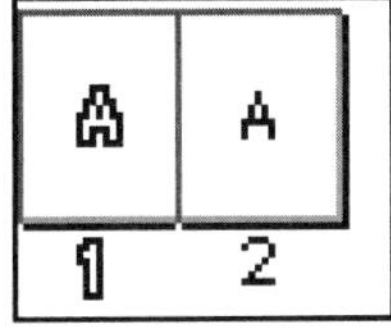

A two-page spread positions two adjacent pages horizontally.

Macintosh Commands

⌘-N File/New/Document
⌘-Y Edit/Preferences/Document

Windows Commands

Ctrl-N File/New/Document
Ctrl-Y Edit/Preferences/Document

MASTER PAGE ITEMS

Master Page Items options tell XPress to keep or delete any changes you made to master page items when you reapply a master page to a document page. For example, if you place a black solid line between two columns on the master page and change that black solid line to a red dotted line on page 3 of the document, XPress will place the black line over the red line when you drag the master page over document page 3 if you select Keep Changes. If you select Delete Changes, XPress will delete the red line *and* replace it with the black line from the master page.

GREEKING

Greeking is changing the appearance of text and graphics to gray bars (text) and a gray box (graphics). This allows for speedy screen redraw and does not affect the text or image, just its screen appearance. If you greek pictures, clicking on the picture box removes the greeking and displays the image.

LESSON 2 IMPORTING TEXT

FYI

You can't type in the automatic text box on a master page. Always create a separate text box for page numbers on the master page.

QuarkXPress 4.0 ships with filters (XTensions) for many word processors. To activate a filter for Microsoft Word, for example, move the MS Word filter into the XTensions folder before launching QuarkXPress. Select a text box and use the Get Text command to open a word processing file created in Microsoft Word. This process applies to importing text created in any word processor.

EXERCISE A

1. Choose File/New/Document and apply the values displayed in Figure 4.3. Click on OK to display a one-page facing page document with an automatic text box containing two columns.
2. Choose Edit/Preferences/Document, select inches as the horizontal and vertical unit of measure, and make sure that Auto Page Insertion is set to End of Document—actually, end of anything works. Click on OK to return to the first page of the document. Choose View/Show Document Layout Palette (F10/Macintosh; F4/Windows). Notice that the master page and document page icons display a turned corner, indicating that this is a facing pages document (Figure 4.4).

New Document
Page
Size: US Letter
Width: 8.5"
Height: 11"
Orientation:
Margin Guides
Top: 1
Bottom: 1
Inside: 1
Outside: 1
☒ Facing Pages
Column Guides
Columns: 2
Gutter Width: 0.167"
☒ Automatic Text Box
Cancel OK

Figure 4.3. These options select an automatic text box with one-inch margins, facing pages, and two columns for the new document. Because this is a facing pages document, the Left and Right margin settings are replaced by Inside and Outside.

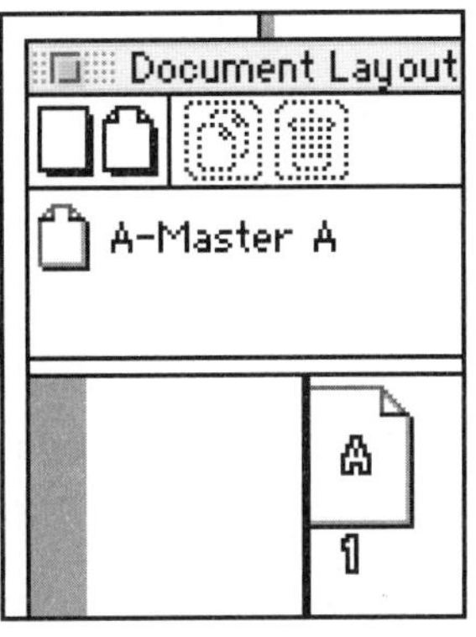

Figure 4.4. When the Facing Pages option is selected in the New Document dialog box, additional facing pages are added as left and right pages. The turned corner on the icon indicates that this is a facing page.

3. Click on the text box on the document page to select it and make sure the Content tool is selected. Choose File/Get Text. Navigate to the Unit 04 folder on the CD-ROM and highlight the *Text.txt* file. Click on Open or double-click on the file name to import the text file. The size of the file causes another page to automatically be added to the document, because Auto Page Insertion is on.

4. Double-click on the icon for page 1 in the Document Layout palette to go to the first page. Choose Edit/Select All to select the entire story. Choose Style/Font/Times (or any font installed in your system). Then choose Style/Size 14.

5. Choose File/Save. Because this file has not yet been saved, the Save as dialog box appears. Type *Face.qxd* in the name field and navigate to your Projects folder. Click on Save. Close this file (File/Close).

Macintosh Commands

⌘-E File/Get Text/Picture
⌘-A Edit/Select All
⌘-S File/Save
⌘-W FIle/Close

Windows Commands

Ctrl-E File/Get Text/Picture
Ctrl-A Edit/Select All
Ctrl-S File/Save
Ctrl-F4 File/Close

Fonts

Feel free to use any fonts installed in your system. No one is paying you for these files, so create some of your own specs!

Macintosh Commands

⌘-O FIle/Open
⌘-0 [zero] View/Fit in Window
⌘-M Item/Modify

Windows Commands

Ctrl-O File/Open
Ctrl-0 [zero] View/Fit in Window
Ctrl-M Item-Modify

LESSON 3 MODIFYING TEXT BOXES

A text box, whether it's a standard-shape text box or a Bézier text box, does not have to be drawn to any specifications. There are three ways to modify a selected text box: manually, resize and reposition it by dragging on any of its resizing handles and use the Item tool (standard-shape text boxes only) to drag the box to a new location; use the Measurements palette to change any of the values on the left side of the palette to modify the box's position, size, corner radius, column number, and angle; or choose Item/Modify and click on the Box tab to change the box's characteristics.

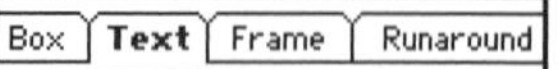

Access multiple dialog boxes by clicking on the appropriate tab.

MODIFY DIALOG BOXES

When you select a box or line and select Item/Modify, a series of tabbed dialog boxes appears. Here you select the attribute you wish to modify, click on its tab, and then change the values in the various fields. You can change the size of the item, its text characteristics if it's a text box, its frame if it is a box, and the runaround specifications that define how text wraps around the item. Each specifications dialog box contains an Apply button that lets you apply the change without leaving the dialog box. If you don't like the options you've selected, click on Cancel to close the dialog box without applying any of the changes.

Some of the word processing filters that ship with QuarkXPress 4.0 for the Macintosh. Similar XTensions ship with the Windows version.

TEXT INSET

When you select a text box and choose Item/Modify, click on the Text tab to get to the Text Inset field. Text defaults to being inset from all the sides of a text box by one point. If you want to change this value—to give your text more white space on all four sides, for example—increase the value in the Text Offset field. Just remember, the Text Offset value applies the space to all sides of the text box, not just to the top and bottom or left and right sides of the box.

EXERCISE B

1. If necessary, open the *Face.qxd* file you created in the last exercise (File/Open) or open the *Face.qxd* file in the Unit 04 folder on the CD-ROM. Choose View/Fit in Window. Click on the text box on the first document page and choose Item/Modify to display the four tabbed specifications dialog boxes. The Box dialog box is the active box (Figure 4.5).

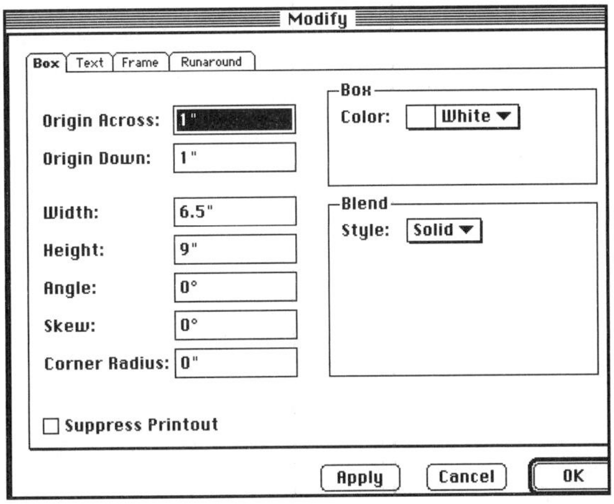

Figure 4.5. The Modify dialog box gives you access to box, text, frame, and runaround (wrap) options for the selected box.

FYI

When you are resizing a text box, press the Command/Ctrl key to resize both the text box and the text simultaneously.

2. The Origin values indicate that this text box is positioned one inch from the left edge of the paper (Origin Across) and one inch from the top edge of the paper. Double-click to select 1″ in the Origin Across field. Type 2 in the Origin Across field and click on Apply. The box moves one inch to the right, and is now positioned two inches from the left edge of the paper.
3. Select 9 in the Height field and type 7. Click on Apply to change the height of the text box to 7 inches.
4. Select the 0 in the Corner Radius field and type 1 to give the corners of the text box a one-inch corner radius. Click on Apply.
5. In the Box field, use the Color pull-down menu to select Blue. Use the Shade pull-down menu to select 50%. Click on OK to apply the changes and return to the document page. Your screen should resemble Figure 4.6.

FYI

When you apply a Shade value to a color, you are screening the color back from its normal 100% shade.

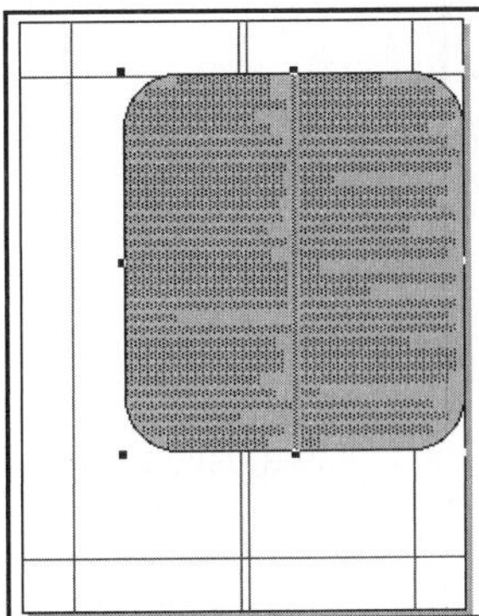

Figure 4.6. The text box displays the changes made in the Box modify dialog box.

Macintosh Commands

⌘-Z Edit/Undo
⌘-M Item/Modify
⌘-W File/Close

Windows Commands

Ctrl-Z Edit/Undo
Ctrl-M Item/Modify
Ctrl-F4 File/Close

6. Before doing anything else, choose Edit/Undo Item Change to undo all the changes you made in the Box modify dialog box and return it to its original values.

7. With the text box still selected, choose Item/Modify again. Click on the Text tab and apply the values in Figure 4.7.

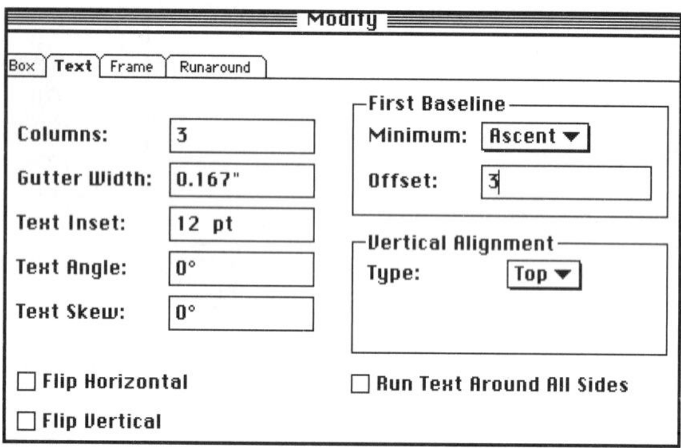

Figure 4.7. The text box now contains three columns, the text is inset 12 points from all four sides of the text box, and the baseline of the first line of text starts 3 inches down from the top of the text box.

8. Click on the Frame tab and apply the values in Figure 4.8. As you make selections from the Width, Style, Frame, and Gap menus, the frame appears in the Preview field. Click on OK to apply the changes. Your first document page should resemble Figure 4.9. Close this file. Don't save your changes.

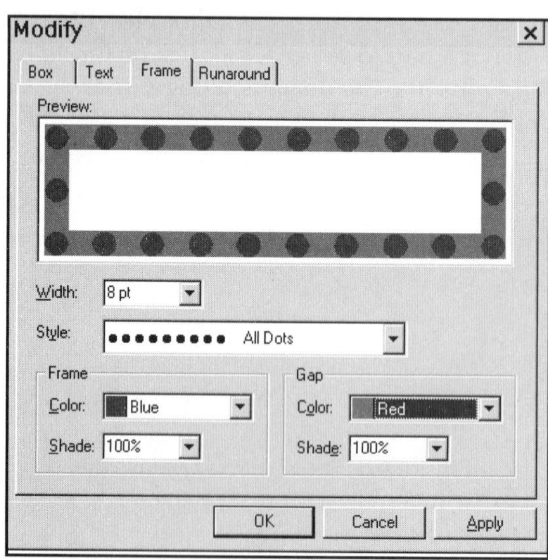

Figure 4.8. The Frame dialog box is where you specify style values for the frame (border) of a box.

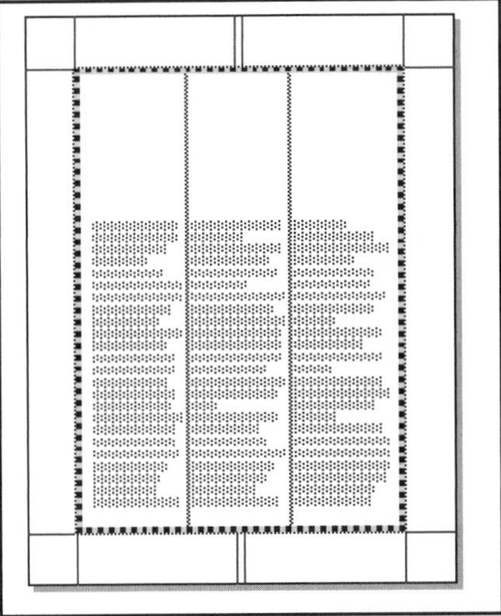

Figure 4.9 displays the changes made in the Text and Frame Modify dialog boxes.

Speed demon!

Press the Tab key to move from one field to another in the Measurements palette. The new field is highlighted and ready for you to enter values without deleting the original values.

LESSON 4
MEASUREMENTS PALETTE

An easy way to apply many specifications to a box and its contents is to use the Measurements palette (Figure 4.10). Press F9 to display and hide the Measurements palette. You can also click in the Close box of the palette to hide it. If the palette appears empty, that's because nothing is selected and there are no measurements to display. When a text box is selected and the Measurements palette is displayed, all the values to the left of the center line apply to the box. All the values to the right of the line apply to the text.

FYI

Remember to press the Return/Enter key after typing anything in the Measurements palette. You don't have to press the Return/Enter key when clicking on the arrows, only when typing in a value.

Figure 4.10. The Measurements palette for a selected text box.

It's important to remember that when you type values in the Measurements palette, you must press the Return/Enter key to execute the command. If you don't press the Return/Enter key, nothing will happen to your selection.

Macintosh Commands

⌘-O File/Open

Windows Commands

Ctrl-O FIle/Open

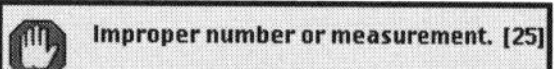

Angry? Frustrated?

If you find the alert constantly beeping or if you get an error message while you are entering a value in the Measurements palette, press Command/Ctrl-Z and press the Return key. You'll see the offending value highlighted in the Measurements palette. Change the value and continue.

Later in life...

It's fine to rotate items a few degrees in XPress, but ordinarily, any heavy-duty rotating should be done in the originating graphics application. Extensive rotating in XPress takes a long time and ties up the printer.

EXERCISE C

1. Open the *Face.qxd* file from your Projects folder or from the Unit 04 folder on the CD-ROM. Click to select the text box on the first page and press F9 (Macintosh) or F4 (Windows) to display the Document Layout palette. It displays the values in Figure 4.10. All the values from the black horizontal and vertical arrows to the left apply to the box. Values to the right of the arrows apply to the box contents, in this case, the text.
2. Double-click on 1″ in the X field and type 2. Press Return/Enter. The selected text box moves two inches from the left edge of the paper, just as it did when you used the Box Modify dialog box in Exercise B.
3. Select the W(idth) value and type 5; select the H(eight) value and type 6. Press the Return/Enter key to execute the commands.
4. With the resized text box still selected, select the 0° value in the box rotation field. Type 45 and press Return/Enter to rotate the text box 45 degrees to the left. Type 0 in the box rotation field and press Return/Enter to return the box to its original position. Type -45 in the box rotation field and press Return/Enter to rotate the box 45 degrees to the right.
5. Select the 2 in the Cols (Columns) field, type 3, and press Return/Enter to change the selected two-column text box to a three-column text box.
6. Click the horizontal and vertical flip arrows to flip the box.
7. Choose File/Revert to Saved to revert to the last saved version of the file. At the prompt, click on OK. When you revert to the last saved version, all changes not saved with this version are discarded. Keep this file open; you will need it for the next exercise.

LESSON 5
LEADING

In the old days (a few years ago), typesetters used bars of different widths of hot lead to separate lines of type, which is why the vertical space between lines of type is called leading (pronounced "ledding"). Leading is the distance measured in points from the baseline of one line of type to the baseline of the line of type above or below it. The more leading between lines, the more elegant and open the type looks. Less leading creates a crowded, jumbled look, but is often used to produce interesting type effects. When designers and editors say something like, "Make it 10 on 12," they are specifying 10 point type on 12 points of leading.

Thus far we have been talking about character-level attributes—typeface and type size. A paragraph can have any number of typefaces at different type sizes, but it can have only one leading value. This is because leading is not a character-level attribute, but a paragraph-level attribute. And unlike specifying character-level attributes where you must select every text character you want to affect, you need only click anywhere inside a paragraph to select the whole paragraph when specifying paragraph-level attributes.

Macintosh Commands

⌘-1 View/Actual Size

Windows Commands

Ctrl-1 View/Actual Size

SPECIFYING LEADING

There are two places to specify paragraph leading: in the Paragraph Attributes dialog box and in the Measurements palette. Selecting Formats and Leading from the Style menu displays the Paragraph Attributes dialog box, where you type a value in the Leading field. You can also type a value in the leading field of the Measurements palette. And because this is QuarkXPress, there are keyboard shortcuts for applying leading.

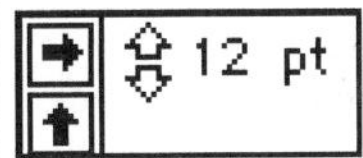

Use the Leading arrows to increase or decrease paragraph leading.

AUTO LEADING

When you first create a document, the Leading value defaults to Auto, which is always 20 percent of the largest font size on a given line of type. For example, if the largest font size on a given line is 10 points, the Auto(matic) leading value will become 12 points (10 X .20 = 2; 10 + 2 = 12). The problem with automatic leading is that you have no control over it—it's automatic—so always specify an absolute leading value for your type.

EXERCISE D

1. In the *Face.qxd* file, choose View / Actual Size. Display the Measurements palette (F9). To select the first paragraph, quadruple-click on it. Click on the arrow in the typeface field on the Measurements palette and drag to select Times Bold (or any other font installed in your system). Click on the arrow in the size field of the Measurements palette and drag to select 18. Click anywhere to deselect the paragraph.

Macintosh Commands

⌘-W File/Close
⌘-Shift-F Style/Formats

Windows Commands

Ctrl-F4 File/Close
Ctrl-Shift-F Style/Formats

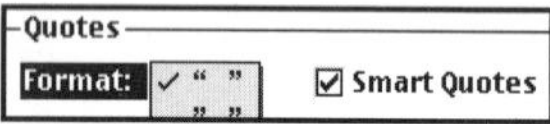

Smart Quotes

Make sure the Smart Quotes check box is selected in the Quotes field of the Application Preferences dialog box (Interactive tab). This ensures that straight quotes (") are replaced with curly quotes (") when you import a text file and check Convert Quotes in the Get Text dialog box.

Straight Quotes

To create straight quotes ("), press the Control key (Macintosh) while pressing the single or double quote key. Windows users type Ctrl-' for foot marks and Ctrl-Alt-' for inch marks (").

2. Click once anywhere inside the first paragraph (the one you just formatted), and double-click on auto in the Measurements palette. Type 24 and press Return/Enter. Your type for that paragraph is now 18/24 (18 on 24) or 18 point type on 24 points of leading.
3. Drag to select the first three words of the paragraph. Use the Measurements palette to specify a different typeface and different type size. You don't have to press Return/Enter because you used a menu instead of typing a value.
4. Double-click on 24 in the Leading field of the Measurements palette and type 26. Press Return/Enter. Click on the up arrow in the leading field four times until the leading value measures 30. Your paragraph should resemble Figure 4.11.

I pointed to **where our village lay, on the flat in-shore among the alder-trees and pollards, a mile or more from the church.**
The man, after looking at me for a moment, turned me upside down, and emptied my

Figure 4.11 displays paragraphs with several different leading values.

5. With the cursor anywhere in that first paragraph, use the leading arrows to increase and decrease the leading values.
6. Choose Style/Formats to display the Paragraph Attributes dialog box and notice that the leading value displayed in the leading field of the Measurements palette is also displayed in the Leading field of the Paragraph Attributes dialog box. Type 36 in the Leading field and click on OK. Notice that 36 also appears in the Leading field of the Measurements palette.
7. Choose Style/Leading to display the Paragraph Attributes dialog box and notice that it displays 36 in the Leading field. Click on Cancel. Close this file (File/Close). Don't save your changes.

LESSON 6
PARAGRAPH ALIGNMENT

Paragraph alignment defines the relation of type in a paragraph to the left and right sides of the text box. Type can be left aligned, right aligned, centered, justified, or force justified. Again, because paragraph alignment is a paragraph-level attribute, it applies to the entire paragraph and not to individual characters or lines in a paragraph.

INDENT HERE COMMAND

To indent part of the paragraph under any text character in the paragraph, use the Indent Here command. This inserts an invisible vertical line under which all subsequent text in the paragraph is aligned. To insert the Indent Here marker, press Command-\ (backslash) on the Macintosh or Ctrl-\ (Windows). To remove the Indent Here marker, place the cursor immediately after the marker and press the Delete/Backspace key.

EXERCISE E

1. Create a new document with an automatic text box. Use the Document Preferences dialog box to select inches as the unit of measure (Edit/ Preferences/Document).
2. Type your name at the top of the text box. Display the Measurements palette (F9) and notice that the Left Align icon is highlighted, indicating that this line of type is aligned to the left side of the text box. Left aligned (called *rag right*) is the default paragraph alignment.
3. Click on the Right Align icon in the Measurements palette and the type moves to the right side of the text box. Right aligned type is called *rag left* because the uneven lines of type appear to the left of the paragraph.
4. Click on the Center Align icon in the Measurements palette to center the type.
5. Select the W value in the Measurements palette, type 2 in the W field, and press Return/Enter. Click after your name and type a few lines of text. Click on the Justify Align icon in the Measurements palette and notice that the lines of text flow to fit exactly from the left to the right sides of the text box. There is no rag or uneven line of type.
6. Close this file; don't save your changes.

Macintosh Commands

⌘-N File/New/Document
⌘-W File/Close

Windows Commands

Ctrl-N File/New/Document
Ctrl-F4 File/Close

The paragraph alignment icons in the Measurements palette.

Facts: I can cater to only one person per day.¶
Today is not your day.¶
Tormorrow doesn't look too good either.

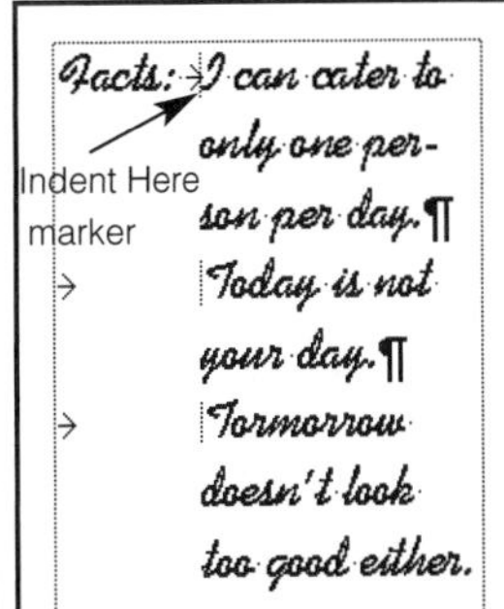

The Indent Here command moves all subsequent lines under the invisible vertical marker.

Macintosh Commands

⌘-N File/New/Document
Shift-F12 Edit/Colors

Windows Commands

Ctrl-N File/New/Document
Shift-F12 Edit/Colors

LESSON 7
TEXT BOX SHAPES

Even though you create a text box with the standard-shape Text Box tools, you can always reshape that text box from the Item menu. Select the text box, choose Item/Shape, and drag to select another shape. Any text you have in that text box will reflow within the new shape. You can even select the Bézier box shape and have the text box converted to a Bézier text box, with anchor points for reshaping instead of just the eight resizing handles. And for an even wilder design change, select one of the line shapes to change the text box from a box to a text path. In that case, the text will flow on the path, not inside a box.

LESSON 8
COLOR LESSON 1
SPOT COLOR

Color in a print document comes in two flavors: spot color and process color. A spot color is any custom color that is applied using one ink. The Pantone numbered color models are all spot colors. If you select Pantone 170 from the Pantone Uncoated library, a single color, a soft peach color, is applied to all selected text and items. If you specify Pantone 170 as spot color in the XPress document, when the document is printed, every item and text character tagged with Pantone 170 will print on one separation plate.

Process color, however, is color comprised of percentages of cyan, magenta, yellow, and black. If you specify Pantone 170 as a process color, XPress will separate Pantone 170 into the percentages of cyan, magenta, yellow, and black needed to create that color, and will print a separation plate for each of the four colors. This is called process separation or four-color printing.

EXERCISE F

1. Create a new document (File/New/Document) with an automatic text box. Type a few words in the text box. Choose Edit/Colors to display the Colors for [filename] dialog box. The Show menu defaults to displaying all the colors in the active document. Currently the three RGB colors (Red, Green, and Blue), the four process colors (Cyan, Magenta, Yellow, and Black), White, and Registration appear.

2. Click on New to display the Edit Color dialog box. Use the Model pull-down menu (Figure 4.12) to select Pantone Uncoated. The Pantone Uncoated library of color swatches appears. This is a good model for printing spot color on uncoated paper, which is probably what you have in your color printer.

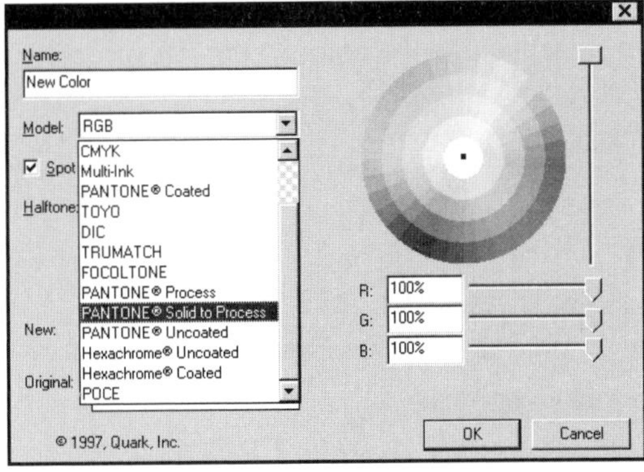

Figure 4.12. Use the Model pull-down menu to select a color model for your individual color selections.

3. As lovely as these swatches are, they are very deceiving. You are viewing color on a monitor that creates color using red, green, and blue phosphors. When this document is printed, the color will be created using ink. The difference between light and ink is enormous, so never, never, specify color from the screen. Use a swatch guide from the manufacturer, in this case the Pantone Uncoated swatch guide. Select your color from the guide and plug in its number in the Edit/Color dialog box. Type 339 in the Pantone field under the library on the right side of the dialog box (Figure 4.13).

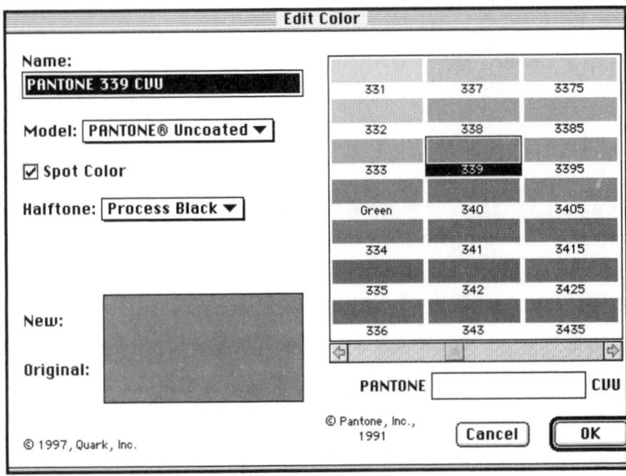

Figure 4.13. Scroll to locate a color or type in the Pantone color number from a Pantone Uncoated swatch book.

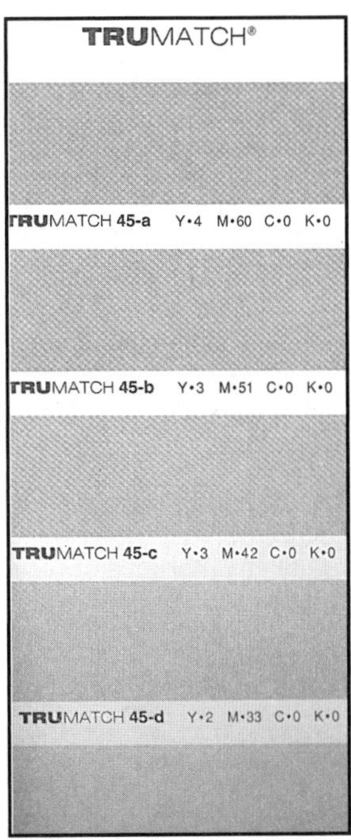

A page from the Trumatch Swatching System displays hues numbered sequentially around a wheel of the visible spectrum, the tint or strength of the hue, and the tint value identifying the percentage of black in 6% increments.

Macintosh Commands

⌘-W File/Close

Windows Commands

Ctrl-F4 File/Close

☑ Spot Color

Select this option in the Edit Color dialog box to specify a color as a spot color that will print on a single plate.

Rectangle Text Box tool

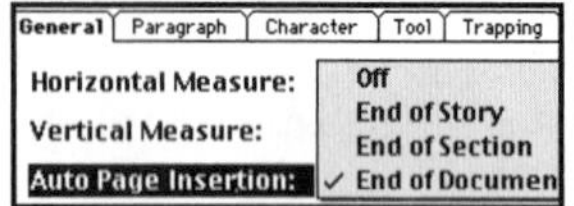

Select one of the last three options from the Auto Page Insertion menu to have XPress automatically add pages to accommodate all the imported and/or typed text in a document.

FYI

You can have only one automatic text link chain in the document. If you want more than one text link chain, you will have to manually link the boxes.

4. When you do this, the Pantone color's name appears in the Name field on the left side of the dialog box. Make sure that Spot Color is selected so that only one plate will print. If you deselect the Spot Color option, XPress will separate Pantone 339 into percentages of cyan, magenta, yellow, and black, making the four-plate job more expensive than the two-plate job (Pantone 339 and black).

5. Click on OK. Click on Save to save the color in the document's colors list (Figure 4.14).

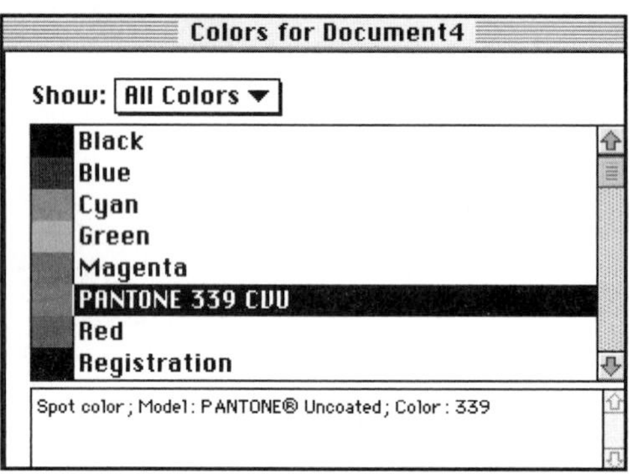

Figure 4.14. Once a color has been selected and named in the Edit Color dialog box, it is automatically added to a document's color list.

6. Drag to select the text you typed earlier. Choose Style/Color and drag to select Pantone 339.

7. Use the Rectangle Text Box tool to draw a text box. With the box selected, choose Item/Modify to display the Box Modify dialog box. In the Box field on the right side of the dialog box, use the Color pull-down menu to select Pantone 339. Use the Shade menu to select 50%. Click on OK. The text box displays a 50% screen tint percentage of Pantone 339.

8. Close this file (File/Close). Don't save your changes.

LESSON 9
LINKING AND UNLINKING TEXT BOXES

Rule #1: All text must be imported or typed in a text box or typed on a text path. Rule #2: If a text box is not big enough to hold all the text, you have two options—edit the text or create another text box. Rule # 3: If you create a new document with an automatic text box and turn Auto Page Insertion on, XPress will automatically create as many pages—with linked text boxes—as necessary to display all the text.

The Automatic Text Box and Auto Page Insertion options solve the linking problem automatically, so flowing text from one page to another becomes an issue only when you don't choose these options.

MANUAL LINKING

Manual linking is used to link text boxes so that text will flow from one text box to another text box. That other text box does not have to be on the same page as the original text box; it can be anywhere in the document. To link text boxes, use the Linking tool, click on the text box with the overflow text, and click on an *empty* text box. You cannot link to any text box that contains text.

UNLINKING

To unlink text boxes, use the Unlinking tool and click on one of the two text boxes you want to unlink. Click on the arrow's point or on its tail to unlink the two boxes connected by the linking arrow. All the linked text boxes before the break remain linked; all the text boxes after the break are unlinked.

EXERCISE G

1. Create a new file without an automatic text box (File/New/Document). Use the Rectangle Text Box tool to draw a text box on the top of the page about three inches high and six inches wide.
2. With the text box selected, choose File/Get Text. Navigate to the Unit 04 folder on the CD-ROM and double-click on the *Link .text* file to import it into the text box. This is a text file and does not require a word processor filter to be installed. The text fills the text box and the Overflow Indicator appears in the bottom right corner of the text box, indicating that there is too much text to fit into the box.
3. Draw another text box about one inch high below the first text box. Click on the Linking tool and click on the first text box. A dotted marquee runs around the text box, indicating that the empty text box you click on will be linked to the one with the flashing marquee. Click on the lower text box. A linking arrow appears, indicating that the text in the top text box is linked to the text in the lower text box . Although the two boxes are linked, there is still not enough room to hold all the text, so the Overflow Indicator now appears in the lower, linked box (Figure 4.15). Click *immediately* on the Content tool. If you inadver-

Macintosh Commands

⌘-N File/New/Document
⌘-E File/Get Text/Picture
⌘-W File/Close

Windows Commands

Ctrl-N File/New/Document
Ctrl-E File/Get Text/Picture
Ctrl-F4 File/Close

his head, 'and
ombstone on

The Overflow Indicator appears when there is more text than can fit in a text box.

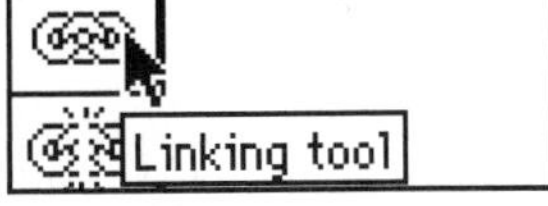

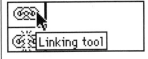

Linking tool

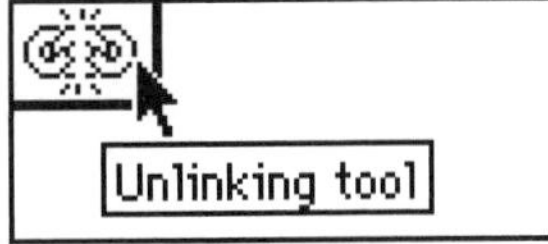

Unlinking tool

Content tool

Macintosh Commands

⌘-W FIle/Close

Windows Commands

Ctrl-F4 FIle/Close

WARNING!

Linking text boxes cannot be undone. Save first!

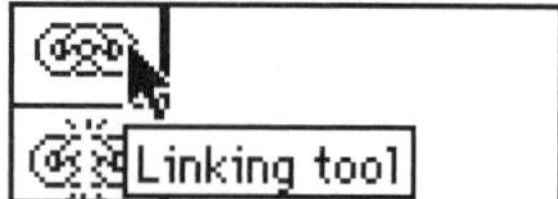

Linking tool

Unlinking tool

tently click on another text box with the Linking tool you can destroy the original text links.

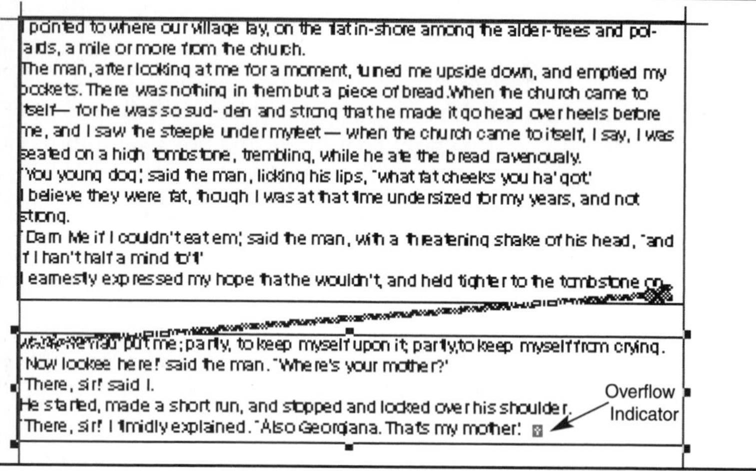

Figure 4.15. A linking arrow displays the linking sequence from one text box to another.

4. Draw another text box about four inches high below the second text box. Click on the Linking tool and click on the middle text box to display the flashing marquee. Click inside the third, bottom text box. The rest of the text flows into the last text box. The Overflow Indicator does not appear because all the text fits into the three text boxes.

5. Click on the Unlinking tool and click on the top text box. The linking arrows appear displaying the links from the first, to the second, to the third text box. Click on the arrow point of the second arrow. The third box becomes unlinked and the text flows in only the first two boxes. The Overflow Indicator appears again in the second text box because there is more text than can fit in that single text box.

6. Close this file (File/Close). Don't save your changes.

LESSON 10
CREATING JUMP LINES

Magazines and newspapers often start an article on one page and then (annoyingly) continue the story on another page. To move the text from a text box on one page to a linked text box on another, non-consecutive page, use the Next Box and Previous Box page number commands.

EXERCISE H

1. Create a new document with an automatic text box (File/New/Document). Display the Document Layout palette (F10/Macintosh; F4/Windows).
2. Select the text box on the first page of the document and choose File/Get Text. Locate the *Text.txt* file in the Unit 04 folder on the CD-ROM and double-click on it to import it into the selected text box. Because the document was created with an automatic text box, XPress adds a second page to hold all the text. Click on the Master Page A icon in the Document Layout palette and drag a third page down onto the document area of the palette.
3. Double-click on the page 1 icon in the Document Layout palette to get to page 1. Use the Rectangle Text Box tool to draw a text box on the bottom of the page but inside the large text box. Make this new text box the entire width of the page. Type *Continued on page,* press the Spacebar, then press Command-4 (Macintosh) or Ctrl-4 (Windows) to insert the Next Box Page Number command. The number 2 appears because this story is now linked from page 1 to page 2.
4. Click after the last text character in the large text box on page 1. Press Command-Option-Shift-Down Arrow (Macintosh) or Ctrl-Alt-Shift-Down Arrow (Windows) to select all the text from the insertion point. Choose Edit/Cut. Keep the cut text in memory.
5. Click on the Linking tool. Click on the large text box on page 1 to display the flashing marquee. Double-click on the page 3 icon in the Document Layout palette to get to page 3. Click inside the large text box on page 3 to link page 1 to page 3. Select the Content tool immediately.

Macintosh Commands

⌘-N File/New/Document
⌘-E File/Get Text/Picture
⌘-X Edit/Cut
⌘-V Edit/Paste
⌘-4 Continued on Page Number symbol

Windows Commands

Ctrl-N File/New/Document
Ctrl-E FIle/Get Text/Picture
Ctrl-X Edit/Cut
Ctrl-V Edit/Paste
Ctrl-4 Continued on Page Number symbol

Important info

The jump line commands must be typed in a separate text box. You cannot type Command/Ctrl-4 or Command/Ctrl-2 in an automatic text box on the document page.

Linking tool

Content tool

Macintosh Commands

⌘-V Edit/Paste
⌘-2 Continued from Page Number symbol
⌘-W File/Close

Windows Commands

Ctrl-V Edit/Paste
Ctrl-2 Continued from Page Number symbol
Ctrl-F4 File/Close

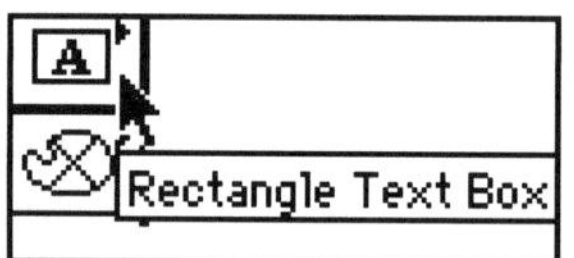

Rectangle Text Box tool

6. Click inside the large text box on page 3 and choose Edit/Paste to paste the cut text onto page 3.
7. Use the Rectangle Text Box tool to draw another small text box on top of the automatic text box on page 3. Type *Continued from page,* press the Spacebar, and press Command-2 (Macintosh) or Ctrl-2 (Windows). This is the Previous Box Page Number command. The number 1 appears, telling you that this story was continued from page 1.
8. Double-click on the page 1 icon in the Document Layout palette. Notice that the small text box now displays Continued on page 3.
9. Close this file (File/Close). Don't save your changes.

Image scanned from a photograph by Joseph A. Dai

Standard-Shape Picture Boxes

OVERVIEW

In this unit you will learn how to:

Draw standard-shape picture boxes
Resize, rotate, move, and skew picture boxes
Import pictures
Resize, crop, flip, and position images
Specify process colors
Create libraries and entry labels
Print images at the correct resolution

TERMS

aspect ratio
bitmap images
Entry label
EPS
image resolution
library
linked image
Offset Across/Offset Down
output resolution
process colors
Scale Across/Scale Down
TIFF
vector images

HOW IT WORKS:

Import the image and resize it to fit the picture box. Create the Unit 5 type and convert the text to boxes. Fill the new Bézier picture box with a black-(80%) to-white linear gradient from the Colors palette. Finally, apply a 1-point frame to the box outline for emphasis.

LESSON 1
CREATING PICTURE BOXES

Concave-Corner Picture Box tool

A selected picture box's values are displayed to the left of the divider in the Measurements palette. The values to the right of the divider apply to the picture itself.

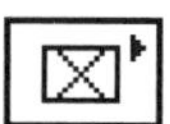

Standard-Shape Rectangle Picture Box tool

Any graphic image (picture) used in a QuarkXPress document must be imported into a selected picture box, and QuarkXPress 4.0 provides two sets of tools for creating picture boxes. The first is the standard-shape toolset. This includes the Rectangle Picture Box tool, the Concave-Corner Picture Box tool, the Beveled-Corner Picture Box tool, and the Oval Picture Box tool. The second is the Bézier toolset, which contains the FreeHand Bézier Picture Box tool and the Bézier Picture Box tool (Figure 5.1). The tools in the standard-shape set draw boxes with eight resizing handles. Clicking and dragging on these handles makes the box larger or smaller. You cannot reshape these boxes, only resize them. Bézier picture boxes, however, contain Bézier points, called anchor points in the PostScript illustration world. These boxes can be resized and reshaped without transforming the pictures they contain. To reshape a standard-shape picture box, select it, and choose Item/Shape. Drag to select another box shape.

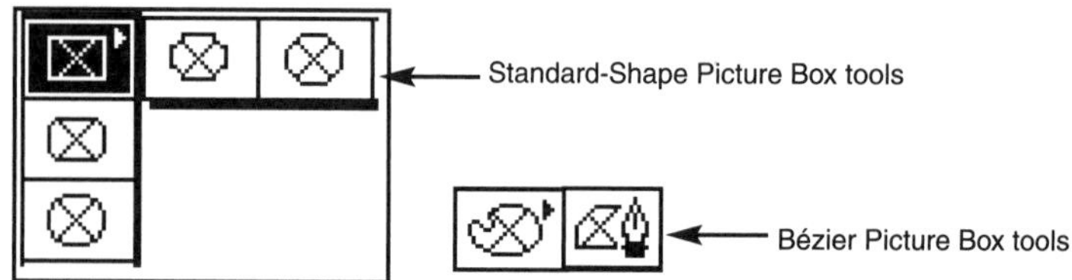

Figure 5.1. The standard-shape Picture Box tools in QuarkXPress 4.0: Rectangle Picture Box, Concave-Corner Picture Box, and Beveled-Corner Picture Box tools (top); and the Rounded-Corner and Oval picture box tools (below). The Bézier Picture Box tools include the Freehand Bézier Picture Box tool (left) and the Bézier Picture Box tool (right).

There are five standard-shape picture box tools in QuarkXPress 4.0, and all can be resized and reshaped without resizing the pictures in them. In order to display a picture (graphic) in an XPress document, a picture box must be created and selected. If you find the Get Picture command under the File menu dimmed, that's because you have not selected a picture box into which you want to import the picture.

GRAPHIC FILE FORMATS

Although XPress imports many different file types, the most common ones are EPS (Encapsulated PostScript) files created in PostScript drawing programs like Adobe Illustrator, Corel Draw, and

Macromedia FreeHand. EPS files can be resized in XPress without affecting their display. TIFF (Tagged Image File Format) files created in bitmap image manipulation programs like Adobe Photoshop and Fractal Design Painter can also be imported into XPress documents, but they should be resized in the image application, because enlarging them in XPress causes them to become pixelated when XPress creates the pixels necessary to make the image larger. Although you can import PICT and Paint images (low-resolution bitmap images) into XPress, it's not a good idea to use PICT files, as XPress doesn't always behave politely when processing PICT images.

Many of the TIFF images used in the lessons were saved with the LZW Compression option selected. Others were saved with JPEG compression. You must have the LZW Import and JPEG Import filters active before you will be able to import these images into XPress picture boxes. Make sure the LZW Compression filter and JPEG Import filter are in the XTension folder before you launch QuarkXPress.

MEASUREMENTS PALETTE FOR PICTURES

Whenever any kind of picture box containing a picture is selected, every value to the left of the dividing line (after the Flip arrows) on the Measurements palette refers to the picture box; every value to the right of the divider refers to the contents of the box, the picture. Whenever you type a value in the Measurements palette, whether it's a box value or a picture value, you must press the Return/Enter key to execute the command.

EXERCISE A

1. Create a new document (File/New/Document) without an automatic text box. Click on the standard-shape Rectangle Picture Box tool to select it. Click on the page and drag to draw a small picture box. Release the mouse when the box is drawn.
2. With the picture box still selected (it displays eight handles), choose Item/Modify. The Modify dialog box appears with the Box tab in front.
3. Type 2 in the Width field; press the Tab key and type 2 in the Height field. Make sure the Color pull-down menu in the Box field is set to white. Click on OK to resize the box.
4. With the picture box still selected, click on the Content tool or on the Item tool and choose File/Get Picture. Navigate to the Unit 05 folder on the CD-ROM and click on the *Marble* image.

Macintosh Commands

⌘-N File/New/Document
⌘-M Item/Modify
⌘-E File/Get Text/Picture

Windows Commands

Ctrl-N File/New/Document
Ctrl-M Item/Modify
Ctrl-E File/Get Text/Picture

ble	Name	Status
✓	Cool Blends	Active
✓	CPSI Fixer	Active
	FRÆMZ PS XT	Active
	Immedia Project Menu	Inactive
	Index	Active
✓	JPEG Import	Active
✓	LZW Import	Active

Make sure a check mark appears next to the selected XTension. Any inactive XTension remains inactive until you relaunch QuarkXPress.

Tip

Press the Tab key to get to a field in any dialog box. Then press the Tab key to get to the next box and select the value in that box. This saves you the trouble of selecting one value before typing another value.

Content tool

Item tool

Macintosh Commands

⌘-B Item/Frame
⌘-W File/Close
⌘-E File/Get Text/Picture
⌘-W File/Close

Windows Commands

Ctrl-B Item/Frame
Ctrl-F4 File/Close
Ctrl-E File/Get Text/Picture
Ctrl-F4 File/Close

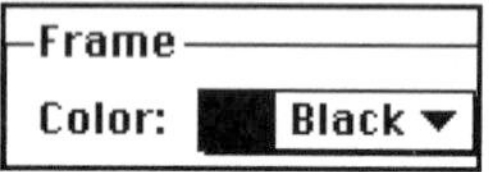

FYI

A black triangle in any options box indicates a pull-down men. Click on the menu to automatically drop the menu and drag to select an option. Release the mouse button when you've made your selection.

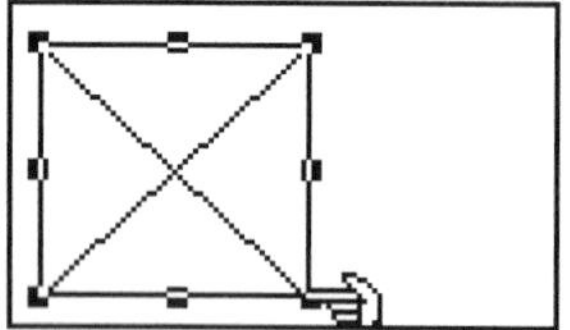

Clicking on the handle of a selected picture box turns the cursor into the Pointer cursor. Use this cursor to resize the box.

This is a TIFF file created in Photoshop. Double-click on the file name or click on Open to import the picture into the selected picture box. Notice that the picture is smaller than the box.

5. Click on the picture box handle in the lower right corner and drag to resize the box so that it fits snugly against the picture.
6. With the picture box still selected, choose Item/Frame. Choose 4 from the Width pull-down menu. Leave the Style as Solid and select a color from the Frame pull-down menu. Click on OK to apply a frame (border) to the picture box. Your screen should resemble Figure 5.2.
7. Close this file (File/Close). Don't save your changes.

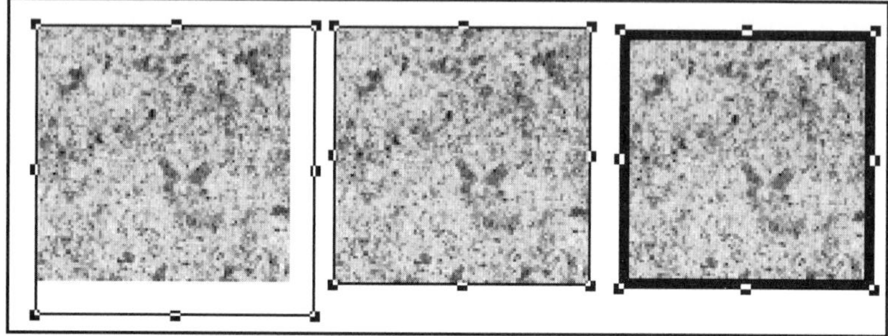

Figure 5.2. The original picture box (left), the resized picture box (center), and the framed picture box (right).

LESSON 2
RESIZING, ROTATING, SKEWING, AND MOVING PICTURE BOXES

You can resize a picture box by dragging any of the box handles with the Pointer cursor. If you press the Shift key while resizing, you will constrain the box to a square. If you press the Command-Option-Shift keys (Macintosh) or Ctrl-Alt-Shift keys (Windows), you will constrain the box's aspect ratio, that is, the height-to-width proportions of the box.

When a picture box is selected, the Measurements palette displays the attributes of the box on the left side of the palette and the attributes of the picture inside the box on the right side of the palette. As always with values typed in the Measurements palette, you must press the Return/Enter key to execute the attribute command.

To rotate a *selected* picture box, select the Rotate tool, click on one of the handles of the box and drag to rotate. As you drag the box, a line appears jutting out of the box handle. The longer the handle, the more control you have over the box's rotation. You can also rotate a box by typing a value in the Angle field of the Box Modify dialog box. Typing a negative number rotates the item to the right.

To move a picture box, select the Item tool and click on the box. Drag to a new location. Remember that before any item such as a picture box can be transformed, it must first be selected.

Skewing slants a box to the right or left. To skew a picture box, type a value in the Skew field of the Modify dialog box. Just as with the rotate command, typing a negative number skews a box to the right.

EXERCISE B

1. Create a new document without facing pages and without an automatic text box (File/New/Document). Click on the standard-shape Rectangle Picture Box tool. The cursor changes to a crosshair. Click and drag on the page to draw a small box. With the box selected, choose Item/Modify to display the Modify dialog box. Click the Box tab (Figure 5.3). Type 2 in the Width field. Press the Tab key once and type 3 in the Height field. Click on OK and notice that the box has been resized.

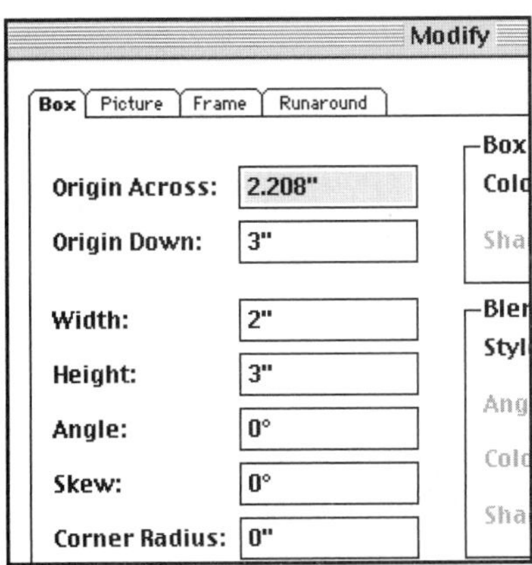

Figure 5.3. The Modify dialog box displays the Box tab. Typing values in the Width, Height, and Angle fields will resize and rotate the selected box.

2. Display the Measurements palette (View/Show Measurements or F9) and notice that the W and H fields on the left side of the palette reflect the values you typed in the Modify dialog box.

Macintosh Commands

⌘-N File/New/Document
⌘-M Item/Modify
F9 View-Show Measurements

Windows Commands

Ctrl-N File/New/Document
Ctrl-M Item/Modify
F9 View-Show Measurements

Item tool

Standard-Shape Rectangle Picture Box tool

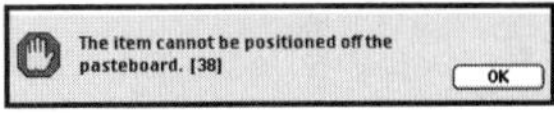

Can't rotate?

If you keep hearing alert sounds when you're trying to rotate, it's because you've typed an angle of rotation that will take the item off of the page. Click OK in the alert dialog box. Press Command/Ctrl-Z and Return/Enter to restore the original rotation value. Then use the Item tool to move the item closer to the center of the page before applying the Rotate command again.

Macintosh Commands

⌘-M Item/Modify
⌘-S File/Save

Windows Commands

Ctrl-M Item/Modify
Ctrl-S File/Save

It doesn't add up

Resize, rotate, angle, and skew values are not incremental. For example, if you rotate a box 30 degrees and then decide to rotate it 45 degrees, you simply type 45 in the Angle field of either the Modify dialog box or the Measurements palette. Typing 0 in the Rotate, Angle, and Skew fields removes the transformation completely.

FYI

You don't have to type the angle symbol in the Measurements palette or in any Modify dialog box.

25°
0"

The Corner Radius field (below the Rotation field on the Measurements palette) specifies how round a box's corners are.

3. With the box still selected, choose Item/Modify (the Box tab is automatically active), and type 25 in the Angle field to rotate the box 25 degrees. Press the Tab key and type -30 in the Skew field to slant the box 10 degrees to the left. Click on OK. Notice that the left side of the Measurements palette displays the same height, width, and rotation values that you typed in the Modify dialog box (Figure 5.4). The Skew value is not displayed in the Measurements palette.

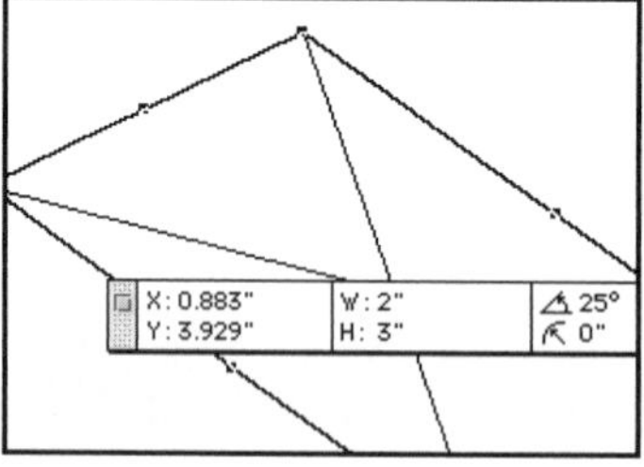

Figure 5.4. The Measurements palette for the selected picture box displays its position, size, and angle of rotation (25 degrees).

4. Type 2 in the Corner Radius field of the Measurements palette to make the box corners round. Your box should resemble Figure 5.5. Save this file (File/Save) as *Box.qxd*. Because this file was not saved previously, the Save as dialog box appears. Type the file name and save the file in your Projects folder.

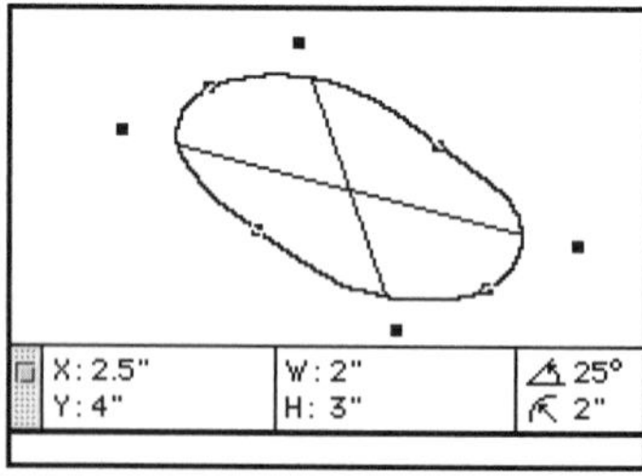

Figure 5.5. The Measurements palette for the selected picture box displays its position, size, angle of rotation (25 degrees), and corner radius (2 inches).

LESSON 3 IMPORTING PICTURES

Once a picture box is created, you can import a picture into that box and resize, rotate, skew, and move the picture with or without transforming the box. In order to import a picture, the picture box must be selected and the image to be imported must be in a file format that QuarkXPress recognizes. The most commonly used images in an XPress document are TIFF, EPS, JPEG, PICT, BMP, Paint, and PhotoCD files.

LINKING PICTURES

Whenever you import a high-resolution image like a TIFF or EPS image into a QuarkXPress picture box, XPress creates a low-resolution PICT version of that image and links that low-resolution image to the original high-resolution image in the folder on the drive from which you imported that picture. When you go to print the file with the picture, XPress scurries to the original location (drive and folder), locates the high-resolution image, applies any editing you made to the image in the document, and prints the edited high-resolution image. If it can't find that high-resolution image, it alerts you and gives you the opportunity to update the file by specifying the new location for the high-resolution image.

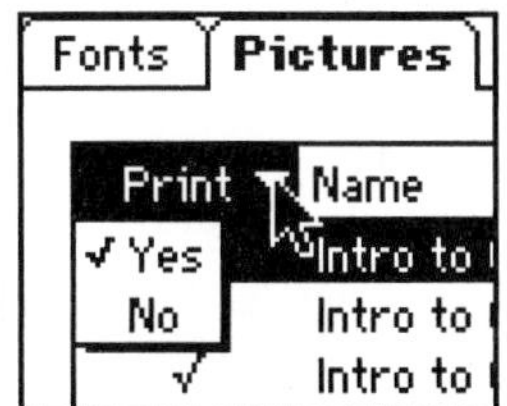

Use the Print pull-down menu in the Pictures Usage dialog box to turn printing on or off for each image.

PICTURE USAGE DIALOG BOX

To avoid any delays at printing, use the Picture Usage dialog box. Choose Utilities/Usage and click on the Picture tab. The status of all the images used in the file appears. If OK appears, then XPress can access the high-resolution image. (Figure 5.6). If it can't, it will display Missing in the Status field. Click the Update button to establish a link to that image at its new location. If you can't remember what the image looked like, click on the image name to select it and click the Show button. XPress will jump to the page with that image and select its picture box. If you click the More Information check box, the original location of the image, as well as its size, resolution, and modification date, will appear in the display box.

Usage

Fonts | Pictures

Print	Name	Page	Type	Status
√	Macintosh HD:...:EPS Files:Chop Suey.eps	1	EPS	OK
√	Macintosh HD:...:Tapestry Border.tiff	2	TIFF	OK
√	Macintosh HD:...:JPEG Files:LATINSUN.JPG	3	JPEG	OK

More Information | Done | Show | Update...

Figure 5.6. The Picture Usage dialog box displays the status of every image used in the document. OK in the Status column indicates that XPress can access all three images for printing. The check marks in the Print column specify that all three images will print. Click the check mark to deselect the Print option if you don't want the image to print (when you're just proofing for text, for example).

Graphic Import Filters

Certain graphic formats like JPEG and PhotoCD files can be imported into a picture box only if the appropriate XTension is available in the XTension folder and selected in the XTensions Manager (Utilities/XTensions Manager). Select the JPEG Import and PhotoCD Import filters, making sure a check mark appears next to the filter's name in the Enable column. Then quit QuarkXPress and relaunch to activate the XTension.

Macintosh Commands

⌘-O File/Open
⌘-M Item/Modify
⌘-E Get Text/Picture

Windows Commands

Ctrl-O File/Open
Ctrl-M Item/Modify
Ctrl-E Get Text/Picture

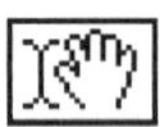

Content tool

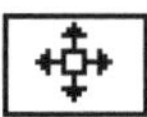

Item tool

FYI

If you import an image and only white space appears in the picture box, that's because the image was saved with a white background. Click on the image with the Content tool and drag it around the box until the image itself appears. You can also press Command-Shift-M (Macintosh) or Ctrl-Shift-M (Windows) to center the image.

What happens when you can't locate the original high-resolution file and print the document anyway? XPress will print the low-resolution PICT image it created when it imported the high-resolution TIFF or EPS image. Of course, you won't get the same quality from a low-resolution image that you can expect from TIFF and EPS images, and you may find your graphic printing with the jagged outline of a pixelated image.

EXERCISE C

1. If necessary, open the *Box.qxd* file you created in the previous exercise or open the *Box.qxd* file in the Unit 05 folder on the CD-ROM. To restore the box to its original position, select the box with either the Content tool or the Item tool and choose Item/Modify. The Modify dialog box appears with the Box tab active.
2. Leave the Width and Height values at 2 and 3 inches, but type 0 in the Angle, Skew, and Corner Radius fields. Click on OK. The box is now just a rectangle.
3. With the picture box still selected and either the Content tool or the Item tool active, choose File/Get Picture. Navigate to the Unit 05 folder on the CD-ROM and click on Open. Double-click on the *Cilan* file (a TIFF file), or highlight the file and click on Open. The image appears centered in the picture box. Because the graphic is larger than the box, part of the image is not displayed (Figure 5.7).

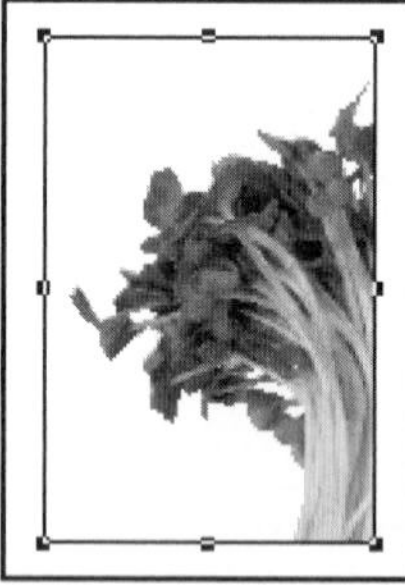

X%: 100%
Y%: 100%

Figure 5.7. A graphic is imported at 100% or at exactly the same size it was saved in the graphic application like Photoshop or Illustrator.

4. Notice that the X% and Y% values on the Measurements palette display 100% because an image is always imported at 100% of the size or at exactly the same size as it was saved in the graphic application where it was created.

5. Click on the original image to select it and click on the lower center handle. When the cursor changes to the Pointer cursor, drag the side of the box down until the whole image is revealed. Drag one of the side handles on the picture box to make the box wide enough to display the entire image. You are resizing only the box, not the image inside the box. Save this file (File/Save as) in your Projects folder as *Image.qxd*.

LESSON 4
POSITIONING IMAGES

When you import an image into a picture box, the image appears at the same size and in the same location on the page as it was when it was saved in the graphic application. This means that if an image was created in a program like Illustrator, Photoshop, FreeHand, or Painter and was 4 inches high and 5 inches wide when it was saved as an EPS or TIFF file, it will come into an XPress picture box at that same size and be positioned in the upper left corner of the picture box. To center the image in the picture box, press Command-Shift-M (Macintosh) or Ctrl-Shift-M (Windows). You can also use the X + and Y+ fields in the Measurements palette or the Offset Across and Offset Down fields in the Modify dialog box.

EXERCISE D

1. If necessary, open the *Image.qxd* file you just created or open the *Image.qxd* file in the Unit 05 folder on the CD-ROM (File/Open). Display the Measurements palette (F9). Notice that the X+ and Y+ (Picture Offset) values on the right side of the Measurements palette display 0, meaning that the picture has not yet been moved.
2. Select the Content tool and click inside the picture box, where the cursor changes to the Picture Mover pointer. Click and drag the image around the box. Notice that the Picture Offset values change to reflect the new position of the image.
3. Choose Item/Modify and click on the Picture tab to display the picture specifications. Notice that those same values in the Measurements palette are reflected in the Offset Across and Offset Down fields. Click on OK to return to the image.

Macintosh Commands

⌘-O FIle/Open
⌘-M Item/Modify
⌘-Option-S File/Save as

Windows Commands

Ctrl-O File/Open
Ctrl-M Item/Modify
Ctrl-Alt-S File/Save as

FYI

Once you position the image, lock the picture box and image by selecting the box and choosing Item/Lock.

Sorry!

You cannot import a Photoshop, Painter, or Illustrator file directly into XPress. Save the Photoshop and Painter files as TIFF files and the Illustrator files in the EPS format.

FYI

Clicking with the Content tool inside a picture box into which you have imported an image changes the cursor into the Picture Mover Pointer, and lets you drag the image around the picture box.

Content tool

Macintosh Commands

⌘-O File/Open
⌘-M Item/Modify
⌘-Shift-M Centers the image in the picture box
⌘-W File/Close

Windows Commands

Ctrl-O File/Open
Ctrl-M Item/Modify
Ctrl-Shift-M Centers the image in the picture box
Ctrl-F4 File/Close

FYI

Click on the Close box in the upper left corner of the window (Macintosh) or click on the X box in the upper right corner of the window (Windows) to close a file.

Content tool

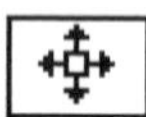

Item tool

4. Press Command-Shift-M (Macintosh) or Ctrl-Shift-M (Windows) to center the image in the picture box. Its new position is reflected in the Picture Offset fields of the Measurements palette. Close this file (File/Close). Don't save your changes.

LESSON 5 RESIZING IMAGES

You can resize an image from the Measurements palette, from the Picture tab of the Modify dialog box, or from the keyboard. The important thing to remember is that to maintain the aspect ratio or the same relationship between the height and width of the graphic's dimensions, the Scale Across and Scale Down fields in the Modify dialog box or the X% and Y% fields in the Measurements palette must be exactly the same. For example, if you resize an image by typing 75 in the X% field and 150 in the Y% field, you will have an image that is disproportionately longer than it is wide. There may be times when you want this to achieve a certain effect, but ordinarily you will want your pictures to be proportionately scaled.

EXERCISE E

1. Open the *Image.qxd* file in your Projects folder or the *Image.qxd* file in the Unit 05 folder on the CD-ROM. Select either the Content tool or the Item tool. Click on the resized picture box that displays the entire image and press Command-Shift-M (Macintosh) or Ctrl-Shift-M (Windows) to center the graphic in the picture box.
2. Type 50 in the X% field, press the Tab key, and type 50 in the Y% field. Press the Return/Enter key. The image is scaled down to half its size.
3. With the picture box still selected, choose Item/Modify. Because you are modifying the picture, not the box, click on the Picture tab. Type 110 in the Scale Across field and click on OK. The image is now wider than it is high (Figure 5.8).
4. Type 100 in the X% and Y% fields of the Measurements palette to restore the image to its original size.

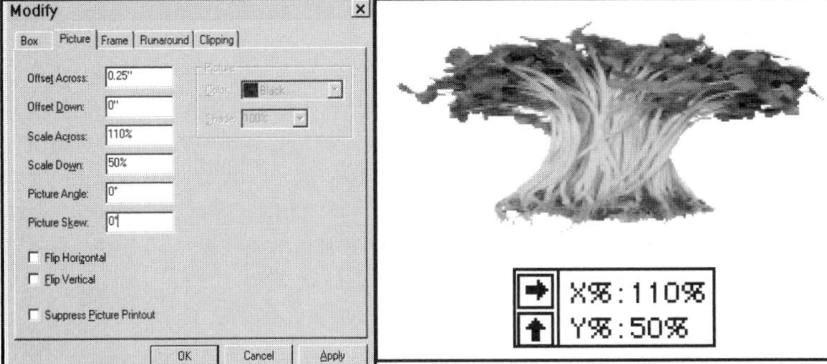

Figure 5.8. The values in the Picture Modify dialog box and Measurements palette indicate that this image is 60% wider than it is high.

5. Type 45 in the Picture Rotation field on the right side of the Measurements palette to rotate the image 45 degrees. Press the Tab key and type -20 in the Picture Skew field of the Measurements palette to skew the picture 20 degrees to the left. Press Return/Enter to execute the commands. Your screen should resemble Figure 5.9.

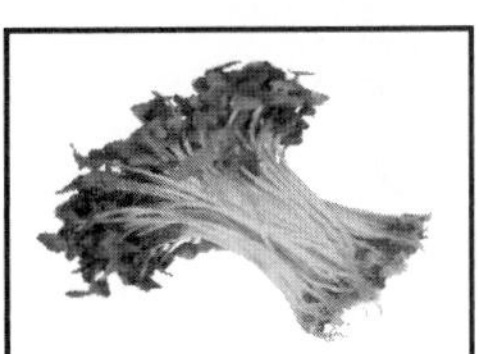

Figure 5.9. The image is rotated 45 degrees and skewed 20 degrees to the left.

6. Choose File/Revert to Saved. Click OK in the alert box to revert to the last saved version of the file. When the original image appears, select the Content tool and click on the picture box. Press Command-Shift-F (Macintosh) or Ctrl-Shift-F (Windows) to fit the picture into the picture box. Notice, however, that to fit the box, it was disproportionately resized, as indicated by the different values in the X% and Y% fields on the Measurements palette. Choose Edit/Undo to restore the original image.

7. With the picture box still selected and the Content tool active, press Command-Option-Shift-F (Macintosh) or Ctrl-Alt-Shift-F (Windows) to resize the image proportionately. Notice that now the X% and Y% values in the Measurements palette are the same.

8. Choose Item/Modify and click on the Picture tab. The proportional values are displayed in the Scale Across and Scale Down fields. Close this file (File/Close). Don't save your changes.

Macintosh Commands

⌘-Shift-F Fit a picture in a box
⌘-Option-Shift-F Fit a picture proportionally in a box
⌘-M Item/Modify
⌘-W File/Close

Windows Commands

Ctrl-Shift-F Fit a picture in a box
Ctrl-Alt-Shift-F Fit a picture proportionally in a box
Ctrl-M Item/Modify
Ctrl-F4 File/Close

Content tool

Tip

Convert any tool to a temporary Item tool by pressing the Command key (Macintosh) or Ctrl key (Windows). Keep the modifier key pressed until you have moved the item. When you release the modifier key, the Item tool cursor returns to the original tool cursor.

Image info

The *Cilan* image is from *Complete Produce Library 2* by Jeff Burke/Lorraine Triolo, for Artville.

Macintosh Commands

⌘-N File/New/Document
⌘-E File/Get Text/Picture

Windows Commands

Ctrl-N File/New/Document
Ctrl-E File/Get Text/Picture

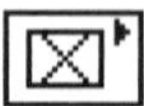

Standard-Shape Rectangle Picture Box tool

Content tool

Item tool

Figure 5.10. Only one pattern is displayed and only this pattern will print.

LESSON 6
CROPPING IMAGES

When you crop an image in a program like Photoshop, you actually remove pixels and make it a smaller image. However, when you crop an image in QuarkXPress, you only *display less of the image*; you don't remove any part of the image. This means that although only part of the image appears in the picture box, the entire image must be processed when the file is printed. For example, if you import a picture of a flock of geese flying over an environmentally protected area and you use the Picture Mover pointer to move the image so that only one goose appears in the picture box, only one goose will print, but the entire flock of geese will be processed by the printer. If the image is very large and if you have many graphics in a document, you may run into problems when printing the image either to your laser printer or to an imagesetter. If an image requires heavy cropping, do it in the graphic application where it was created and import the cropped image into XPress.

EXERCISE F

1. Create a new document without facing pages and without an automatic text box. Display the Measurements palette (F9). Make sure the unit of measure is inches (Edit/Preferences/Document).
2. Select the standard-shape Rectangle Picture Box tool and drag to draw a small picture box. Type 4 in the W field of the Measurements palette. Press the Tab key and type 3 in the H field. Press Return/Enter.
3. Select the Content tool or the Item tool and, with the picture box selected, choose File/Get Picture. Navigate to the Unit 05 folder on the CD-ROM and click on Open. Double-click on the *Patterns* file (an EPS file) to import it into the selected picture box. Notice that the graphic, which consists of six patterns, is larger than the box.
4. Use the Picture Mover pointer to move the image around the box until you find a pattern you like. Then resize the box to display only that pattern. In Figure 5.10 (sidebar), only the star pattern is displayed and it is the only pattern that will be printed. However, all the other five patterns will be processed, even though they will not be printed, because they are still part of the image.

5. Turn your printer on. Choose File/Print. Click on the Setup tab and make sure your printer (or a generic printer) appears in the Printer Description menu. Click on the Output tab and select Grayscale from the Print Colors menu. Type the correct output resolution of your printer in the Resolution field. Click on Print in the lower right corner of the dialog box to print the image. Close this file (File/Close). Don't save your changes.

Macintosh Commands

⌘-P File/Print
⌘-N File/New/Document
⌘-E File/Get Text/Picture
⌘-W File/Close

Windows Commands

Ctrl-P File/Print
Ctrl-N File/New/Document
Ctrl-E File/Get Text/Picture
Ctrl-F4 File/Close

LESSON 7
FLIPPING IMAGES

Images can be flipped horizontally or vertically inside the picture box. This is a handy function when you want to create facing images or a mirror image. To flip an image, select the picture box and click on the Horizontal flipping arrow to flip the image from right to left. Click on the arrow again to restore the image. To flip the image vertically, click on the Vertical flipping arrow, and click on that arrow again to restore the image.

EXERCISE G

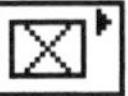

Standard-Shape Rectangle Picture Box tool

1. Create a new document (File/New/Document) without facing pages and without an automatic text box. Display the Measurements palette (F9).
2. Use any standard-shape Picture Box tool to draw a picture box. Choose File/Get Picture and navigate to the Unit 05 folder on the CD-ROM. Import the *Lady* file (an EPS file). Resize the box to fully display the image. Choose Item/Duplicate and use the Item tool to move the duplicate image next to the original.
3. Click on the first image and click the Horizontal Flipping arrow on the Measurements palette or choose Style/Flip Horizontal. Click on the duplicate image and click on the Vertical Flipping arrow on the Measurements palette or choose Style/Flip Vertical. Your screen should resemble Figure 5.11.
4. Close this file (File/Close). Don't save your changes.

Image info

The *Lady* file is from *Roundhead Executives*, by Barton Stabler for Artville. The *Bridge* and *Tolls* images are from *Metropolis* by Rob Porazinski, for Artville.

Figure 5.11. The original image (left) is flipped horizontally (center) and vertically (right).

Macintosh Commands

⌘-N File/New/Document

Windows Commands

Ctrl-N File/New/Document

FYI

All the default colors in the Colors palette, including Red, Green, and Blue, are spot colors. Unless you specify these default colors as process colors they will print on a separate plate. You would never use the RGB colors (Red, Green, Blue) in printing, so delete them before specifying any spot or process colors.

LESSON 8
COLOR LESSON 2
PROCESS COLORS

A process color is one color comprised of percentages of the four process colors, cyan, magenta, yellow and black. Regardless of how many colors in a document you specify as process colors, only four plates will print. This allows you to specify an infinite number of colors for a document's colors list without having to pay for more than four plates. There are some color models that require an extra plate, but these are not used regularly. Also, some clients insist that their corporate logos be printed on a separate plate even though the document uses process colors. In this case five plates will be printed, four for the cyan, magenta, yellow, and black process colors and one for the spot color.

EXERCISE H

1. Create a new document (File/New/Document) without an automatic text box. Choose Edit/Colors. Click on the New button to display the Edit Color dialog box.
2. Use the Model pull-down menu to select Pantone Process. The screen displays the Pantone Process Color swatch library. Scroll to find a deep blue color or type 192-1 in the Pantone S field below the library's scroll bar. The number for the process color appears in the Name field in the upper left corner of the dialog box (Figure 5.12). Click on OK.

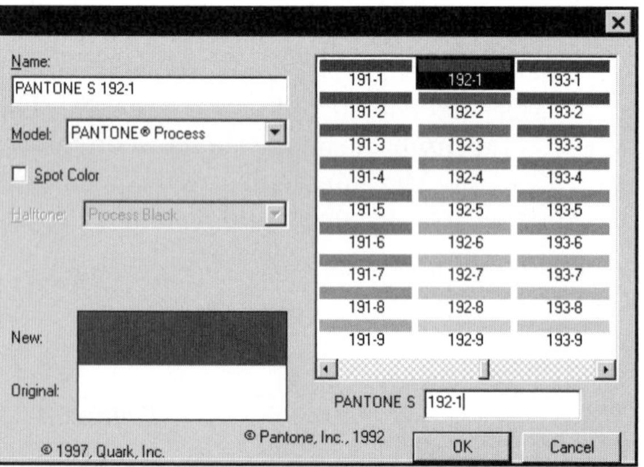

Figure 5.12. When you select a color from the Pantone Process Color swatch library, its name automatically appears in the Name field.

3. Still in the Edit Color dialog box, click on New again. Choose CMYK from the Model dialog box. Type *Deep Rose* in the Name field. You should use a process color swatch to specify the percentages of cyan, magenta, yellow, and black, but for now use the slider bars beneath the Color Picker or type the following values for the colors: C(yan): 55%; M(agenta): 100%; Y(ellow): 27%. Leave K (black) at 0%.
4. Make sure that the Spot Color check box on the left side of the dialog box is unchecked so that the color will print on four plates as a process color (Figure 5.13). Click on OK.

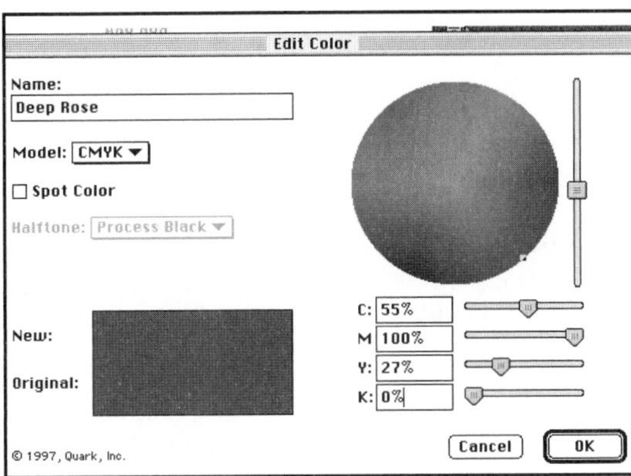

Figure 5.13. Always deselect the Spot Color check box when creating process colors colors based on percentages of CMYK.

5. Use the Show menu at the top of the Colors for Document dialog box to select Process Colors. The four default process colors and the two new process colors appear in alphabetical order in the Show menu. Click on Save to add the new process color to the document's colors list (Figure 5.14).

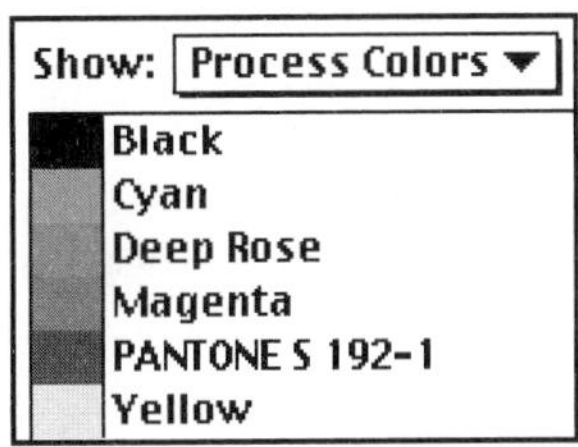

Figure 5.14. Use the Show menu to display only certain kinds of colors in a document.

6. Use any of the picture box tools to draw picture boxes. Choose Item/Modify and apply the new process colors in various shades to the backgrounds of the different boxes.

Macintosh Commands

⌘-P File/Print
⌘-W File/Close

Windows Commands

Ctrl-P File/Print
Ctrl-F4 File/Close

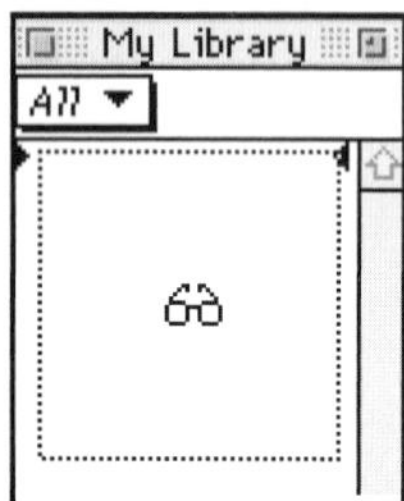

When the Library pointer and two icon arrows appear, the item has been added to the library.

Selecting one label displays all the entries tagged with that label.

7. Choose File/Print. Click the Separations check box in the Document tab of the Print dialog box and select Centered from the Registration pull-down menu. This will print registration and crop marks on each of the four pages. Click on Print. Four pages should print, one for each of the four process colors.
8. Close this file (File/Close). Don't save your changes.

LESSON 9 USING LIBRARIES

A library is an electronic storage bin for thumbnails of text boxes, picture boxes, lines, text paths, and groups. When you create a new library file, a palette appears on the page. Drag-copy items into and out of this palette just as you would if you were pulling pages from a file drawer. Library entries can be edited (Cut, Copy, Paste, Clear) in the palette, but any changes made to library items on the page are not reflected in the Library palette. You must drag an edited item from the document page into the Library again if you want to keep a copy of it in the Library file.

Any text and graphics stored in a Library must first be created in or imported into a box. You can't store an image or a text file unless they have been imported into picture boxes or text boxes. It's important to remember that when you store a high-resolution image in a library, the link between the low-resolution preview of that image and the actual high-resolution somewhere on disk is maintained.

ACCESSING LIBRARIES

Once you create a library, it remains open until you close it by clicking on its Close box. Whenever you launch QuarkXPress, any library palettes that were open when you last quit XPress are opened automatically and displayed at their previous positions. If you closed a library and want to reopen it, use the Open command under the File menu, just as you would for any XPress document file.

LABELS

Once you have added entries to a library, double-click on the entry to display the Label Entry dialog box. You can assign a different name to every entry or you can assign the same name to a group of related entries. If you have already assigned a label, you can access that name from the Label List instead of typing it in again.

EXERCISE I

1. Create a new file without an automatic text box (File/New/Document). Make sure the JPEG Import and LZW Import XTensions are active. Use any of the picture box tools to draw two picture boxes on the page.
2. Select the first picture box and choose File/Get Picture. Navigate to the Unit 05 folder on the CD-ROM and double-click on the *Bridge* image (a JPEG file) to import it into the picture box. Repeat with the second picture box and import the *Tolls* image (a JPEG file).
3. Draw a text box on the page. Click inside the text box and type *Give me all your chocolate and no one gets hurt!* Draw another text box on the page and type *Touch my Twinkies and you die!*
4. Choose File/New/Library. Navigate to your Projects folder. Type *My Library* in the Library Name field and click Create. The Library palette appears on the page.
5. Select the Item tool, click on the first picture box, and drag it into the library. You are drag-*copying* the image, not moving it. When the Library pointer appears, release the mouse button. A thumbnail of the image appears in the Library. Repeat for the second image.
6. With the Item tool still selected, click on the first text box and drag-copy it into the library. Repeat for the second text box. You now have four items in the library.
7. Double-click on the Bridge image in the Library to display the Library Entry dialog box. Type *Bridge* in the Label Name field and click OK. Double-click in the *Tolls* image and type *Tolls* in the Label Name field. Click on OK.
8. Double-click on the first text box in the library. Type *Threats* in the Label Entry field. Click on OK. Double-click on the second text box. Drag the Label List pull-down menu and select Threats. Click on OK (Figure 5.15).

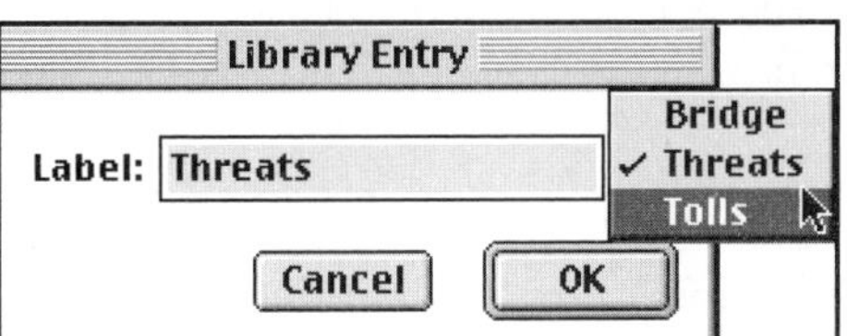

Figure 5.15. Use the Label List to select a label for a selected library item. The selected label appears in the Label field.

Macintosh Commands

⌘-N File/New/Document
⌘-E File/Get Text/Picture
⌘-Option-N File/New/Library

Windows Commands

Ctrl-N File/New/Document
Ctrl-E File/Get Text/Picture
Ctrl-Alt-N File/ New/Library

√	JPEG Import
√	LZW Import

These XTensions must be active before importing a JPEG file saved with LZW compression.

FYI

Library palettes are just like any other palette in XPress. You can close, move, and resize them. Unlike other palettes, however, a library is a separate file that must be opened from the File menu. A Library palette can contain up to 2,000 entries.

Macintosh Commands

⌘-X Edit/Cut
⌘-W File/Close

Windows Commands

Ctrl-X Edit/Cut
Ctrl-F4 File/Close

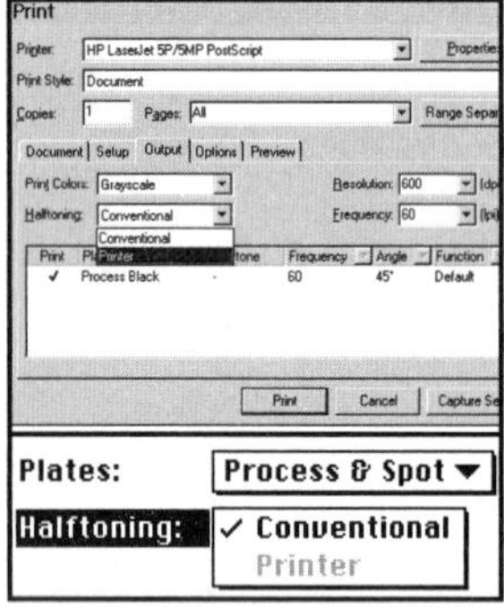

The Conventional option is the only one available when Separations is checked in the Document tab.

9. Use the Library palette's Labels pull-down menu to select *Threats*. Only the two text boxes labeled *Threats* are displayed (Figure 5.16). Click on one of the text boxes and choose Edit/Cut from the main menu. Click OK at the alert. The selected text box is deleted from the library—but not from the document.

Figure 5.16. Selecting a label from the Library palette's menu displays only those thumbnails tagged with that label.

10. Click on the Library palette's close box in the upper corner of the palette. Choose File/Open, navigate to the Projects folder, and double-click on *My Library* to open the library. The palette appears on the page.

11. Close this file (File/Close). Don't save your changes.

LESSON 10 PRINTING LESSON 2 DEVICE AND IMAGE RESOLUTION

The term *resolution* refers to the degree of detail in an image or in the quality of text output. Different output devices have different resolutions, usually measured in dots per inch. Images, depending on how they were created and saved in the graphics program, have image resolution.

OUTPUT RESOLUTION

Output devices such as laser printers and Linotronic imagesetters have various output resolutions. A laser printer, for example, can have an output resolution of 300 dots per inch or 600 dots per inch. An imagesetter, however can have output resolutions of 1240, 1500, or more dots per inch.

IMAGE RESOLUTION

There are two basic kinds of graphic files: bitmap files created in programs like Adobe Photoshop and Fractal Design Painter, and object-oriented images created in PostScript illustration programs like Adobe Illustrator, Macromedia FreeHand, and Corel Draw. Bitmap images are composed of pixels. Image resolution for bitmap images is usually measured in pixels per inch. The more pixels in the image, the larger the image resolution and the greater the detail and color fidelity. Object-oriented images are composed of paths drawn on X and Y coordinates.

FILE FORMATS

Bitmap graphics are usually saved in TIFF (Tagged Image File Format), PICT, Paint, JPEG (Joint Photographic Expert Group), or PhotoCD formats, whereas object-oriented images, sometimes called vector images, are usually saved in EPS (Encapsulated PostScript) format. When you import a bitmap image into a QuarkXPress picture box, it comes in at the exact size and resolution that it was saved in the graphics program. If you enlarge a bitmap image in XPress, you arbitrarily enlarge pixels and therefore reduce the resolution or detail in the image. For example, if you import a 1″ X 1″ image with a resolution of 200 pixels per inch (ppi) and scale it to 2″ X 2″, its effective resolution drops to 100 pixels per inch because you enlarged the pixels to create the larger image. Try not to enlarge bitmap images. You can reduce them without losing detail, but enlarging them beyond 10% of their original size can cause you problems. EPS images, can be resized to any dimension because they aren't composed of pixels, but of mathematical algorithms.

EXERCISE J

1. Create a new file (File/New/Document) with one-inch margins and without an automatic text box. Display the Measurements palette (F9). Use any standard-shape picture box tool to draw a picture box on the page. Choose File/Get Picture. Navigate to the Unit 05 folder on the CD-ROM and double-click on *Tolls* (a JPEG file) to import it into the picture box. Resize the *picture box* to accommodate the image by dragging on the box's resizing handles.
2. With the picture box selected, choose Item/Duplicate twice to create two copies of the image. Use the Item tool to position them one next to the other. Choose File/Document Setup. Click the Landscape icon (right) in the Orientation field to position the page horizontally in the file. Click on OK.

Macintosh Commands

⌘-D Item/Duplicate
⌘-Option-Shift-P File/Document Setup

Windows Commands

Ctrl-D Item/Duplicate
Ctrl-Alt-Shift-P File/Document Setup

FYI

When a Windows Metafile is imported into any QuarkXPress picture box, it is converted to PICT format.

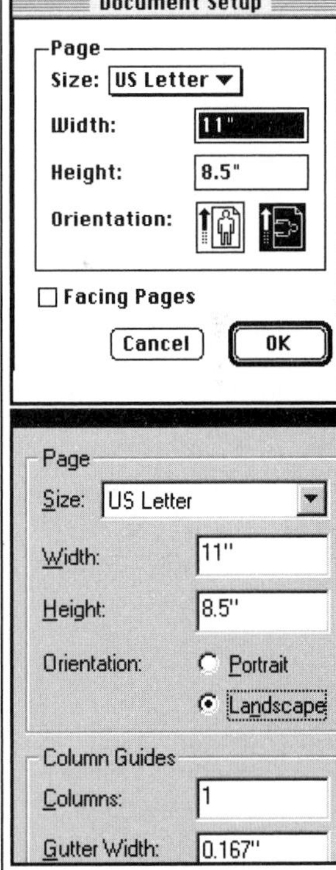

Select a vertical or horizontal Orientation in the Macintosh (top) or Windows (bottom) Document Setup dialog box.

Important info!

You must press the Return/Enter key to execute any command you type in the Measurements palette. Until you press Return/Enter, the new values do not take effect.

Item tool

PPDs

PPDs are PostScript Printer Description files. Select the appropriate PPD for your printer to ensure that the default information in the Print dialog box matches your output device. You can customize this list of PPDs by selecting PPD Manager from the Utilities menu and clicking on the check mark for any unneeded devices to remove them from the Include field. Click the Update button to execute the command.

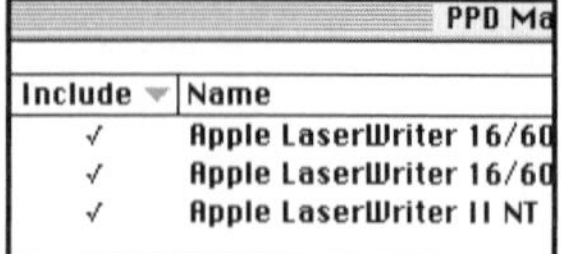

3. Click on the second image and use the X% and Y% fields in the Measurements palette to enlarge the image to 150%. Typing this same value in both the X% and Y% field enlarges the image proportionally. Press Return/Enter after typing the values.
4. Click in the third image and use the X% and Y% fields to proportionally reduce the image to 50% of its original size. Press Return/Enter.
5. Choose File/Print. Make sure the correct options, especially the Printer Description option, are selected in the Document tab. Click the Setup tab and click the Landscape icon (right) in the Orientation field in the lower right corner of the dialog box.
6. Click the Output tab and select Composite Color (if you have a color printer selected) or Grayscale from the Print Colors pull-down menu. If you selected the correct PPD in the Document tab, the Resolution field for that output device displays the maximum dots per inch the selected device can print. Below it, the lpi (lines per inch) value is displayed for the selected printer.
7. Choose Printer for the Halftoning option to use the selected printer's calculated halftone screen values. Make sure that the Process Black plate is selected in the Plate area. Usually the default values in the Plate fields are correct. Click on Print. This image may take a long time to print because the printer has to process the image three times.

UNIT 6 Bézier Boxes

OVERVIEW

In this unit you will learn how to:

Create and modify Bézier text boxes and picture boxes
Reshape Bézier boxes
Add and delete Bézier points
Convert Bézier points
Convert standard-shape boxes to Bézier boxes

TERMS

Bézier point
corner point
smooth point
symmetrical point
direction handles

HOW IT WORKS:

In Photoshop, crop the image and change its mode to grayscale. Then import it into a standard-shape rectangle picture box. Select the picture box, and select the Bézier shape from the Item/Shape menu. Add Bézier points to the sides of the boxes and convert many of the corner points to smooth points. This allows you to use the direction handles on the smooth points to shape the box around the outline of the picture. Finally, add a frame around the box for emphasis.

LESSON 1
CREATING BÉZIER BOXES

In a previous lesson you learned how to use the standard-shape Picture Box tools to create picture boxes with only eight resizing handles. Although you can resize those boxes, you cannot reshape them beyond the shape options under the Item/Shape menu—unless you convert them to boxes with Bézier points via the Item/Shape command. To reshape a picture box you must create a Bézier picture box with Bézier points and curve handles. Dragging these anchor points and handles and adding and deleting points will reshape the picture box, allowing you to create any shape you wish.

Bézier Picture Box tool

BÉZIER PICTURE BOX TOOL

When you draw a picture box with the Bézier Picture Box tool, you don't click and drag as you do with the standard-shape Picture Box tool. Instead, you click and release the mouse to place one anchor point (point A), then move the cursor somewhere else on the page and click to set another anchor point (point B). This creates a straight line between anchor points A and B. When creating straight lines with a Bézier tool, you don't drag because dragging creates curves. Just click.

Freehand box under the Shape menu

All of the information about Bézier picture boxes applies to Bézier text boxes. In fact, any box, whether it's a picture box or a text box, can be created as a Bézier picture or text box or converted to a Bézier picture or text box.

EDITING BÉZIER BOXES

You can reshape a Bézier box (picture box or text box) by manipulating the anchor points, the direction handles that are attached to those Bézier points, and the line segments themselves. To edit a Bézier point, click on the point to select it. Then drag that point to reshape the item. If a point has accessible curve handles, click on the tip of the handle and drag to reshape the item.

When you select (click on) a Bézier point, the Measurements palette displays the kind of point it is. To change a point from one type of point to another, select the point and click on one of the Point icons in the Measurements palette. To change a line segment, click on the line segment to select it, and click on one of the two Line icons in the Measurements palette to change a line segment to a curve or a curve segment to a straight segment.

Bézier Pointer Icons and Point Icons

The Point pointer appears when you move the cursor over a Bézier point. Click the Bézier point and drag to reshape the item.

The Line Segment pointer appears when you move the cursor over a straight or curved line segment. Click on the line and drag to reshape the line segment.

LESSON 2
IMPORTING PICTURES INTO BÉZIER PICTURE BOXES

Once you create a Bézier picture box of any shape, you can import a graphic file into that Bézier picture box. Make sure the picture box is selected, then select either the Content tool or the Item tool, and choose File/Get Picture. Navigate to the folder with the image you want to import and double-click on its file name in the Get Picture dialog box. Because the shape of a Bézier picture box may make it difficult to see the graphic once the graphic is imported (the crossed black lines disappear and the Picture Mover pointer appears in the box), press Command-Shift-M (Macintosh) or Ctrl-Shift-M (Windows) to center the image in the picture box. Once you see it, you can reposition it.

Macintosh Commands

⌘-N File/New/Document

Windows Commands

Ctrl-N File/New/Document

The Corner Point icon is a triangle.

EXERCISE A

1. Create a new document (File/New/Document) without an automatic text box. Click on the Bézier Picture Box tool to select it. Click on the page and release the mouse button to create one point. Move above and to the right and click and release the mouse button to create a second point with a line between the two points. Continue to click and release the mouse to draw a house—or at least something that resembles human habitation. When you come around to the first anchor point, click on it to close the box. The cursor will display the Close Box pointer indicating that the next click will close the box (Figure 6.1). Just click and release, don't drag. Once the box is drawn, you can edit the points.

Bézier Picture Box tool

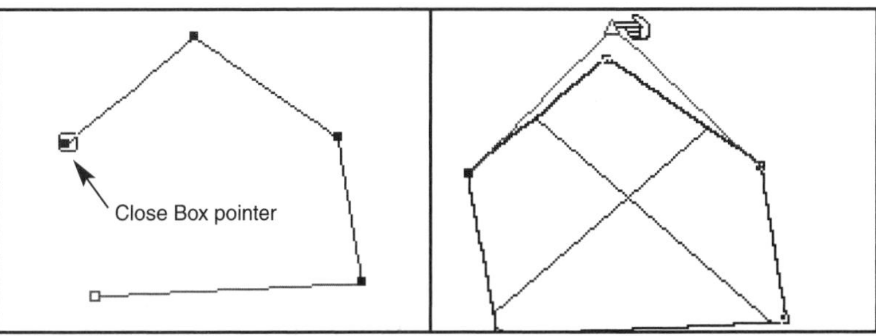

Figure 6.1. Click on top of the first point to close the box (left). Click on any single point to reshape the segments connected by that point.

Closing boxes

There are three ways to close a freehand Bézier box: Click on top of the first point, double-click anywhere on the page, or select another tool.

Macintosh Commands

⌘-W File/Close

Windows Commands

Ctrl-F4 File/Close

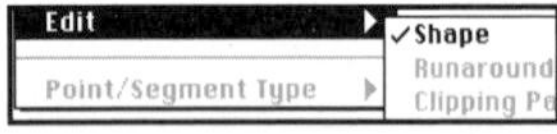

Shape must be selected (Item/Edit) before you can edit the Bézier points on a box.

Bézier Point Icons

The Curve Handle icon is a white square. Drag this icon to move the curve handles and reshape the item.

The Corner Point icon is a black square. Selecting a corner point displays a white triangle.

2. There are three ways to reshape a Bézier box: manipulate the anchor points, move the curve handles, and move the line segments. Choose Item/Shape (Shift F4) and make sure that Shape is selected. This displays the anchor points and allows you to manipulate them. To reshape the box you just created, click on the topmost anchor point and drag it up or down to edit the "roof" of the box (Figure 6.1).
3. Double-click on any anchor point to select the whole item and use the Item tool to drag it around the page (Figure 6.2). Because this item is composed of all corner points, the selected points display as triangles. When all the anchor points are selected, you can also click on any anchor point and drag the item.

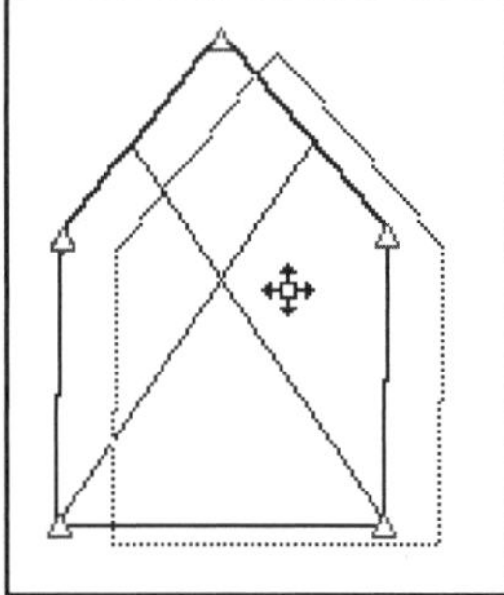

Figure 6.2. Double-clicking on any single point selects all the points and segments in the item and lets you move it around the page with the Item tool or by dragging on any anchor point. As you move the item, the original placement remains behind the item.

4. Click on the picture box to select it. Choose Item/Content/Text to convert the Bézier picture box into a Bézier text box. Now you can type in this house-shaped text box just as you can in any standard-shape text box. And because it is a Bézier text box, you can reshape the box. When you do, the type will adjust to the boundaries of the box.
5. Close this file (File/Close). Don't save your changes.

LESSON 2
CONVERTING STANDARD-SHAPE BOXES TO BÉZIER BOXES

You can always convert a standard-shape box (text or picture) to a Bézier box by using the Item menu (Figure 6.3). You can also convert a standard-shape picture box to a different shape without making it a Bézier box, or you can convert it to a Bézier picture box from the Shape menu (Item/Edit/Shape) and then assign it another shape.

EXERCISE B

1. Create a new document (File/New/Document) without an automatic text box and use any of the three standard-shape Picture Box tools to draw a box. Keep the box selected and choose Item/Shape. Its current shape appears in the list of box shapes under the Shape menu. Drag to select the Bézier box icon, the sixth shape in the list.
2. Pull down the Item menu and under Edit make sure that Shape is selected (Figure 6.3). The eight resizing points on the original standard-shape picture box have now become Bézier points. Click and drag these points to reshape the box.

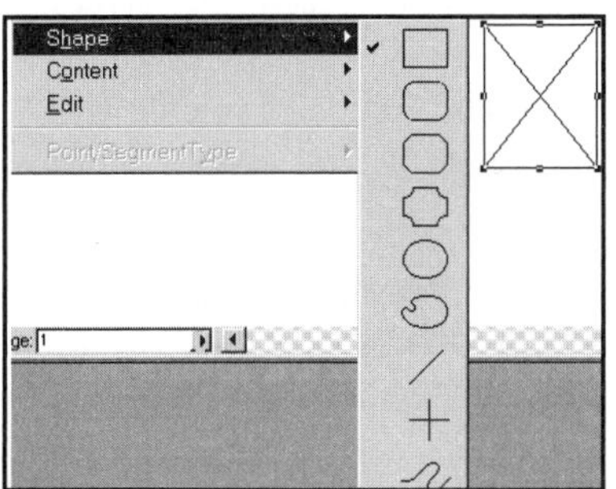

Figure 6.3. The standard-shape picture box can be changed to another shape or to a Bézier picture box by selecting a Shape option under the Item menu.

3. Use any of the standard-shape Text Box tools tool to draw a text box. Type some words in the box. With the box still selected, choose Item/Shape and drag to select the Bézier box icon. Make sure that Shape is selected under the Item/Edit menu. Click and drag the anchor points to reshape the Bézier text box.
4. Close this file (File/Close). Don't save your changes.

LESSON 3 RESHAPING SMOOTH AND SYMMETRICAL POINTS

When a Bézier point connects two curved lines, that point is a smooth point and displays two direction handles that can be manipulated independently of each other. When you click and release the mouse with a Bézier tool, and then click somewhere else on the page, you create a straight line segment. To create a curve line segment, you must click *and drag.*

Macintosh Commands

⌘-N File/New/Document
⌘-W File/Close

Windows Commands

Ctrl-N File/New/Document
Ctrl-F4 File/Close

Standard-shape Picture Box tools

Standard-shape Text Box Tools

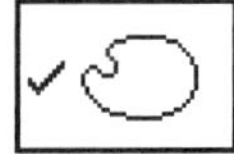

Selecting this icon from the Item/Shape menu converts a conventional box to a Bézier box.

✓Shape Any box displaying eight handles is a standard-shape box. Select the box and select Item/Shape (Shift-F4/Macintosh or F10 (Windows) to access the reshape mode. *Shape* must be checked (selected).

Macintosh Commands

⌘-N File/New/Document
⌘-Z Edit/Undo

Windows Commands

Ctrl-N File/New/Document
Ctrl-Z Edit/Undo

Symmetrical Point icon in the Measurements palette

Bézier Picture Box tool

Moving the cursor near a Bézier point displays a black square. Click on that point to select it.

If the Bézier point connecting two curved lines is a symmetrical point, it also displays two direction handles, but these handles are always equidistant from the point. You can drag the point, the curve segment, and/or the direction handle to reshape the item.

EXERCISE C

1. Create a new file (File/New/Document) without an automatic text box. Select the Bézier Picture Box tool. The cursor changes to a crosshair. Remember, if you make a mistake, choose Edit/Undo. You can also wait until you have completed the item and then edit the Bézier points and segments.
2. You are going to draw a heart which is comprised of curve segments. This means you must click *and drag* to set the direction of the curve. Click and drag up about an inch and release the mouse button (Figure 6.4). You have set the first anchor point (A) and determined the direction of the curve.
3. Click below that first anchor point and drag down about an inch (B) to set the second anchor point and create the actual curve. Release the mouse button.
4. Click across from the second anchor point and drag up and to the right (C) to create the second curve, the V curve in the heart.
5. Click across from the first anchor point at (D) and drag down to create the top of the heart.
6. Click on the first anchor point (E), which displays the Close Box cursor and closes the box.

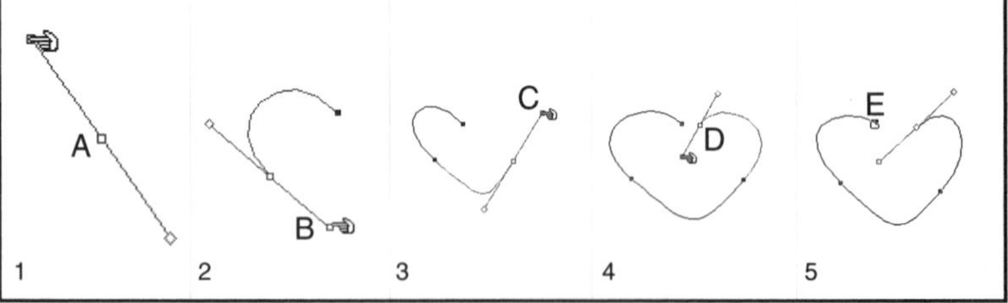

Figure 6.4. Clicking and dragging up sets the direction of the first curve (#1). Clicking and dragging down actually creates the curve (#2). Clicking and dragging up sets the third point and completes the second segment (#3). Clicking across from the first point and dragging down forms the top of the heart and completes the third segment (#4). Clicking on the first Bézier point closes the box.

7. Click to select any smooth Bézier point and use the direction handles to reshape the box. You can also move the Bézier point itself to reshape the item, or click on the segment itself and drag it to reshape the item.
8. When you are satisfied with the box, close the file (File/Close). Don't save your changes.

LESSON 4
ADDING AND DELETING BÉZIER POINTS

Sometimes it's easier to reshape a Bézier item by adding or deleting Bézier points. To add a point to a line segment, move the cursor over the segment; when the Line Segment pointer appears, Option-click (Macintosh) or Alt-click (Windows) to create a new point. To delete a Bézier point, move the cursor over the point you want to delete; when the Point pointer appears, Option-click (Macintosh) or Alt-click (Windows) to delete the Bézier point.

EXERCISE D

1. Create a new file without an automatic text box. Display the Colors palette (F12). Use the standard-shape Picture Box tool and press the Shift key while drawing to create a square picture box. With the box still selected, choose Item/Shape and drag to select the Bézier icon. Make sure that Shape is checked under the Item/Edit menu.
2. Move the cursor over one of the line segments where it changes to the Line Segment pointer. Press the Alt key (Windows) or the Option key (Macintosh) and click to create another Bézier point. Continue to add points around the square (Figure 6.5).

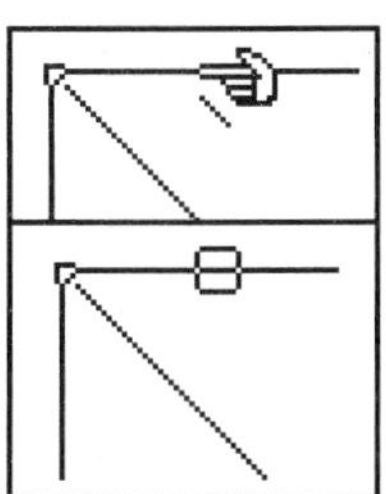

Figure 6.5. When you move the cursor over a line segment on a Bézier box, the Line Segment pointer appears (above). Press the Alt/Option key and the cursor changes to indicate that a new Bézier point will be created on the line segment (below).

Macintosh Commands

⌘-N File/New/Document
⌘-W File/Close

Windows Commands

Ctrl-N File/New/Document
Ctrl-F4 File/Close

The Line Segment pointer appears when you move the cursor over a straight or curved line segment. Click on the line and drag to reshape the line segment. Or, Alt/Option-click to add a Bézier point.

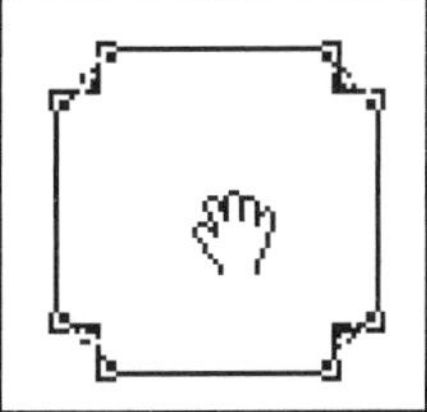

The crossed black lines disappear and the Grabber hand appears in a picture box that contains a graphic.

Macintosh Commands

⌘-W File/Close

Windows Commands

Ctrl-F4 File/Close

Moving the cursor over a Bézier point displays a delete point cursor. Alt/Option clicking with this cursor deletes the Bézier point.

Symmetrical Point icon highlighted on the Measurements palette when a symmetrical point is selected.

Corner point

A corner point connects two straight lines, a straight line and a curved line, or two noncontinuous curved lines. When the corner point connects two curved line segments, the corner point's curve handles can be manipulated independently and form a sharp transition between the curve segment and the straight line segment.

3. With the box still selected, click on the Background icon in the Colors palette and click on a color (name or swatch) to fill the box with color. Click on the Bézier points you created and drag them to form a design.
4. To delete a Bézier point, move the cursor over the point and press the Alt/Option key. When the cursor changes to a rectangle with two lines through it, Alt-click (Windows) or Option-click (Macintosh) to delete the anchor point. Continue to add, delete, and move points to reshape the item (Figure 6.6).

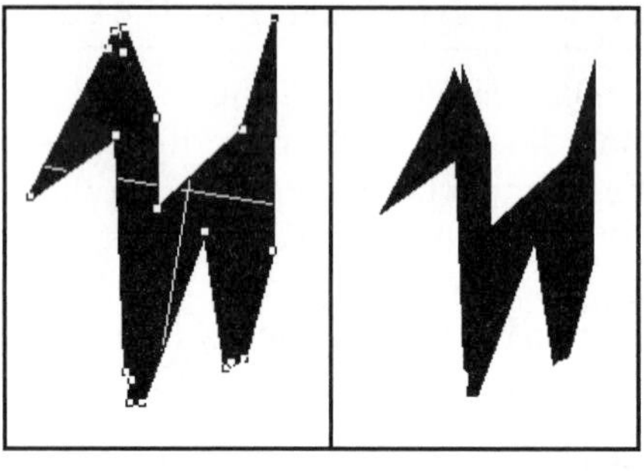

Figure 6.6. Adding, deleting, and moving points lets you reshape Bézier boxes.

5. When you are comfortable with creating and deleting points or when your design resembles something someone would pay for, close the file (File/Close). Don't save the changes.

LESSON 5
CONVERTING BÉZIER POINTS

When drawing Bézier boxes, sometimes adding and deleting Bézier points is not enough to create the box shape you want. It is frequently necessary to reshape a box by changing the points themselves. There are three kinds of Bézier points that affect the way a box is shaped. A *corner point* is used to connect straight lines, a straight and curved line, or two noncontinuous curved lines. A *smooth point* connects two curved lines to form a continuous curve. The direction handles on a curve point rest on a straight line through the point and can be moved independently. A *symmetrical point* connects two curved lines to form a continuous curve, but its direction handles always remain equidistant from its Bézier point.

You can change a Bézier point by first selecting it and then clicking the icon for the type of Bézier point in the Measurements palette. You can also change a point or line segment by using keyboard shortcuts (Figure 6.7).

	Macintosh Command	Windows Command
Change point or line segment		
Corner point	Option-F1	Ctrl-F1
Smooth point	Option-F2	Ctrl-F2
Symmetrical point	Option-F3	Ctrl-F3
Straight line segment	Option-Shift-F1	Ctrl-Shift-F1
Curved line segment	Option-Shift-F2	Ctrl-Shift-F2
Change in point or curve handles		
Add point	Option-click on line segment	Alt-click on line segment
Delete point	Option-click on point	Alt-click on point
Smooth to corner point (vice-versa)	Control-drag on curve handle	Ctrl-Shift-drag on curve handle
Retract curve handles	Control-click on point	Ctrl-Shift-click on point
Expose curve handles	Control-drag on point	Ctrl-Shift-drag on point

Figure 6.7. Use these keyboard commands to reshape Bézier boxes.

FREEHAND BÉZIER PICTURE BOX TOOL

The Freehand Bézier Picture Box tool works like a pencil. Click and drag to draw a box of any shape with both curve and straight line segments. Unlike a pencil, however, the Freehand Bézier Picture Box tool does not create lines, only boxes. If you release the mouse before closing the box, XPress will close the box for you by connecting the last point you created to the first point that was created.

Freehand Bézier Picture Box tool

EXERCISE E

1. Create a new file without an automatic text box. Select the Freehand Bézier Picture Box tool. This tool is used to create closed shapes. Click and drag on the page to draw a fish. Remember, clicking and dragging creates a curve segment. Clicking, releasing the mouse, and moving the cursor before clicking again creates a straight line segment. To end the drawing and close the box, click on top of the first Bézier point. Your aquatic art should resemble Figure 6.8.

Bézier Picture Box tool

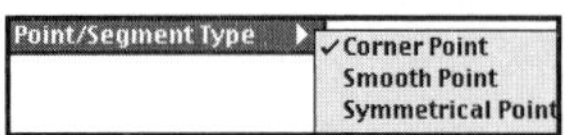

When a Bézier point is selected, you can change the shape of the point from the Item menu.

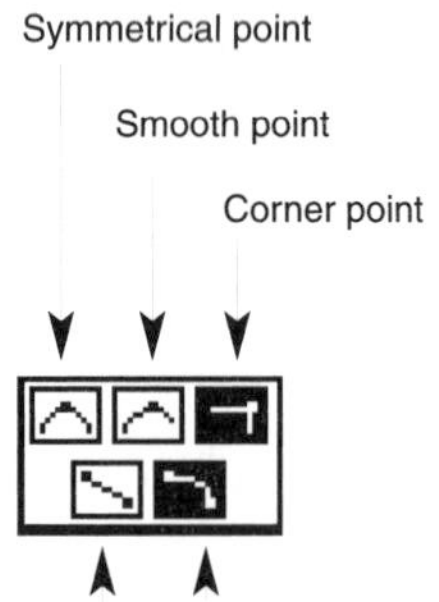

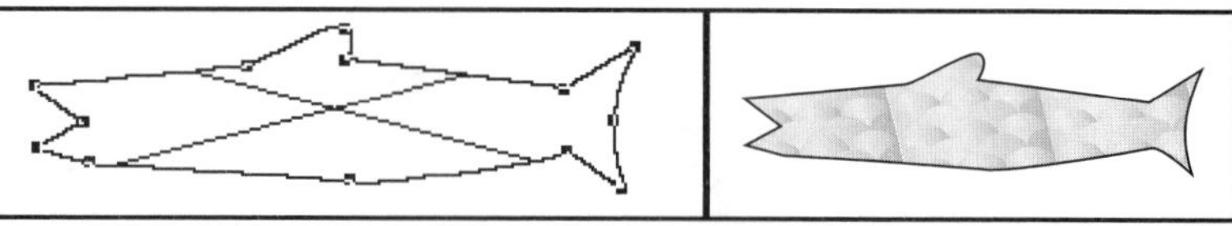

Figure 6.8. A design created with the Freehand Bézier Picture Box tool is really a picture box. An EPS file was imported into the "fish" box.

2. Display the Measurements palette (F9). Click on any Bézier point in the fish box and notice which point icon is highlighted in the Measurements palette (Figure 6.9).

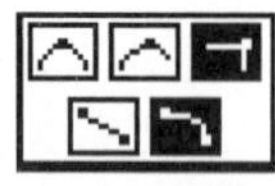

Figure 6.9. Click the Point icons on the Measurements palette to change the shape of a Bézier point. The Straight Line and Curve Line icons appear beneath the Point icons.

3. Click on a different Point icon in the Measurements palette and notice how the shape of the fish changes. To see the name of a selected point, choose Item/Point/Segment Type. The type of the selected point appears with a check mark in the menu.
4. Control-drag (Macintosh) or Ctrl-Shift-drag (Windows) on a curve point to display its two direction handles. Click on the tip of either direction handle to reshape the curve.
5. With the curve point still selected, click on the Symmetrical Point icon in the Measurements palette. Drag one of the direction handles and notice that the handles always rest on a straight line through the point and remain equidistant from the point.
6. Continue to select points, Control-drag (Macintosh) or Ctrl-Shift-drag (Windows) to display direction handles, and convert points to reshape the fish. When you are satisfied, close the file (File/Close). Don't save your changes.

UNIT 7 WORD PROCESSING

OVERVIEW

In this unit you will learn how to:

Create, select, and style type
Set and modify tabs
Apply vertical alignment
Use the spell check and create auxiliary dictionaries
Open, close, and save QuarkXPress documents
Import and export text files

TERMS

auxiliary dictionary
Invisibles
Overflow Indicator
vertical alignment

HOW IT WORKS:

Create the type in Adobe Illustrator and convert it to outlines. Fill the type with 30% black and no stroke. Convert the type to outlines. This lets you print the XPress document without installing the fonts used in the Illustrator document. Save the file in the Illustrator EPS format and import it into an XPress picture box. Because an EPS file can be enlarged without losing detail, the image was enlarged to fit the picture box. Set the unit type in a text box with a background of None to make it transparent against the EPS graphic. Select the text box and apply Centered vertical alignment from the Text Modify dialog box. Apply tracking to the text so that it isn't lost in the large text box.

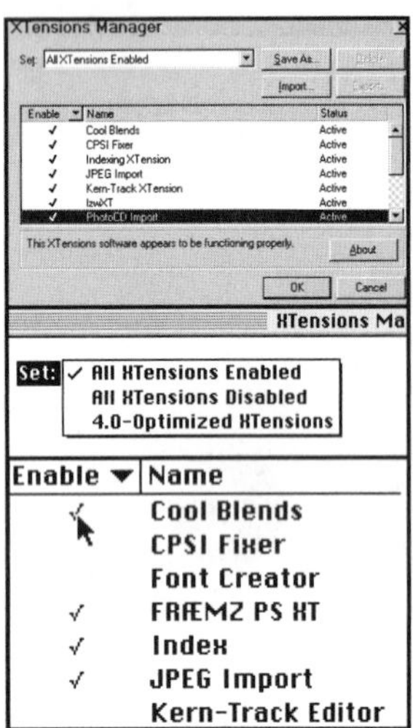

The XTensions Manager is available under the Utilities menu. Use it to turn XTensions on and off and to create sets of frequently used XTensions.

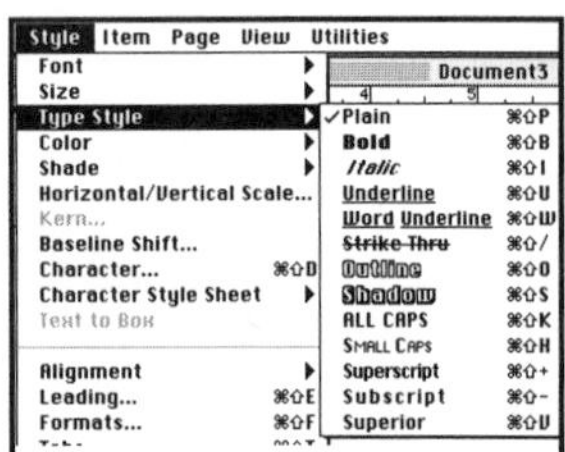

Apply a type style to selected text from the Type Style pull-down menu.

LESSON 1
CREATING AND SELECTING TYPE

To create type in QuarkXPress, you must have a text box or text path active and the Content tool selected. When the I-beam cursor appears in a text box or on a text path, you can begin typing. To style type, that type must be selected. To select one word, double-click on the word; to select a single line, triple-click anywhere in the line; and to select an entire paragraph, quadruple-click anywhere in the paragraph. To select contiguous lines of text, click at the start of the text to be selected; press the Shift key and keep it pressed while you scroll to the last character to be selected. Then click after that last character. You can always click and drag over characters to select them.

IMPORT/EXPORT FILTERS

To import text created in word processing files into QuarkXPress, the correct filter for that word processor must be present in the XTension folder in the QuarkXPress 4.0 folder on the hard drive. For example, if you want to import a Microsoft Word file into an XPress document, the MS Word XTension must be in the XTension folder. If it isn't, drag the MS Word filter from the XTension disabled folder in the QuarkXPress 4.0 folder into the XTension folder. You must relaunch QuarkXPress for the filter to be recognized by the program. Likewise, using the Save Text command, you can export text from XPress in formats that can be read by word processors.

XTENSIONS MANAGER

QuarkXPress 4.0 includes an XTensions manager (Utilities/XTensions Manager) that lets you create sets of different XTensions for different kinds of work. For example, you can select all the word processing filters you use, click the Save As button, and save them as a set of filters. Then use the Set pull-down menu to select the set of XTensions you want to use for a particular project. Any changes you make in the XTensions Manager dialog box take effect the next time you launch XPress.

FORMATTING TEXT

Formatting text includes applying a specific typeface in a specific size and color. Type can also be styled with any of the options from the Style/Type Style menu. Most of these formatting options are also available from the Measurements palette (View/Show Measurements) when a text box is selected. The important thing to remember about styling type is that every text character to be styled must first be selected.

INVISIBLES

While you're typing, XPress places the following invisible code marks in your text:

1. A raised dot indicates that you pressed the spacebar.
2. A right-pointing arrow indicates that the Tab key was pressed.
3. The ¶ mark indicates that you pressed the Return/Enter key at the end of the paragraph.
4. The down-arrow mark indicates that you pressed the Enter key to create the New Column mark.
5. A left-pointing arrow indicates a New Line Marker by pressing Shift-Return.

You can display these code marks, called Invisibles, by choosing View/Show Invisibles. Choosing View/Hide Invisibles hides the code marks.

INTERACTIVE TEXT RESIZING

Ordinarily, clicking and dragging on one of the resizing handles of a text box resizes only the text box. You can, however, modify the point size of type, its auto leading, and horizontal and vertical scaling, as well as the box, *at the same time*. To do this, press the Command key (Macintosh) or the Ctrl key (Windows) as you drag a resizing handle on the text box.

EXERCISE A

1. Create a new, non-facing pages document without an automatic text box (File/New/Document). Display the Measurements palette (View/Show Measurements or F9). Make sure inches is the unit of measure (Edit/Preferences/Document).
2. Use the standard-shape Text Box tool to draw a text box on the page by clicking and dragging, just as you did when creating picture boxes. Use the Measurements palette and type 2 in the W(idth) field; press the Tab key and type 3 in the H(eight) field. Press Return/Enter to resize the selected text box. Make sure the Content tool is selected.

Macintosh Commands

⌘-N File/New/Document
⌘-Y Edit/Preferences/Document
F9 View/Show Measurements

Windows Commands

Ctrl-N File/New/Document
Ctrl-Y Edit/Preferences/Document
F9 View/Show Measurements

Space·tab→ 

The dot, arrow, and ¶ are Invisibles.

FYI

Pressing the Command-Option-Shift keys (Macintosh) or Ctrl-Alt-Shift keys (Windows) will resize the text in proportion to the original box dimensions as you drag on the text box's resizing handle.

Standard-Shape Text Box tool

Macintosh Commands

⌘-I View/Show Invisibles
⌘-E File/Get Text/Picture

Windows Commands

Ctrl-I View/Show Invisibles
Ctrl-E File/Get Text/Picture

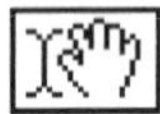

Content tool

Important info

Macintosh users cannot press the Enter key to end a paragraph, only the Return key. Windows users must press the Enter key on the keyboard, not the Enter key on the numeric keypad.

Do it this way!

Always quadruple-click to select a paragraph instead of dragging. Quadruple-clicking selects the entire paragraph, even text hidden by the Overflow Indicator.

3. Notice the I-beam cursor at the top of the text box. This tells you that you can start typing at this point. Type *This is a text box.* Press the Return/Enter key.
4. Choose View/Show Invisibles. Select the Zoom tool and click twice on the text you just typed to magnify your view to 150%. Notice the ¶ mark at the end of the paragraph indicating that you pressed the Return/Enter key to end the paragraph. Also notice the raised dots between each word that indicate where the spacebar was pressed (Figure 7.1).

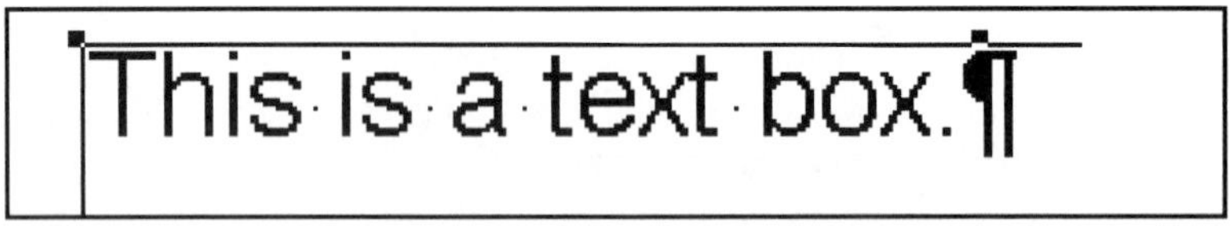

This·is·a·text·box.¶

Figure 7.1. The raised dots (they're higher than the period dot) indicate that the Spacebar was pressed, and the ¶ indicates that the Return key was pressed to end the paragraph.

5. Select the Content tool. Double-click on the word *This*. Use the Style menu or the Measurements palette to select a font and a type size to format the single word.
6. Click below the line of type and choose File/Get Text. Because you have a text box selected and the Content tool active, the Get Text command is available. Navigate to the Unit 07 folder on the CD-ROM and click on Open. Double-click on the file named *Sample.txt.* to import the text into the selected text box. It appears in the same font and type size as the last word in the previous paragraph. That's because the ¶ mark carries that information with it. Notice the box with an X in the lower right corner of the text box. This is called the Overflow Indicator and tells you that you imported more text than will fit in the text box.
7. Triple-click anywhere in the first line of the imported text. Use the Measurements palette or the Style menu to format the selected text in a different font and in a smaller type size.
8. Quadruple-click anywhere in the paragraph of the imported text to select the entire paragraph and notice that the Font and Size fields on the Measurements palette are blank (Figure 7.2). This is because you have selected type with more than one font and in more than one size.

This is a text box.

The marshes were just a long black horizontal line then, as I stopped to look after him; and the river was just another horizontal line, not nearlyso broad nor yet so black; and the sky was just a row of long angry red lines and dense black lines intermixed. On the edge of the river I could faintly make out the only two black things in all the prospect that seemed to be standing upright; one of these was the beacon by which the sailors steered—like an unhooped cask upon a pole—an ugly thing when you were near it; the other a gibbet, with some chains hanging to it which had once held a pirate.

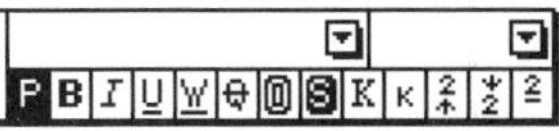

Figure 7.2. The blank Font and Size fields in the Measurements palette indicate that more than one typeface and type size have been selected.

9. With all the text still selected, choose another font from the Font menu and 12 from the Size menu to format the entire paragraph. Because you selected a smaller type size, the entire paragraph should now fit in the text box and the Overflow Indicator should disappear.
10. With the text box still selected, click on the Item tool to select it and press the Delete key (Macintosh) or the Backspace key (Windows) to delete the text box. Because you are deleting an item (the text box) and not its contents (text), you must use the Item tool. Choose Edit/Undo to restore the deleted text box.
11. Save this file as *Format.qxd* in your Projects folder.

EXERCISE B

1. Create a new file (File/New Document) without an automatic text box. Display the Document Layout palette (F10/Macintosh; F4/Windows) and the Measurements palette (F9). Double-click on the first page to get to it. Use the standard-shape Rectangle Text Box tool to draw a text box 3 inches square. (Use the Measurements palette to resize the box, or press the Shift key while drawing the box to constrain it to a square.)
2. Click inside the text box and type *HELLO*. Double-click on the word to select it and format it in 36 pt. Ariel/Helvetica. Select Bold from the Type Style menu or B from the style area at the bottom right corner of the Measurements palette.

Macintosh Commands

⌘-N File/New/Document
⌘-W File/Close
⌘-Z Edit/Undo
⌘-Option-S File/Save as
F10 View/Show Document Layout

Windows Commands

Ctrl-N File/New/Document
Ctrl-F4 File/Close
Ctrl-Z Edit/Undo
Ctrl-Alt-S File/Save as
F4 View/Show Document Layout

Item tool

FYI

Type size is not type weight. Weight describes type as thick or thin. The type in the sidebars of this book is set in Helvetica Light, as opposed to Helvetica Regular. Other type weights include ultralight, book, demibold, and heavy.

Standard-Shape Text Box tool

Macintosh Commands

⌘-O File/Open
⌘-W File/Close

Windows Commands

Ctrl-O File/Open
Ctrl-F4 File/Close

Inter ¶ Max option

This value tells XPress the maximum amount of space it can insert between vertically justified paragraphs to justify them and make them fit from the top to the bottom of the box with equal amounts of space between each paragraph. Leaving the Inter ¶ Max default value at 0" means that if all the vertically justified paragraphs in a text box still do not extend from the top to the bottom of the text box, XPress will override the leading values and insert an equal amount of space between the lines of the paragraph to vertically justify the paragraphs.

FYI

Vertical alignment applies to every paragraph in the text box. You cannot apply different vertical alignments to different paragraphs as you can with the paragraph alignment commands.

3. Press the Command key (Macintosh) or Ctrl key (Windows) and drag one of the resizing handles to make the box about one inch wide and four inches high. Release the mouse button. Check the Measurements palette and notice that the text has been disproportionately resized with the box (Figure 7.3).

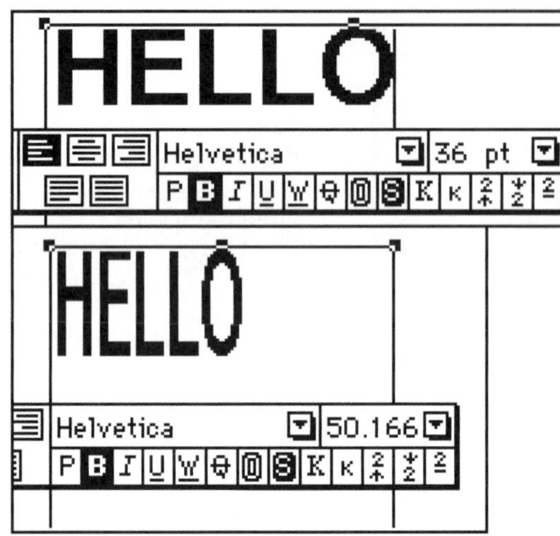

Figure 7.3. Pressing the modifier key while resizing the text box also resized the text inside the box.

4. Close this file (File/Close). Don't save your changes.

LESSON 2
VERTICAL ALIGNMENT

Paragraph alignment defines the relationship of type in a paragraph, whether that paragraph is one line or several lines, to the left and right edges of the text box. Vertical alignment defines the position of the type relative to the top and bottom edges of the text box. Vertical alignment positions the text (1) from the first baseline at the top of the text box; (2) centers it in the text box; (3) starts it from the bottom of the text box, or (4) adds enough space to vertically justify the text, spread it evenly from the top to bottom sides of the text box.

EXERCISE C

1. If necessary, open the *Format.qxd* file you created in the last exercise or open the *Format.qxd* file in the Unit 07 folder on the CD-ROM.

2. With the Content tool selected, click once on the text box to select it. Choose Item/Modify and click on the Text tab. Use the Vertical Alignment pull-down menu on the right side of the dialog box to select Centered. Click on Apply and drag the window to view the centered text. Click on OK. The text appears centered between the top and bottom sides of the text box (Figure 7.4).

Figure 7.4. The first line of text is centered using the paragraph alignment command. The paragraph below it is left-aligned with the paragraph alignment command. Both paragraphs are vertically aligned to the center of the text box with equal space from the top and bottom sides of the text box.

3. With the text box still selected, choose Item/Duplicate twice to create two more text boxes. Position them on the page so they are visible. Choose View/Fit in Window or press Control-V (Macintosh) or Ctrl-Alt-V (Windows) and type a value like 70 in the View Box in the lower left corner of the document window. Press Return/Enter to execute the magnification command.

4. Click in the second text box to select it. Choose Item/Modify and in the Text tab, choose Bottom from the Vertical Alignment pull-down menu. Click on OK. The type starts from the bottom of the text box and works its way up.

5. Click in the third text box to select it. Choose Item/Modify again and select Justified from the Vertical Alignment pull-down menu. Click on OK to justify the lines of text from the top to the bottom of the text box. Your screen should resemble Figure 7.5. Close this file (File/Close). Don't save your changes.

Macintosh Commands

⌘-M Item/Modify
⌘-D Item/Duplicate
⌘-W File/Close

Windows Commands

Ctrl-M Item/Modify
Ctrl-D Item/Duplicate
Ctrl-F4 File/Close

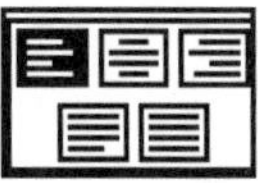

Paragraph alignment can be left, center or right aligned (top row) or justified and force justified (bottom row).

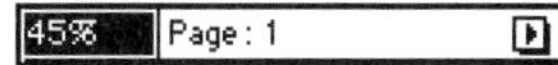

Pressing Control-V (Macintosh) or Ctrl-Alt-V (Windows) highlights the View Box in the lower left corner of the document window. Type a magnification value and press Return/Enter to increase or reduce magnification.

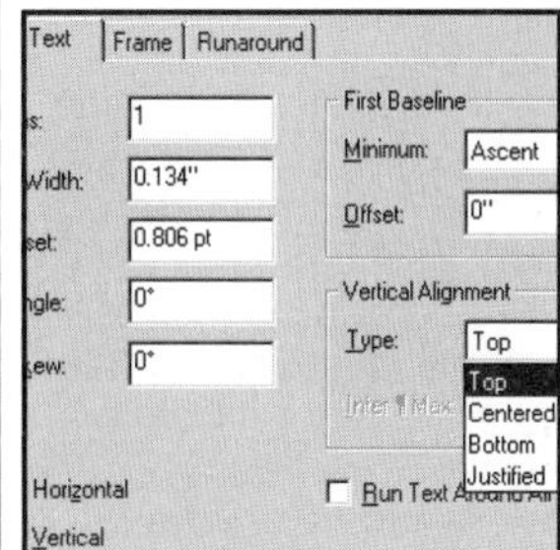

Vertical alignment is specified in the Text Modify dialog box.

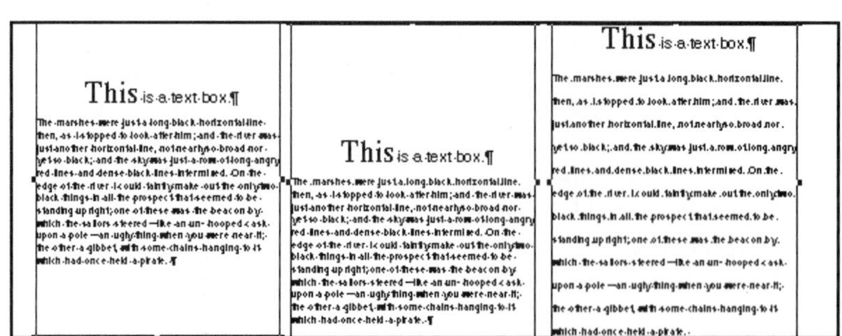

Figure 7.5. Text boxes vertically aligned center, bottom, and justified.

Problems?

When text isn't behaving properly, the first thing to do is display Invisibles and check for tab marks and extra paragraph returns.

LESSON 3 USING TABS

Use tabs to align rows and columns of entries. To set a tab, you must press the Tab key before or after you specify the tab position in the Tabs dialog box. Once the Tab key is pressed, any values you type in the Tabs dialog box will be applied.

Tabs are a paragraph-level format, which means that the entire paragraph is affected by the tab, not just one line. You must press the Return/Enter key to end the paragraph before applying tabs. And because Tabs are paragraph-based, you don't have to select the entire paragraph; clicking anywhere in the paragraph selects the paragraph whenever you are applying a paragraph-based command. If you find that a line is too long to be tabbed effectively, consider reducing the type size or the number of text characters in the entries.

Sorry

Placing boxes or other items in a column of text that is vertically justified will cancel the vertical justification.

Tabs can be aligned on the left character in the entry, on the right character in the entry, on the center character in the entry; aligned on a text character like the dollar sign; aligned on a comma; or aligned on a decimal point (Figure 7.6). You can also include a tab leader, like a period, between tab stops to make it easier for the eye to follow the tab.

More problems?

If your type is not aligning vertically with the different Vertical Alignment commands, you probably (1) have paragraph returns running loose in the paragraph. Turn on Invisibles (View/Show Invisibles), select and delete the paragraph returns. Or, (2) you don't have a text box selected.

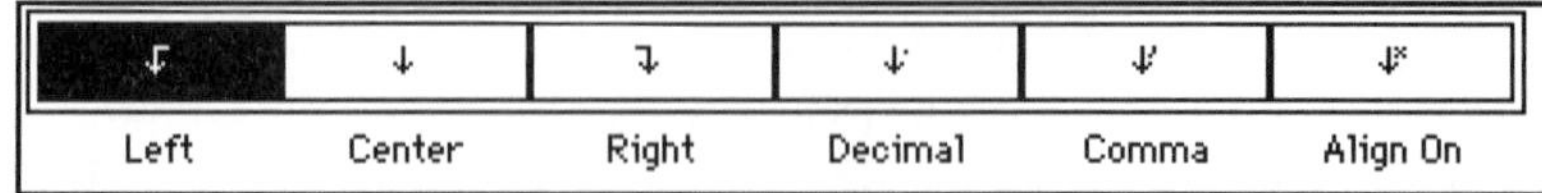

Figure 7.6 displays the six different tab stops in QuarkXPress 4.0.

EXERCISE D

1. Create a new document with an automatic text box (File/New/Document). Display the Measurements palette (F9). Choose Edit/Preferences/Document and make sure the unit of measure is set to inches. Select the Content tool, click inside the text box on the first page of the document, and choose File/Get Text.
2. Navigate to the Unit 07 folder on the CD-ROM drive and open the file named *Tabs.text.* Choose View/Show Invisibles to display the text codes and notice the spaces between the words and the paragraph returns after each line.
3. Click between each entry, delete the space, and press the Tab key. The text will not format properly until you specify the tab stops (Figure 7.7).

```
School·Cookie·Sale¶
Student→Cookies→        Price→  Boxes·Sold→    Total·¶
Katie→  Seriously·Sinful·Chocolate→    $1.98→  37→     $73.26¶
Liz→    Tofu·Treasures→$1.69→  2→      $1.38¶
Trish→  Butterscotch·Bubbles→  $1.59→  22→     $34.98¶
```

Figure 7.7. Delete the spaces between the entries and press the Tab key before setting the tabs. With Invisibles on, the arrow indicates that the Tab key was pressed.

4. Triple-click to select the first line of text, the title. Format it in 14 pt. Times bold. Click on the Center Align icon in the Measurements palette to center the line of text in the text box.
5. Triple-click to select the second line of text and the headings, and format in Times at 12 points.
6. Click anywhere inside that second line of text and choose Style/Tabs. The Paragraph Formats dialog box appears with the Tabs tab active. There are two ways of setting tabs: (1) clicking in the tab ruler at the top of the dialog box (not the ruler on the document page) or (2) typing a tab position in the Position field, then clicking Set in the dialog box. Click on the Center tab icon to indicate a center tab. Click inside the Position field and type 1.3. Click on the Set button. Click the Apply button. A tab appears on the tab ruler, and the second element in the heading line, Cookies, is centered on the 1.3-inch mark on the page.

Macintosh Commands

⌘-N File/New/Document
⌘-Y Edit/Preferences/Document
⌘-E File/Get Text
⌘-I View/Show Invisibles
⌘-Shift-T Style/Tabs

Windows Commands

Ctrl-N File/New/Document
Ctrl-Y Edit/Preferences/Document
Ctrl-Y File/Get Text/Picture
Ctrl-I View/Show Invisibles
Ctrl-Shift-T Style/Tabs

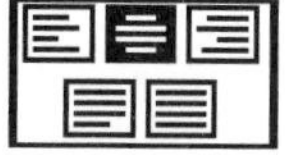

The Center Align icon is selected in the Measurements palette.

FYI

The tab stops in XPress default to setting a left-aligned tab every half inch.

Macintosh Commands

⌘-Z Edit/Undo
⌘-Shift-T Style/Tabs

Windows Commands

Ctrl-Z Edit/Undo
Ctrl-Shift-T Style/Tabs

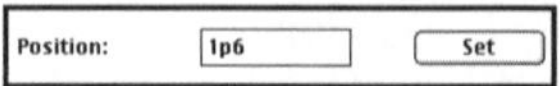

Until you click the Set button or click on OK, the tab is not permanently set in the paragraph.

Setting tables

Use the Rule Above or Rule Below command to create tables. Then use the Orthogonal Line tool to create vertical lines between the tabs. Group all the lines with the text box so the table stays intact.

TABLE

One	Two	Three
Four	Five	Six
Seven	Eight	Nine

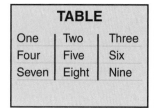

7. Make sure the Center tab icon is still selected. Type 2.8 in the Position field and click on Set. Click on Apply. Type 3.6 in the Position field and click on Set. Type 5 in the Position field and click on Set (Figure 7.8). You can also click the Apply button to set the tab. If you make a mistake, press Command-Z (Macintosh) or Ctrl-Z (Windows) to undo your last action or click on the tab icon in the ruler and drag it off the ruler. Click on OK to exit the Tabs dialog box.

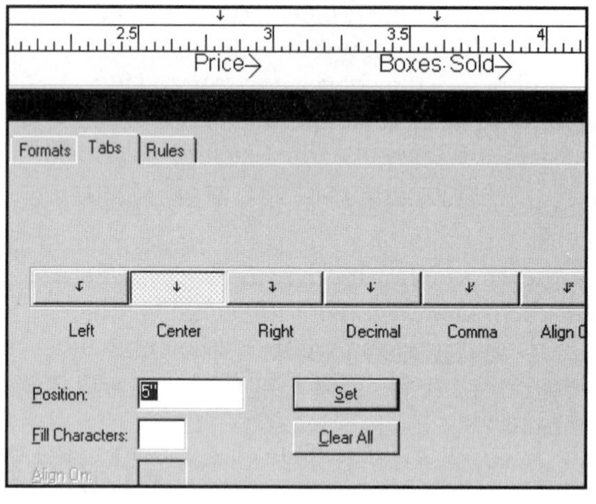

Figure 7.8. This Tabs dialog box displays a selected center tab stop at the 5-inch mark.

8. Drag to select at least one character in the last three lines of text, the girls' sales records. Choose Style/Tabs to display the Tabs dialog box.

9. Click on the Left Align tab icon and click around the .75 mark on the ruler. Notice the value that appears in the Position field when the tab stop is selected. To modify the tab stop, click on the tab indicator in the ruler (Figure 7.9) and drag it along the tab ruler. Then click on the tab indicator and drag it to the left off of the ruler. Type .75 in the Position field and click on Set.

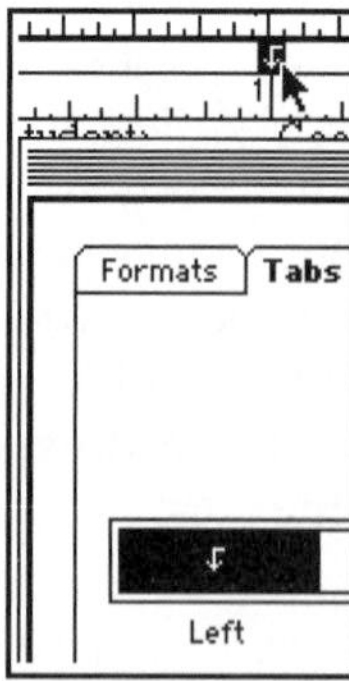

Figure 7.9. Click on a tab stop to select it. To remove it, drag it to the left off of the ruler. To modify it, drag it along the tab ruler.

10. Click on the Decimal tab and click on the 2.8 mark on the ruler. Move the tab indicator or drag it from the ruler and type 2.8 in the Position field. Click on Set.
11. Click on the Left Align tab icon and position a tab at the 3.6 mark on the ruler.
12. Click on the Right Align icon and position a tab at the 5.25 mark on the ruler to align the Total values along the rightmost character in the values.
13. Click on Set. Click the Apply button to apply the tabs and see where they are placed. Drag them off the ruler and reapply or drag them along the ruler to reposition them. When you are finished, click on OK. Your screen should resemble Figure 7.10.

Student→	Cookies→	Price→	Boxes·Sold→	Total¶
Katie→	Seriously·Sinful·Chocolate→	$1.98→	37→	$73.26¶
Liz→	Tofu·Treasures→	.69→	2→	$1.38¶

Figure 7.10. The last three lines of text are tabbed using left, center, decimal, and right align tab stops.

14. Save this file as *Tabs.qxd* (File/Save as) in your Projects folder.

LESSON 4
MODIFYING TAB STOPS

You can modify any tab stops in any document from the Tabs dialog box. Tab stops can be modified by dragging the tab indicator to a new location or by adding and deleting tab stops. Sometimes it's easier to click the Clear All button in the Tabs dialog box and start over again. You can also drag a tab indicator off the ruler to delete it. QuarkXPress 4.0 allows you to place thousands of tab stops on one line, which makes it easier to set heavy tabular documents like spreadsheets saved as text files and imported into XPress text boxes.

EXERCISE E

1. If necessary, open the *Tabs.qxd* file you just created or open the *Tabs.qxd* file in the Unit 07 folder on the CD-ROM (File/Open). You need to adjust the position of *Boxes Sold* in the heading line.

Macintosh Commands

⌘-O File/Open
⌘-Option-S File/Save as

Windows Commands

Ctrl-O File/Open
Ctrl-Alt-S File/Save as

Tip

Because the Tabs dialog box is large and consumes lots of screen real estate, reduce the level of magnification to about 90% so you can move the dialog box around and see what happens when you click the Apply button.

Important info

To modify an existing tab stop, first click on the tab stop in the tab ruler to select it. Then either change its position in the Position field or drag the tab stop along the ruler to reposition it.

Macintosh Commands

⌘-N File/New/Document
⌘-E File/Get Text/Picture
⌘-W File/Close

Windows Commands

Ctrl-N File/New/Document
Ctrl-E File/Get Text/Picture
Ctrl-F4 File/Close

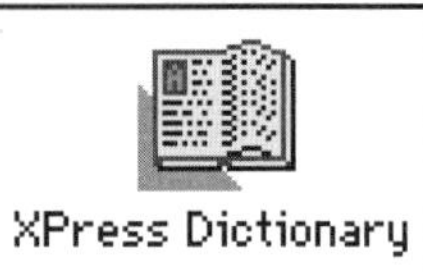

The QuarkXPress dictionary must be present in the QuarkXPress 4.0 folder for the spell check to work.

Story time

A story is text in the selected text box and in all text boxes linked to that text box.

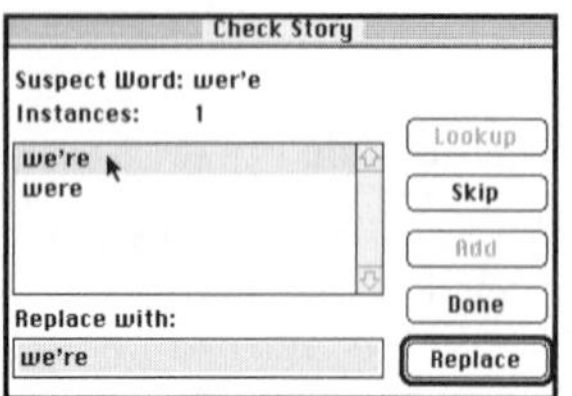

Click to select one of the suggested replacement words in the scroll panel, and click on Replace.

2. Click in the second line of text, the headings line, and choose Style/Tabs. Click on the third tab stop in the tab ruler, a center tab, and drag it to the 3.75 mark on the tab ruler. Click on OK to set the tab. Close this file (File/Close). Don't save your changes.

LESSON 5 SPELL CHECKING

Like any good word processor, QuarkXPress contains a spell checking function, and like all spell checkers it should be used judiciously and not as a substitute for careful proofreading. There are three levels of spell checking in XPress: word check, story check, and document check. All three kinds of spell checking rely on the XPress Dictionary, which is installed in the QuarkXPress folder when you install QuarkXPress 4.0. You can also create auxiliary dictionaries that contain words often used in your documents.

EXERCISE F

1. Create a new file with an automatic text box. Click the automatic text box on the first page and choose File/Get Text. Open the *Spell1.txt* file in the Unit 07 folder on the CD-ROM. You will begin by spell checking a single word. Double-click on the word *chocolatte,* and choose Utilities/Check Spelling/Word. A dialog box appears telling you that *chocolatte* is a suspect word—it's not in the XPress Dictionary—and suggests that you replace it with *chocolate*. Click on *chocolate* to select it as the replacement word and click on Replace (Figure 7.11). The correctly spelled word appears in the document.

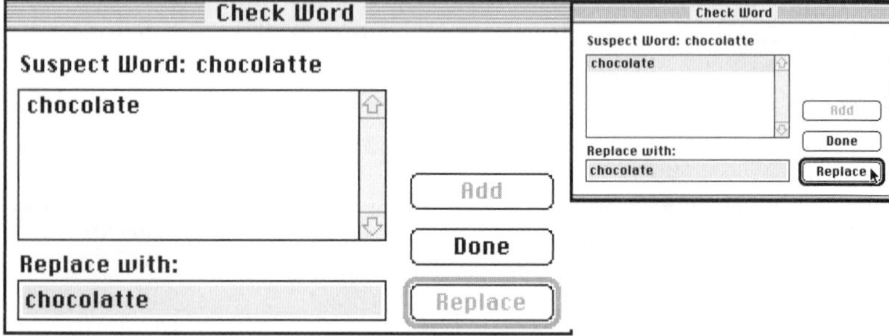

Figure 7.11. The suspect word appears in the Replace with field. To replace the suspect word with the correctly spelled word, click on it in the scroll panel and click Replace. Or, double-click on the replacement word in the scroll list.

2. To spell check a story (a chain of linked text), choose Utilities/Check Spelling/Story. The Word Count dialog box appears giving you the number of words in the active story (Total), the total number of different words in the story (Unique), and the number of unique words that can't be found either in the XPress Dictionary or in any open auxiliary dictionaries (Suspect).
3. Click on OK to display the Check Story dialog box. *Mae* is listed as a suspect word that occurs once in the document. Click on Lookup to see what XPress suggests you replace this word with (Figure 7.12).

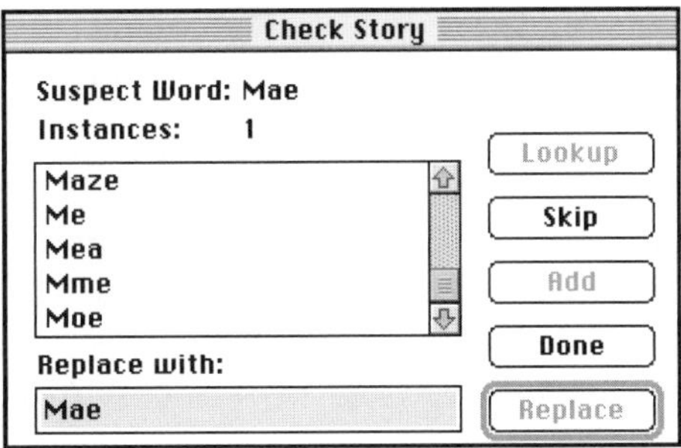

Figure 7.12. When the spell check finds a word that is not in any of the open dictionaries, it tags it as Suspect. Click on Lookup to list suggested replacement words. Click on Skip to leave the suspect word untouched.

4. *Mae* is the correct word, so click on Skip. *Mae* is left untouched, and the Spell Check displays the next suspect word. Click on Lookup and click on *frequently* to replace the suspect word.
5. Continue to Lookup, select a replacement word, and click the Replace button. When the entire document has been spell checked, the Check Story dialog box closes automatically and returns you to the document.
6. Close this file (File/Close). Don't save your changes.

LESSON 6
AUXILIARY DICTIONARIES

An auxiliary dictionary is a custom dictionary that you create just as you create a library or any other file. You can add words to this dictionary that do not appear in the XPress Dictionary. When you open this auxiliary dictionary and encounter a suspect word during the spell check, you have the option of adding the suspect word to the auxiliary dictionary. You can edit an auxiliary dictionary, adding and deleting words, without being in the spell check function. Unlike the XPress Dictionary, which opens automatically

Macintosh Commands

⌘-Option-L Utilities/Check Spelling/Story
⌘-W File/Close

Windows Commands

Ctrl-Alt-W Utilities/Check Spelling/ Story

The Word Count dialog box gives the number of words in a story or document (39) and the number of words that don't appear in any of the open dictionaries (5).

Lookup

The Lookup function displays a list of words that are similar to the suspect word. If there are no similar words, all you get is a message.

Done

Click the Done button to stop the spell check at any point in the process. When you return to the document, any choices made in the Check Story or Check Document dialog boxes prior to clicking Done are applied to the text.

Macintosh Commands

⌘-N File/New/Document
⌘-E File/Get Text/Picture
⌘-Option-Shift-L Utilities/Check Spelling/Document

Windows Commands

Ctrl-N File/New/Document
Ctrl-E File/Get Text/Picture
Ctrl-Alt-Shift-W Utilities/Check Spelling/Document

Cancel out

Clicking the Cancel button in any dialog box closes the dialog box without applying any of the values you set in that dialog box.

FYI

You can create as many auxiliary dictionaries as you need, but you can use only one auxiliary dictionary at a time with an active document. However, you can use that same auxiliary dictionary with several documents.

when you begin to spell check, an auxiliary dictionary, must be opened manually the first time you use it in a document. The next time you spell check that same document, the auxiliary dictionary will load automatically as long as you haven't moved the document file from its original location.

EXERCISE G

1. Create a new file with an automatic text box (File/New/Document). Select the automatic text box on the first page and choose File/Get Text. Open the *Spell2.txt* file in the Unit 07 folder on the CD-ROM.
2. This file contains several proper nouns, words that probably won't be found in the XPress Dictionary. Choose Utilities/Auxiliary Dictionary. In Mac OS, click the New button and navigate to your Projects folder. Type *Company Dictionary* in the New Auxiliary Dictionary field, and click on Create. In Windows, after choosing Utilities/Auxiliary Dictionary, navigate to your Projects folder. Type *Company Dictionary* in the File name field. Then click on New. The auxiliary dictionary is created and you are returned to the document.
3. Choose Utilities/Check Spelling/Document. The Word Count dialog box indicates that there are two suspect words in the document. Click OK to begin spell checking. When *GraphTech* is tagged as a suspect word, click on the Add button to add *GraphTech* to the auxiliary dictionary. Repeat for *Dilbert*. The spell check returns you to the document.
4. Choose Utilities/Check Spelling/Document once more. The Word Count dialog box displays 0 as the number of suspect words because it read the two words you added to the auxiliary dictionary.
5. Choose Utilities/Edit/Auxiliary. In the Edit Auxiliary Dictionary dialog box, type *IBM* in the text field at the bottom of the dialog box. Although you are typing in uppercase, the characters appear in lowercase in the auxiliary dictionary. Click the Add button to add *IBM* to the Company Dictionary auxiliary dictionary (Figure 7.13).

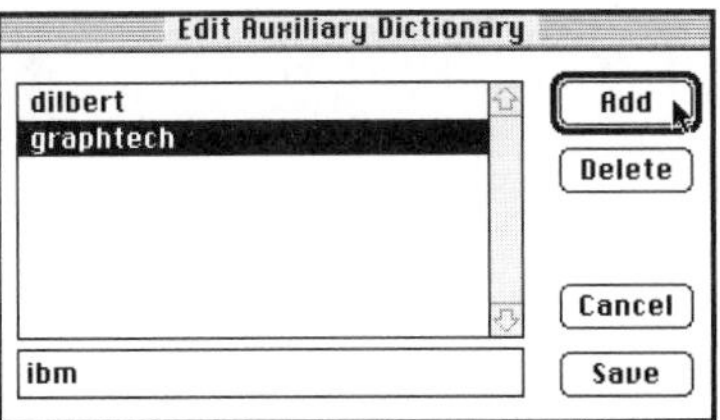

Figure 7.13. Add words to and delete words from the auxiliary dictionary in the Edit Auxiliary Dictionary dialog box.

6. Select *dilbert* from the scroll list and click on Delete to delete that word from the auxiliary dictionary. Click Save to save the edits.
7. In the document, type *IBM is a big company.* after the last sentence. Choose Utilities/Check Spelling/Document and notice that only one word is tagged as suspect. Click OK, and when *Dilbert* is tagged as a suspect word, click Skip to leave it untouched.
8. Close this file (File/Close). Don't save your changes.

LESSON 7 EXPORTING TEXT

Any text imported into or created in XPress can be exported as a text file in one of three formats. The Save Text command lets you export either selected text in the XPress document or the entire story as an ASCII text file, as a Microsoft Word file, or as text with XPress tags. Text exported in the ASCII format can be opened as raw text in many word processing, page layout, and graphic applications, and then formatted in those applications. If you have applied paragraph styles to the text in XPress and export it in Microsoft Word format, Microsoft Word will read those styles and keep them with the Microsoft Word document.

XPRESS TAGS

QuarkXPress lets you import and export text in the ASCII format. If you have the XPress Tags filter loaded in the XTension folder *before* launching QuarkXPress, you can export text in the XPress Tags format. This format lets you embed the codes XPress uses to display character and paragraph attribute information in the ASCII file when you export it. Any text exported in the XPress tags format can be imported into an active text box in XPress. Check the Include Style Sheets option in the Get Text dialog box to translate the XPress Tags codes to character and paragraph attributes.

Macintosh Commands

⌘-Option-Shift-L Utilities/Check Spelling/Document
⌘-W File/Close

Windows Commands

Ctrl-Alt-Shift-W Utilities/Check Spelling/Document
Ctrl-F4 File/Close

Skip

Click the Skip button to leave every instance of the suspect word untouched. Click Skip when documents contain names and places—spelled correctly, of course!

Use the Format menu in the Save Text dialog box to select an export format.

Macintosh Commands

⌘-N File/New/Document
⌘-E File/Get Text/Picture
⌘-Option-E File/Save Text
⌘-W File/Close

Windows Commands

Ctrl-N File/New/Document
Ctrl-E File/Get Text/Picture
Ctrl-Alt-E File/Save Text
Ctrl-F4 File/Close

EXERCISE H

1. Create a new document with an automatic text box (File/New/Document). Click inside the text box on page 1 and choose File/Get Text. Double-click on the *Sample.txt* file in the Unit 07 folder on the CD-ROM to import the text.
2. Choose File/Save Text. Navigate to your Projects folder. Type *Export.txt* in the Save text as field (Macintosh) or in the Save as type field (Windows). Use the Format pull-down menu to select ASCII or a Microsoft Word format. Click on Save.
3. Close this file (File/Close). Don't save your changes. If you have Microsoft Word on your hard drive, launch it and use the File/Open command to open the *Export.txt* file in Microsoft Word.

UNIT 8 Formatting Paragraphs

OVERVIEW

In this unit you will learn how to:
Apply paragraph formatting
Set leading and spacing values
Control paragraph flow
Create drop caps
Lock text to the baseline
Apply and edit hyphenation values

TERMS

absolute leading
auto leading
baseline
baseline grid
drop cap
increment
leading
orphan
widow

HOW IT WORKS:

Create the unit text and select Create Effect from the QX-Effects menu. Choose Bevel for the Box option rather than the Contents option (which would have applied the bevel to the type). Choose Grayscale at 300 dpi in the Attributes dialog box because this file will be printed at a line screen of 133 lines per inch, and the rule is to print at a resolution double the line screen. Leave the other options at their default values and click on Finish. When the beveled box appears, select the text box, choose Item/Bring to Front, and change its background to None. QX-Effects creates a high-resolution TIFF file called *Bevel 1* in the same folder as the XPress document. You will need this file to print the effect properly.

LESSON 1
PARAGRAPH ATTRIBUTES

The paragraph is the basic unit of a document. Its characteristics include leading, the space between lines of type, indents from the left and right side of the text box as well as for the first line of the paragraph, drop caps, spacing before and after the paragraph, as well as the paragraph's relation to the paragraph that immediately follows it. In this unit you will learn how to format a paragraph so that it behaves properly, that is, it displays the proper indents, spacing, and leading values and lives in harmony with subsequent paragraphs. You will also learn how to create drop caps in a paragraph and how to lock paragraphs to the baseline grid so they align evenly across multiple columns. Hyphenation and justification values (H&Js) and paragraph alignment are also covered.

These paragraph attributes are all assigned from the Paragraph Formats dialog box, which at first glance can seem overwhelming, but is really a powerful and easy dialog box to use. It will also help you to break some bad typesetting habits like pressing the spacebar to indent a paragraph and allowing single paragraph lines to appear at the end of a column (orphans) and at the top of a column (widows) of text.

Very important info

Always use the First Line indent command to indent a paragraph. Using the Spacebar or the Tab key is absolutely the wrong thing to do because these keys generate extra characters over which you have little or no control. In a long document this can make you weep.

PARAGRAPH INDENTS

A paragraph is any number of lines of text where the last character is the paragraph mark (¶). Every time you press the Return/Enter key while typing text characters, a paragraph mark is generated. You won't see this paragraph mark in the XPress document unless you turn on Invisibles (View/Show Invisibles). Paragraph marks never print, but they indicate the end of a paragraph. Paragraph formats, then, apply to every text character and every line of text in that paragraph. You cannot, for example, have a paragraph with more than one leading value, because leading is the vertical space between lines of type in a single paragraph. The entire paragraph must be left, right, center, or justified aligned, not just selected lines in the paragraph. And you can apply space before and after only the entire paragraph, not between individual lines in a paragraph.

In QuarkXPress a paragraph is aligned relative to the left and right sides of the text box. Its distance from those sides is first determined by the value specified in the Text Inset field of the Text Modify dialog box. The default value is 1 point, which means that the text is inset 1 point around all four sides of the box. Any change you make to this value applies that value to all four sides of the text box.

Beyond the Text Inset value are the paragraph indent values. Here you specify the distance of only the left side of the paragraph text from the left side of the text box (Left Indent value), from the right side of the text box (Right Indent), or the distance of the first line of the paragraph from the left side of the text box (First Line indent).

Because paragraph formatting commands apply to the entire paragraph, you simply click anywhere in a paragraph to select the paragraph. You don't have to highlight any of the characters in a paragraph to select a paragraph.

EXERCISE A

1. Create a new document with one-inch margins, non-facing pages, and an automatic text box (File/New/Document).
2. Choose Edit/Preferences/Document and in the General Preferences dialog box make sure that inches is the unit of measure. Click on OK.
3. Click inside the automatic text box on the page and choose File/Get Text. Locate the *Para1.txt* file in the Unit 08 folder on the CD-ROM and double-click on the file or highlight the file name and click on Open to load the text file into the XPress document. Choose View/Show Invisibles and notice the paragraph return marker at the end of both paragraphs.
4. Click anywhere in the first paragraph and choose Style/Formats to display the Paragraph Attributes dialog box (Figure 8.1).

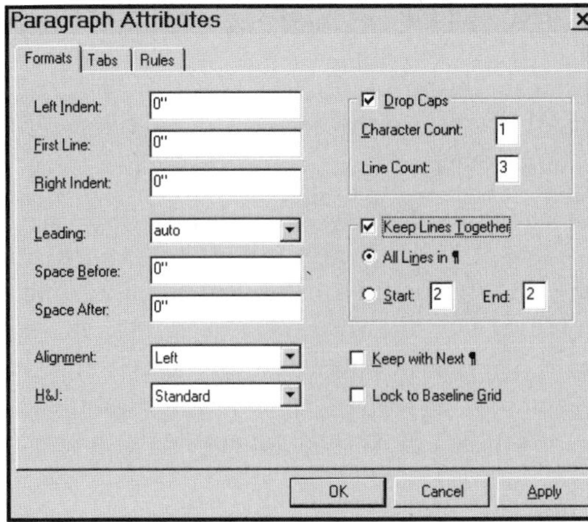

Figure 8.1. The Paragraph Attributes dialog box.

Macintosh Commands

⌘-N File/New/Document
⌘-Y Edit/Preferences Document
⌘-E File/Get Text/Picture
⌘-I View/Show Invisibles

Windows Commands

Ctrl-N File/New/Document
Ctrl-Y Edit/Preferences/ Document
Ctrl-E File/Get Text/Picture
Ctrl-I View/Show Invisibles

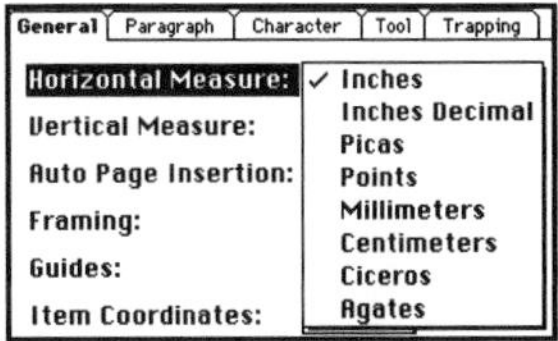

Select from a variety of horizontal and vertical units of measure in the General Preferences dialog box.

FYI

When you work with the Paragraph Attributes dialog box (Style/Formats), you are specifying values for only the selected paragraph, not for every paragraph in the document.

Macintosh Commands

⌘-Shift-F Style/Formats

Windows Commands

Ctrl-Shift-F Style/Formats

5. The first three options, Left Indent, First Line, and Right Indent, refer to the distance of the paragraph lines from the left and right sides of the text box. Type 1 in the Left Indent field, press the Tab key, type .5 in the First Line field, press the Tab key and type 2 in the Right Indent field. Click on the Apply button to apply those values without leaving the dialog box. You may have to move the dialog box by dragging its title bar so you can see the first paragraph. Your screen should resemble Figure 8.2. Notice how the paragraph is indented from both sides of the text box and that the first line is indented one-half inch into the paragraph. Click on OK to execute the changes.

The Leading field defaults to auto. The auto value defaults to 20% of the type size but can (and should) be changed to an absolute value such as 12 points, for example, in the Paragraph Preferences dialog box.

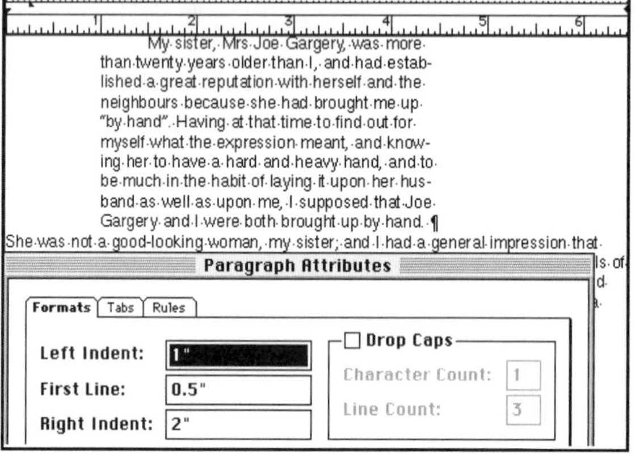

Figure 8.2. This paragraph reflects the indent values in the Paragraph Attributes dialog box. The paragraph marker (¶) is displayed when Invisibles are turned on from the View menu.

6. Quadruple-click inside that first paragraph to select the entire paragraph. Use the Measurements palette or the Style menu to change the font to 10 pt Helvetica. Click to deselect the characters but keep the cursor inside the paragraph. Choose Style/Formats (Command/Ctrl-Shift-F) and in the Paragraph Formats dialog box select auto in the Leading field and type 12. This applies 12 points of leading to the paragraph even though the unit of measure is inches.

7. Press the Tab key twice to get to the Space After field. Type 1p to apply one pica of space after the paragraph. Even though inches is the selected unit of measure for the document, typing p after any value overrides the unit of measure and applies the value in picas. Click on Apply and notice that the XPress has translated the pica value into inches, the specified unit of measure. Click on OK. Your paragraph should resemble Figure 8.3.

Free math lesson

There are 12 points in one pica.

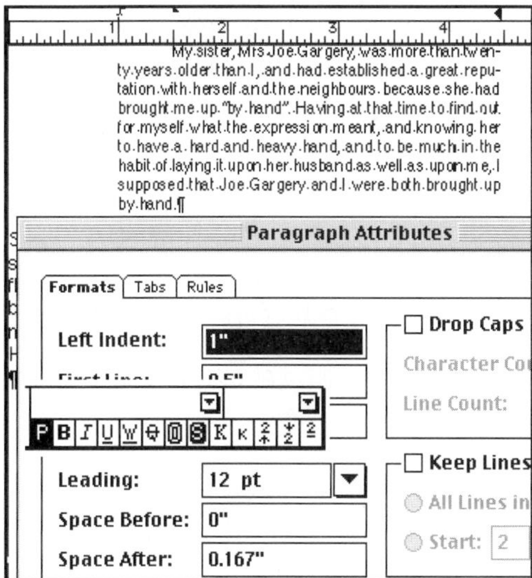

Figure 8.3. Leading and spacing values affect the entire paragraph. The pica value in the Space After field is translated into inches, the document's specified unit of measure.

8. With the paragraph still selected, choose Style/Formats (Command-Shift-F/Macintosh or Ctrl-Shift-F/Windows) again. Type 0 in the Left Indent field, press the Tab key twice, and type 0 in the Right Indent field. Use the Alignment pull-down menu to select Justified. Click on OK. Only the first line of the paragraph is indented from the left side of the text box and the entire paragraph is horizontally aligned from the left to right sides of the text box. The paragraph also displays the one pica of space after the paragraph.

9. Choose File/Save and save this file as *Para1.qxd* in your Projects folder. You will need it for the next exercise.

LESSON 2 SETTING LEADING AND SPACING VALUES

Because leading, the vertical space between lines of type, is applied to every line in a paragraph, a Leading field is available in the Paragraph Attributes dialog box. Two other spacing values are also available that allow you to specify an amount of space before and/or after a paragraph. One of the cardinal sins of typesetting is to press the Return/Enter key twice at the end of the paragraph to create space after the paragraph. This extra paragraph return is a character, albeit an invisible character, and like an infectious disease, it carries font, font size, leading, and other format information

Macintosh Commands

⌘-Shift-F Style/Formats
F9 View/Show Measurements
⌘-S File/Save

Windows Commands

Ctrl-Shift-F Style/Formats
F9 View/Show Measurements
Ctrl-S File/Save

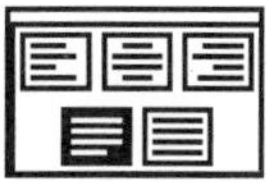

FYI

When you choose a horizontal alignment from any dialog box, that alignment is reflected in the Measurements palette. Here, the Justified icon is highlighted, indicating that Justified alignment was selected in a dialog box.

Auto Leading

QuarkXPress calculates the auto leading value by multiplying the largest point size in a paragraph by the amount specified in the Auto Leading field. For example, a paragraph of 10 point type at the default 20% Auto Leading value would have a leading of 12 points:
10 x .20 = 2; 10 (type size) + 2 (auto leading percentage) = 12 points of paragraph leading.

Macintosh Commands

⌘-O File/Open
⌘-Shift-F Style/Formats
⌘-Option-S File/Save As
F9 View/Show Measurements

Windows Commands

Ctrl-O File/Open
Ctrl-Shift-F Style/Formats
Ctrl-Alt-S File/Save As
F9 View/Show Measurements

Watch your ps and ps

Typing a p after a value applies the value in picas. Typing a p before the value applies the value in points. 7p2p applies a value of 7 picas and 2 points. Pica values are not case-sensitive. If you don't type a p, the value defaults to points.

with it. Having these paragraph returns floating around in a document is the easiest way to lose control of your document, because different paragraph returns will carry different formatting information that will throw your document design off and result in an inconsistent publication.

The correct way to add space before and after paragraphs is to use the Space Before and Space After commands in the Paragraph Attributes dialog box. Just remember that if you apply a half inch of space *after* one paragraph and a half inch of space *before* the next paragraph, those two paragraphs will be separated by one full inch of space. Use the Space Before and Space After commands to set spacing before and after a paragraph—always.

EXERCISE B

1. If necessary, open the *Para1.qxd* file you created in the last exercise or open the *Para1.qxd* file in the Unit 08 folder on the CD-ROM.
2. Click inside the second paragraph, the one you didn't format, and quadruple-click to select the entire paragraph. Format the type in 12 pt. Times from either the Style menu or the Measurements palette (F9).
3. Click anywhere inside that paragraph to select the entire paragraph. Choose Style/Formats to display the Paragraph Attributes dialog box. Type 0 in the Left Indent field, press the Tab key twice, and type 0 in the Right Indent field.
4. Press the Tab key again to highlight the Leading field. Type 15 in the Leading field and press the Tab key to highlight the Space Before field. Type p6 to apply 6 points of space before the paragraph.
5. Press the Tab key to highlight the Space After field. Type 1p to apply one pica of space after the paragraph. Click on OK. Your screen should resemble Figure 8.4.
6. Save this file as *Space.qxd* (File/Save as).

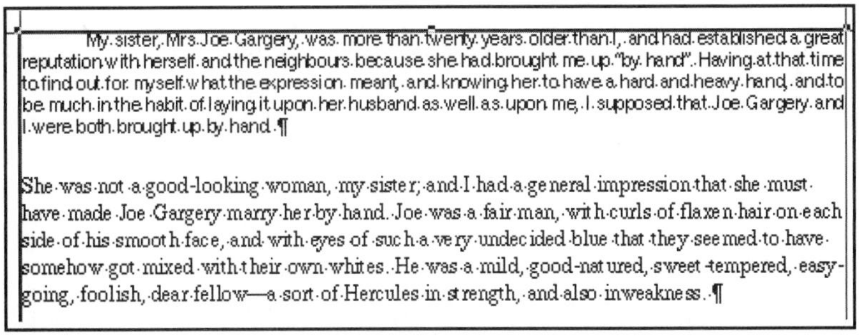

My sister, Mrs. Joe Gargery, was more than twenty years older than I, and had established a great reputation with herself and the neighbours because she had brought me up "by hand". Having at that time to find out for myself what the expression meant, and knowing her to have a hard and heavy hand, and to be much in the habit of laying it upon her husband as well as upon me, I supposed that Joe Gargery and I were both brought up by hand.¶

She was not a good-looking woman, my sister; and I had a general impression that she must have made Joe Gargery marry her by hand. Joe was a fair man, with curls of flaxen hair on each side of his smooth face, and with eyes of such a very undecided blue that they seemed to have somehow got mixed with their own whites. He was a mild, good-natured, sweet-tempered, easy-going, foolish, dear fellow—a sort of Hercules in strength, and also in weakness.¶

Figure 8.4. Applying the values in the Paragraph Formats dialog box results in the second paragraph displaying 15 points of leading with 6 points of space before and 1 pica of space after the paragraph.

Macintosh Commands

⌘-O File/Open
⌘-Shift-F Style/Formats

Windows Commands

Ctrl-O File/Open
Ctrl-Shift-F Style/Formats

LESSON 3 DROP CAPS

A drop cap is one or more initial characters in a paragraph that, rather than sitting on the baseline of the first line of text, drop down one or more lines into the paragraph. You can format drop caps separately from the rest of the paragraph, but you may have to fiddle with them to get them positioned perfectly in the paragraph. Although the Measurements palette reflects the drop cap character at its original size, selecting just the drop character(s) changes the type size from a numerical value to 100%. You can resize that drop character(s) in percentages, not in point sizes.

EXERCISE C

1. If necessary, open the *Space.qxd* file you created in the last exercise or open the *Space.qxd* in the Unit 08 folder on the CD-ROM. Display the Measurements palette (View/Show Measurements). Click anywhere in the first paragraph to select it and choose Style/Formats (Command/Ctrl-Shift-F) to display the Paragraph Attributes dialog box.
2. On the right side of the dialog box, click in the Drop Cap check box to turn on the drop cap option. It defaults to one character (Character Count value) dropping down into the first three lines of the text (Line Count). To give the drop cap more room, drag the First Line indent marker on the ruler over the text box to the left until the First Line field in the dialog box reads 0″. You can also just type 0 in the First Line field. Click on OK. Your screen should resemble Figure 8.5.

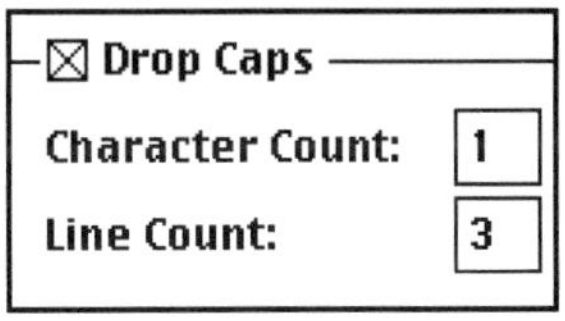

☒ Drop Caps
Character Count: 1
Line Count: 3

Select the Drop Caps check box in the Formats tab of the Paragraph Attributes dialog box.

Macintosh Commands

⌘-Shift-F Style/Formats
⌘-W File/Close

Windows Commands

Ctrl-Shift-F Style/Formats
Ctrl-F4 File/Close

Drop Cap size

Highlight a drop cap to display its size as percentage of the font size as displayed in the Size field of the Measurements palette. To reduce or enlarge the drop cap, type a value in that field between 20 and 400%.

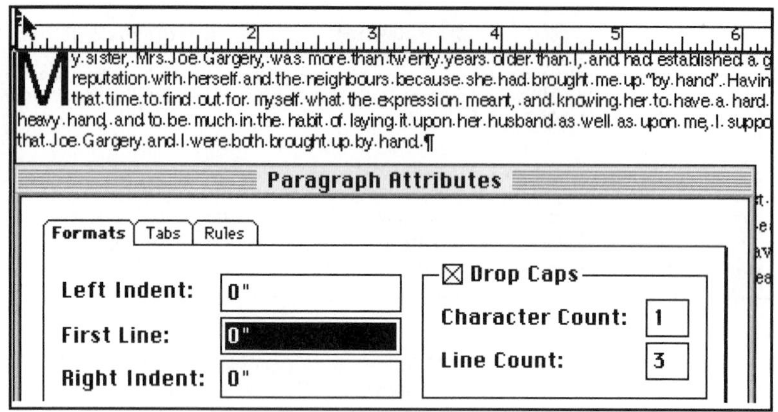

Figure 8.5. The First Line indent marker on the ruler over the text box is moved to the 0 mark, and one character is dropped 3 lines into the paragraph.

3. With the paragraph still selected, choose Style/Formats again and in the Drop Cap field change the Character Count value to 2 and the Line Count value to 2. Click on OK.

4. Drag to select the two drop characters and notice that the type size value in the Measurements palette displays 100%. Select the 100% and type 110. Press Return/Enter to increase the size of the two drop characters. Your screen should resemble Figure 8.6.

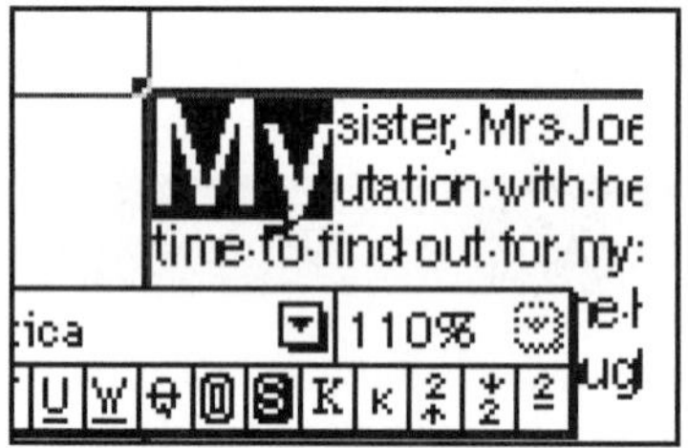

Figure 8.6. The selected drop cap characters are enlarged by 10%,

5. Click in the second, unformatted paragraph to select it. Press the Option-Shift keys (Macintosh) or Alt-Shift keys (Windows) and click anywhere in the first paragraph, the one with the drop caps. All the paragraph formatting from the first paragraph (leading, spacing, alignment, and drop caps) is automatically applied to the second paragraph. The only formatting that is not applied is character formatting, in this case, the 10-pt. Helvetica. To see this for yourself, click anywhere in the second paragraph and notice that the Measurements palette reflects the leading change. Your screen should resemble Figure 8.7. Close this file. Don't save your changes.

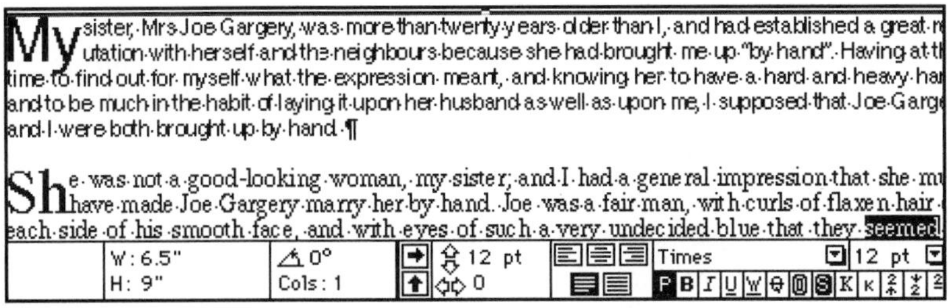

My sister, Mrs Joe Gargery, was more than twenty years older than I, and had established a great re utation with herself and the neighbours because she had brought me up "by hand". Having at t time to find out for myself what the expression meant, and knowing her to have a hard and heavy ha and to be much in the habit of laying it upon her husband as well as upon me, I supposed that Joe Garg and I were both brought up by hand.¶

She was not a good-looking woman, my sister; and I had a general impression that she mu have made Joe Gargery marry her by hand. Joe was a fair man, with curls of flaxen hair each side of his smooth face, and with eyes of such a very undecided blue that they seemed

Figure 8.7. Selecting any paragraph (target paragraph) and Alt/Option-Shift clicking in another paragraph (source paragraph) applies all the paragraph formatting from the source paragraph to the selected target paragraph.

LESSON 4
KEEP LINES TOGETHER COMMAND

When setting type, editorial constraints often include keeping some or all of the lines in a paragraph together to avoid widows and orphans. A widow is the last line of a paragraph that, because of the text flow, ends up at the top of a column or page. An orphan is the first line of a paragraph that ends up as the last line in a column or text box. The Keep Lines Together command in the Paragraph Attributes dialog box lets you decide how many lines in a paragraph must appear at the bottom of a column or page and how many must appear at the top of a column or page. If the paragraph cannot meet these requirements, then the entire paragraph moves to the next column or page.

EXERCISE D

1. Open the *Keepara*.qxd file in the Unit 08 folder on the CD-ROM (File/Open). Choose View/Show Invisibles. Notice the headings in red boldfaced type. The third heading, Description, displays only one line, the first line ("My sister, Mrs."), from the following paragraph at the bottom of the second column. This line is a widow.
2. Click anywhere in the first paragraph below the Description paragraph and choose Style/Formats to display the Paragraph Attributes dialog box.
3. At the right side of the dialog box, click in the Keep Lines Together check box to activate the function. XPress defaults to keeping all the lines in a paragraph together. This is the correct

Macintosh Commands

⌘-O File/Open
⌘-I View/Show Invisibles
⌘-Shift-F Style/Formats

Windows Commands

Ctrl-O File/Open
Ctrl-I View/Show Invisibles
Ctrl-Shift-F Style/Formats

FYI

Most editors want at least the first two lines of a paragraph at the bottom of a column or page (Start field) and at least two lines of a paragraph at the top of a column or page (End field). However, you can set any value in these fields.

Macintosh Commands

⌘-Option-S File/Save As

Windows Commands

Ctrl-Alt-S File/Save As

option to choose for heads, but not for a body paragraph. Instead, click the Start button, which defaults to a minimum of 2 lines at the end of a column or page and a minimum of 2 lines at the beginning of the next column or page. Click on OK.

4. Because two lines could not fit at the bottom of the column, the entire paragraph moved to the top of the third column, thus meeting the Start and End requirements of at least two lines at the end of a column or page and two lines at the top of a column or page (Figure 8.8).

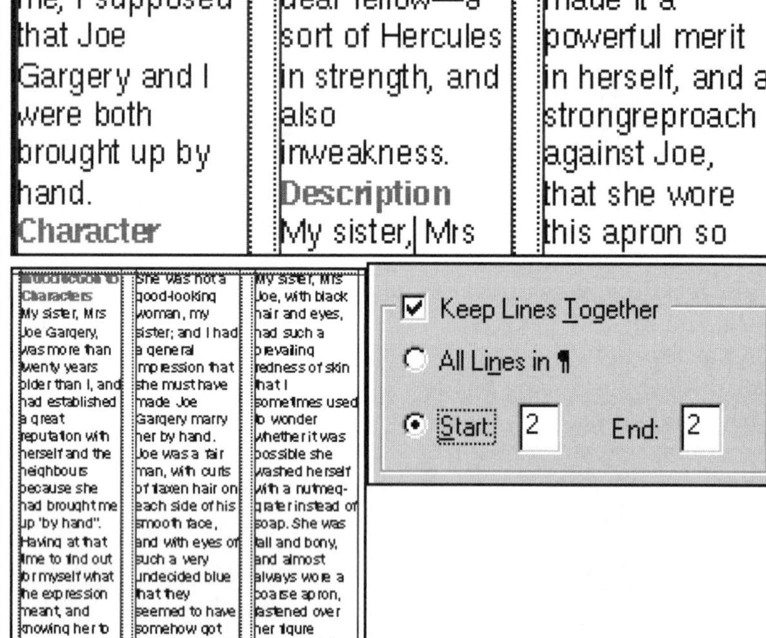

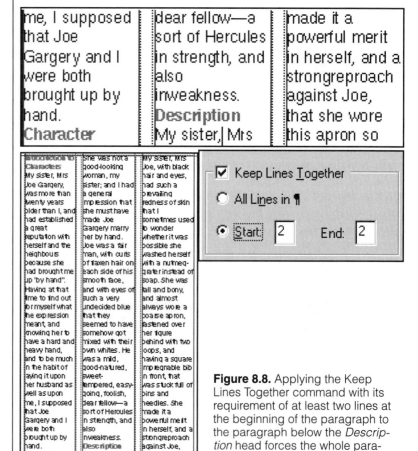

Figure 8.8. Applying the Keep Lines Together command with its requirement of at least two lines at the beginning of the paragraph to the paragraph below the *Description* head forces the whole paragraph to move to the next column.

5. Save this file as *Linestog.qxd* in your Projects folder. You will need it for the next exercise (File/Save As).

LESSON 5
KEEP WITH NEXT PARAGRAPH COMMAND

When a document contains headings before paragraphs, it's important that the heading remain with its paragraph and not end up at the bottom of a column or page while the paragraph moves to the top of the next column or page. The Keep Lines Together command in the Paragraph Attributes dialog box is used to link headings with their paragraphs. When this command is applied to a heading paragraph, if there is not enough room at the bottom of a column or of a page for both the heading paragraph and the following paragraph to fit, both paragraphs will travel together to the top of the next column or page.

Macintosh Commands

⌘-O File/Open
⌘-Shift-F Style/Formats

Windows Commands

Ctrl-O File/Open
Ctrl-Shift-F Style/Formats

EXERCISE E

1. Open the *Linestog.qxd* file in the Unit 08 folder on the CD-ROM (File/Open). Display the Document Layout palette (View/Show Document Layout) and double-click on page 1 to get to the first page. Scroll through the first page of the file and notice the headings in red boldfaced type. The Character and Description headings are at the bottom of the first and second columns of text and are, therefore, separated from their subsequent paragraphs.
2. Click anywhere in the red Description paragraph to select it. Choose Style/Formats to display the Paragraph Attributes dialog box.
3. Click in the Keep with Next ¶ check box to turn on the function. This forces the selected paragraph to travel with the paragraph following it. Click on OK. Notice that the Description head now moves to the top of the third column (Figure 8.9).

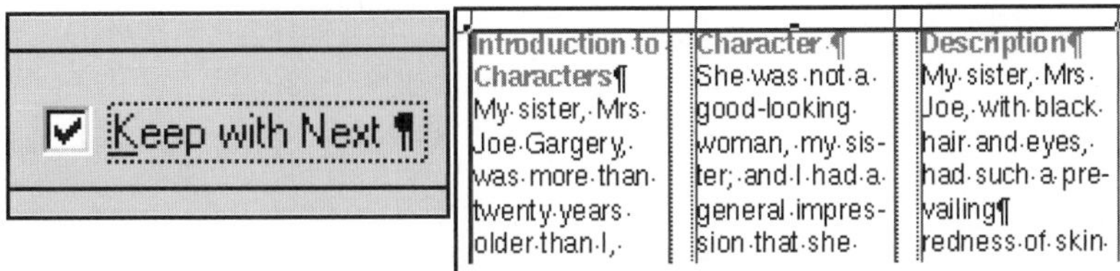

Figure 8.9. Applying the Keep with Next ¶ command to the Character and Description paragraphs forces them to move to the top of the next column to stay with their subsequent paragraphs.

Macintosh Commands

⌘-W File/Close

Windows Commands

Ctrl-F4 File/Close

4. Even if text is added or deleted from this text box, the Description head will always remain the paragraph following it. Click anywhere in the red Character paragraph. Press the Option-Shift keys (Macintosh) or Alt-Shift keys (Windows) and click in the red Description paragraph to apply the Description formatting to the Character paragraph. The Character paragraph moves to the top of the second column.
5. Close this file (File/Close). Don't save your changes.

LESSON 6
LOCK TO BASELINE GRID

Lines of type sit on an invisible line called the *baseline*. These lines of type run merrily from left to right in a text box divided by vertical space called *leading*. The more leading between lines of type, the more open and elegant the type looks. Not enough leading, and type looks like an ad for a sleazy appliance store. Leading across multiple columns isn't a critical issue for type set in one column, but it can be for multiple-column text like that in newspapers and magazines. In these kinds of documents, type must sit on the same baseline in all the columns and not appear up and down across the columns (Figure 8.10).

Tip

When applying space before or space after values to a paragraph locked to the baseline grid, specify the spacing value in increments of the leading. For example, if you have locked a paragraph with 14 points of leading to the baseline grid, apply a spacing value of 3½ points (p3.5) or 7 points (p7). You can always specify values in any unit of measure, regardless of the option selected in the General Preferences dialog box.

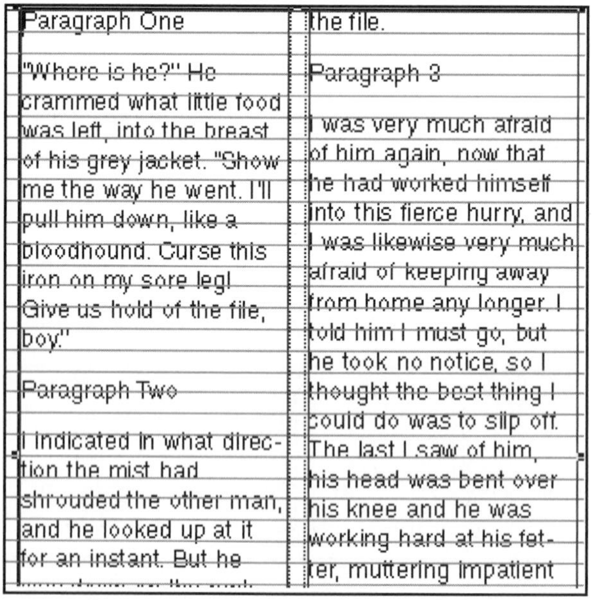

Paragraph One

"Where is he?" He crammed what little food was left, into the breast of his grey jacket. "Show me the way he went. I'll pull him down, like a bloodhound. Curse this iron on my sore leg! Give us hold of the file, boy."

Paragraph Two

I indicated in what direction the mist had shrouded the other man, and he looked up at it for an instant. But he

the file.

Paragraph 3

I was very much afraid of him again, now that he had worked himself into this fierce hurry, and I was likewise very much afraid of keeping away from home any longer. I told him I must go, but he took no notice, so I thought the best thing I could do was to slip off. The last I saw of him, his head was bent over his knee and he was working hard at his fetter, muttering impatient

Figure 8.10. Displaying the Baseline Grid indicates that the type is not aligned on the baseline across the two columns.

To see the baseline for lines of type, choose Show Baseline Grid from the View menu. The position for the baseline grid is determined by the Increment value in the Baseline Grid field of the Paragraph Preferences dialog box (Figure 8.11). When this value equals the leading value and a paragraph is locked to that baseline grid, the lines of text will sit at the same position across multiple columns.

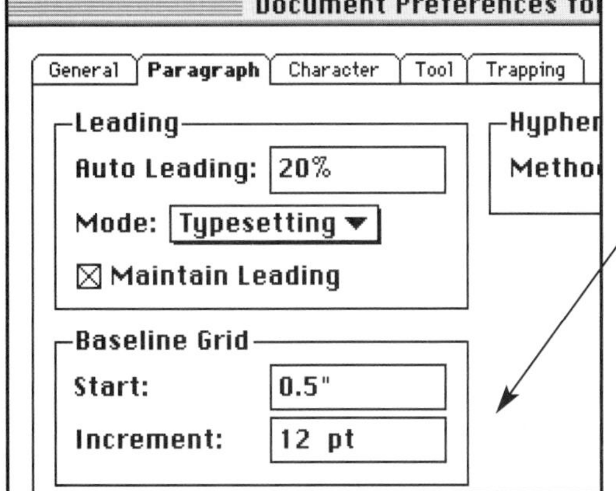

Figure 8.11. The Increment value in the Baseline Grid field in the Paragraph Preferences dialog box must equal the leading value of the paragraph if type is to sit at the same position across multiple columns.

Aligning text across multiple columns is a three-step process:

1. Assign an absolute leading value to the paragraphs, specified in points.
2. Assign that *same leading value* to the Increment in the Baseline Grid field of the Paragraph Preferences dialog box (Edit/Preferences/Document/Paragraph).
3. Lock the paragraphs to the baseline grid from the Paragraph Attributes dialog box.

EXERCISE F

1. Open the *Baseline.qxd* file in the Unit 08 folder on the CD-ROM. Click inside the text box to select it. Choose View/Show Baseline Grid to display the current baseline in the document. Notice that the lines of type do not line up across both columns. Display the Measurements palette (View/Show Measurements). The Leading field displays auto for the entire document.
2. Choose Edit/Select All. Double-click to select auto in the Leading field of the Measurements palette, type 18, and press Return/Enter to apply 18 points of space from one baseline to the one above or below it.

Macintosh Commands

⌘-O File/Open
⌘-A Edit/Select All
Option-F7 View/Show Baseline Grid

Windows Commands

Ctrl-O File/Open
Ctrl-A Edit/Select All
Ctrl-F7 View/Show Baseline Grid

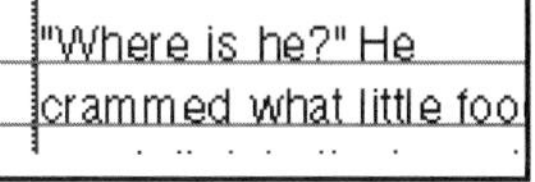

The absolute leading value measures the space from one baseline to the one above or below it.

Absolute Leading

Absolute leading remains fixed, regardless of the point size of any character in a paragraph. Absolute leading is applied in the Paragraph Attributes dialog box and in the Leading field of the Measurements palette.

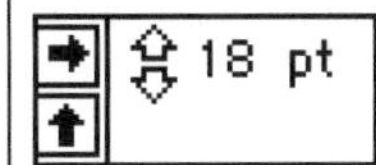

☒ Lock to Baseline Grid

You must select this option in the Paragraph Attributes dialog box after setting leading and increment values before the paragraphs will align properly across multiple columns.

Macintosh Commands

⌘-Y Edit/Preferences/Document
⌘-Shift-F Style/Formats
⌘-W File/Close

Windows Commands

Ctrl-Y Edit/Preferences/Document
Ctrl-Shift-F Style/Formats
Ctrl-F4 File/Close

Maintain Leading

Select Maintain Leading to control the placement of a line of text that falls immediately below a box or item in a column of text. With this option selected, the line's baseline is placed according to its assigned leading value. Deselecting this option causes the line's ascenders (tops of capital letters, ls, ds, etc.) to abut the bottom of the item.

WARNING!

It's a good idea to assign an increment value in the Baseline Grid area equal to your leading. If your Increment value is less than or equal to the specified leading, the lines of text will lock to every grid line. If you specify a grid increment greater than the leading, the line of text will lock to the next grid line and create ugly gaps of space between lines.

3. Choose Edit/Preferences/Document and click on the Paragraph tab to display the Paragraph Preferences for this document. Type 18 in the Increment field under Baseline Grid on the left side of the dialog box. Click on OK.
4. With all the text still selected, choose Style/Formats and click to select the Lock to Baseline Grid check box. Click on OK. The lines of type now align across the three columns (Figure 8.12).

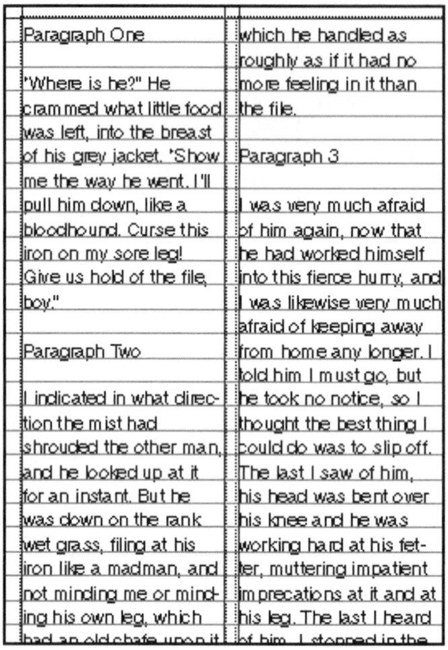

Paragraph One

"Where is he?" He crammed what little food was left, into the breast of his grey jacket. "Show me the way he went. I'll pull him down, like a bloodhound. Curse this iron on my sore leg! Give us hold of the file, boy."

Paragraph Two

I indicated in what direction the mist had shrouded the other man, and he looked up at it for an instant. But he was down on the rank wet grass, filing at his iron like a madman, and not minding me or minding his own leg, which had an old chafe upon it which he handled as roughly as if it had no more feeling in it than the file.

Paragraph 3

I was very much afraid of him again, now that he had worked himself into this fierce hurry, and I was likewise very much afraid of keeping away from home any longer. I told him I must go, but he took no notice, so I thought the best thing I could do was to slip off. The last I saw of him, his head was bent over his knee and he was working hard at his fetter, muttering impatient imprecations at it and at his leg. The last I heard of him, I stopped in the

Figure 8.12. Once leading and increment values are the same, locking the paragraphs to the baseline grid in the Paragraph Attributes dialog box will align the paragraphs properly across multiple columns.

5. Choose Edit/Preferences/Document and click on the Paragraph tab. In the Paragraph Preferences dialog box, type 9 in the Increment field. Click on OK. The lines still align properly across the columns because 9 is an increment of 18, the leading value.
6. Close this file. Don't save your changes.

LESSON 7
SETTING PARAGRAPH ALIGNMENT AND HYPHENATION

The Paragraph Formats dialog box also allows you to set paragraph alignment just as you did from the Measurements palette. It also lets you choose a method of hyphenating the paragraph. QuarkXPress defaults to hyphenating a word as small as six characters if that six-character word is not capitalized. It allows for unlimited hyphens in a row across the full width of the text box. However, most editors want to see no more than two hyphens in a row in any paragraph and sometimes allow for hyphenating capitalized words.

EXERCISE G

1. If necessary, open the *Space.qxd* file you saved earlier or open the *Space.qxd* file in the Unit 08 folder on the CD-ROM. Choose Edit/H&Js to display the H&Js (Hyphenation and Justification) dialog box for the active document. You can either edit the Standard H&J settings or create a new setting. Click on New. Type *My H&J* in the Name field and apply the values displayed in Figure 8.13.

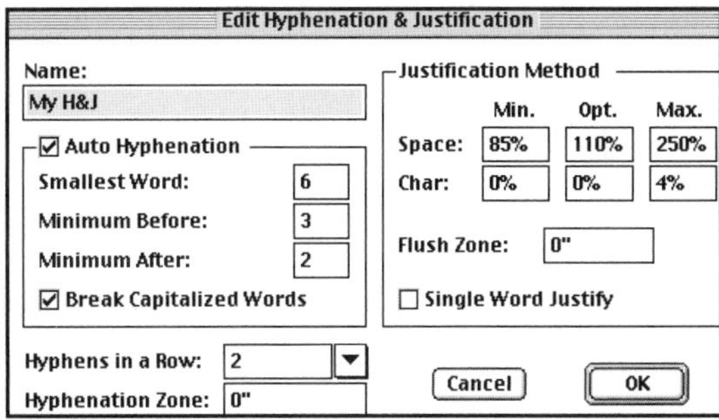

Figure 8.13. The new hyphenation values call for automatically hyphenating words of at least six characters, but limiting the hyphens to no more than two in a row. If the last paragraph consists of only one word, that paragraph is not justified.

2. Leave Auto Hyphenation selected and leave the smallest word set to 6 characters, with the minimum number of characters before the hyphen set to 3 and the minimum number of characters after the hyphen set to 2. This means that XPress will hyphenate a word like *double* but won't hyphenate a word like *doubt*.

Macintosh Commands

⌘-O File/Open

Windows Commands

Ctrl-O File/Open

READ THIS FIRST!

QuarkXPress has an unusual and generally unacceptable hyphenation dictionary. My editor for every book I have typeset in XPress has scribbled "bad break" next to many hyphenated words because the program's hyphenation algorithm does not conform to conventional editorial standards. Although Version 4.0 claims to have an excellent hyphenation dictionary instead of a hyphenation algorithm, you should carefully check hyphenated words in your documents.

Discretionary hyphens

If you want to insert a hyphen in a paragraph that will disappear if the text flow changes, use the discretionary hyphen—sometimes called a soft hyphen. Type Command/Ctrl-hyphen. If the text flow changes, then the discretionary hyphen will disappear.

Macintosh Commands

⌘-W File/Close

Windows Commands

Ctrl-F4 File/Close

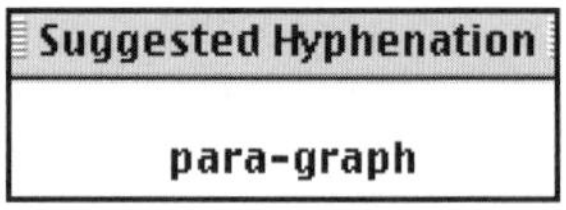

3. Click to select Break Capitalized words. Type 2 in the Hyphens in a Row field to limit the number of consecutive hyphens in a paragraph to no more than two. Deselect Single Word Justify on the right side of the dialog box so that if a single word falls on the last line of the paragraph it will not be tracked to fit the width of the text box. Click on OK. Click on Save.

4. Use the Measurements palette (F9) to resize the text box to 12 picas wide by typing 12p in the W field and pressing Return/Enter. Click anywhere in the first paragraph to select it. Choose Style/Formats. Choose Justified from the Alignment pull-down menu. Choose My H&J from the H&J pull-down menu. Click on OK. Your first paragraph should resemble Figure 8.14. Notice that there are only two consecutive hyphens in the first paragraph.

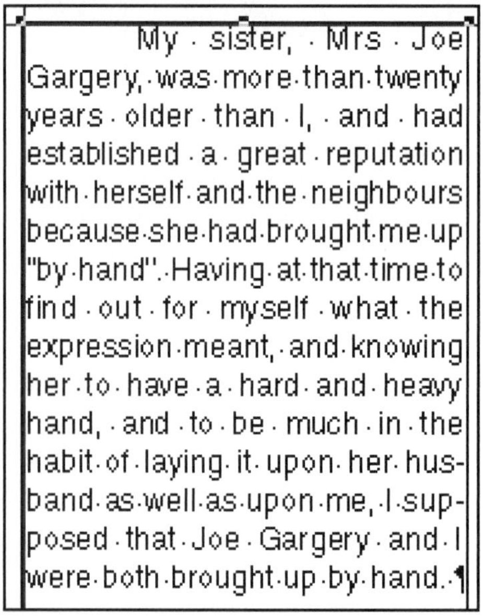

How it hyphenates

To see how XPress will hyphenate a word, select the word and choose Utilities/Suggested Hyphenation (Command/Ctrl-H).

Suggested Hyphenation

para-graph

My · sister, · Mrs · Joe
Gargery,·was·more·than·twenty
years · older · than · I, · and · had
established · a · great · reputation
with·herself·and·the·neighbours
because·she·had·brought·me·up
"by·hand".·Having·at·that·time·to
find · out · for · myself · what · the
expression·meant,·and·knowing
her·to·have·a·hard·and·heavy
hand, · and · to · be · much · in · the
habit·of·laying·it·upon·her·hus-
band·as·well·as·upon·me,·I·sup-
posed · that · Joe · Gargery · and · I
were·both·brought·up·by·hand.·¶

Figure 8.14 displays the H&J and Alignment values applied in the Paragraph Attributes and H&Js dialog boxes.

5. Drag the text box, making it wider and narrower, to see how the different lines in that second paragraph become hyphenated. Close this file (File/Close). Don't save your changes.

Image from *Metropolis* by Rob Porazinski, for Artville

OVERVIEW

In this unit you will learn how to:

Create, edit, and apply paragraph style sheets
Create, edit, and apply character style sheets
Apply styles from the Style Sheets palette
Append styles from another document

TERMS

Append
character style sheet
global formatting
local formatting
New Line Marker
No Style
Normal style
paragraph style sheet

HOW IT WORKS:

In Photoshop, change the color image to grayscale and reduce its size it to fit the XPress picture box. After importing it into XPress, use the Bézier Text Box tool to create a text box around the outside of the mailbox to hold the Unit 9 type. Then create several text boxes with a background of None and with None runaround to hold the number 9s. Rotate the boxes and reduce the type size of the individual numbers. Finally, position the boxes around the picture box.

LESSON 1
CREATING PARAGRAPH STYLES

When formatting paragraphs, it can sometimes take twenty trips to the menus and dialog boxes to apply attributes to a single paragraph. If you want to apply those same attributes to another paragraph in the document, you have to go through those same steps to create another similarly formatted paragraph. And if you change one formatting attribute in the first paragraph, you must manually make that same formatting change in every other similar paragraph—unless you use style sheets. A paragraph style sheet is a single command that executes any number of formatting commands to a *selected paragraph*. A character style sheet is a single command that executes any number of text formatting commands to *selected text*.

FYI

The Style Sheets palette will highlight the name of a character style only when one or more of the characters tagged with that character style are selected, or if the cursor is somewhere in the word tagged with that character style.

To make changes in a paragraph's format that has been tagged with a style sheet, just change the style sheet and the change is made to any paragraph tagged with that style. Likewise, any text characters in any paragraph tagged with a character style can be changed by simply changing the character style sheet.

Every paragraph consists of text characters with their own formatting attributes such as typeface, type size, type color, etc. These characters, from the first character to the paragraph return (¶), form a paragraph. The paragraph itself has its own formatting attributes, such as leading, drop cap, alignment, tabs, rules, etc.

A paragraph style consists of any or all of the formatting attributes available from the Paragraph Attributes dialog box and any or all of the character attributes available from the Character attributes dialog box. So, a paragraph displays text and paragraph formatting attributes, all of which can be defined and placed in a style sheet.

WARNING!

You cannot undo many actions performed in the Style Sheets palette, so it's a good idea to save your file before you begin using these functions. This lets you revert to the last saved version of the file.

SELECTING PARAGRAPHS

To select a paragraph, click anywhere in the paragraph. It isn't necessary to highlight the entire paragraph because any paragraph formatting applies to every line in the paragraph. You can't split lines in a paragraph to create two paragraphs unless you split the paragraph into two or more distinct paragraphs by pressing the Return/Enter key.

NEW LINE COMMAND

You can split the lines in a paragraph using the New Line command. Show the Invisibles (View/Show Invisibles) then click right before where you want the new line to begin. Press Shift-Return

(Macintosh) or Shift-Enter (Windows). This inserts the New Line marker at that point, and all the text after the New Line marker drops to the next line. Those lines after the New Line marker, however, are still formatted with the paragraph style applied to the paragraph. Just because you split the lines doesn't mean you also split the paragraph.

STYLE SHEETS PALETTE

The Style Sheets palette (View/Show Style Sheets) is used to apply styles and to access the Edit Style Sheets dialog box. The upper panel displays the paragraph styles for the document, which are preceded by the paragraph symbol (¶) as they are in the dialog boxes and menus where they are also displayed.

The lower panel of the Style Sheets palette displays the character styles for the document. These are preceded by an underlined A (A), as they are in the dialog boxes and menus.

Both panels default to Normal style, the default style automatically applied to any text created in XPress, and No Style, which strips a paragraph of any local or global formatting codes and prepares it to receive another style.

Macintosh Commands

⌘-N File/New/Document
⌘-C Edit/Copy
⌘-V Edit/Paste

Windows Commands

Ctrl-N File/New/Document
Ctrl-C Edit/Copy
Ctrl-V Edit/Paste

move↵

The New Line Marker is created by pressing Shift-Return.

EXERCISE A

1. Create a new file with an automatic text box. Use the Measurements palette to make the text box on the first page 3 inches wide.
2. Type *This is the first paragraph.* Don't press the Return/Enter key. Triple-click to select the sentence, choose Edit/Copy, click after the first sentence and choose Edit/Paste. Do this a few times until you have a few lines. Press the Return/Enter key to create the paragraph.
3. Type *This is the second paragraph.* Copy and paste, and press the Return/Enter key to create the second paragraph (Figure 9.1).

This·is·the·first·paragraph.·This·is·the·first·paragraph.·This·is·the·first·paragraph.·This·is·the·first·paragraph.This·is·the·first·paragraph.·This·is·the·first·paragraph.This·is·the·first·paragraph.·This·is·the·first·paragraph.¶
This·is·the·second·paragraph.·This·is·the·second·paragraph.This·is·the·second·paragraph.¶

Figure 9.1 displays two unformatted paragraphs. The paragraph return symbol (¶) indicates that the Return/Enter key was pressed.

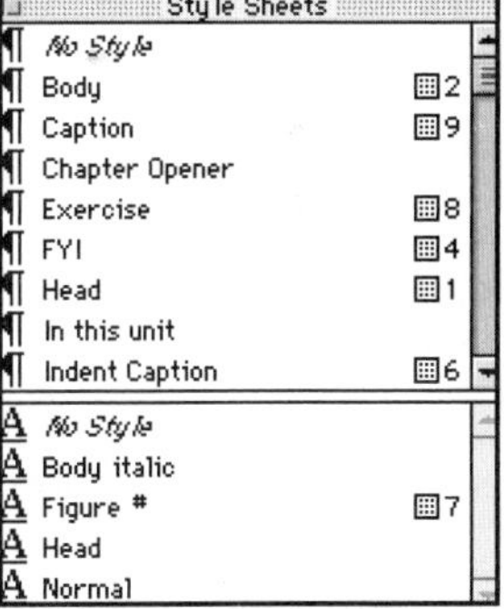

The Style Sheets palette displays paragraph styles (top panel) and character styles (bottom panel).

Macintosh Commands

⌘-I View/Show Invisibles
⌘-E File/Get Text/Picture
⌘-Shift-F Style/Formats
Shift-F11 Edit/Style Sheets

Windows Commands

Ctrl-I View/Show Invisibles
Ctrl-Y File/Get Text/Picture
Ctrl-Shift-F Style/Formats
Shift-F11 Edit/Style Sheets

FYI

A rule is a paragraph format, and you must select the paragraph before applying the rule. Likewise, to delete a rule, select the paragraph, or the paragraph return mark if it's an empty ruled line (¶), and use the Rules dialog box to deselect the rule option.

4. The easiest way to create a paragraph style sheet is by example. Using this method, you format the paragraph exactly the way you want and then create the style sheet based on those formatting attributes. Quadruple-click in the first paragraph to select the entire paragraph. Use the Style menu or Measurements palette to format it in 14 pt Times. Because you are applying text attributes, you must select all the text characters.
5. Choose Style/Formats to display the Paragraph Attributes dialog box. Type 24 in the Leading field, 1p in the Space After field. In the Drop Caps area, type 1 in the Character Count field and 2 in the Line Count field. Don't press Return/Enter.
6. Click on the Rules tab. Click the Rule Below box. Leave the Length option set to Indents with the default 0 values so the rule will run the full length of the paragraph. Type 1p in the Offset field. Choose Dotted 2 from the Style menu, 6 from the Width menu, and Red from the Color menu. Click on OK. All of these attributes are applied to the paragraph (Figure 9.2).

This·is·the·first·paragraph.·This·is·the·first·paragraph.·This·is·the·first·paragraph.·This·is·the·first·paragraph.·This·is·the·first·paragraph.·¶

This·is·the·second·paragraph.This·is·the·second·paragraph.This·is·the·second·paragraph.This·is·the·second·paragraph.This·is·the·second·paragraph.·¶

Figure 9.2. The first paragraph displays specified text and formatting attributes.

7. Click anywhere in the paragraph. Choose Edit/Style Sheets (Shift F11) to display the Style Sheets for [filename] dialog box. Use the New pull-down menu in the lower part of the dialog box to select Paragraph. This displays the Edit Paragraph Style Sheet dialog box (Figure 9.3).

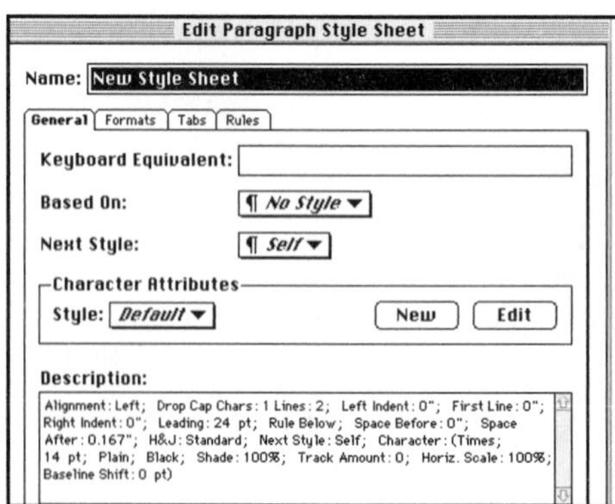

Figure 9.3. The Edit Paragraph Style Sheet dialog box contains the same tabbed areas as the Paragraph Formats dialog boxes.

8. Notice that the Description field displays all the text and paragraph formatting options you selected earlier. Type *First Paragraph* in the Name field. Right now the default text attributes for the paragraph are 14 pt. Times, which is what you want, so leave the default character attributes. Click OK. Click Save to create the style sheet and add it to the document's Style Sheets palette.

9. Display the Style Sheets palette (View/Show Style Sheets). Just because you created a style sheet based on a selected paragraph doesn't mean that the paragraph is automatically tagged with that style. You must do this manually. With the paragraph still selected, choose Style/Paragraph Style Sheet and drag to select First Paragraph (Figure 9.4). Although nothing appears to happen to the text, it has been tagged with the First Paragraph style and its style name is highlighted in the Style Sheets palette (Figure 9.5).

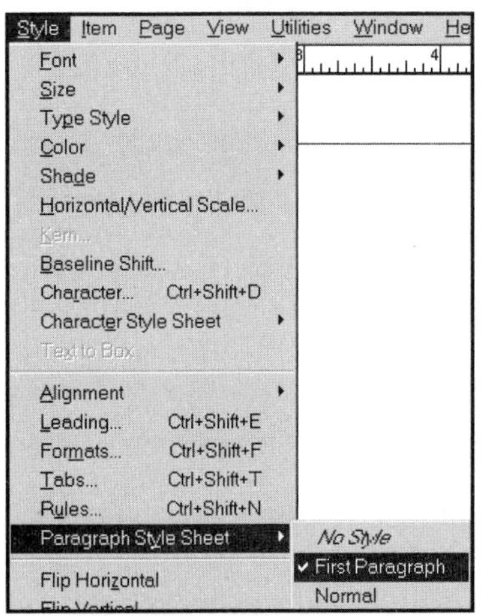

Figure 9.4. Select a paragraph style sheet from the Style menu.

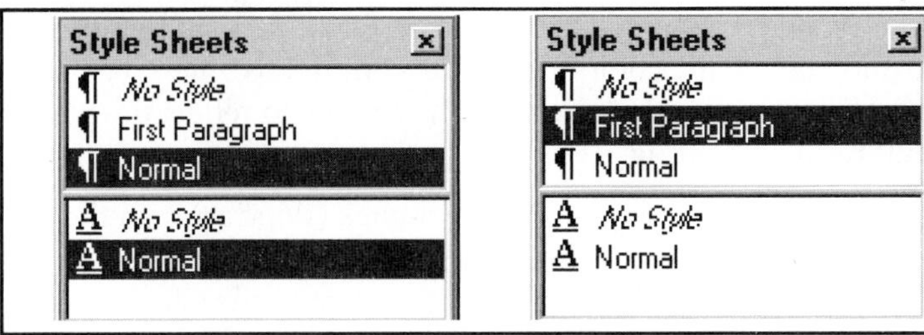

Figure 9.5. Before the First Paragraph style is actually applied to the paragraph, the Style Sheets palette highlights Normal as the default style for that paragraph (left). Once the style is applied to the paragraph, however, the palette highlights the style's name (right).

Macintosh Commands

F11 View/Style Sheets

Windows Commands

F11 View/Style Sheets

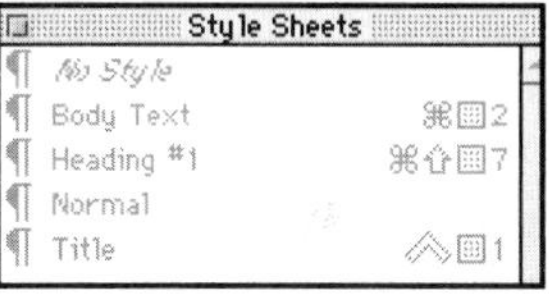

You can assign keyboard equivalents for styles from the numeric keypad or from function keys F5 through F15. However, if you use the function keys for style sheet keyboard equivalents, you override Quark's built-in keyboard shortcuts. To avoid this, use a modifier key such as the Ctrl/Command, or Alt/Option key with the function key.

Macintosh Commands

⌘-O File/Open
⌘-Alt-S File/Save As
F11 View/Show Style Sheets
Shift-F11 Edit/Style Sheets

Windows Commands

Ctrl-O File/Open
Ctrl-Alt-S File/Save As
F11 View/Show Style Sheets
Shift-F11 Edit/Style Sheets

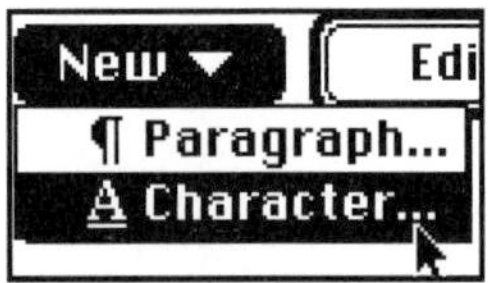

Select Character from the New dialog box to create a new character style.

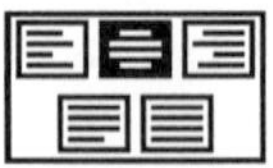

The Center Align icon is highlighted in the Measurements palette.

FYI

The advantage of creating style sheets by example is that you can use the Apply button to see how the options you've chosen appear in the paragraph, something you can't do in any of the style sheet dialog boxes.

10. Click anywhere in the second paragraph. Click on the First Paragraph style in the Style Sheets palette to apply it to the selected paragraph.
11. Save this file as *Styles.qxd* in your Projects folder (File/Save As). You will need it for the next exercise.

LESSON 2
EDITING PARAGRAPH STYLES

Any paragraph style can be edited so that it reflects different text and formatting attributes. When you change a paragraph style, any paragraph that was tagged with that style automatically changes to reflect the new text and paragraph attributes.

Because every paragraph style includes both paragraph and type style options, you can edit either or both of these options when editing a paragraph style. The paragraph and text changes are applied to any paragraph tagged with that paragraph style.

EXERCISE B

1. If necessary, open the *Styles.qxd* file in your Projects folder or open the *Styles.qxd* file in the Unit 09 folder on the CD-ROM. Click on the text box to select it. Display the Style Sheets palette (F11). The file displays three paragraph styles (*No Style*, First Paragraph, and Normal) and two character styles, *No Style* and Normal. Choose Edit/Style Sheets. Highlight the First Paragraph style and click on Edit to display the Edit Paragraph Style Sheets dialog box.
2. Click on the Formats tab and choose Centered from the Alignment pull-down menu. Don't click on OK. Click on the Rules tab and change the color of the rule from red to blue. Click on OK. Click on Save. Both paragraphs change to reflect the new paragraph formatting.
3. Command-click (Macintosh) or Ctrl-click (Windows) on the First Paragraph style in the Style Sheets palette. First Paragraph is highlighted. Click the Edit button. In the Character Attributes field, leave the default text attributes selected and click on Edit.

4. In the Edit Character Style Sheet dialog box, change the font to Ariel/Helvetica, the size to 18 pt., the color to Magenta, and the style to All Caps. Click on OK twice. Click on Save. The two paragraphs tagged with the First Paragraph style now reflect the edits.
5. Close this file (File/Close). Don't save your changes.

LESSON 3 CREATING AND EDITING CHARACTER STYLES

You probably noticed from the previous exercise that when you make character attributes changes to a paragraph style, every text character displays those attributes. For example, *all* the text characters became 18-point Helvetica and all caps in Magenta. This is called global formatting, where formatting applies to every character in the paragraph or document. To change only certain characters in a paragraph—whether or not that paragraph has been tagged with a paragraph style—you must create a character style.

Like paragraph styles, character styles can be edited and those changes will apply to all the text characters anywhere in the document that have been tagged with that particular character style. However, unlike paragraph styles, which are applied to paragraphs selected by just clicking in the paragraph, character styles must be applied to highlighted text characters.

LOCAL FORMATTING

Even though you apply a paragraph style to a selected paragraph, you can still apply local formatting to that paragraph. For example, a paragraph may be styled in 24 pt Helvetica, but if you select even a single character and change its formatting, that change is called *local formatting*. Or, if you change any of the paragraph formats like indents or space before and after, that too is local formatting.

EXERCISE C

1. Open the *Styles.qxd* file in your Projects folder or in the Unit 09 folder on the CD-ROM. Click on the text box to select it. Display the Style Sheets palette (F11). Drag to select the drop cap *T* at the beginning of the first paragraph. Choose Edit/Style Sheets. Select Character from the New Menu to display the Edit/Character Style Sheet dialog box.

Macintosh Commands

⌘-M Item/Modify
⌘-D Item/Duplicate
⌘-W File/Close
Shift-F11 Edit/Style Sheets

Windows Commands

Ctrl-M Item/Modify
Ctrl-D Item/Duplicate
Ctrl-F4 File/Close
Shift-F11 Edit/Style Sheets

Important info

Always use the First Line indent command to indent a paragraph. Using the Spacebar or the Tab key is absolutely the wrong thing to do because it generates extra characters over which you have little or no control. In a long document this can make you weep. (This was said before, but it bears repeating.)

Important info

You must select a text box to view and use any of the styles in the Style Sheets palette.

Drop Cap size

Highlight a drop cap to display its size as percentage of the font size as displayed in the Size field of the Measurements palette. To reduce or enlarge the drop cap, type a value in that field between 20% and 400%.

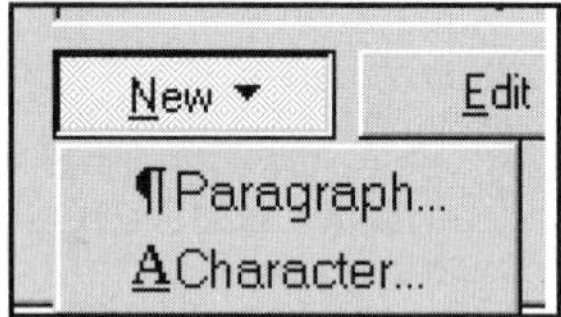

The New menu lets you select options for either a paragraph or character style.

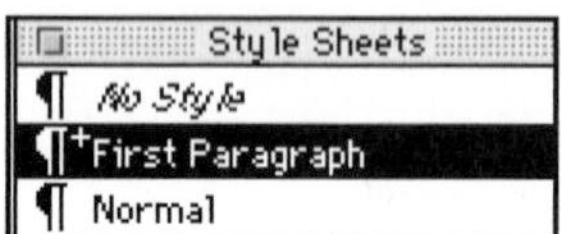

The + sign before the style name indicates that local paragraph formatting was applied to the paragraph. If the local character formatting was applied to the paragraph, the cursor would have to be in the formatted word for the + to be displayed in the Style Sheets palette.

2. Type *Drop Cap* in the Name field. Assign a keyboard shortcut from the keypad by clicking in the Keyboard Equivalent field and pressing the 2 key on the extended keypad. Change the Times font to Helvetica, the color to Red, and the Type Style to Bold. Click on OK. Click on Save.
3. With the drop cap character still selected, click on the Drop Cap style in the lower panel of the Style Sheets palette or press 2 on the extended keypad to apply the style.
4. Drag to select the *T* in the second paragraph, and click on the Drop Cap style in the Style Sheets palette to tag that character with the Drop Cap style.
5. Command-click (Macintosh) or Right-click (Windows) on the Drop Cap style in the Style Sheets palette and click on Edit to display the Edit Character Style Sheet dialog box.
6. Change the text size to 24 points, and the color of the text to blue. Click Underline in the Type Style field. Click on OK. Click on Save. Both drop caps reflect the edits (Figure 9.6).

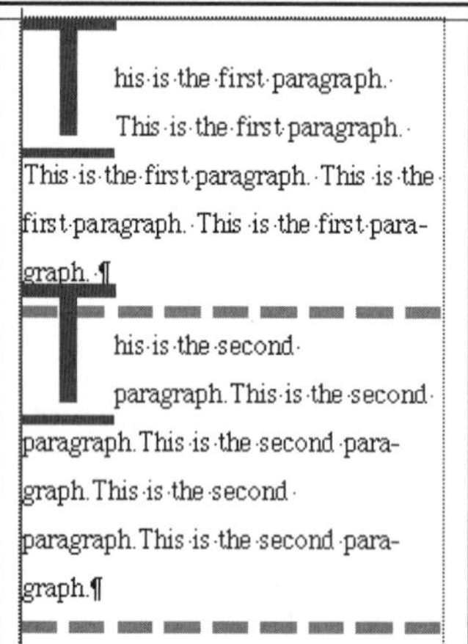

Figure 9.6. The Drop Cap style is edited, changing the original drop cap to a larger, underlined text character.

7. Drag to select the word *first* or double-click on *first* anywhere in the paragraph. Click on the Drop Cap style in the Style Sheets palette to apply that character style to the selected characters (Figure 9.7).
8. Notice that although the paragraph is tagged with the First Paragraph style, the style name displays a + sign indicating that local formatting has been applied to the paragraph, as indeed it has in the way of the 24 pt. underlined blue text (Figure 9.7).

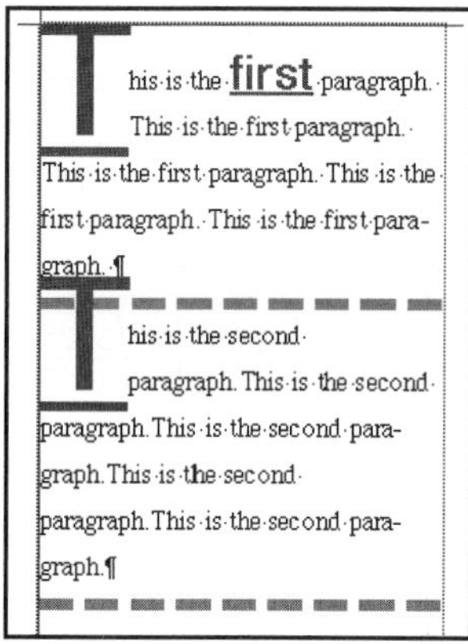

Figure 9.7. The Drop Cap character style is applied to the selected word. The First Paragraph style displays a + indicating that local formatting, in this case the attributes from the Drop Cap style sheet, have been applied to the paragraph.

9. To restore the paragraph to its original First Paragraph style, click anywhere in the paragraph to select it. Option-click (Macintosh) or Alt-click (Windows) on the First Paragraph style in the Style Sheets palette. The paragraph displays only the text and paragraph attributes of the First Paragraph style.
10. Close this file (File/Close). Don't save your changes.

Macintosh Commands

⌘-W File/Close

Windows Commands

Ctrl-F4 File/Close

LESSON 4 NORMAL STYLE AND NO STYLE

Whenever you create a new document, the Style Sheets palette always displays two paragraph styles and two character styles, *No Style* and Normal. A better name for Normal would be Default because that is what the Normal style is, the default paragraph and character styles applied to any text you type in a new document or import into a newly created document. You can edit the Normal style so that whenever you type non-styled text, it appears in the font, size, etc. of your choice.

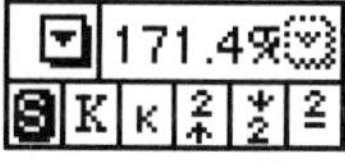

FYI

Although you can change the type size of a drop cap in a dialog box, that size is not reflected in points in the Measurements palette. Instead, the new size is displayed as a percentage of the original type size.

The *No Style* paragraph and character styles are really not styles at all. In fact, unlike every other paragraph and character style, *No Style* is displayed in italics, indicating that it is somehow different from the other styles. Rather than *apply* a style, when you click a paragraph and select *No Style,* or when you select text characters and apply *No Style,* that paragraph and those text characters are stripped of any style sheet that was applied to them. Although nothing is visible on the screen when you apply *No Style,* any local formatting like bold or italics, or any character and paragraph styles, will be overridden when you apply another paragraph or character style. When you Alt/Option-clicked on the First Para-

Macintosh Commands

⌘-N File/New/Document
⌘-Z Edit/Undo

Windows Commands

Ctrl-N File/New/Document
Ctrl-Z Edit/Undo

FYI

There are two ways to apply *No Style* to a paragraph before applying another style. The first is to click on *No Style* in the Style Sheets palette and then to click on another style. The second is to Alt/Option-click on the new style. This automatically applies the *No Style* before applying the new style.

graph style sheet in the previous exercise, you automatically applied the *No Style* before applying the First Paragraph style. That's why the Drop Cap text attributes disappeared, because character styles are considered local formatting and applying *No Style* strips a paragraph of all local formatting.

EXERCISE D

1. Create a new file (File/New/Document) with an automatic text box. Display the Style Sheets palette (F11) and the Measurements palette (F9). Click inside the text box and type *One if by land and two if by sea*. Press the Return/Enter key.
2. Click inside the paragraph and notice that the paragraph and character styles for the paragraph are Normal. Unless the Normal style has been edited in your version of QuarkXPress, the Measurements palette should display 12-pt. Helvetica (Macintosh) or Ariel (Windows). Quadruple-click to select the entire paragraph and use the Measurements palette to format it in Times, 24 pt. bold. These three attributes—typeface, type size, and type style—are local formatting, that is, they are departures from the Normal style's defined attributes of 12 pt Ariel/Helvetica. Therefore, a + sign appears before the Normal paragraph and character styles in the Style Sheets palette.
3. Click at the end of that paragraph. Press the Return/Enter key to start a new paragraph and type *This is not Normal*. It appears tagged with the Normal style sheet, but because you carried over the local formatting from the first paragraph to the second when you pressed the Return/Enter key, you carried over the local formatting attributes and the Normal style displays the + sign in the Style Sheets palette.
4. Click anywhere in that second paragraph and click on *No Style* in the paragraph style panel of the Style Sheets palette. Nothing appears to happen. The text attributes do not display the original Normal attributes of 12 pt Ariel or Helvetica—yet. But the paragraph has been disassociated from any style.
5. With the paragraph still selected, click the Normal paragraph style in the Style Sheets palette and notice that it now displays the original Normal style of 12 pt Ariel or Helvetica. Notice also that the + sign no longer appears before the Normal style name, because all the local formatting which the + sign indicates as being present was stripped from that paragraph when you applied *No Style* (Figure 9.8).

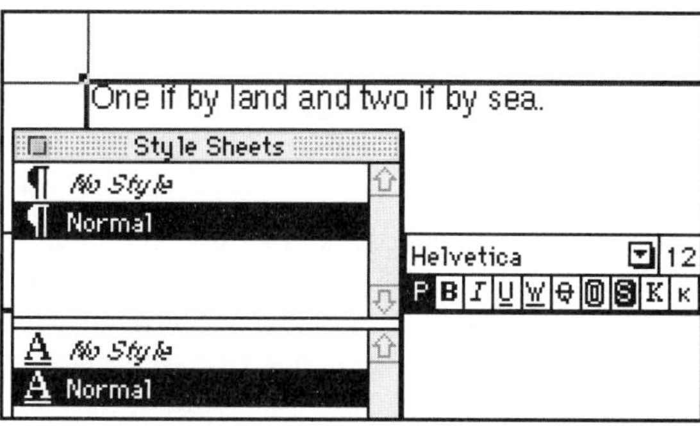

Figure 9.8. When you first type or import text into a new document, the default style is Normal and the default text attributes are 12-pt. Ariel or Helvetica.

6. Quadruple-click to select the second paragraph. Format it in a different typeface and in a large type size. The Style Sheets palette displays the highlighted Normal style with the + sign, because you applied local formatting to the original Normal style (Figure 9.9).

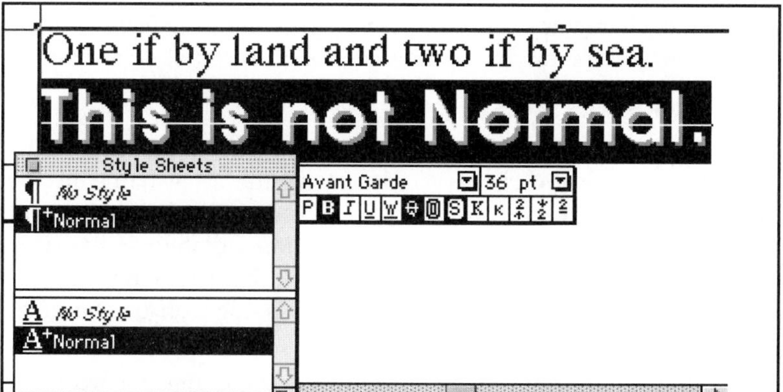

Figure 9.9. The Normal style displays the + sign, indicating that local formatting was applied to the paragraph tagged with the Normal style.

7. With the paragraph still selected, Alt/Option-click on the Normal style in the upper panel of the Style Sheets panel to strip the local formatting and return the paragraph to the original Normal style.

8. Close this file (File/Close). Don't save your changes.

Macintosh Commands

⌘-W File/Close

Windows Commands

Ctrl-F4 File/Close

LESSON 5
APPLYING COMMANDS FROM THE STYLE SHEETS PALETTE

Macintosh Commands

⌘-O File/Open

Windows Commands

Ctrl-O FIle/Open

Thus far you have used the Style Sheets palette to apply paragraph and character styles. You can also use it to edit, duplicate, and delete style sheets, as well as to create new paragraph and character style sheets. All of these functions are available from menus and dialog boxes, but it is usually easier to execute these functions from the Style Sheets palette.

APPLYING CHARACTER STYLES

Because character styles are attached to individual text characters instead of to every character in the paragraph, you must manually select those characters before applying a character style. Unlike paragraph styles that are applied after just clicking anywhere in a paragraph, character styles require that you highlight (select) those specific characters to which you want the character style applied.

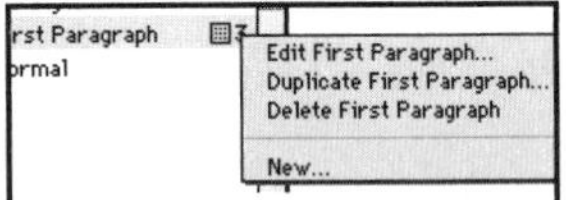

Control-click (Macintosh) or Right-click (Windows) on a style to display a menu from which you can select editing options.

DELETING STYLE SHEETS

There are two ways to delete a style sheet. You can Control-click (Macintosh) or Right-click (Windows) on the style name in the Style Sheets palette and drag to select Delete. If the style has not been used in the document, it is deleted immediately. If the style sheet has been applied to a paragraph or to characters in the document, an alert asks you to select another paragraph or character style as a replacement.

EXERCISE E

1. Open the *Styles.qxd* file in your Projects folder or in the Unit 09 folder on the CD-ROM (File/Open). Display the Style Sheets palette (F11). Click anywhere in the first paragraph.
2. Press the Control key (Macintosh) or Right-click (Windows) and click down on the First Paragraph style in the Style Sheets palette to display another menu (Figure 9.10). Drag to select Edit First Paragraph. Click on the Formats tab and deselect the Drop Caps check box to remove the drop cap. Don't click on OK.
3. Click on the Rules tab and change the color of the rule to green. Click on OK. Both paragraphs reflect the edit.

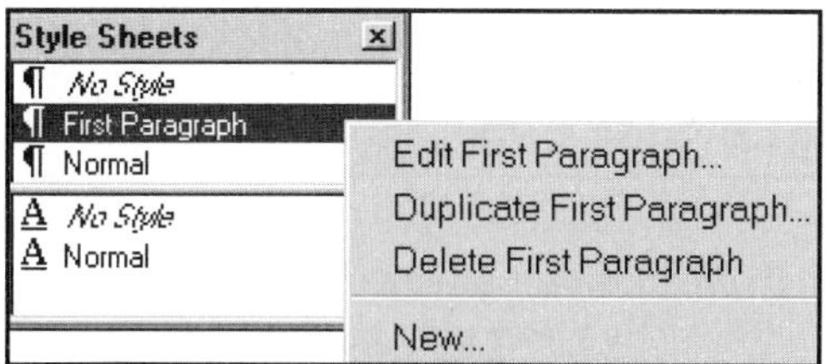

Figure 9.10. Control-clicking (Macintosh) or Right-clicking (Windows) on a style name in the Style Sheets palette displays another menu.

4. Double-click on the first word in the paragraph. Format it in another typeface, larger type size, and in a different color. Keep it selected and Control-click (Macintosh) or Right-click (Windows) on Normal in the lower panel of the Style Sheets palette. Drag to select New. In the Edit Character Style Sheet dialog box, type First Word in the Name field. Click on OK. You have created a character-based style sheet by example.
5. With the word still selected, click on the First Word style in the lower panel (character styles panel) of the Style Sheets palette to tag those characters with that style.
6. Control-click (Macintosh) or Right-click (Windows) on the First Paragraph style and drag to select Duplicate First Paragraph. The Edit Style Sheet dialog box appears with First Paragraph copy displayed in the Name field. Type *Subhead* in the Name field. In the Character Attributes field, click on New. Type *Subhead Type* in the Name field. Change the font to Helvetica, the size to 12 points, and the color to red. Click on OK twice to return to the document. *Subhead* appears in the upper panel (paragraph styles panel) of the Style Sheets palette as a paragraph style. *Subhead Type* appears in the lower panel of the palette as a character style.
7. Control-click (Macintosh) or Right-click (Windows) on the First Word style in the lower panel of the palette. Drag to select Delete First Word. Because the First Word style was applied to text, the alert asks what style you want to use to replace the deleted First Word style. Drag to select Subhead Type. Click on OK. Any text tagged with the First Word type is now styled with the Subhead Type. The First Word style is deleted from the Style Sheets palette.
8. Close this file or choose File/Revert to Saved. Don't save your changes.

FYI

When you Control-click (Macintosh) or Right-click (Windows) on a paragraph style and choose New, the Edit Paragraph Style Sheet dialog box is displayed. When you Control/Right-click on a character style and select New, the Edit Character Style Sheet dialog box is displayed. It's just like using the New menu in the Style Sheets dialog box.

Macintosh Commands

⌘-Option-A File/Append

Windows Commands

Ctrl-Alt-A File/Append

LESSON 6
APPENDING STYLE SHEETS

Many times styles sheets that have taken a long time to create and tweak are part of a document created previously. You can, however, append these style sheets to the active document using the Append command from the File menu or by clicking the Append button in the Style Sheets for [filename] dialog box.

If a style sheet in the active document has the same name (not necessarily the same formatting attributes), you have to tell XPress how to resolve the conflict by selecting one of three options:

RENAME

You can simply rename the appended style sheet's name, which changes the name of the appended style sheet and places it as a new style in the Style Sheets palette. This does not affect the formatting of any of the style sheets in the active document.

AUTO-RENAME

This option renames the appended style sheet by adding an asterisk before its name in the Style Sheets palette. The auto-renamed style appears as another style in the palette and is not applied to any of the paragraphs or text in the active document.

USE NEW

This is the option that can do the damage if you select it when you really don't mean to select it. Choosing Use New *replaces* the style sheet with the same name in the active document; in doing this, it replaces all the paragraph and text attributes of the original style sheet with those from the appended style sheet.

USE EXISTING

Choosing Use Existing essentially cancels the Append command and uses the style sheet in the active document instead of appending the selected style from the new document.

FYI

If you transfer a style sheet by mistake from the Available field to the Including field, highlight the style in the Including field and click the large black backward arrow.

EXERCISE F

1. If necessary, open the *Styles.qxd* file and click on the text box to select it. Display the Style Sheets palette (F11). It currently displays one new paragraph style sheet, First Paragraph.
2. Choose File/Append and navigate to the Unit 09 folder on the CD-ROM. Highlight the *Append.qxd* file and click on Open. The

file does not open, but rather displays the Append to [filename] dialog box with the Style Sheets tab selected (Figure 9.11).

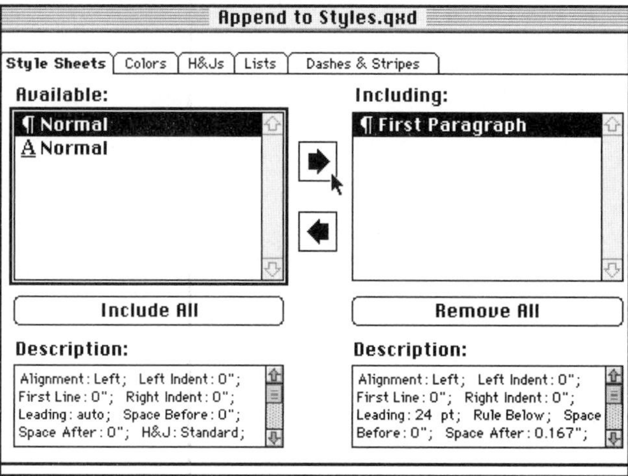

Figure 9.11. Use the Append dialog box to transfer style sheets and other formatting options from one file to the active document.

FYI

You can append Colors, H&Js, Lists, and Dashes & Stripes as well as style sheets from other XPress documents.

3. The Styles Sheet palette for the *Append.qxd* file displays the same First Paragraph paragraph style as the *Styles.qxd* file. The Available field on the left lists all the style sheets in the new document that are available to be appended to the active document. Click on the First Paragraph style, and click the large black forward arrow to copy the First Paragraph style to the Including field.
4. Click on OK and at the alert, click OK again to display the Append Conflict dialog box (Figure 9.12). Notice that Drop Cap Chars is boldfaced in the Description field for the active (existing) document and that it doesn't appear in the description field for the New document. Click the Rename button to rename the appended style sheet's name.

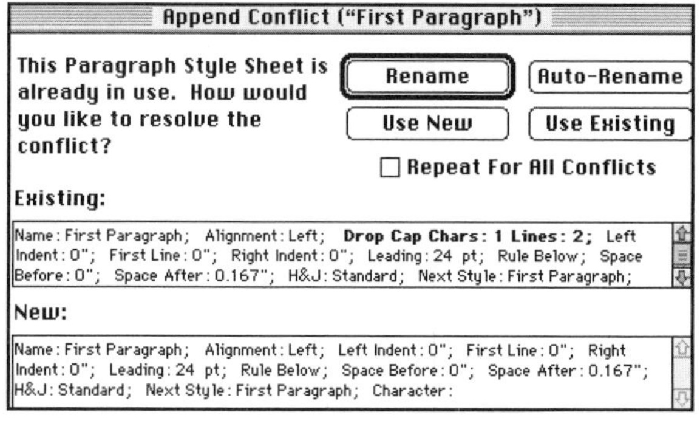

Figure 9.12. Make choices in the Append Conflict dialog box about how the appended style sheet is to behave and be named in the active document.

5. Type *Appended First Paragraph* in the New Name field and click on OK. The Appended First Paragraph style appears as a new paragraph style in the Style Sheets palette (Figure 9.13). The two paragraphs in the *Styles.qxd* document styled with the First Paragraph styles do not change because you have only *appended* a style sheet, not replaced or edited an existing style sheet.

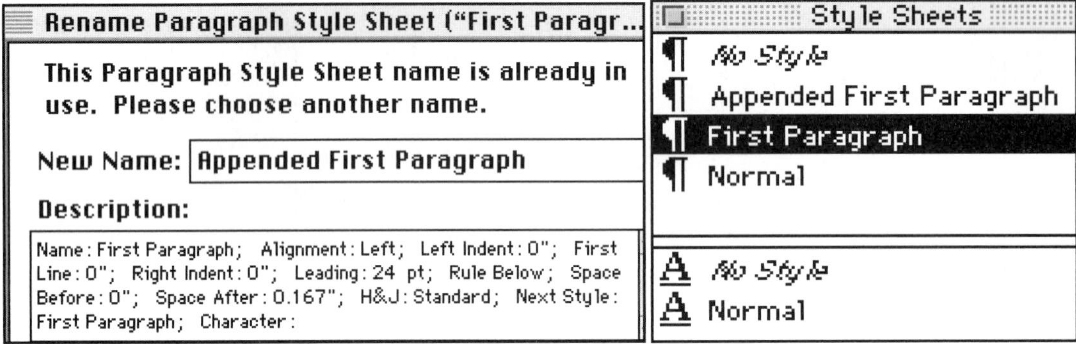

Figure 9.13. Type a new name for a style sheet with the same name as the appended style sheet. The appended style sheet name appears as a new style in the Style Sheets palette for the active document.

6. Repeat steps 2 and 3. In the Append Conflict dialog box, click the Auto-Rename button and click OK twice. The First Paragraph style appears as a separate style in the Style Sheets palette for the *Styles.qxd* file, but it displays an asterisk before its name, indicating that it is an appended style sheet with the same name as a style sheet in the active document. Again, no change is made to the two paragraphs in the *Styles.qxd* file that are styled with the First Paragraph style, because the *First Paragraph style is only appended, not applied.
7. Repeat steps 2 and 3 again. In the Append Conflict dialog box, click the Use New button. You are returned to the document. Notice that the two paragraphs originally styled with the First Paragraph style no longer display the drop cap because the new appended style did not specify drop caps.
8. Close this file. Don't save your changes.

UNIT 10

FIND/CHANGE

OVERVIEW

In this unit you will learn how to:
Find and change words
Find and change non-printing characters
Find and change text attributes
Find and change style sheets

TERMS

Find Attributes
Find First
Find Next
story

HOW IT WORKS:

Create and format the text. Select the text box and make a note of its height. Use the Step and Repeat command to create 1 repeat with 0 Horizontal Offset and a Vertical Offset equal to the height of the text box. Give the duplicate box a runaround on None. Select the text and click on the Flip Vertical arrow (lower arrow) in the Measurements palette. With the text box still selected, click on the Item tool and use the Up Arrow on the keyboard to move the duplicate box up until the letters barely touch the letters in the original box. Select the text in the duplicate box and use the Shade command under the Style menu to screen the text back to 30% to create the shadow. If you want to miter the two backslashes, use the Bézier Picture Box tool to create boxes with None runaround to conceal the points of the lines.

Macintosh Commands

⌘-O File/Open
⌘-F Edit/Find/Change

Windows Commands

Ctrl-O File/Open
Ctrl-F Edit/Find/Change

FYI

The Find/Change commands are accessed from the Find/Change palette—not dialog box—that stays open unless you click in its close box.

Change

Clicking the Change button changes the highlighted characters to the contents of the Change To field, and disables all other options except the Find Next button.

LESSON 1
FIND/CHANGE COMMAND

One of the most powerful text editing functions in QuarkXPress 4.0 is the Find/Change command. This command can be used to find, highlight, and change text, non-printing characters, such as paragraph returns and tabs, text attributes, such as font size and type style, and style sheets. This allows you to make global and local formatting changes to every text character in a document, quickly and consistently.

FINDING AND CHANGING WORDS

Use the Find/Change command to find and replace any word or any part of a word in a document. You can replace the text characters with new characters or use this command to simply remove the selected text. To do this, however, you must understand how XPress starts the search for your text. Unless you select the Document check box in the Find/Change dialog box, XPress begins the search from the insertion point and concludes the search with the last text character in the active (selected) text box or text chain. It does not wrap to the beginning of the story or text chain. However, if you do select the Document check box in the Find/Change dialog box and no text box is active, XPress will wrap to search the entire document for the characters in the Find What field.

To search for text, non-printing characters, or style sheets on master pages, display the master pages, but do not select any of the text boxes on those master pages.

EXERCISE A

1. Open the *Find.qxd* file in the Unit 10 folder on the CD-ROM (File/Open). If you get an alert telling you that kerning and tracking settings are different, ignore the alert and click the Use XPress Preferences button. Click on the text box to select it and display the Style Sheets palette (F11). It consists of four paragraphs. The Style Sheets palette indicates that there are two paragraph styles (Head and Body), and one character style, First Word. Click the close box on the Style Sheets palette to close the palette.

2. Click outside the margins to deselect the text box. Choose Edit/Find Change. In the Find What field type *the*. Press the tab key and type your first name in the Change To field. Click

the Document check box to search the entire document. Don't select the Whole Word option. You're looking for *the* in any string of text. Make sure the Ignore Case check box is selected to find both upper and lower case instances of the Find What text and replace them with the upper- or lowercase version of the Change to text. Also make sure the Ignore Attributes check box is selected so that font size, type style, etc. will be ignored during the search (Figure 10.1).

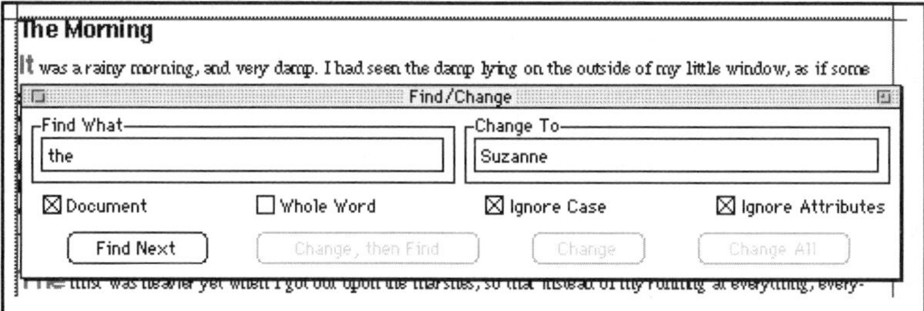

Figure 10.1. With no text box selected, selecting the Document check box will cause the search to wrap and check the entire document for the Find What text.

3. Click the Find Next button. The first word of the document, *The*, appears highlighted because no text box was selected when you began the search. Four options now appear in the Find Change dialog box: Find Next, Change then Find, Change, and Change All (Figure 10.2). Click the Find Next button and notice that the *The* in the first heading remains untouched and that the word *the* before *damp* in the first line is highlighted.

Figure 10.2. When it encounters a match for the contents of the Find What field, the Find command provides four options for replacing, ignoring, or deleting those contents.

4. Click Change, then Find and the word *the* before the word *damp* is changed to the contents of the Change To field, in this case your first name. Also, the word *the* before the word *outside* is highlighted, indicating that it is a match. Click Change. The word is changed to match the contents of the Change To field, and only the Find Next button is active. Click the Find Next button.

Change All

Clicking Change All automatically changes every instance of the Find What field to the contents of the Change To field—based on the selections you made in the Find/Change dialog box—without giving you the option to override any change.

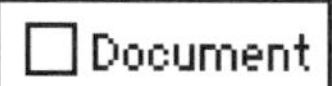

Click to select or click to deselect a check box. When Document is checked, the Change To text applies to every story (chain of linked text) in the document.

Find Next

Clicking Find Next when the contents of the Find What field are encountered leaves those contents untouched and continues the search for the next match.

Change, then Find

Clicking Change, then Find, changes the highlighted characters to the contents of the Change To field, and then highlights the next contents of the Find What field.

Macintosh Commands

⌘-F Edit/Find/Change

Windows Commands

Ctrl-F Edit/Find/Change

Whole Word

Selecting the Whole Word option will find only the exact match for a word. If *the* is the Find What text, and Whole Word is checked, then only the whole word will be highlighted. Words such as *there*, *other*, *their*, etc. will not be selected.

5. The characters *the* in the word *there* are highlighted. Click the Change All button and every instance of *the* in any word is changed to the contents of the Change To field. An alert tells you that 21 instances (of the Find What contents) were changed to the contents of the Change To field. Because the Whole Word option was not selected, several of those changes should not have been made and the document doesn't read correctly at all (Figure 10.3). Close the Find/Change dialog box.

It was a rainy morning, and very damp. I had seen suzanne damp lying on suzanne outside of m
if some goblin had been crying suzannere all night, and using suzanne window for a pocket-han
saw suzanne damp lying on suzanne bare hedges and spare grass, like a coarser sort of spiders'
from twig to twig and blade to blade. On every rail and gate, wet lay clammy; and suzanne mar
thick, that suzanne wooden finger on suzanne post directing people to our village—a direction
never accepted, for suzanney never came suzannere—was invisible to me until I was quite close
Suzannen, as I looked up at it, while it dripped, it seemed to my oppressed conscience like a ph
to suzanne Hulks.

Suzanne Marshes

Suzanne mist was heavier yet when I got out upon suzanne marshes, so that instead of my
thing, everything seemed to run at me. This was very disagreeable to a guilty mind. Suzanne ga
banks came bursting at me through suzanne mist, as if suzanney cried as plainly as could be, "A
Somebody else's pork pie! Stop him!" Suzanne cattle came upon me with like suddenness, starin
eyes, and steaming out of suzanneir nostrils.

Figure 10.3. Because Whole Word was not checked, every instance of the Find What text was replaced by the Change To text, even a word like *there*, which is not what you would want to do. Because Ignore Case was selected, any lowercase words that matched the Find What text were replaced with lowercase versions of the Change To text.

Space Saver

When navigating a document with the Find/Change dialog box, click the Close button (Macintosh only) to hide all the search and replace parameters and display only the option buttons.

6. Choose File/Revert to Saved to revert to the last saved version of the file.

7. Click outside the margins to deselect the text box. Choose Edit/Find/Change. Type *The* in the Find What field, press the Tab key and type your first name in the Change To field. Make sure that Document, Whole Word, and Ignore Attributes are checked. Ignore Case should be *deselected* because you want to change only those instances of *The* with a capital *T* and replace them with the uppercase version of your name.

8. Because you have so narrowly limited your selection, click the Find Next button. The first word in the document is highlighted. Click the Change All button. The alert tells you that a total of 5 instances (of *The*) were changed.

9. Click the Close button in the Find/Change dialog box to close the box. Close this file or choose File/Revert to Saved. You will need it for the next exercise. Don't save your changes.

LESSON 2
FINDING AND CHANGING NON-PRINTING CHARACTERS

Whenever you press the Spacebar, the Return/Enter key, the Tab key, or other keyboard combinations, XPress inserts marks called Invisibles. You can view these invisibles by choosing View/Show Invisibles. It may be necessary for you to delete some of these invisibles to properly format a document, and it will be easier for you, as well as result in a consistently formatted document, if you use the Find/Change command to do this.

EXERCISE B

1. If necessary, open the *Find.qxd* file in the Unit 10 folder on the CD-ROM. Choose View/Show Invisibles.
2. Click after the word *damp* in the first line and press the Shift key while pressing the Return/Enter key. Windows users should press the Enter key on the keyboard. This is called a Shift-Return and produces the New Line invisible symbol. Repeat after the word *handkerchief* and after the word *blade* (Figure 10.4). Leave the cursor where it falls at the beginning of the next line.

The·Morning¶
It·was·a·rainy·morning,·and·very·damp.↵
·I·had·seen·the·damp·lying·on·the·outside·of·my·little·w
and·using·the·window·for·a·pocket-handkerchief.↵
·Now,·I·saw·the·damp·lying·on·the·bare·hedges·and·spa
from·twig·to·twig·and·blade·to·blade.·↵
On·every·rail·and·gate,·wet·lay·clammy;·and·the·marsh·
directing·people·to·our·village—a·direction·which·they·
me·until·I·was·quite·close·under·it.·Then,·as·I·looked·up
science·like·a·phantom·devoting·me·to·the·Hulks.¶

Figure 10.4. Pressing Shift-Return/Enter creates the New Line invisible in a paragraph.

3. Choose Edit/Find/Change. Type Command-Shift-Return (Macintosh) or Ctrl-Shift-Enter (Windows) in the Find What field. This displays the New Line code—not the symbol—for the search (\n). Delete any text in the Change To field because you just want to delete the New Line marker and restore the original layout of the paragraph.

Macintosh Commands

⌘-O File/Open
⌘-I View/Show Invisibles
⌘-F Edit/Find/Change

Windows Commands

Ctrl-O File/Open
Ctrl-I View/Show Invisibles
Ctrl-F Edit/Find/Change

Windows info

In Windows, press the Enter key on the keyboard, not on the extended keypad.

Play a wild card

Search for any text character by typing the wild card command (Command/Ctrl-?) in the Find What field.

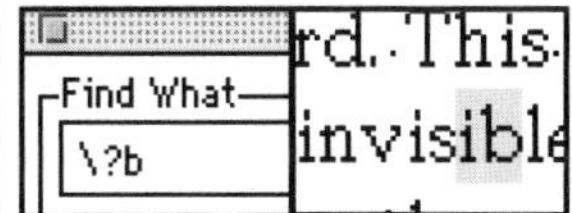

Macintosh Commands

⌘-F Edit/Find/Change
⌘-W File/Close

Windows Commands

Ctrl-F Edit/Find/Change
Ctrl-F4 File/Close

4. With the Find/Change dialog box displayed, press (and keep pressed) the Alt key (Windows) or the Option key (Macintosh) to change the Find Next button to the Find First button. Click on the Find First button to find the first instance in the document of the New Line code/symbol. When it is highlighted, click the Change button. Because no text or code appears in the Change To field, the New Line symbol is deleted. Click the Find Next button, and click the Change All button to remove the last two New Line symbols from the paragraph and restore it to its original formatting. Close the Find/Change box.

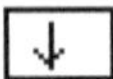

Pressing the Enter key creates the invisible New Column marker.

5. Choose File/Revert to Saved. Select the text box and choose View/Show Invisibles. Display the Measurements palette (F9). Type 5 in the Cols field to make the single-column text box a five-column text box. Press Return/Enter.

6. Scroll down to the end of the paragraph before the second head, and click after the word *Hulks*. Press the Enter key (Windows users should press the Enter key on the numeric *keypad*) and notice that the New Column marker appears and that the subsequent text has moved to the top of the next column (Figure 10.5).

Finger dance

When pressing the Command-Return keys (Macintosh) or Ctrl-Enter keys (Windows), first press the modifier key and keep it pressed while pressing the Return/Enter key.

to·my·oppressed·
conscience·like·a·
phantom·devoting·
me·to·the·Hulk↓

Figure 10.5. Press the Enter key anywhere to move all the subsequent text to the next column or, in a single-column text box, to the next text box.

7. Choose Edit/Find/Change. Type Command-Enter (Macintosh) or Ctrl-Enter (Windows) in the Find What field to display the search code for the New Column marker. Leave the Change To field blank.

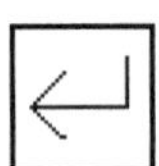

The New Line symbol is created when you press Shift-Return/Enter. This creates a new line in a paragraph without disassociating the new and subsequent lines from the paragraph's formatting. Select Character from the New dialog box to create a new character style.

8. Alt-or Option-click on the Find Next button to change it to the Find First button. Keeping the modifier key pressed, click the Find First button. When the New Column marker is highlighted, click the Change All button. The alert tells you that one instance was changed.

9. Click the Close button in the Find/Change dialog box to close the box. Close this file (File/Close). Don't save your changes.

LESSON 3
FINDING AND CHANGING TEXT ATTRIBUTES

Not only can you find and change text characters, but you can also find and change text attributes. For example, you could find every instance of Times Roman that is italicized and change it to another typeface, type style, and/or type size, etc. To do this, you must be sure to deselect the Ignore Attributes check box in the Find/Change dialog box. You must also be very specific about which attributes you want the search to consider. If one of the search parameters doesn't exist, XPress will ignore all the search parameters and find nothing. When this happens, check to see that you have selected and/or deselected the appropriate check boxes and made the correct selections from the pull-down menus in the expanded Find/Change dialog box.

EXERCISE C

1. Open the *Find.qxd* file in the Unit 10 folder on the CD-ROM again. Display the Measurements palette (F9).
2. Double-click on *rainy* in the first body paragraph and click on the Italics symbol in the Measurements palette to make the selected word Times italics. Repeat for the word *damp* in the same line (Figure 10.6).

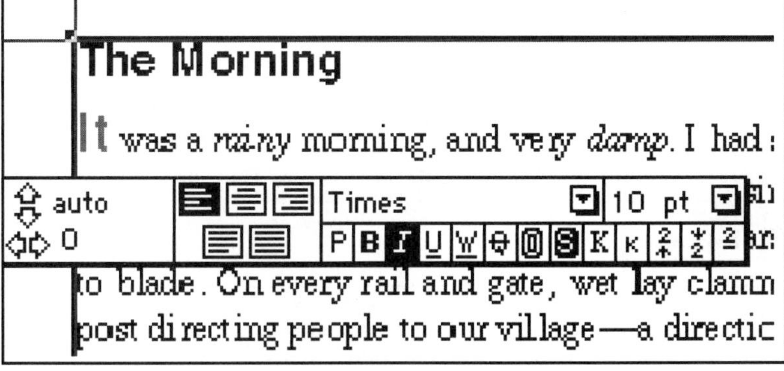

Figure 10.6. Use the Measurements palette to style the selected words in italics.

Macintosh Commands

⌘-O File/Open

Windows Commands

Ctrl-O File/Open

Ignore Case

If Ignore Case is selected, any Find What characters, whether they are upper- or lowercase, will be replaced with the Change To characters—based, of course, on your selection or deselection of the Document, Whole Word, and Ignore Attributes check boxes. If you search for Sandy and deselect Ignore case, a word like sandy would not be affected.

Don't do this!

Never use the Style menu or style options on the Measurements palette to style bold and italic text. Instead, use the actual bold and italic fonts that are part of every professional PostScript type library. Otherwise, you force the printer to create the bold and italic faces, and it never, ever looks right.

Macintosh Commands

⌘-F Edit/Find/Change

Windows Commands

Ctrl-F Edit/Find/Change

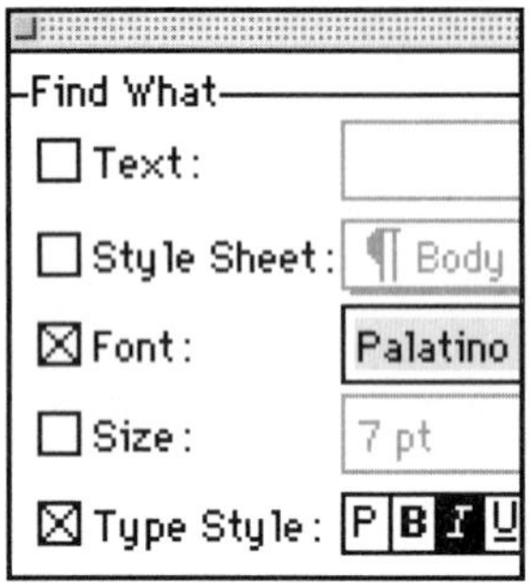

This search will locate any text set in any size in Palatino styled with Italic from the Measurements palette or Type Style menu. Because Text is unchecked in the Find What field, the search will replace *attributes* only, not text characters.

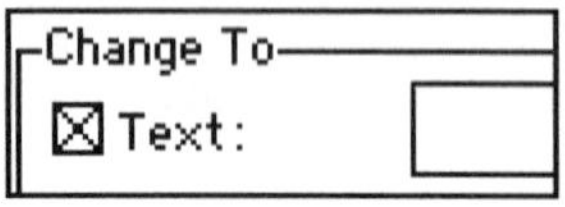

Because Text is not selected, in the Change To field the found text will be deleted.

3. Choose Edit/Find/Change. Deselect the Ignore Attributes check box to display the expanded Find/Change dialog box. Because you are searching for only a type style, the Whole Word and Ignore Case options don't have to be selected. In the Find What panel of the expanded Find/Change dialog box, deselect the Text check box—you're not interested in finding specific words, only a specific style. Deselect the Style Sheet check box—you're not searching for a style sheet, but for a type style.
4. Select the Font check box and use the pull-down menu to select Times. The menu displays every font used in the document.
5. Deselect the Size check box—you're searching for type style, not type size.
6. Select the Type Style check box and click on the italics symbol (*I*) in the panel that resembles the same panel in the Measurements palette.
7. In the Change To panel, deselect the Text and Style Sheet check boxes. Select the Font check box and use the pull-down menu to select any font installed in your system.
8. Select the Size check box and choose 36 from the pull-down menu.
9. Select the Type Style check box and click on the P in the Style panel. This will make the changed text plain style—no bold, italic, etc. Your screen should resemble Figure 10.7.

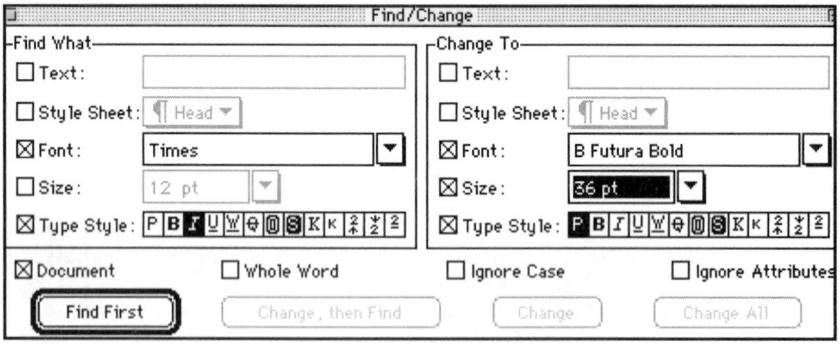

Figure 10.7. Select a font and style for the search and then select another font, font size, and style for the replacement text.

10. Alt-click or Option-click on the Find Next button and click on the Find First button. When the first word is highlighted, click the Change All button to change both instances of the Times italic type to the larger type in the new typeface and plain type style.
11. Click the Close button in the Find/Change dialog box to close the box. Close this file or choose File/Revert to saved. Don't save your changes.

Macintosh Commands

⌘-O File/Open
⌘-F Edit/Find/Change

Windows Commands

Ctrl-O File/Open
Ctrl-F Edit/Find/Change

LESSON 4
FINDING AND CHANGING STYLE SHEETS

An easy way to apply the paragraph and character attributes of one style sheet to paragraphs tagged with a different style sheet is to use the Find/Change command. You can also replace a style sheet with new text attributes.

EXERCISE D

1. If necessary, open the *Find.qxd* file in the Unit 10 folder on the CD-ROM. Choose Edit/Find/Change and deselect Ignore Attributes to display the expanded dialog box. Deselect every check box in the Find What panel except the Style Sheet check box. With the Style Sheet check box selected, use the pull-down menu to select Head, a paragraph style. In the Change To panel, deselect every check box except the Style Sheet check box. Use the pull-down menu to select First Word, a character style (Figure 10.8).

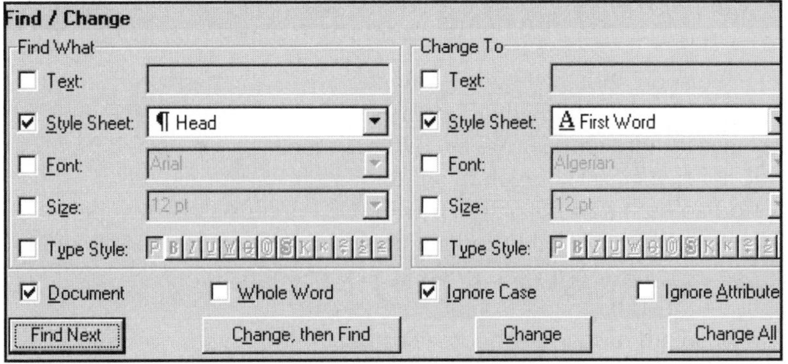

Figure 10.8. Use the Style Sheet options in the expanded Find/Change dialog box to swap style sheets for paragraphs tagged with those styles.

Find First

Press (and keep pressed) the Alt or Option key when the Find/Change dialog box is open to change the Find Next button to the Find First button. This lets you begin the search from the start of the document even if the Document option is deselected.

Macintosh Commands

⌘-W File/Close

Windows Commands

Ctrl-F4 File/Close

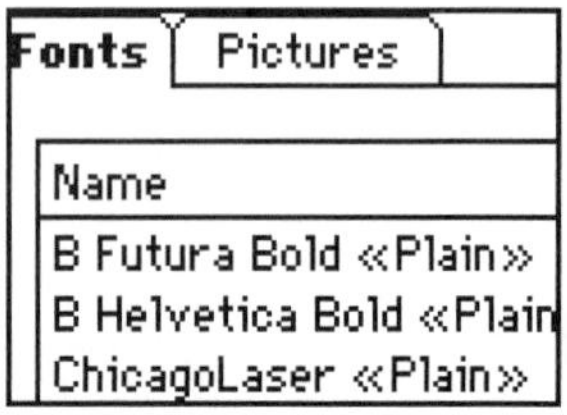

Fonts | Pictures

Name
B Futura Bold «Plain»
B Helvetica Bold «Plain
ChicagoLaser «Plain»

The Fonts Usage dialog box (Utilities/Usage) should display all the typefaces in Plain style, not styled from the Measurements palette. Use the Find/Change dialog box to change any such styled type to the specific typeface.

2. Alt-click or Option-click on the Find Next button and then click on the Find First button to find the first instance of the Head style sheet. When it is highlighted, click on Change All. The alert tells you that both instances (of the Head style) have been changed (to the First Word style).
3. Display the Style Sheets palette (F11) and notice that the Head style displays a +, indicating that the original style has been changed by local formatting, in this case, the size and color of the First Word style.
4. In the Find What panel of the expanded Find/Change dialog box, use the Style Sheet pull-down menu to select the Body style. Leave all the other options in this panel deselected.
5. In the Change To panel, deselect the Style Sheet check box. Click to select the Font check box and use the pull-down menu to choose another typeface installed in your system. Click the Size check box and use the pull-down menu to select 14 or type another value in the Size field (Figure 10.9).

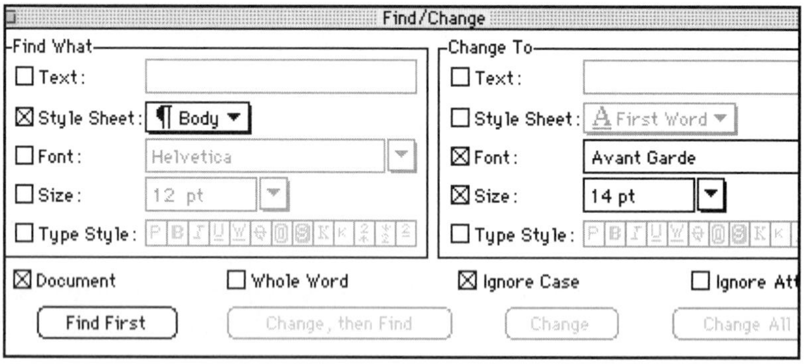

Find/Change

Find What
Text:
Style Sheet: Body
Font: Helvetica
Size: 12 pt
Type Style:

Change To
Text:
Style Sheet: First Word
Font: Avant Garde
Size: 14 pt
Type Style:

Document | Whole Word | Ignore Case | Ignore Att

Find First | Change, then Find | Change | Change All

Figure 10.9. Use the Find/Change dialog box to change the font and type size of all paragraphs tagged with a style sheet.

6. Alt-click or Option-click on the Find Next button and then click the Find First button. When the first instance of the Body style is highlighted, click the Change All button. The alert tells you that two instances have been changed.
7. Display the Style Sheets palette and notice that the Body style displays a +, indicating that local formatting has been applied to that style.
8. Close this file. Don't save your changes.

UNIT 11

OVERVIEW

In this unit you will learn how to:
Set typographical preferences
Append H&Js
Apply baseline shift
Apply Horizontal/Vertical scaling
Specify hyphenation and justification values

TERMS

Baseline Shift
em dash
hyphenation and justification
kerning
tracking

HOW IT WORKS:

Create the type in a serif typeface with each text character in a separate text box. Utopia, Utopia Italic, and Utopia Semibold are used here. Assign each text box a runaround of None and a background color of None. This allows you to move the boxes on top of each other without losing the text. Select each text character and make it a different size and apply a different shade of black or color from the Style menu. Then play with the boxes until you get an arrangement that is visually pleasing.

LESSON 1
TYPOGRAPHIC PREFERENCES

Tip

Use the superior style instead of superscript, because superior type is reduced in size and won't interfere with the leading.

Many of the typographic settings in QuarkXPress are default settings that can be changed in the Character Preferences dialog box (Figure 11.1). You could leave these specifications at their default values and live happily ever after, but if you want to tweak your type globally, this is the first dialog box to check. The percentage values in the Superscript, Subscript, Small Caps, and Superior fields indicate the position and size of the characters. Superscript and subscript characters are not resized, just offset 33% above and below the baseline. Small caps are proportionally reduced to 75% of the specified type size, and superior characters are reduced to 50% of the specified type size.

Accents for All Caps

Keep this option selected to include accent marks on accented uppercase characters.

Ligatures (available only on the Macintosh) are two characters entwined to form a single character like the *fl* in *affluent* and the *fi* in *affiliation*. If you are tracking or kerning headline text and don't want ligatures, type a value such as 5 in the Break Above field. Any characters tracked or kerned above 5 won't display the ligatures; the fl or fi will "break" apart.

LESSON 2
KERNING

FYI

You can also apply kerning from the Style menu and from the Measurements palette if the cursor is placed between two text characters.

Kerning, or letterspacing, is the process of adding or deleting space between two adjacent characters or letter pairs. XPress will automatically kern, or adjust the space between two adjacent letters, if the Auto Kern Above field in the Document Preferences Character dialog box is checked. With this option selected, XPress will adjust the spacing between characters above the value in the Auto Kern Above field using the kerning values built into the program's kerning tables (Figure 11.1).

Affluent
Affiliation

When ligatures are selected in the Character modify dialog box (Macintosh only), fl and fi are displayed as one character—in fonts that support ligatures.

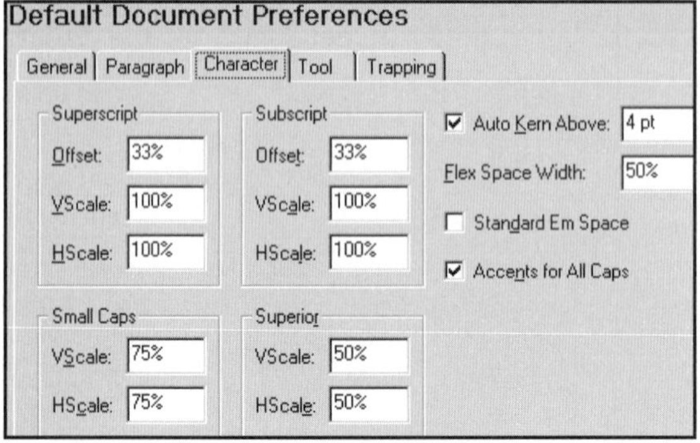

Figure 11.1. Select the Auto Kern Above option in the Character Modify dialog box to automatically kern characters above a specified point size.

EXERCISE A

1. Create a new non-facing pages document with one-inch margins and an automatic text box (File/New/Document). Click inside the text box on the first page and type *Tomorrow.* Press the Return/Enter key to create a paragraph return. Double-click on the word to select it and use the Measurements palette (View/Show Measurements) to format it in 72-pt. Helvetica. Triple-click on the word to select the entire line and choose Edit/Copy. Click below the word and choose Edit/Paste to paste a copy of the word. You will work with the copy, using the original as a reference.
2. Click in the vertical ruler on the left side of the page and drag a ruler guide to the left side of the first *o* in *Tomorrow.*
3. With the Content tool selected, click between the *T* and the *o* in the lower word. Use the Zoom tool to draw a marquee around those two letters, and notice the wide space between the letters. To reduce the space between text characters, you will apply kerning.
4. With the cursor between the first two letters, choose Style/Kern to display the Character Attributes dialog box. In the lower right side of the dialog box, type -7 in the Kern Amount field. Click on OK. Notice how the *o* moves to the left, closer to the T. Applying a negative kerning value reduces space; a positive value increases space (Figure 11.2).

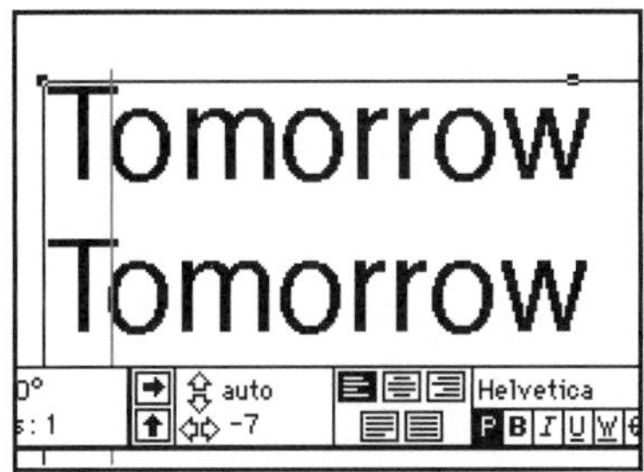

Figure 11.2. Typing a negative value in the Kerning field of the Measurements palette reduces space between characters.

5. With the cursor still between the first two characters, double-click on the -7 in the Kerning field of the Measurements palette and type 10. Press Return/Enter. The *o* moves further to the right because by typing a positive number you have added space between the two characters.

Macintosh Commands

⌘-N File/New/Document
⌘-C Edit/Copy
⌘-V Edit/Paste

Windows Commands

Ctrl-N File/New/Document
Ctrl-C Edit/Copy
Ctrl-V Edit/Paste

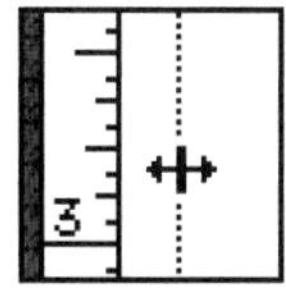

Click inside the vertical ruler and drag it out onto the page.

Content tool

☑ Auto Kern Above: 8 pt

Auto Kern Above

This value in the Character Preferences dialog box specifies the point size at which XPress will automatically kern letter pairs. For laser printing, 10 points is a good setting. Keep this value at about 8 points for documents printed from an imagesetter.

Macintosh Commands

⌘-W File/Close

Windows Commands

Ctrl-F4 File/Close

6. Kerning is applied in 10 units with every click of the kerning arrow in the Measurements palette. Click the left kerning arrow to return the kerning value to 0. Click the right arrow again to add 10 units of space between the *T* and the *o*. Click again to add 20 units of space between the characters.
7. To apply kerning in 1-unit increments with every click on an arrow, press the Option key (Macintosh) or Alt key (Windows) while clicking on the arrows. Press the Alt/Option key and click on the forward arrow four times to add 4 units of space between the letters (Figure 11.3).

Clicking is not typing

When you click any of the arrows in the Measurements palette, you don't have to press Return/Enter to execute the command. You only press Return/Enter when you type a value in the palette.

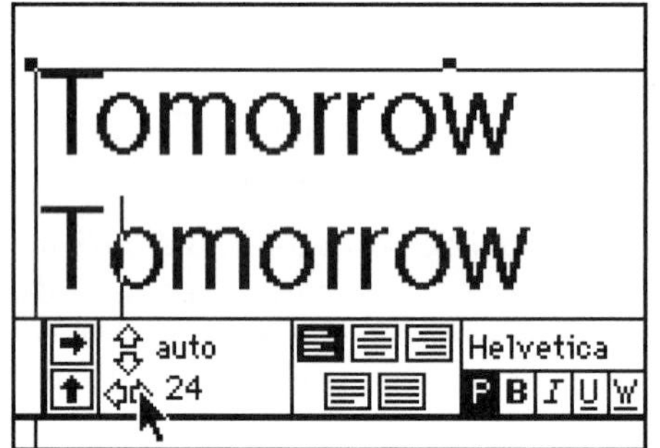

Figure 11.3. Clicking the right kerning arrow adds 10 units of space between the characters each time you click. Press the Alt/Option key to add or subtract space in 1-unit increments.

8. Close this file (File/Close). Don't save your changes.

Standard em-space

An em is a standard typographical measure upon which other measurements are based. This option in the Character Preferences dialog box tells XPress how to calculate the width of an em. The wider world measures the em as the width of the capital M in a typeface. XPress uses the width of two zeros. Either choice is fine because typographers assigned number characters the width of half an em space (an en space) to make number alignment in setting tables easier.

LESSON 3 TRACKING

Tracking, also called *range kerning* and *letterspacing*, is the process of adding or deleting space between *two or more* selected characters. When two or more adjacent characters are selected, the Kern command in the Style menu becomes the Track command. You can also apply tracking values from the Measurements palette if you have more than one character selected in the document.

Because tracking is applied to a range of selected characters, it is a powerful tool in getting rid of widows, single lines of type that fall at the top of a new column. By selecting the entire paragraph and applying single units of tracking, you can usually get the wandering word to fall back into the paragraph at the bottom of the paragraph where it belongs. Always remember that typography is a visual art, and as long as you can fool the eye, your pages will be fine. Too much tracking, however, is visible and distracting to the eye, so be careful when using this feature.

EXERCISE B

1. In a new document without an automatic text box or in another page in the active document, use the standard-shape Rectangle Text Box tool and the Measurements palette (View/Show Measurements) to draw a text box 5 inches wide and 3 inches high.
2. Click inside the text box and type *Typesetters Earn Big Bucks in Industry!* Format it in 18-pt. Helvetica. If this were a headline, you would want it to fit across the width of the column. Triple-click to select the whole line and choose Style/Track. Type 10 in the Track Amount field and click on OK. The letters almost reach to the right edge of the text box.
3. Keep the words selected, press the Alt/Option key, and click on the forward tracking arrow in the Measurements palette until you add enough space between all the characters and space between the words to fit the sentence across the full width of the text box. If you add too much space, press the Alt/Option key and click until the characters jump from the second line back to the first line.
4. Close this file (File/Close). Don't save your changes.

Macintosh Commands

⌘-N File/New/Document
⌘-W File/Close

Windows Commands

Ctrl-N File/New/Document
Ctrl-F4 File/Close

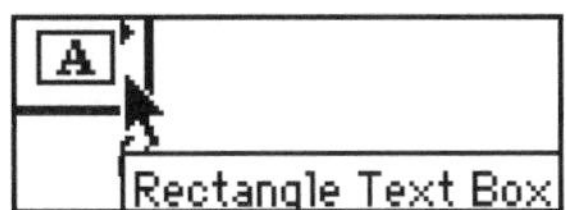

Rectangle Text Box tool

When a range of text is selected, click on the forward tracking arrow to add space between the characters and the spaces between words.

LESSON 4
BASELINE SHIFT

Just because text characters are supposed to sit on the baseline, that invisible horizontal line, doesn't mean they always do. Sometimes, for stylistic reasons, you may want to move characters above and below the baseline. To do this, select the character and apply a positive baseline shift value from the Style menu to move the selected character(s) above the baseline or a negative value to move them below the baseline.

The Baseline Shift command should not be used indiscriminately. Using it to position blocks of text like paragraphs in a text chain makes it difficult to control spacing before and after a paragraph and plays havoc with text flow. Use it only when you want to create special effects, or when fitting lines vertically in a tight space like a series of boxes across the page, or when typesetting tables and forms. To remove the Baseline Shift values, select the affected characters, choose Style/Baseline Shift, and type 0 in the Baseline Shift field of the Character Attributes dialog box.

Dot, dot, dot

A menu command followed by an ellipse (...) indicates that selecting that command will display a dialog box. That's why there are no keyboard shortcuts for any of these commands.

EXERCISE C

1. Create a new document without an automatic text box (File/New/Document). Use the Document Preferences dialog box (Edit/Preferences/Document) to choose In Front from the Guides pull-down menu. Use the Rectangle Text Box tool and the Measurements palette to draw a text box 5 inches wide and 2 inches high. Type *Up and down and all around*. Select the type and format it in 24-pt. Helvetica. Deselect the text.

2. With the text box still selected, choose Item/Modify and click on the Text tab. Use the Vertical Alignment pull-down menu to select Centered. Click on OK. The sentence is now centered vertically in the text box.

3. Click in the horizontal ruler at the top of the page and drag a ruler guide down to the baseline of the words. You'll use this as the reference point when you use the Baseline Shift command to move words up and down.

4. Double-click to select *Up*. Choose Style/Baseline Shift and type 10 in the Baseline Shift field in the lower left side of the Character Attributes dialog box. Click on OK. The word moves 10 points above the baseline.

5. Double-click to select *down*. Choose Style/Baseline Shift and type -30 in the Baseline Shift field. A negative number moves the selected characters below the baseline. Click on OK. Your screen should resemble Figure 11.4. The Baseline Shift commands also work with text on any of the text paths.

Up and and all around
down

Figure 11.4. The Baseline Shift command moves selected characters above and below the baseline.

6. Select any word and press Command-Option-Shift- + (Macintosh) or Ctrl-Alt-Shift- + (Windows) and watch the word move above the baseline. Using the keyboard command lets you see how far the selected text is moving above or below the baseline as you're moving it.

Macintosh Commands

⌘-N File/New/Document
⌘-Y Edit/Preferences/Document
⌘-M Item/Modify
⌘-Option-Shift-+/- Baseline Shift

Windows Commands

Ctrl-N File/New/Document
Ctrl-Y Edit/Preferences/Document
Ctrl-M Item/Modify
Ctrl-Alt-Shift-+/- Baseline Shift

Em dash

Never use two hyphens—that means never—to set off text. Instead, use an em dash. Create an em dash by pressing Option-Shift-hyphen (Macintosh) or Ctrl-Shift-+ (Windows).

Standard em space

An em space is created by combining two en spaces. The standard em space is the width of two hyphens in the current point size. Deselect this option to create Quirky Quark's em spaces based on the width of two zeros.

LESSON 5
HORIZONTAL/VERTICAL SCALE

When a typographer designs a typeface, he or she puts a great deal of thought into the height and width of the character strokes. Some typefaces like Stone, Palatino, and Times are so beautifully designed that they have become famous for readability and style. If you feel that you want to tamper with perfection, use the Horizontal and Vertical Scale commands to increase or decrease a character's size. Sometimes this can create interesting designs, but once you change the horizontal or vertical scale of a character, you no longer have the typeface you started with. However, using the Horizontal Scale function judiciously will get your headlines to justify properly between the two sides of a column.

Macintosh Commands

⌘-N File/New/Document
⌘-M Item/Modify

Windows Commands

Ctrl-N File/New/Document
Ctrl-M Item/Modify

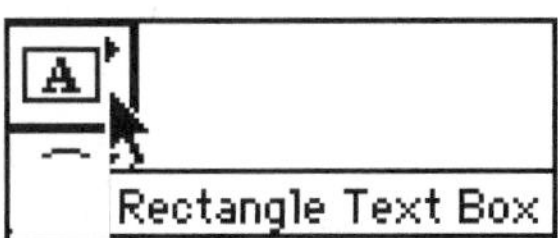

Rectangle Text Box tool

EXERCISE D

1. Create a new document without an automatic text box (File/New/Document). Use the Rectangle Text Box tool and the Measurements palette to draw a text box 6 inches wide and 4 inches high. Type *WOW!* and format it in 24-pt. Times.
2. With the text box still selected, choose Item/Modify and click on the Text tab. Use the Vertical Alignment pull-down menu to select Centered. Click on OK. The word is centered vertically in the text box.
3. Triple-click to select the word and its punctuation. Choose Style/Horizontal/Vertical Scale to display the Character Attributes dialog box. Use the pull-down menu in the lower left corner of the dialog box to select Horizontal. It currently displays a value of 100% because the selected characters are the size of their original design. Type 200 in the Horizontal field to double the width of the characters. Click on OK.
4. Select the *W* and choose Style/Horizontal/Vertical Scale. Use the pull-down menu to select Vertical. Type 300 in the field and click on OK. The *W* is now three times its designed height.
5. Drag to select *OW!* and choose Style/Horizontal/Vertical Scale again. Use the pull-down menu to select Horizontal and type 50 in the field. Click on OK. The three characters are now half the width of their original design (Figure 11.5).

Headline

Si meliora dies, ut vina, poemata reddit, scire velim, chartis aste pretium quotus utar arroget annus. scriptor abhinc annos centum qui decidit, inter perfectos sunt veteresque quae referri debet an inter vilis atque novos? Exclud

at iurgia finis, "Est vetus atque probus, centum qui perficit annos." Quid, qui deperiit minor uno mense vel anno, inter quos referendus erit? Veteresne poetas, an quos et praesens et postera respuat aetas?

"Iste quidem veteres inter ponetur honeste, qui vel mense brevi v"Iste quidem late veteres inter ponetur honeste, qui vel mense brevi v"Iste quidem veteres inter ponetur honeste, qui vel mense brevi v"Iste quidem fue veteres inter ponetur hon-

Reducing the Horizontal Scale value from 100% to 98% fits the Headline text across the column.

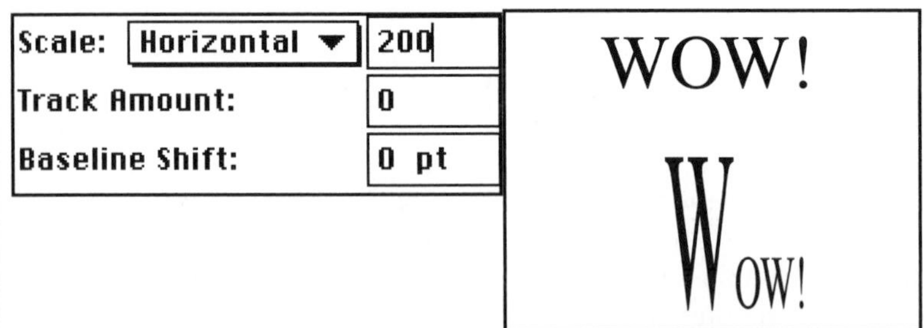

Figure 11.5. Typing 200 in the Horizontal field doubles the width of the selected characters. Typing 300 in the Vertical field triples the height of the initial W. Typing 50 in the Horizontal field reduces the last three characters to one half of their original width.

Creating ellipses

Press the Option-; (semicolon) keys (Macintosh) or the Alt-0133-Enter keys on the keypad (Windows) to create an ellipse. *Never* press the period key three times.

LESSON 6 HYPHENATION AND JUSTIFICATION

One of the features that makes QuarkXPress such a superb typesetting tool is the control it allows over the way words are hyphenated and how closely characters and words are spaced to create a beautiful page. The color of a page is as important as its contents, and by color we mean the evenness of the black type against the white background of the page. To achieve good color, type, especially justified type, must be properly set in the column.

Hyphenation Method: Standard / Enhanced / ✓ Expanded

Standard and Enhanced Hyphenation methods refer to algorithms in earlier versions of XPress. Expanded uses the same algorithm as Enhanced but also checks for any built-in hyphenation dictionaries before using the Enhanced algorithm.

There are three ways of controlling the way type fits in the column. You can hyphenate words, you can increase or reduce the space between words, and you can increase and reduce the space between text characters. In QuarkXPress this control over hyphenation, word spacing, and character spacing is called Hyphenation and Justification or H&Js, and is specified in the Edit Hyphenation and Justification dialog box (Figure 11.6). Every paragraph you set is governed by the default values in this dialog box unless you edit the Standard H&J or create a new H&J style and apply it to a paragraph.

HYPHENATION

Minimum Before: 2

Less of two evils

Set the Minimum Before value to 2 (characters) to avoid text with large gaps at the end of lines. Some editors don't like this, but it allows words such as *re-prisals* and *un-done* to hyphenate.

The left side of the dialog box specifies hyphenation rules and defaults to hyphenating a word with at least six characters, as long as at least three of those characters appear before the hyphen and at least two of them appear after the hyphen. This means that a word like *donuts* would not hyphenate because, although it has six letters, the hyphen would fall after the *do* and the Minimum Before value is set to 3 characters. Using this default hyphenation, capitalized words would not break and you would have unlimited hyphens in a row, giving the paragraph a jagged look. Most editors want to see no more than two hyphens in a row. The Hyphenation Zone is used to limit the number of hyphens in the paragraph and should be left at 0, giving XPress the full column width to use for

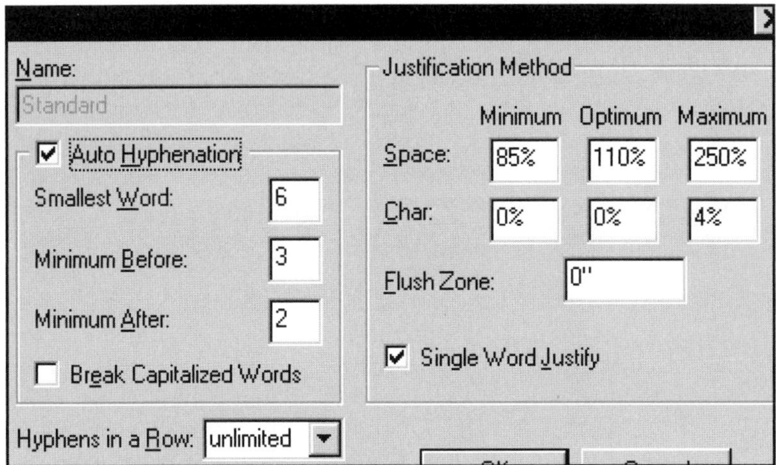

Figure 11.6. The Edit Hyphenation and Justification dialog box is where you specify hyphenation and word and character spacing for a paragraph.

hyphenation.

WORD SPACING AND CHARACTER SPACING

Every typeface is designed with a specific amount of space between characters and words and it is in the right panel of the dialog box, Justification Method, where you can adjust word spacing (Space) and character spacing (Char) based on the type designers' built-in values. The Optimum value (Opt) is the value specified by the type designer and should always be changed from the default 110% to 100%. The Min value is percentage of the optimum value that is allowed to justify the text. The Max value is the highest amount of space allowed between words to justify the text. At the Min default 85% and a default Max value of 250%, XPress will reduce the optimum word space by at least 15% and increase it no more than 150% of the Opt value to justify the line. Because 250% is usually too much word spacing, a good value for this option is 105%.

In the character spacing field (Char) where the values are based on the width of an en space, the default 0% optimum setting is the best. You can also leave the minimum value at 0% which tells XPress not to add or reduce the space between characters. The default 4% maximum value (of an en space) is about as much additional space between characters as type can handle before it looks too loose.

FYI

The general rule for word spacing is the wider the column of type, the more space you can have between words.

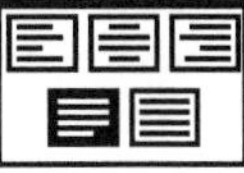

The Justify Align icon is selected. The Last Word Justify Align icon to the right should rarely be used.

En spaces

In XPress, an en space is the width of one zero. Type Option-Spacebar (Macintosh) or Ctrl-Shift-6 (Windows) to create an en space which behaves like a space character created with the Spacebar.

Macintosh Commands

⌘-N File/New/Document
⌘-Y File/Get Text/Picture
⌘-Option-H Edit/H&Js

Windows Commands

Ctrl-N File/New/Document
Ctrl-Y File/Get Text/Picture
Ctrl-Shift-F11 Edit/H&Js

Content tool

The Justify Align icon is selected in the Measurements palette.

Choosing the Append command gives you access to the five functions that permit you to append specifications.

Em dash

Never use two hyphens (--) when you should use an em dash. Create an em dash by pressing Option-Shift-hyphen (Macintosh) or Ctrl-Shift-= (Windows).

APPENDING AND DELETING H&JS

Any H&J style can be appended from another document or deleted from the active document. To do this, choose H&Js from the Edit menu and click the Append button. Open the file with the H&J styles you want to append and select the H&J. Use the black forward arrow to copy the style to the Including panel and click on OK. You can also choose Append from the File menu, click on the H&Js tab, and select the document with the H&Js you want to append.

EXERCISE E

1. Create a new, non-facing pages document with one-inch margins, three columns, and an automatic text box (File/New/Document). Display the Document Layout palette (F10/Macintosh; F4/Windows) and double-click on the first document page to get to page 1. Display the Measurements palette (F9).
2. Click with the Content tool to select the text box on the page and choose File/Get Text. Navigate to the Unit 11 folder on the CD-ROM and double-click on the *HJ.txt* file to import the text file into the selected text box.
3. Use the Measurements palette to make the box 4 inches high and 4 inches wide with 2 columns. Choose Edit/Select All and click on the Justify Align icon in the Measurements palette to justify all of the text. Click to deselect the text.
4. Choose Edit/H&Js to display the Edit H&Js dialog box. The default H&J style is Standard, and right now its options are applied to every paragraph in the document. Click on Edit to display the default H&J settings (Figure 11.7). Notice that unlimited hyphens in a row are allowed, capitalized words won't hyphenate, and if a single word falls in the last line of a justified paragraph, it will be tracked out to the end of the text column. Notice also that the optimum word spacing option is set to 110% and the maximum word spacing is set to 250%. Both of these values are too large to set justified type. Click on OK to close the dialog box and return to the H&Js for the document dialog box.

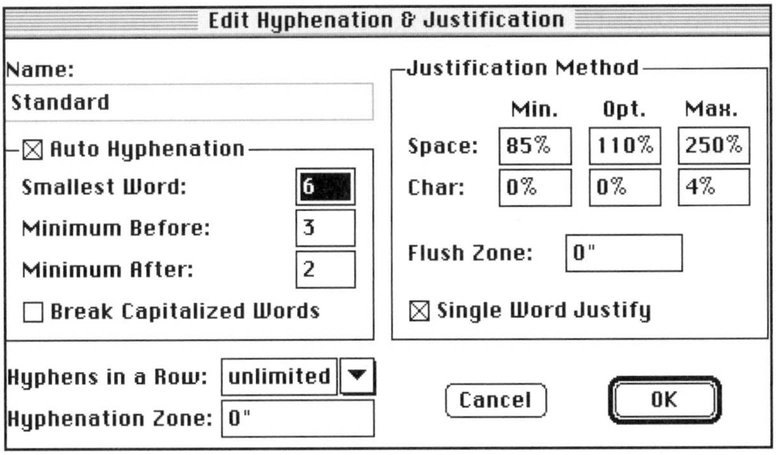

Edit Hyphenation & Justification

Name: Standard

☒ Auto Hyphenation
Smallest Word: 6
Minimum Before: 3
Minimum After: 2
☐ Break Capitalized Words

Hyphens in a Row: unlimited
Hyphenation Zone: 0"

Justification Method

	Min.	Opt.	Max.
Space:	85%	110%	250%
Char:	0%	0%	4%

Flush Zone: 0"
☒ Single Word Justify

Cancel OK

Figure 11.7. The default H&J dialog box allows for unlimited hyphens in a row and single word justify.

5. Click on New in the Edit H&Js dialog box and type *Tight* in the Name field. Change the options in the Justification Method area so that they match the values in Figure 11.8. Because you are reducing the values in the Optimum and Maximum fields, justified lines will display less space between words. Also, the -5% minimum letter spacing will squeeze the text more attractively in the narrow column. Don't click on OK yet.

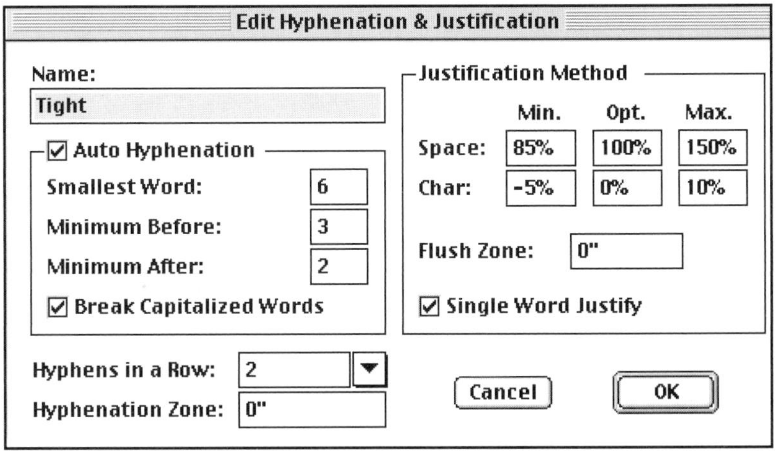

Edit Hyphenation & Justification

Name: Tight

☑ Auto Hyphenation
Smallest Word: 6
Minimum Before: 3
Minimum After: 2
☑ Break Capitalized Words

Hyphens in a Row: 2
Hyphenation Zone: 0"

Justification Method

	Min.	Opt.	Max.
Space:	85%	100%	150%
Char:	-5%	0%	10%

Flush Zone: 0"
☑ Single Word Justify

Cancel OK

Figure 11.8. Reducing the Space and Char values in the Justification Method fields creates tighter text.

Min & Opt & Max

The **Min** (minimum) value refers to the smallest amount of space that XPress can add between words or characters to justify the text. The **Opt** (optimum) value specifies the amount of space *you want* between words and characters. XPress will try to apply that value. The **Max** (maximum) value specifies the limit of space XPress will add between words and characters to justify the text.

Rolling rivers

Excessive space between words in a block of text is called a *river*. Hold a page up to the light. If you see too much white space, you have rivers, and you need to tighten that space up to achieve good (page) color.

Macintosh Commands

⌘-Shift-F Style/Formats
⌘-W File/Close

Windows Commands

Ctrl-Shift-F Style/Formats
Ctrl-F4 File/Close

FYI

You can include H&Js in any style sheets to apply custom H&Js to paragraphs tagged with those style sheets.

6. Keep Auto Hyphenation selected but limit the number of hyphens in a row to 2 by double-clicking *unlimited* and typing 2 in the field. Click to select Break Capitalized Words. In the word spacing field (Space), type 100 in the Opt field to set word spacing to the exact value specified by the type designer. Press the Tab key and type 150 in the Max Space field. Deselect the Single Word Justify option and click on OK. Click on Save to save the new H&J style.
7. Click anywhere in the first paragraph and choose Style/Formats. Choose Tight from the H&Js pull-down menu and click on OK. The characters move closer together, reducing the space between the characters and the space between the words.
8. Close this file. Don't save your changes.

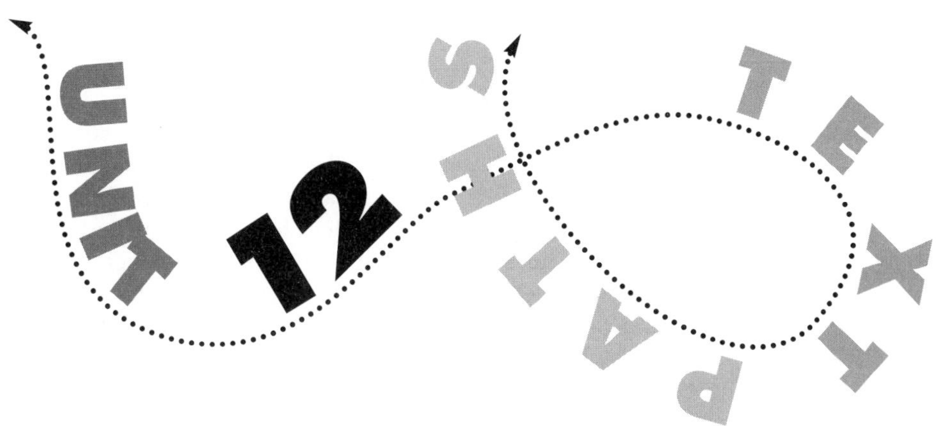

OVERVIEW

In this unit you will learn how to:

Create horizontal and vertical text paths
Create and edit Bézier text paths
Use the Font Usage dialog box
Prepare a document for the printer

TERMS

Bézier text path
Collect for Output
Font Usage
text path

HOW IT WORKS:

Use the Freehand Text-Path tool to create a text path that crosses over itself. Type the text on the path, format it, and track it until it fits the path. You may have to adjust the Bézier points and direction handles to get the path to behave and some kerning may still be necessary. Select the path with the Item tool and assign it a style and width from either the Style menu or the Measurements palette. Finally, quadruple-click on the path with the Content tool to select all the type, and apply a few points of baseline shift to move the text above the path. Remember to use the Content tool to select the type and not the path. Sometimes it's easier when working on a twisted path to click on the path with the Content tool and then select the text by pressing the Shift key and using the arrow keys to select the text.

LESSON 1
TEXT ON A PATH

Ordinarily, text sits on a stationary baseline unless you manually move it up and down using the Baseline Shift command. The only "path" for the text is the baseline; in fact, the term *path* is never used in conjunction with text unless that text is created in an illustration program such as Adobe Illustrator or Macromedia FreeHand. In QuarkXPress 4.0, however, there are four tools used for creating text on straight, slanted, Bézier, and freehand paths (Figure 12.1). Once the path is drawn, the I-beam cursor appears on the path, and you can type and format text as well as edit both the text and its path. Text on a path is "real" text, that is, all of the typographic functions and text effects in XPress can be applied to it.

Figure 12.1. The four Text-Path tools in QuarkXPress 4.0 are the Line Text-Path tool, Orthogonal Text-Path tool, Bézier Text-Path tool, and the Freehand Text-Path tool.

FYI

If you apply a color of None to the path (line), the text path will not appear.

THE LINE TEXT-PATH TOOL

The Line Text-Path tool is used to create text on a straight or diagonal line. To edit all of the text, quadruple-click on the text with the Content tool to select all of the text, even the text that might not appear because the path is too short. As with text in a text box, if there is more type than will fit on the path, the Overflow Indicator appears at the end of the line telling you that the path is not long enough to contain the text.

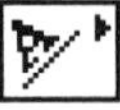

Line Text-Path tool

Any text you select can be formatted from the Style menu or from the Measurements palette. The text path can be modified when the path is selected with either the Item tool or the Content tool. And because it is an item, a text path can have runaround and be grouped with other items.

EDITING LINE TEXT PATHS

To edit a path created with the line tool, first select the path with either the Item tool or the Content tool. Then choose Item/Modify to display the Line specifications dialog box and make your selections.

EXERCISE A

1. Create a new document without an automatic text box. Choose the Line Text-Path tool from the Tool palette and draw a diagonal line about 4 inches long on the page.
2. Type *This is text on a diagonal line.* Quadruple-click to select all the text and then format it in a large point size and a different type. The Overflow Indicator should appear at the end of the path (line) (Figure 12.2).

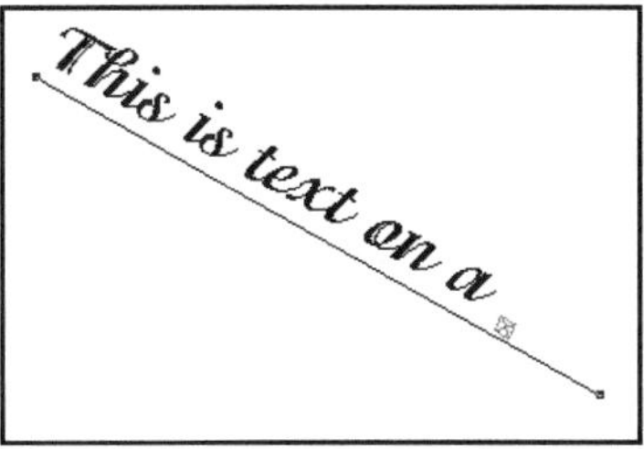

Figure 12.2. Because the text extends beyond the path, the Overflow Indicator appears.

3. With the cursor anywhere on the text, click at one end of the path and drag to lengthen the path so that the type will fit on the line (Figure 12.3). The path is still selected, so choose Item/Modify to display the Line Modify dialog box.

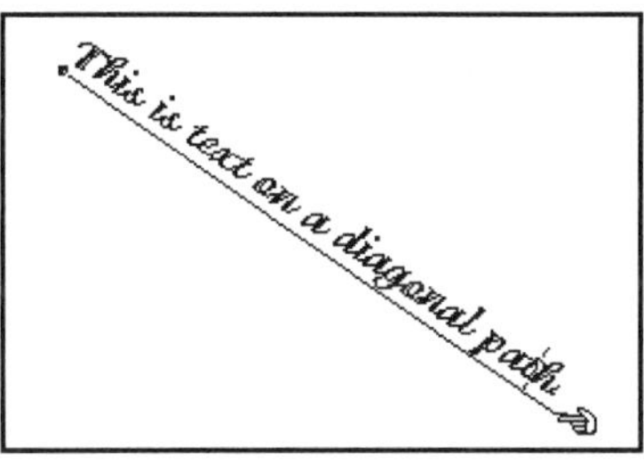

Figure 12.3. Click on the path to select it, then drag the path to lengthen it so that the type fits on the path.

4. Change the width, style, and color of the line. If you choose other than a solid line, you can also assign a gap color. Add arrowheads and click on OK to display the newly formatted path (line).
5. Select the Item tool and click on the path. Once the cursor turns into the Mover pointer, move the path up and down on the page.
6. Close this file (File/Close). Don't save your changes.

Macintosh Commands

⌘-N File/New/Document
⌘-M Item/Modify
⌘-W File/Close

Windows Commands

Ctrl-N File/New/Document
Ctrl-M Item/Modify
Ctrl-F4 File/Close

The Line Text-Path tool is used to create text on a straight or diagonal line.

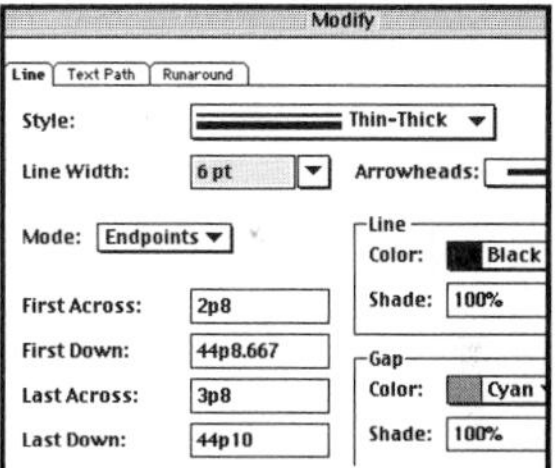

When a text path is selected, all the line attributes from the Line Modify dialog box can be applied to the path.

Use the Item tool to select a text path.

Macintosh Commands

⌘-N File/New/Document
⌘-A Edit/Select All

Windows Commands

Ctrl-N File/New/Document
Ctrl-A Edit/Select All

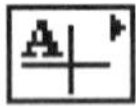

Orthogonal Text-Path tool

Item tool

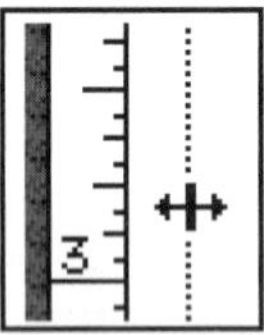

Click inside the vertical ruler and drag it out onto the page.

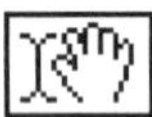

Content tool

LESSON 2
THE ORTHOGONAL TEXT-PATH TOOL

Unlike the Line Text-Path tool, which draws lines (paths) in any direction, the Orthogonal Text-Path tool draws only horizontal or vertical lines (paths). Text created on an orthogonal line is edited by selecting it and choosing options from the Style menu. To edit a path created with the Orthogonal Line tool, first select the path with either the Item tool or the Content tool. Then choose Item/Modify and make your selections in the Line Modify dialog box. Click on the Text Path tab and make further modifications in the Text Path Modify dialog box.

EXERCISE B

1. Create a new document. Display the Measurements palette (F9). Select the Orthogonal Text-Path tool and draw a horizontal line on the page. Once you finish drawing the line, the Content tool is automatically selected. To format the text path itself, select the Item tool and click on the text path to select it. Use the Line Style menu on the Measurements palette to format the path in 2-pt. black. Select the Content tool. When the I-beam cursor appears, type *horizontal line.* Click on the Center Align icon on the Measurements palette to center the text on the line. Choose Edit/Select All to select both words and format them to fit on the path.
2. Select the Orthogonal Text-Path tool again and draw a vertical line intersecting the horizontal line. Select the path with the Item tool and format it in 2 pt black. Select the Content tool and click the Center Align icon in the Measurements palette. Type *vertical line* on the path. Choose Edit/Select All and format the type as you did on the horizontal line.
3. Select the Item tool and move the vertical line to the right of the horizontal line. Your screen should resemble Figure 12.4.
4. Close this file or keep it open to use in the next exercise. Don't save your changes.

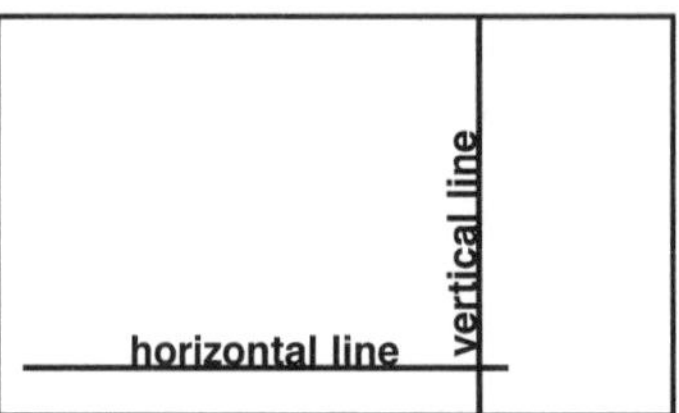

Figure 12.4. Horizontal and vertical text appear on separate paths.

LESSON 3
THE BÉZIER TEXT-PATH TOOL

The Bézier Text-Path tool in XPress works just as it does in any PostScript illustration program. Click to create the first anchor point and release the mouse. Click someplace else and release the mouse to create a straight or diagonal line. You can also click and drag before releasing the mouse button to create a curved path. To end the path, double-click the last anchor point before releasing the mouse button, or click on another tool in the Tool palette.

Bézier Text-Path tool

EDITING BÉZIER TEXT PATHS

To edit the path, select it with either the Item tool or the Content tool, click on one of the anchor points and drag to reshape the path. Anchor points that are diamond-shaped indicate a curve point; triangle points indicate a corner point where the two segments meet at right angles to the triangular anchor point.

Content tool

EXERCISE C

Item tool

1. Use the Item tool to select and delete everything on the page or add a new page to the active document. Select the Bézier Text-Path tool and click once on the page to set the first point. Click about two inches away from that first point to set the first straight line segment. Because you clicked and didn't drag, you are creating straight line segments. Click below that first segment to set the second segment. Continue clicking until you have five segments. Click on another tool to end the path.
2. Select the Content tool, click on the path, and type a sentence. As you type, the text follows the straight lines of the path. Click on any point and drag the segment to reshape the path. Notice how the text follows the new shape (Figure 12.5).

Figure 12.5. Dragging an anchor point or changing a Bézier point from square to smooth reshapes the path and reflows the text along the new path.

FYI

If you don't manually assign a color to the text path, it defaults to no color, displays as a gray line, and will not be visible.

Macintosh Commands

⌘-M Item/Modify

Windows Commands

Ctrl-M Item/Modify

Bézier Text-Path tool

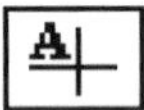

The Orthogonal Text-Path tool draws only horizontal or vertical paths.

The Center Align option is selected on the Measurements palette.

When selecting all of the text on any text-path, don't drag to select. Quadruple-click or use the Select All command to ensure that you've selected all the text, even the text hidden by the Overflow Indicator.

3. Select the Item tool and drag a selection marquee around the entire path to select it. Click on the text path and when the Move cursor appears, drag the path around the page to reposition it. Clicking on the text instead of on the path prevents you from selecting an anchor point and reshaping the path as you move it.
4. Select the Bézier Text-Path tool again, but this time, instead of clicking and releasing the mouse button, click *and drag* upward until a one-inch handle appears. Then release the mouse button. What you see are two direction handles connected to the Bézier point between them. That diamond-shaped anchor point is a smooth point, indicating that the segment connected to it will be a curve. Move the mouse about one inch to the right of that anchor point and click to set the curve (Figure 12.6).

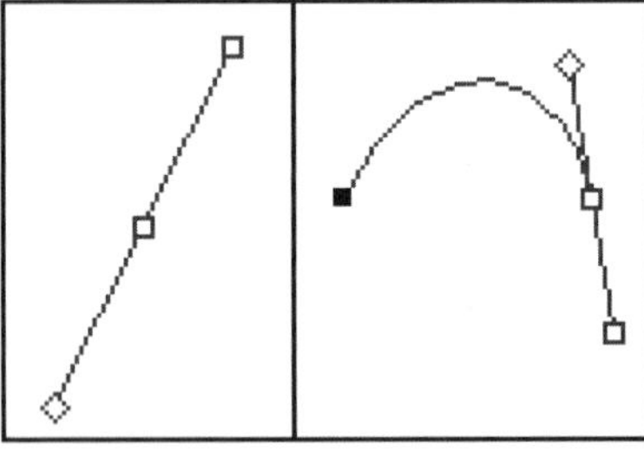

Figure 12.6. Clicking and dragging sets the direction of the curve. Clicking away from that anchor point creates the curve itself.

5. Click any other tool in the Tool palette to complete the path. This deselects the anchor points on the path but leaves the path itself selected. Choose Item/Modify to display the Line Modify dialog box. Select 1 from the Width pull-down menu and Black from the Color pull-down menu. Click on OK. The path remains selected.
6. Click on the Content tool. Type a few words on the path and notice how they follow the direction of the curve. Choose Edit/Select All and format the text. Click the Center Align icon in the Measurements palette to center the text on the path. Your screen should resemble Figure 12.7.

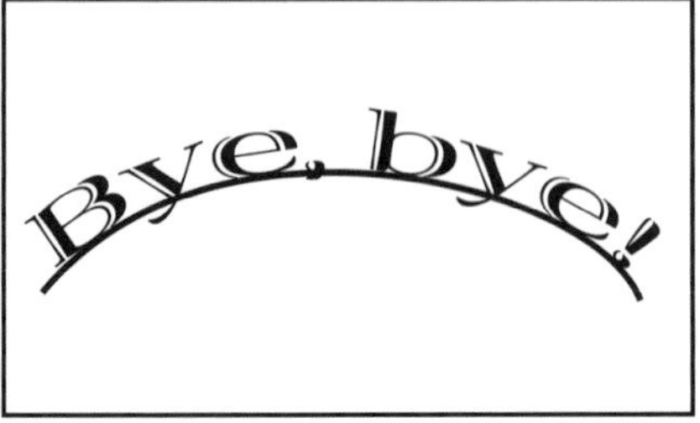

Figure 12.7. Both the path and text have been formatted.

7. Click on the right anchor point to select it and display its direction handles. Click on the anchor point between the two direction handles and drag to change the width of the curve. Click on one of the direction handle points and drag to change the slope of the curve. The text follows the new curves and remains centered on the path (Figure 12.8).

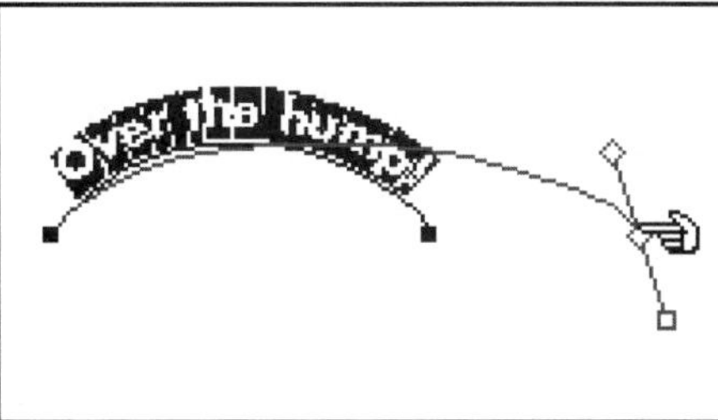

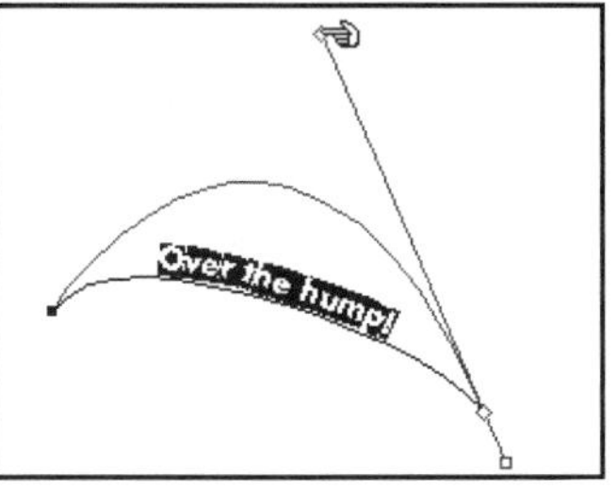

Figure 12.8. Dragging the selected anchor point adjusts the width of the curve (left). Dragging the direction handle adjusts its slope (right).

Macintosh Commands

⌘-A Edit/Select All

Windows Commands

Ctrl-A Edit/Select All

Freehand Text-Path tool

LESSON 4 THE FREEHAND TEXT-PATH TOOL

The Freehand Text-Path tool is used to draw open freehand paths in any shape. Use this tool as you would a pencil, drawing a path and then clicking on another tool. Like all Bézier paths, paths created with the Freehand Text-Path tool contain anchor points with direction handles that can be moved to change the shape of the path.

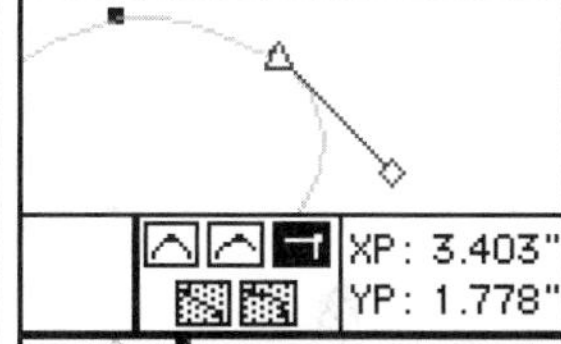

Use the Point icons in the Measurements palette to change the shape of a selected anchor point.

EXERCISE D

1. Delete all the paths on the page by selecting the Item tool, choosing Edit/Select All, and pressing the Delete/Backspace key.
2. Click on the Freehand Text-Path tool to select it and in one motion draw a figure 8 on the page. Click on any other tool to end the path. If you release the mouse button while drawing the figure 8, you cannot join the first path to another. Just start over again. The Freehand Text-Path tool does not create closed paths, so you will have to place your last point next to or on top of the first anchor point.

Tip

Select an anchor point and use the Point icons on the Measurements palette to change it to a Symmetrical or Smooth point, to get a better figure eight.

Macintosh Commands

⌘-W File/Close
⌘-A Edit/Select All

Windows Commands

Ctrl-F4 File/Close
Ctrl-A Edit/Select All

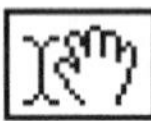

Content tool

The hollow square beneath the selected direction handle point on a Bézier text path indicates that you are moving a direction handle, not an anchor point.

Baseline Shift

When you're trying to position text on a text path to which you have applied a line style, you can use the Baseline Shift command to move the text up or down on the the path. Remember to select the text before applying any text commands.

3. Click on any of the black anchor points to display its direction handles and drag these handles to reshape the path. Click on the anchor point and drag to change the width of the curve. Click on a direction handle point and drag to change the slope of the curve. Continue moving anchor points and direction handle points until you are satisfied with the path. To change an anchor point, select it and click on the appropriate Point icon in the Measurements palette.
4. Make sure the Content tool is selected. When the I-beam cursor appears, type around the figure 8. Choose Edit/Select All to select all the text and format it so that it fits on the figure 8. Use the tracking arrows to add and delete space between the selected characters until they fit on the path. Your screen should resemble Figure 12.9.

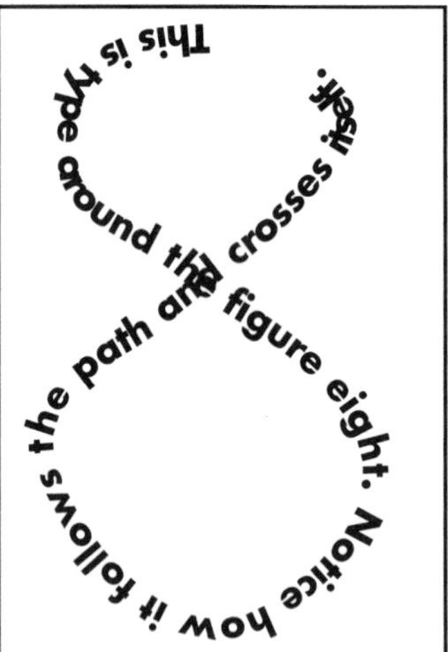

Figure 12.9. The text path (with a color of None) does not show; only the formatted type is displayed.

5. Close this file. Don't save your changes.

LESSON 5
TEXT PATH MODIFY DIALOG BOX

When a text path is selected and you select Item/Modify, the Text Path tab is available. Here you can change the position and orientation of the text on the path and specify the relationship between the text and the text path (Figure 12.10). After making your selections, use the Apply button to see the effect before closing the dialog box.

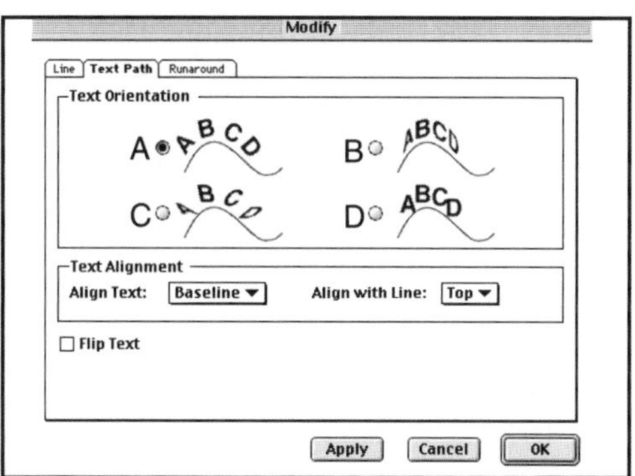

Figure 12.10. The four Text Orientation options include normal orientation (A), where the text characters are rotated but not slanted and sit on the path at the angle determined by the path itself; ribbon orientation (B) where characters are rotated, skewed, and sometimes flipped to produce a 3-D effect; skewed orientation (C) where the characters are slanted but not rotated; and stair-step orientation (D) where the characters are neither rotated nor skewed, but positioned in a stair-step effect depending on the angle of the text path.

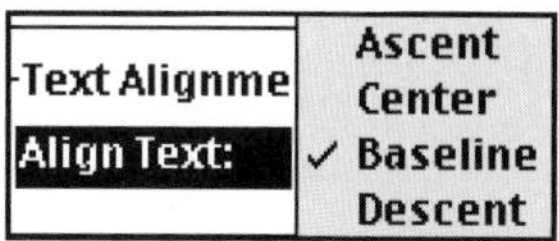

The four text alignment options in the Text Path Modify dialog box.

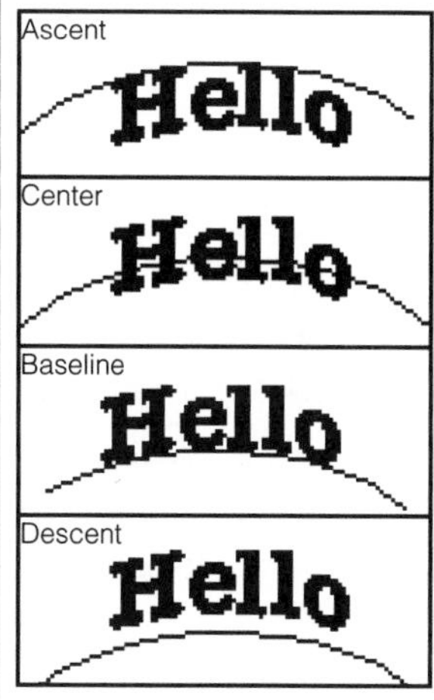

TEXT ALIGNMENT

Use the Align Text pull-down menu to select a text alignment option based on a specific *part of the font.* Text can be aligned on the path using the font's ascenders, center of its x-height, its baseline, or its descenders.

The Align with Line menu lets you choose which *part of the path* is aligned with the selection you made in the Align Text field. Depending on your selection in the Align Text field, text will sit on the top, center, or bottom of the path. Checking the Flip button flips the text 180° and positions it on the opposite side of the text path.

LESSON 6
FONT USAGE

Fonts come in two flavors: Type 1 PostScript fonts and TrueType fonts. Type 1 Postscript fonts consist of screen fonts (bitmap) fonts and Printer (PostScript) fonts. The screen/bitmap fonts are used only to *display* the font on the screen. If you have Adobe ATM installed, the pixel outline of the display fonts will be smoothed for easier reading on the screen. The printer/PostScript fonts are downloaded to the PostScript printer to create the mathematically smooth curves and lines built into the PostScript fonts. If the printer can't access the printer/Postscript font, you'll end up with jagged type on the printed page.

WARNING!

Don't use both Type 1 PostScript and TrueType fonts in the same document. It confuses printers and imagesetters.

ATM

Adobe's Deluxe Type Manager 4.0 lets you open a font suitcase when you are in QuarkXPress and XPress will then apply that font to any open documents that use it.

TrueType fonts, however, have both the screen/bitmap and printer/Postscript information built into one font. When you use TrueType fonts in your document, the PostScript information is built into the screen font and automatically goes to the printer.

Once you use text in any document, printing that document requires that the printer or imagesetter have access to the typefaces used in the document. If you create a file using Times New Roman and Futura Extended Bold, the printer must be able to access those fonts. If it can't, it will substitute (ugly) system fonts, causing text to reflow. That's the good news. The bad news is that the client won't pay for the job.

XPress has three ways of safeguarding against type disasters. When you open a document that uses fonts not installed in your system, an alert appears telling you so and giving you the opportunity to substitute installed fonts for the missing fonts. Click on a font and click the Replace button to replace the missing font with one installed in your system.

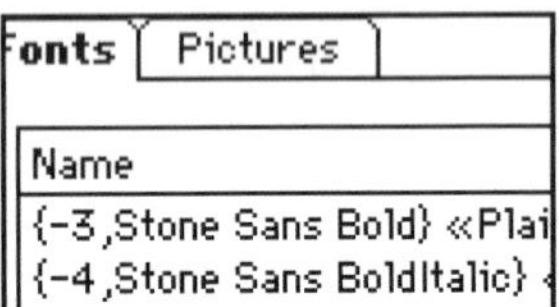

The Fonts Usage dialog box lists these fonts with negative numbers, indicating that the printer can't access them when printing the document.

FONTS USAGE DIALOG BOX

Another safeguard is the Fonts Usage dialog box. Choose Utilities/Usage and click the Fonts tab. The Fonts Usage dialog box lists every font in every font style used in the document. Any font or font style that can't be accessed by the system is displayed with a negative number. Click the Show First button to scroll to the first instance of that font in the document. Then click Replace and select a replacement font from one installed in your system.

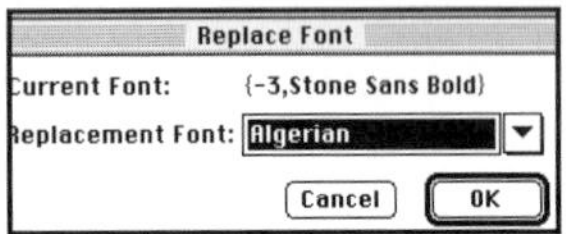

Click the Replace button in the Fonts Usage dialog box to display the Replace Font dialog box, where you can select a replacement font from those installed in your system.

COLLECT FOR OUTPUT

As a final precaution before sending the file to the imagesetter or printer, use the Collect for Output command under the File menu. Collect for Output creates a report listing every component in your document, including fonts used in any EPS files imported into the document with the Get Picture command. For example, if you used Minion Bold in an EPS image created in Illustrator or FreeHand and import that picture into an XPress document, the Collect for Output Report will tell you that Minion Bold was used in a picture file. Make sure all fonts listed in the Report are available to the printer.

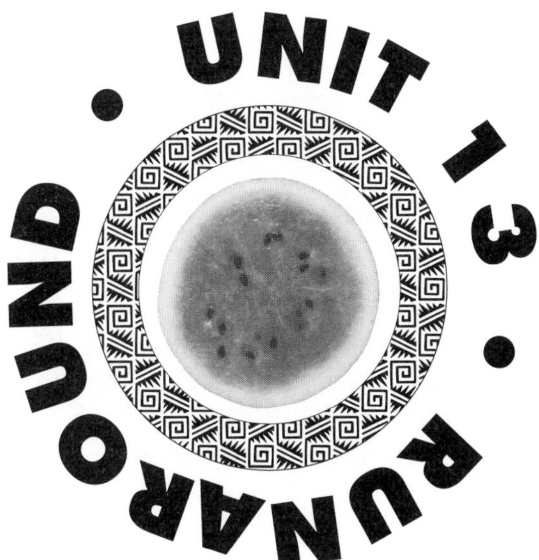

Image from
Produce Library 2
by Jeff Burke and
Lorraine Triolo,
for Artville

OVERVIEW

In this unit you will learn how to:
Wrap text around items and images
Apply different runaround values

TERMS

Auto Image Runaround
clipping path
embedded path
Image Runaround
Item Runaround
noise
None Runaround
smoothness
threshold

HOW IT WORKS:

This TIFF image ships from Artville with a path outline available. In Photoshop, select that Outline path in the Paths palette and select Clipping Path from the Paths palette. Delete the channel mask in the Channels palette so you can save the file as a Photoshop EPS file with the Outline path. In Illustrator, use the Place command to place the EPS melon file in the Illustrator document. Draw a circle with no fill and no stroke around the melon and choose Object/Mask/Make to make the melon image a perfect circle. Draw two larger circles from the center around the melon and fill the inner circle with white for the plate and the outer circle with an Illustrator pattern from the Pattern Fill Library. Use the Layers palette to display the objects in correct order. Select the three objects and align them using the Horizontal Align Center icon in the Align palette. Save the file as an Illustrator EPS file, import it into an XPress picture box, and use the Bézier Text Path tool to draw a path around the plate. Add the type and format it so that it flows around the graphic.

LESSON 1
RUNAROUND

What the rest of the world calls text wrap, QuarkXPress calls runaround. The term runaround describes the way text flows around an item or an item's contents. For example, when text encounters a picture box containing an image, the text has to decide how to deal with the obstruction. Should the text run around the picture box? Run behind the picture box? Or run around the picture? In other words, runaround defines the relationship of text and graphics when they meet on a blind date.

Sorry!

The Embedded Path option is available only when the image was exported from Photoshop with an embedded path.

Text has to make one of eight decisions when it encounters an item like a box, text path, or line. Should it just ignore the item and keep flowing? Should it flow around the picture box or around the picture? Should it ignore the box and flow around an embedded path in the picture? Should it flow around the non-white areas of the picture or should it just flow around the picture bounds? The selection you make in the Runaround Modify dialog box (Figure 13.1) determines just how the text wraps around the item or how it wraps around the graphic inside the picture box. Also be aware that the background color of the box affects how text displays as it runs around the graphic. If the box has any background color applied to it, the text behind the box will not be visible.

What you see is what you get

Whenever you select an option in the Runaround dialog box, the preview screen displays a thumbnail view of what the effect will look like on the document page. In some of the Runaround related dialog boxes, you have to press the Rescan button to display a preview of the changes.

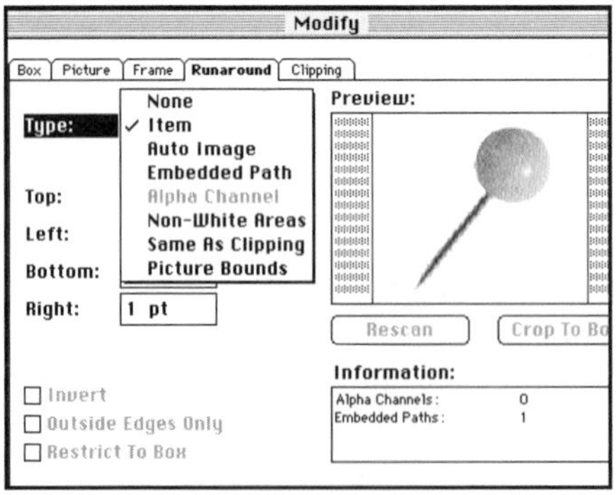

Figure 13.1. Use the Type menu in the Runaround Modify dialog box to specify exactly what the type wraps around: nothing, the box, the image itself, a Bézier path, any pixelated area, or the area adjacent to the picture.

NONE RUNAROUND

When you import a picture into a picture box and lay that box over text, if you select None for the Type from the Runaround Modify dialog box, that's what you get—no text wrap. The text is obstructed by the graphic and any text behind the picture box is not visible and will not print. Unless you change the Box Preferences (Edit/Preferences/General/Tool), the default in XPress is to create a picture box with a white background. So, any picture you import into this default picture box will automatically obscure any text behind the box.

EXERCISE A

1. Create a new document with an automatic text box and two columns. Display the Measurements palette (F9). Click inside the automatic text box on the page and choose File/Get Text. Navigate to the Unit 13 folder on the CD-ROM and double-click on the *Run.txt* file to import it into the selected text box. Reduce the height of the text box so the text fills both columns. Choose Edit/Select All and click the Justified icon on the Measurements palette.
2. Use any of the picture box tools to draw a picture box about two inches wide and three inches high. Use the Item tool to position the picture box in the center of the page between the two columns of text. Click on the Content tool to select it.
3. With the picture box still selected, press the Command/Ctrl key to display the temporary Item tool. Double-click on the picture box with the temporary Item tool and notice that the Box Modify dialog box displays white as the box's background color. Click on Cancel. Keep the picture box selected.
4. Choose File/Get Picture. In the Unit 13 folder on the CD-ROM, double-click on the *Cherries* file (a TIFF image) to import it into the picture box.
5. Press the Command-Option-Shift-F keys (Macintosh) or Ctrl-Alt-Shift-F keys (Windows) to proportionally scale the picture and fit it in the picture box. To increase or reduce the picture's size in 5% increments, press the same key combination, but substitute the < or > keys for the F key.
6. Once the picture is positioned in the box, press the Command/Ctrl key to display the temporary Item tool again. Double-click on the picture box and notice that now the box color is None. Click on Cancel to exit the dialog box and return to the document page.

Macintosh Commands

⌘-N File/New/Document
⌘-E File/Get Text/Picture
⌘-A Edit/Select All
⌘-Option-Shift-F Fits a picture proportionally in a picture box

Windows Commands

Ctrl-N File/New/Document
Ctrl-E File/Get Text/Picture
Ctrl-A Edit/Select All
Ctrl-Option-Shift-F Fits a picture proportionally in a picture box

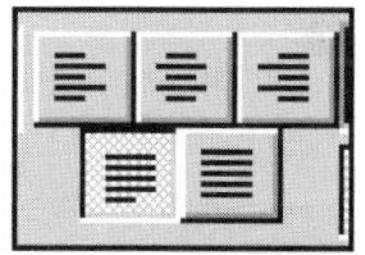

The Justified Align icon is highlighted in the Measurements palette.

FYI

If you import the graphic with the Item tool selected, you must switch to the Content tool before you can manipulate the image.

Image info

The *Cherries*, *Apple*, *Lime*, and *Melon* images are from *Produce Libraries 1* and *2* by Jeff Burke and Lorraine Triolo, for Artville. The *Lady* file is taken from *Roundhead Executives* by Barton Stabler, for Artville.

Macintosh Commands

⌘-T Item/Runaround
⌘-O File/Open
⌘-Option-S File/Save as

Windows Commands

Ctrl-T Item/Runaround
Ctrl-O File/Open
Ctrl-Alt-S File/Save as

7. Choose Item/Runaround to display the Runaround dialog box. Use the Type pull-down menu to select None. A thumbnail of the text wrap—or, as in this case, the lack thereof—appears to the right. Click on OK. The text is obscured by the graphic because there is no text wrap applied (Figure 13.2). Moving the graphic with the Content tool or the picture box with the Item tool hides and displays different text characters behind the graphic and the box.

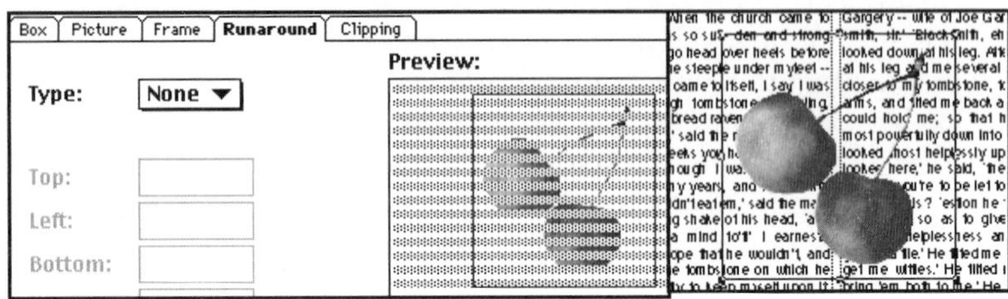

Figure 13.2. When None is selected for Runaround, the text does not run around or wrap around the image, but is obscured by the image. The thumbnail in the Runaround dialog box displays this by showing the text bars running through the graphic instead of around it.

8. Save this file as *None.qxd* in your Projects folder. You will need it for the next exercise.

FYI

When clipping and runaround values are applied to an image, the size and position of the picture box are totally ignored. The text will wrap around the graphic using the values specified in the Runaround and Clipping dialog boxes, not in the Box Modify dialog box.

LESSON 2
ITEM RUNAROUND

In XPress, an item is either a box, a line, or a text path. When you select Item for the runaround, the text wraps around the boundaries of the picture box, line, or text path regardless of the physical dimensions of the item or of the picture background inside a box.

EXERCISE B

Item tool

1. If necessary, open the *None.qxd* file you created in the last exercise or open the *None.qxd* file in the Unit 13 folder on the CD-ROM.
2. Click on the picture box with the Item tool to select it and choose Item/Runaround. Select Item from the Type menu. The thumbnail displays the type running around the item, the picture box. Click on OK. Notice that the text now runs around the outside of the picture box (Figure 13.3).

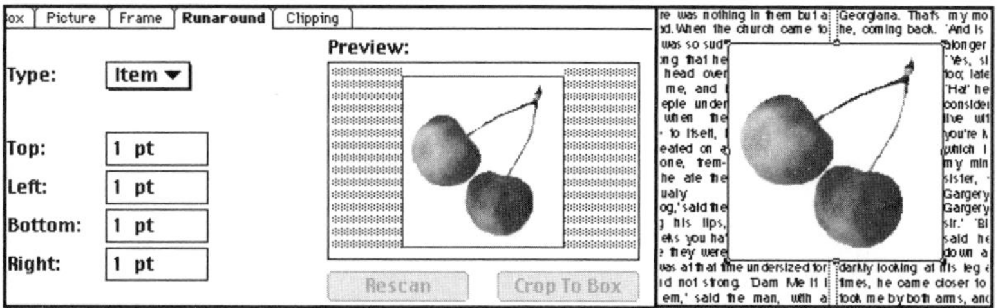

Figure 13.3. When Item is selected for the runaround, the text wraps around the item, in this case, the picture box.

Macintosh Commands

⌘-T Item/Runaround

Windows Commands

Ctrl-T Item/Runaround

3. With the picture box still selected, choose Item/Runaround again and leave Item selected from the Type menu. Type 20 in the Top field, press the Tab key, and type 20 in the Left, Bottom, and Right fields. Click on Apply. The bounding box moves away from the image, leaving more distance between the text and the text box. Click on OK. The text wraps around the boundary of the box (Figure 13.4).

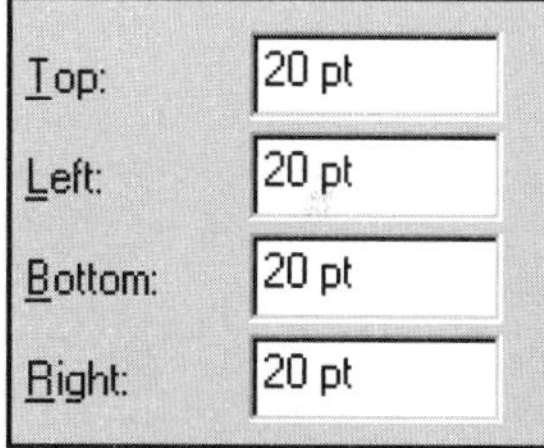

The values you type in the offset fields of the Runaround dialog box determine how much space XPress adds between the text and the item or graphic.

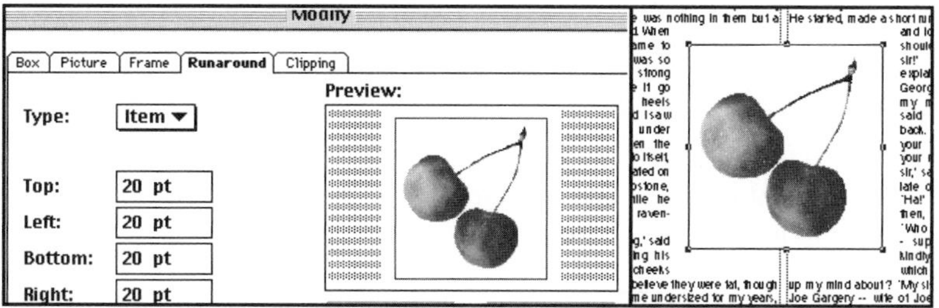

Figure 13.4. Increasing the default values in the Top, Left, Bottom, and Right fields expands the distance between the text and picture box.

LESSON 3 IMAGE RUNAROUND

Thus far you have been running text around the item, the picture box. You can also run text around the image, bypassing both the picture box and the white background that is created whenever an image is saved as a TIFF or EPS image. Even if you specify a transparent background in an image manipulation program like Adobe Photoshop, when that image is saved as a TIFF image, a white background is created, because Photoshop needs to add pixels to complete the rectangular or square image. Likewise, any image saved in an EPS illustration program like Adobe Illustrator or Macromedia FreeHand always includes a white background behind the image.

FYI

Digital artists for high-quality image vendors like Artville frequently export paths with the high-resolution images. This saves you the time and effort of creating those paths with the Pen tool in the graphics application and provides XPress with a path on which to base the runaround path.

There are five options under the Type menu that let you specify how the text wraps around the image: Auto Image, Embedded Path, Alpha Channel, Non-White Areas, and Same As Clipping.

Tip

Double-click on any item with the Item tool to display its Modify dialog box.

AUTO IMAGE

The Auto Image option will run the text around the image using the Outset value to specify how much space to leave between the text and the graphic—not between the text and the picture box. Selecting Auto Image automatically changes the background color of the picture box to None and creates an uneditable path around the image.

NOISE

Rescan

When making changes in the Runaround and Clipping dialog box, if the Rescan button is available, click it to see the effect of your changes before exiting the dialog box.

The Noise, Smoothness, and Threshold options let you specify how closely the automatic path runs around the image. Because a major runaround path can contain several smaller paths, use the Noise field to specify which paths should be deleted and which paths included when creating a single runaround path. For example, a picture of a steaming cup of coffee with spikes of steam coming from it could generate one runaround path for the cup and another for the steam. Both of these paths are considered to be one runaround path. To delete the small steam paths, enter a value in the Noise field that corresponds to the diameter of the steam spike (like 10 points). Click the Rescan button below the thumbnail to apply the new values (Figure 13.5).

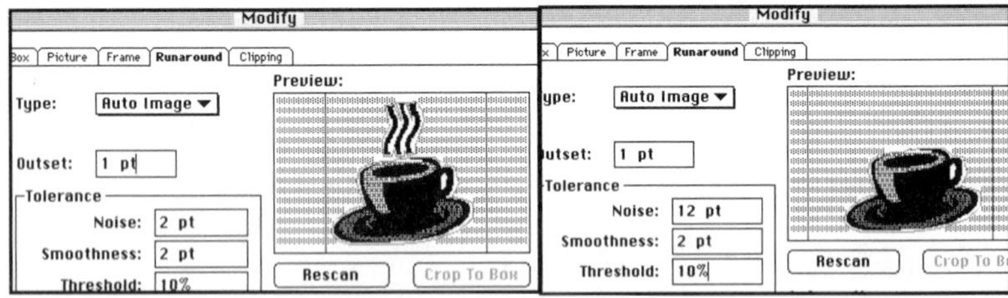

Figure 13.5. When the Noise value is increased to 12 points, the spikes of steam are clipped out of the path and the text will run around only the cup and saucer.

SMOOTHNESS

The Smoothness value specifies how accurate the runaround path is. The lower the value, the more complex the path, with a greater number of points. The higher the value, the less complex and therefore less accurate the path. However, more complex paths may give you problems when printing, so keep the Smoothness value as high as possible and click the Rescan button to check the path.

THRESHOLD

The Threshold value refers to the line between dark pixels and light pixels and tells XPress how to determine which is which. Any pixel lighter than the Threshold value is clipped from the runaround path and any pixel darker than the Threshold value is included in the runaround path. Clicking the Rescan button lets you see how your new values are applied.

EMBEDDED PATH

The Embedded Path option reads a clipping path that was created in the graphic application like Photoshop and exported with the image. This path, embedded in the image when it was exported, is used as the basis of a new clipping path in XPress (Figure 13.6).

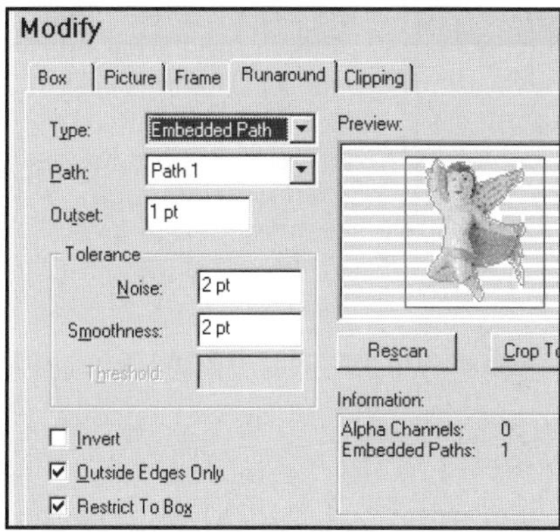

Figure 13.6. This image was saved as a TIFF file in Photoshop with an embedded path that XPress calls Path 1 under the Path menu on the left side of the dialog box.

ALPHA CHANNEL

Like paths, alpha channels can also be embedded in a Photoshop image. You can select the alpha channel from which XPress will create the runaround path.

NON-WHITE AREAS

This option creates a runaround path based on the picture contents using the values in the Threshold field. Use this option to outline a dark object within a larger white or near-white background. You can also check the Invert box to run the path around the white areas and clip out the dark areas. Make changes under Tolerance and click the Rescan button to see how the path looks (Figure 13.7).

Clipping Paths

To practice working with clipping paths, do the following:

1. Launch Photoshop and open the *Sunfl* file (a TIFF image) in the Unit 13 folder on the CD-ROM.
2. Use any of Photoshop's selection tools to select the flower—not the background.
3. Choose Make Work Path from the Paths palette menu.

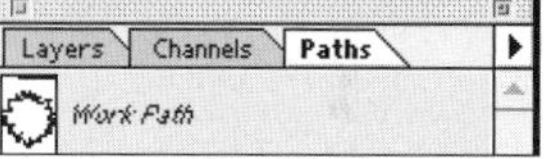

4. Choose Save Path from the Paths palette menu and name the path.
5. Save the file as a TIFF file.

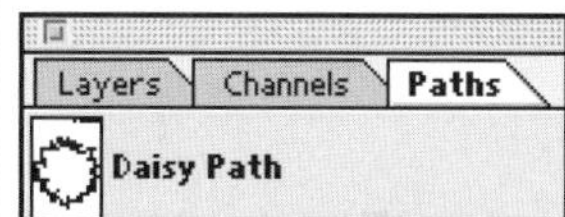

6. In XPress, import the picture into a picture box. Because you "clipped out" the background, only the flower appears. Use the Clipping and Runaround commands to run the text around the flower petals.

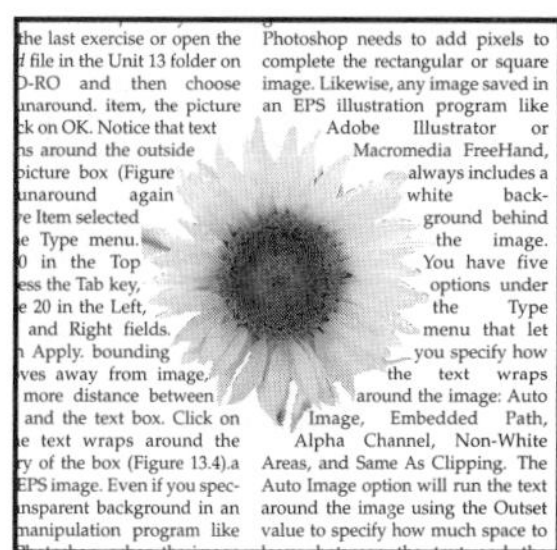

the last exercise or open the
d file in the Unit 13 folder on
D-RO and then choose
unaround. item, the picture
k on OK. Notice that text
ns around the outside
picture box (Figure
unaround again
e Item selected
e Type menu.
0 in the Top
ess the Tab key,
e 20 in the Left,
and Right fields.
n Apply. bounding
ves away from image,
more distance between
and the text box. Click on
e text wraps around the
ry of the box (Figure 13.4).a
EPS image. Even if you spec-
nsparent background in an
manipulation program like
Photoshop needs to add pixels to
complete the rectangular or square
image. Likewise, any image saved in
an EPS illustration program like
Adobe Illustrator or
Macromedia FreeHand,
always includes a
white back-
ground behind
the image.
You have five
options under
the Type
menu that let
you specify how
the text wraps
around the image: Auto
Image, Embedded Path,
Alpha Channel, Non-White
Areas, and Same As Clipping. The
Auto Image option will run the text
around the image using the Outset
value to specify how much space to

Image scanned from a photograph by Joseph A. Dai.

FYI

The clipping path is selected from the Type menu in the Clipping dialog box and specifies which part of the picture will be displayed on the page. Unless you do this first, Same As Clipping will not be available from the Type menu in the Runaround dialog box.

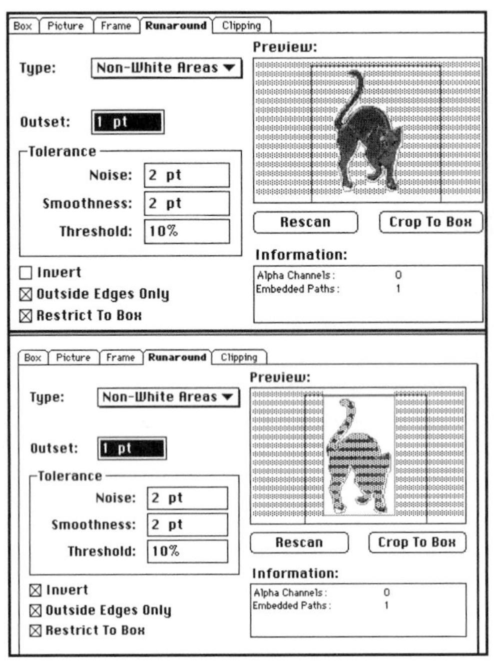

Figure 13.7. Select Non-White areas to run the path around the dark edges of the image. Click to select Invert to run the path around the white areas of the image. The Information area tells you that there is one embedded path in this image, which could also be used to create a runaround path.

SAME AS CLIPPING

This option creates a runaround path based on the specifications you set in the Clipping Modify dialog box. In Figure 13.8 the TIFF image with its embedded path was imported into XPress. In the Clipping Modify dialog box, the Outset value was increased to 12 points and the Outside Edges Only option was selected. This caused the clipping path to appear around the outside boundaries of the image only and not around the inside areas between their hands. In the Runaround dialog box, when Same As Clipping was selected, the runaround path followed the expanded clipping path.

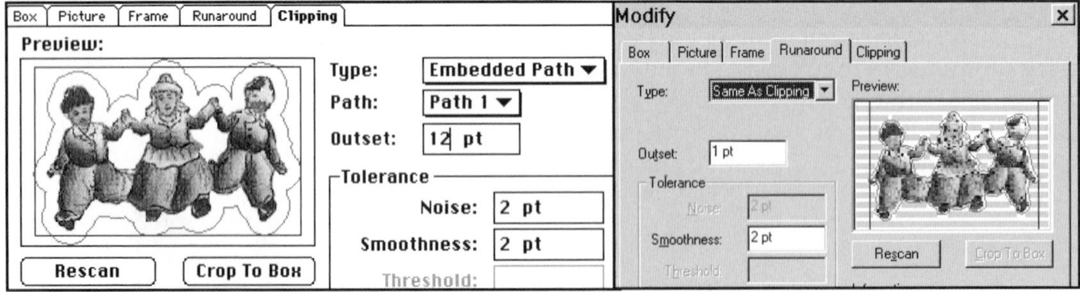

Figure 13.8. The Outset value in the Clipping Modify dialog box expands the embedded clipping path. When Same As Clipping is selected in the Runaround dialog box, the text runs around the expanded path.

PICTURE BOUNDS

The Picture Bounds option runs the text around the rectangular background of the imported picture, including any white background area that was saved with the picture. The values entered in the Top, Left, Bottom, and Right fields specify the distance of the text from the picture boundary (Figure 13.9).

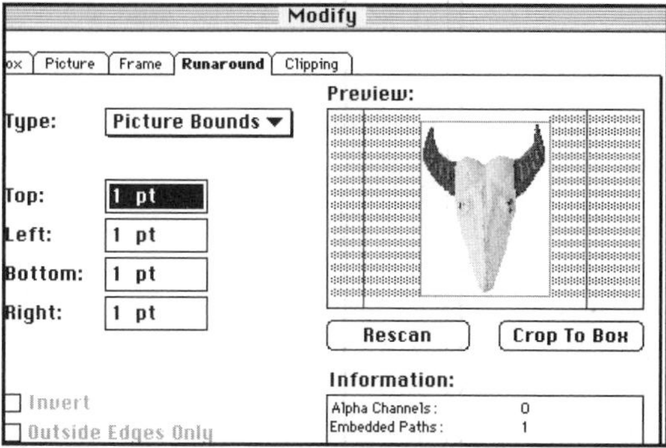

Figure 13.9. The Picture Bounds Runaround option wraps the text around the rectangular bounds of the picture's background.

EXERCISE C

1. Create a new document (File/New/Document) with two columns and an automatic text box. Display the Measurements palette (F9).
2. Click in the text box on the first page of the document and choose File/Get Text. Navigate to the Unit 13 folder on the CD-ROM and double-click on the *Run.txt* file to import it into the text box.
3. Choose Edit/Select All and click the Justify icon on the Measurements palette to justify the text. Copy and paste the text so that it fills both columns.
4. Use any of the picture box tools to draw a picture box about 3 inches wide and 3 inches high. With the box still selected, choose File/Get Picture. Double-click on the *Apple* file (a TIFF image) in the Unit 13 folder on the CD-ROM to import it into the picture box. With the picture box selected, choose Item/Runaround to display the Runaround Modify dialog box. The default Runaround type is Item. Click on OK. The text wraps around the outside of the picture box (Figure 13.10).

Macintosh Commands

⌘-N File/New/Document
⌘-E File/Get Text/Picture
⌘-A Edit/Select All
⌘-T item/Runaround

Windows Commands

Ctrl-N File/New/Document
Ctrl-E File/Get Text/Picture
Ctrl-A Edit/Select All
Ctrl-T Item/Runaround

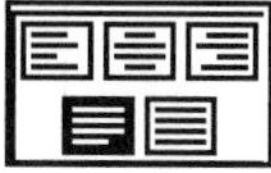

Justified icon selected in the Measurements palette

Standard-Shape Rectangle Picture Box tool

Bézier Picture Box tool

Macintosh Commands

⌘-T item/Runaround

Windows Commands

Ctrl-T Item/Runaround

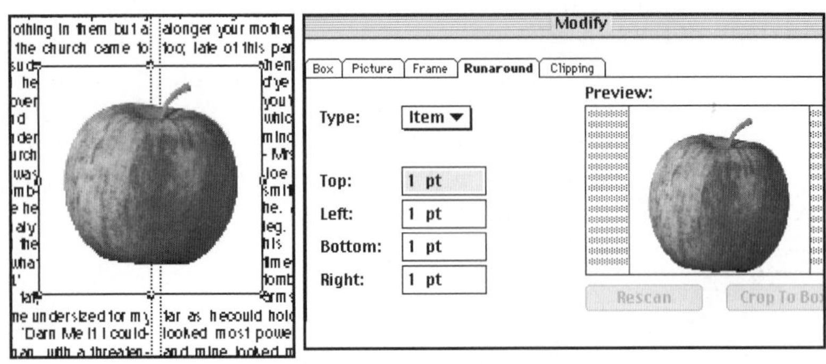

Figure 13.10. Item runaround wraps the text around the item (picture box), not the contents (graphic).

5. With the picture box still selected, choose Item/Runaround again. Select Auto Image from the Type menu. Click OK at the alert to delete the existing clipping path. Increase the Threshold value to 50, and click the Rescan button. Notice that some of the pixels in the left side of the image are clipped out because the higher threshold value defines more pixels as white and excludes them from the clipping path. Return the Threshold value to 10% and click the Rescan button. Click on OK. The text now wraps around the image, not around the box, and the background color of the box is None (Figure 13.11).

FYI

The color of the runaround path defaults to magenta. You can change this default color in the Application/Display Preferences dialog box. Change the Grid color to another color.

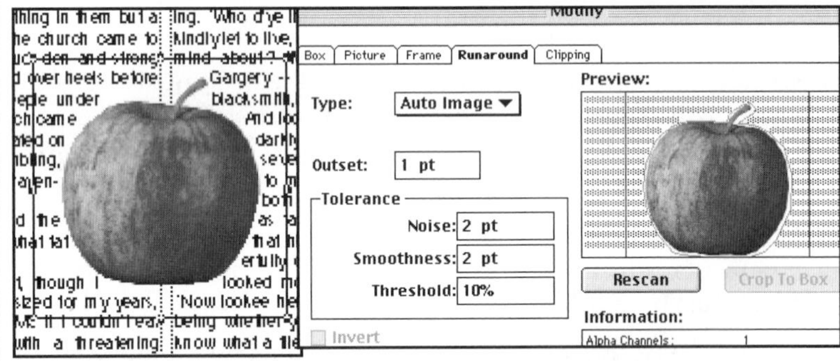

Figure 13.11. The Auto Image option runs the text around the outside of the picture, not the picture box.

6. Choose Item/Runaround again and select Embedded Path from the Type menu. The magenta runaround path appears around the non-white areas of the image, much as it did with the Auto Image command. However, unlike the Auto Image option, Embedded Path creates the runaround based entirely on the outline of the embedded path, not on any algorithm in XPress. Click on OK.

7. Click inside the picture box with the Content tool and press the Delete key to delete just the image, not the box. With the picture box still selected, choose File/Get Picture and import the *Lady* image (an EPS file) from the Unit 13 folder on the CD-ROM. Resize the box to fit the image. Choose Item/Runaround and select Non-White Areas. Click to deselect the Outside Edges Only box and notice the small path that's created inside the graphic, under the lady's neck. Change the Noise value to 20 and click the Rescan button. The interior path disappears because a higher Noise value deletes smaller paths, making them part of the larger path. Click on OK.
8. Choose Item/Runaround again and click on the Clipping tab or choose Item/Clipping. In the Clipping dialog box, choose Non-White Areas from the Type menu and change the Outset value to 8. Notice how the magenta outline expands in the thumbnail image. Click on the Runaround tab and choose Same As Clipping from the Type menu. Click on OK. Your image should resemble Figure 13.12.

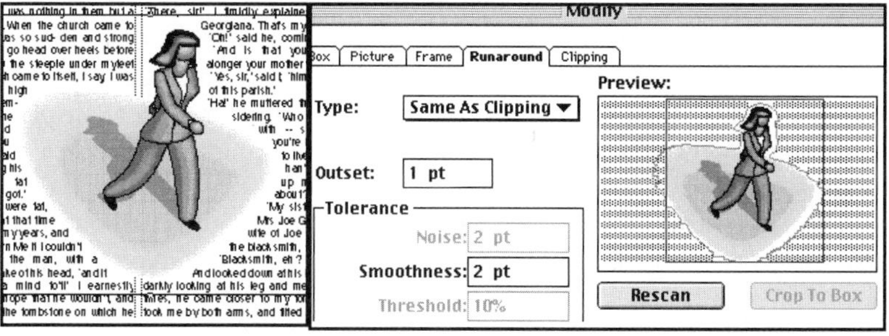

Figure 13.12. The Same As Clipping option in the Runaround dialog box runs the text around the clipping path specified earlier in the Clipping dialog box.

9. Choose Item/Runaround once more and choose Picture Bounds from the Type menu. The runaround path condenses to include only that part of the image background that is the default 1 point away from the image area. Type 10 in the Top field, press the Tab key twice, and type 10 in the Bottom field. Press the Rescan button and notice that the magenta thumbnail is offset 10 points from the top and bottom of the image. Click on OK. Your screen should resemble Figure 13.13.

Macintosh Commands

⌘-E File/Get Text/Picture
⌘-T item/Runaround
⌘-Option-T Item/Clipping

Windows Commands

Ctrl-E File/Get Text/Picture
Ctrl-T Item/Runaround
Ctrl-Alt-T Item/Clipping

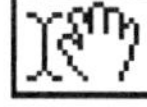

Content tool

FYI

If you click OK to close the Clipping dialog box, choose Item//Runaround to display the Runaround dialog box.

Macintosh Commands

⌘-W File/Close

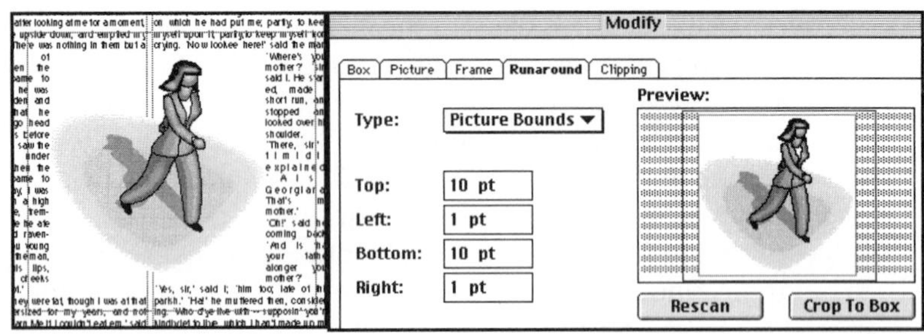

Figure 13.13. When Picture Bounds is selected in the Runaround dialog box, you can expand the boundary of the image background by typing values higher than the default 1 point in the Top, Left, Bottom, and Right fields.

10. Close this file (File/Close). Don't save your changes.

LESSON 4 CLIPPING PATHS

When you import a high-resolution image like a TIFF or EPS file into a picture box, that image comes in with the background against which it was created in the graphic program. For example, if you draw a flower in Adobe Illustrator or Corel Draw and export that file as an EPS file, the flower will appear against a white background even though you do not specify a background color in the drawing program. Even specifying a background of None in the drawing program (Figure 13.14) results in the image being displayed against a white background in XPress (Figure 13.15). It is this white background that you clipped out in the earlier exercise to wrap the text around the graphic.

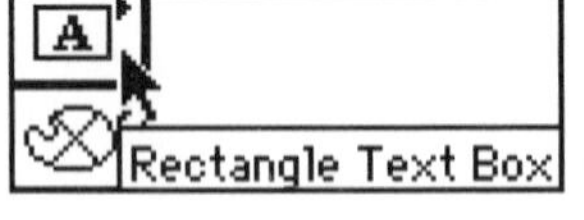

Rectangle Text Box tool

Figure 13.14. The image is specified with no fill and no stroke in both versions of Adobe Illustrator.

Figure 13.15. The image exported as an EPS file and placed in a picture box displays the white area around the image boundaries that obscures the text.

Macintosh Commands

⌘-N File/New/Document
⌘-E File/Get Text/Picture

Windows Commands

Ctrl-N File/New/Document
Ctrl-E File/Get Text/Picture

The only way to avoid having the image background opaque is to create a clipping path in a program like Photoshop and export that clipping path with the image as part of the EPS file format, as was done with the *Lady* image. QuarkXPress has always read such a clipping path, but in version 4.0, you can also create a clipping path.

A clipping path is a boundary around part of the image which makes the image area inside the boundary opaque and the image area outside the boundary transparent.

Export paths to file:
Apple.tiff.ai
Write: Apple Outline Path

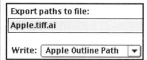

A clipping path is created in Adobe Photoshop and exported to Adobe Illustrator via the Export command in Photoshop.

EXERCISE D

1. Create a new file with an automatic text box and two columns. Display the Measurements palette (F9). Make sure the text box is selected. Select the Content tool. Choose File/Get Text and open the *Run.txt* file in the Unit 13 folder on the CD-ROM. The text almost fills the two columns on the page. Shorten the text box so that both columns are filled with text.

Bézier Picture Box tool

2. Use any rectangle picture box tool to draw a picture box about 3 inches wide and 4 inches high between the two columns and keep it selected.
3. Choose File/Get Picture and highlight the *Lime* file (a TIFF image) in the Unit 13 folder on the CD-ROM. Click on Open.

Standard-Shape Rectangle Picture Box tool

4. Adjust the picture box and the picture so that the image appears centered in the box. Notice the white area around the lime. This is the area that will be clipped out of the image so the text can run around the graphic.

Macintosh Commands

⌘-Option-T Item/Clipping

Windows Commands

Ctrl-Alt-T Item/Clipping

5. With the picture box still selected, choose Item/Clipping to display the Clipping Modify dialog box (Figure 13.16).

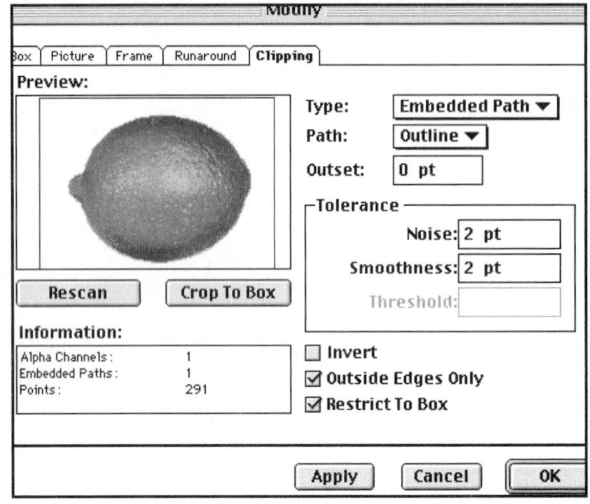

Figure 13.16. When a picture box is selected, the Clipping command is used to specify a clipping path around the image.

6. Use the Type pull-down menu on the right side of the dialog box to select Non-White Areas. This will draw a green clipping path around the colored edge of the image.
7. Set the Outset value to 0 points so that the clipping path will be drawn against the edge of the image without including any of the white space.
8. Make sure that Outside Edges Only and Restrict to Box are selected. Because the Lime image has no interior holes like the Phone image in Figure 13.17, you only need to have the clipping path run around the outside of the image.

Figure 13.17. You would deselect the Outside Edges Only option in the Clipping dialog box in order to draw a clipping path around both the exterior edge of the image and the interior edge next to the cord.

9. Notice the green clipping path running around the outside of the lime (Figure 13.18). The image area inside that green path will be opaque against the page. The white area outside the clipping path will be transparent against the page.

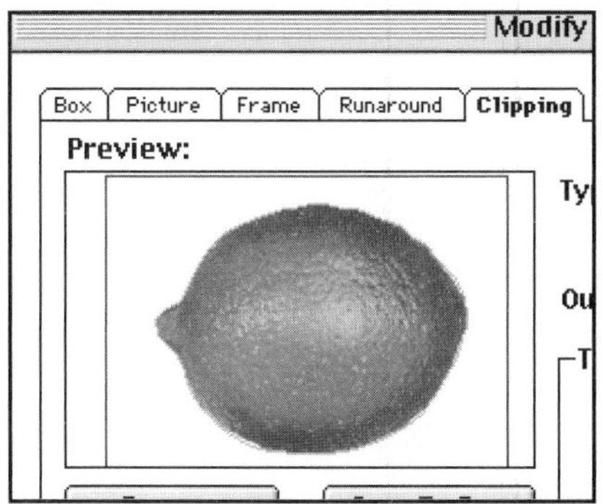

Figure 13.18. The green clipping path appears around the outside edges of the image.

10. Still in the Clipping dialog box, click on the Runaround tab to display the Runaround dialog box (Figure 13.19). Choose Same As Clipping from the Type pull-down menu, and notice that the display text now runs around the image along the edge of the clipping path.

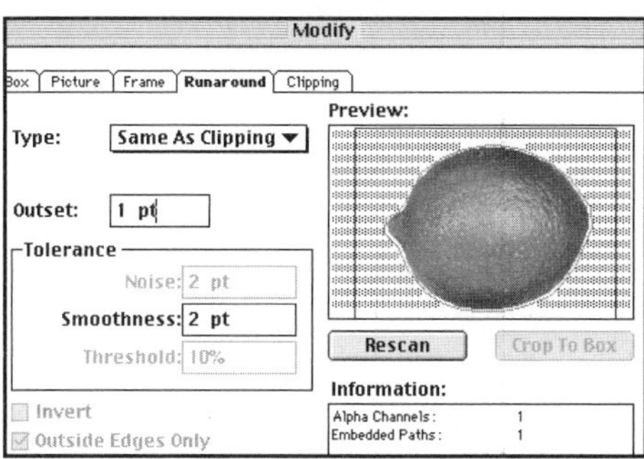

Figure 13.19. Clicking on the Runaround tab in the Modify dialog box displays the Runaround dialog box.

11. Click on OK. Your screen should resemble Figure 13.20. The text now runs around the image because the white background that was originally part of the image was made transparent by the clipping path. In the next exercise you will learn how to edit the clipping path and the distance between the clipping path and the text.

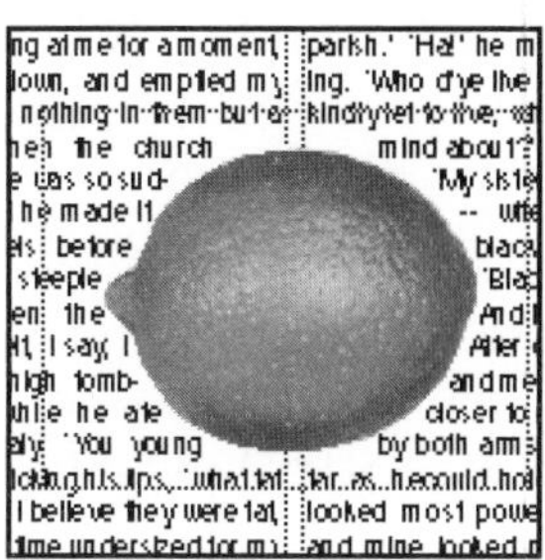

Figure 13.20. Once the clipping path is drawn *and the Runaround command is applied to that clipping path,* the type will wrap around the clipping path, leaving the white background transparent against the text.

Viva la difference!

The difference between the Clipping dialog box and the Runaround dialog box is that in the Clipping dialog box you specify which part of the image is to be displayed in the picture box by creating a clipping path. In the Runaround dialog box you specify how the text runs around that clipping path.

FYI

To center the image in the picture box without affecting the size of the image, press Command/Ctrl-Shift-M.

Macintosh Commands

⌘-N File/New/Document
⌘-Y Edit/Preferences/Document
⌘-E File/Get Text/Picture
⌘-M Item/Modify
⌘-T item/Runaround

Windows Commands

Ctrl-N File/New/Document
Ctrl-Y Edit/Preferences/Document
Ctrl-E File/Get Text/Picture
Ctrl-M Item/Modify
Ctrl-T Item/Runaround

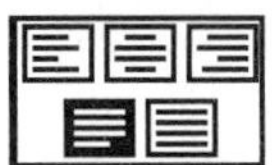

The Justify Align icon is selected in the Measurements palette.

Oval Picture Box tool

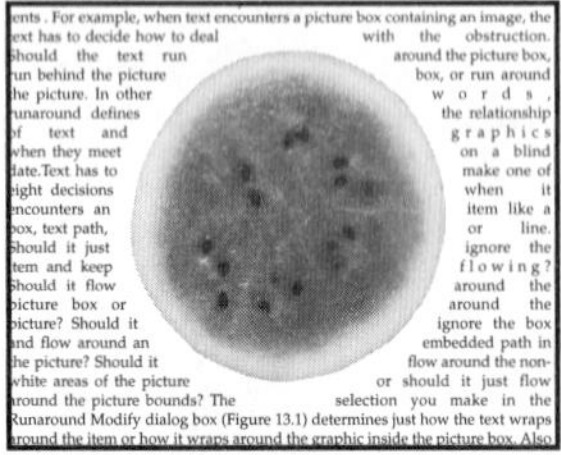

Image from ***Produce Library 2*** by Jeff Burke and Loraine Triolo, for Artville

Figure 13.21. Only after selecting Run Text Around All Sides from the Text modify dialog box can you apply a text offset value from the Runaround dialog box.

LESSON 5
SINGLE COLUMN RUNAROUND

In the old days (Version 3.3), if you wanted to run text around all the sides of an item, you had to position that item somewhere between two columns of text. Version 4.0 lets you run the text around all sides of an item even if the text is in a single column. This runaround command is not available from the Runaround Modify dialog box because it is a function of the *text box*, not the graphic.

EXERCISE E

1. Create a new document (File/New/Document) without facing pages and with two-inch margins, one column, and an automatic text box.
2. Choose Edit/Preferences/Document and choose Off from the Auto Page Insertion pull-down menu. You only need one page in this document. Click on OK.
3. Click inside the single-column text box on page 1. Choose File/Get Text. Navigate to the Unit 13 folder on the CD-ROM and double-click on *Run.txt* to import it into the selected text box. Click the Justify Align icon in the Measurements palette.
4. Select the Oval Picture box tool and press the Shift key while drawing a circle about three inches in diameter. Choose File/Get Picture. Navigate to the Unit 13 folder on the CD-ROM and double-click on the *Melon* file (a TIFF file) to import it into the picture box.
5. With the picture box selected, press Command-Option-Shift-F (Macintosh) or Ctrl-Alt-Shift-F (Windows) to proportionally resize the picture to the box.
6. Click inside the text box to select the text box. Choose Item/Modify. Click on the Text tab to display the Text Modify dialog box. Check the Run Text Around All Sides check box to select that option. Click on OK. The text runs very closely around the picture box.
7. Click on the picture box to select it. Choose Item/Runaround. Type 12 in the Outset field to create 12 points of space between the text and the picture box. Click on OK. Your screen should resemble Figure 13.21 (sidebar).
8. Close this file. Don't save your changes.

UNIT 14
Lines and Frames

OVERVIEW

In this unit you will learn how to:
Draw horizontal, vertical, Bézier, and freehand lines
Reshape and convert lines
Apply frames to boxes
Create and edit custom dashes and stripes
Align items
Specify tool color preferences

TERMS

Bézier line
dash
Endpoints
First Point
frame
Last Point
Midpoint
stripe

HOW IT WORKS:

Use the Edit Dashes & Stripes dialog box to create a new dash. Move the arrows in the ruler area to create breaks in the line. Change the values in the Repeats Every dialog box to adjust the space between the segments. Select a Miter Style to specify how corners will look. Select an Endcap option to determine how the ends of the individual dashes will look. Because this dash was applied to a rectangle, the Stretch to Corners option was selected to make the dash pattern stretch evenly along the dimensions of the box and display symmetrical corners. When the dash was applied to the the box, Frame and Gap colors were selected in the Frame dialog box.

Macintosh Commands

⌘-N File/New/Document
⌘-O File/Open

Windows Commands

Ctrl-N File/New/Document
Ctrl-O File/Open

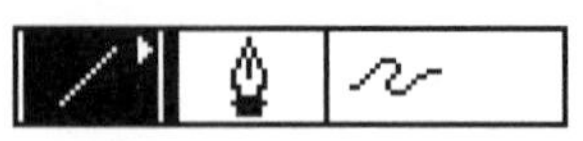

Drag the Line Tool out to select the Bézier Line tool (center).

Very important info!

You must have a line or box selected before you can apply a dash or stripe from the Frame dialog box. And don't forget to assign the dash or stripe a width from the Width field. The Width field in the Frame dialog box defaults to 0 points for the width, and unless you assign a width greater than 0, you won't be able to see the frame—because it isn't there!

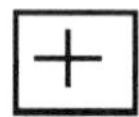

Orthogonal Line tool

LESSON 1
TYPES OF LINES

There are four kinds of lines in QuarkXPress 4.0 and four different tools used to create them (Figure 14.1). The Line tool is used to create straight lines at any angle; the Freehand Line tool creates freehand lines with curved segments connected by Bézier points; the Bézier Line tool creates lines with both straight and curve segments between Bézier points; and the Orthogonal Line tool draws only horizontal and vertical lines.

Figure 14.1. The Line tool, Freehand Line tool, Bézier Line tool, and Orthogonal Line tool in the Tool palette.

Although the Tool palette defaults to displaying only the Line tool and the Orthogonal Line tool, you can display the other two tools in the Tool palette by pressing the Control key (Macintosh) or Ctrl key (Windows) before clicking on the Line tool's triangle and dragging to select another tool. To remove a tool from the Tool palette, Control/Ctrl-click on the tool. At least one tool from a tool's pop-out menu must appear on the Tool palette.

EXERCISE A

1. Create a new, single-column document with one-inch margins and without an automatic text box. Display the Measurements palette (F9) and the Colors palette (F12). Click on the Line tool to select it. Click and drag on the page to draw a line at any angle. Release the mouse button.
2. Select the Line tool again and drag to draw another line. Before releasing the mouse button, press the Shift key to constrain that line to a 45° angle.
3. Click on the Orthogonal Line tool to select it. Drag to draw a horizontal line. Select the Orthogonal Line tool again and drag to draw a vertical line. You cannot draw a diagonal line with the Orthogonal Line tool.

4. With the vertical line selected, use the Measurements palette to select 12 for the width of the line, Dotted for the style, and a left-pointing arrowhead for the top of the line (Figure 14.2). Click on the selection point at either end of the line and drag to lengthen or shorten the line.

Figure 14.2. The W pull-down menu in the Measurements palette is used to select a point size, the left menu to select a line style, and the right menu to select an arrowhead style for a selected line.

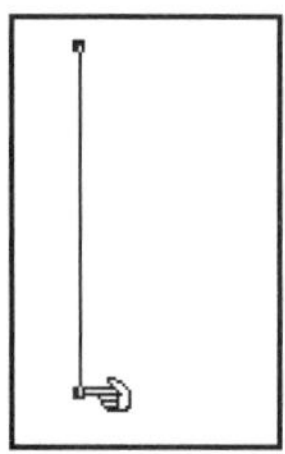

Click and drag on the resizing handle with the Resizing pointer to lengthen or shorten the line.

5. In the Colors palette, with the Line icon selected, click on a color to change the color of the selected line.

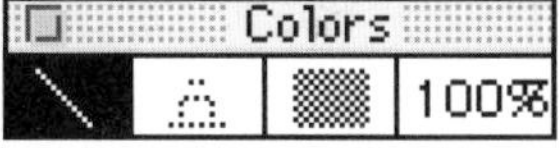

The Line icon is highlighted in the Colors palette when a line is selected.

LESSON 2
FREEHAND LINES

The Freehand Line tool differs from the Freehand Bézier box tools in that it creates an open path called a *line*, not a closed path called a *box*. You can draw with this tool just as you would with a pencil and then adjust the Bézier points to refine the drawing. Just as with straight and diagonal lines, color, width, styles, and arrowheads can be applied.

EXERCISE B

1. In the same file or in a new document, click on the triangle in the Line tool and drag to display and select the Freehand Line tool. Press the Alt/Option key while selecting the Freehand Line tool to keep it selected.

Click on the triangle on the Line tool and then Control/Ctrl-click on any of the other two line tools to add it to the Tool palette.

2. Use the Freehand Line tool to click and drag a few times on the page to create a line drawing or to write your name. When you have finished, the Bézier points will appear on the line(s). Click and drag the points to reshape the item. Click on a single point and click on one of the Point icons in the Measurements palette to change the point's type (Figure 14.3).

Freehand Line tool

Bézier Line tool

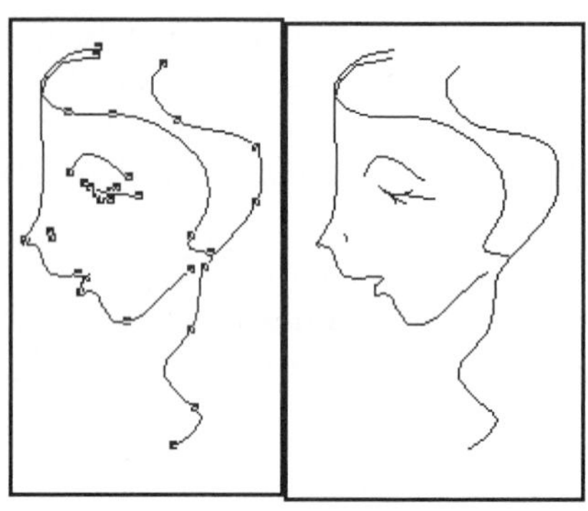

Figure 14.3. An item drawn with the Freehand Line tool displays Bézier points that can be manipulated to change the shape of the item. This drawing contains ten separate lines.

The Bézier Line tool draws both straight and curved lines.

LESSON 3 BÉZIER LINES

Unlike the Freehand Line tool, which allows you to draw only curved segments, the Bézier Line tool lets you draw both curved and straight segments. You can also manipulate the Bézier lines just as you can lines created with the Freehand line tool.

Unlike the Pen tool in Adobe Illustrator and Adobe Photoshop, lines drawn with the Bézier Line tool cannot be connected. In other words, once you complete a line by deselecting the Bézier Line tool, you cannot continue to draw that line. You can, of course, drag one line up to another line so that their endpoints are close to one another. Then choose Item/Merge/Join Endpoints to connect the two endpoints.

To deselect the Bézier Line tool, click on another tool in the Tool palette. You can then select the Bézier Line tool again and draw a new line, unconnected to any previously drawn line.

Join Endpoints

This option under the Merge commands is available only when two lines or text paths are selected. The endpoint from one selected line must overlap an endpoint from the other selected line. Drag a selection marquee around the two overlapping points to select them and choose Join Endpoints from the Item/Merge menu. This command creates a single Bézier corner point that replaces the two overlapping endpoints.

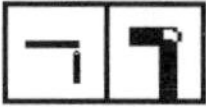

EXERCISE C

1. Click and drag on the Line tool to display and highlight the Bézier Line tool. Click and drag on the page to set the first anchor point, then click away from that point to create the first curve connected to that point. Release the mouse button. Move the cursor away from the curve, press the Shift key, and click to create a straight line connected to the curve segment. Continue to draw a single line with the Bézier Line tool. When you have finished, click on any other tool in the Tool palette which will deselect the Bézier Line tool.

2. When you have created Great Art (Figure 14.4), use the Item tool or temporary Item tool (press the Command or Ctrl key to turn the current cursor into the temporary Item tool) to select individual lines and apply color from the Colors palette and different line weights and line styles from the Measurements palette.

Figure 14.4. This drawing is comprised of different lines created with the Bézier Line tool. Because many of the line segments are not connected, you have to deselect the Bézier line tool and then reselect it before drawing another line.

LESSON 4
MEASURING LINES

When you draw a line with either the Line tool or the Orthogonal line tool, the tip of the line that starts the line is called the First Point. The tip of the line that ends the line is called the Last Point. The First Point and Last Point options under the Mode menu in the Measurements palette let you mathematically position the line and adjust its length from these two points. For example, if you select the First Point option and type 4 in the Measurements palette, the line will become 4 inches long, expanding or contracting from the tip that begins the line—assuming you have selected inches as the unit of measure. If the line is, for example, 4 inches long and any option except Endpoints is selected in the Measurements palette, typing +2 next to the L value in the Measurements palette will lengthen the line to six inches. Likewise, -2, *2, and /2 will subtract, multiply and divide the length of the line.

EXERCISE D

1. Choose Edit/Preferences/Document and click the General tab to set the unit of measure to inches. Click on OK. Display the Measurements palette (F9). Use the Orthogonal Line tool to draw a horizontal line and keep it selected. Choose First Point from the Mode pull-down menu in the Measurements palette.

Macintosh Commands

⌘-Y Edit/Preferences/Document

Windows Commands

Ctrl-Y Edit/Preferences/Document

The Symmetrical, Smooth, and Corner Point icons in the Measurements palette. Notice the Line Segment icons are dimmed because both straight and curve line segments are selected.

Endpoints
✓ First Point
Midpoint
Last Point

Use the Mode menu in the Measurements palette to select a point of measure for a selected line.

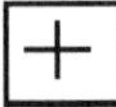

Orthogonal Line tool

Macintosh Commands

⌘-M Item/Modify

Windows Commands

Ctrl-M Item/Modify

2. The Measurements palette displays the X1 and Y1 values for the first (left) point on the line. The X value is the point's distance from the horizontal (left) margin and the Y1 value is the point's distance from the vertical (top) margin. Type 0 in the X1 field, press the Tab key, and type 2 in the Y1 field. Press Return/Enter. The line moves to the left margin (X1=0) and two inches down from the top margin (Y1=2).

3. Double-click the L(ength) value in the Measurements palette and type 5. Press Return/Enter to make the line 5 inches long. Use the W(idth) menu on the Measurements palette to increase the line width to 6 points (Figure 14.5).

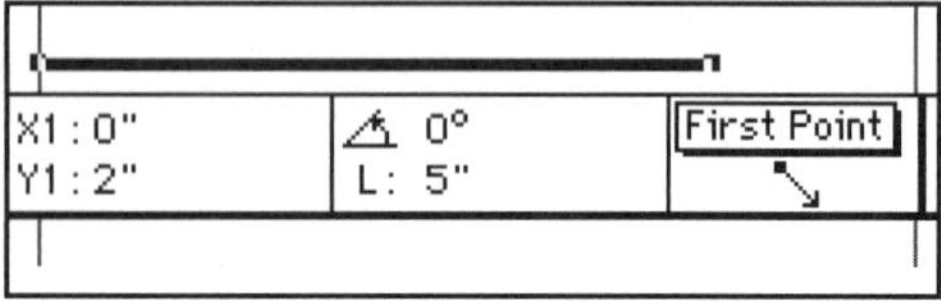

Figure 14.5. The line is positioned directly on the left margin (X1) and two inches down from the top margin (Y1).

FYI

To keep a tool selected until you choose another tool, press the Alt/Option key when selecting the tool.

4. With the line still selected, choose Item/Modify. In the Line Modify dialog box, use the pull-down menus to select the values displayed in Figure 14.6. Click on Apply to see your changes. Click on OK. The line becomes a vertical line with arrowheads at each end.

FYI

The L(ength) value is not available in Endpoints mode.

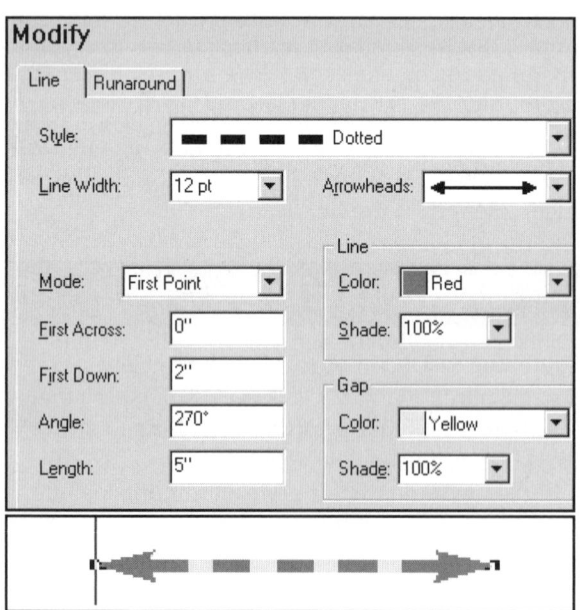

Figure 14.6. The Line Modify dialog box is where you specify line weight, length, position, and color.

FYI

You can select all the line options from the Line Modify dialog box. Otherwise, you have to make some selections from the Measurements palette and others from the Style menu. When a line is selected, all the options under the Style menu apply to that line.

5. With the line still selected, type /2 in the Y1 field to divide the current vertical position by 2. Click next to 5″ in the L field and type +2 in the L field to add 2 inches to the current length (Figure 14.7). Press Return/Enter to move the line up to the one-inch mark on the ruler (2÷2=1) and increase its length to 7 inches (5+2=7).

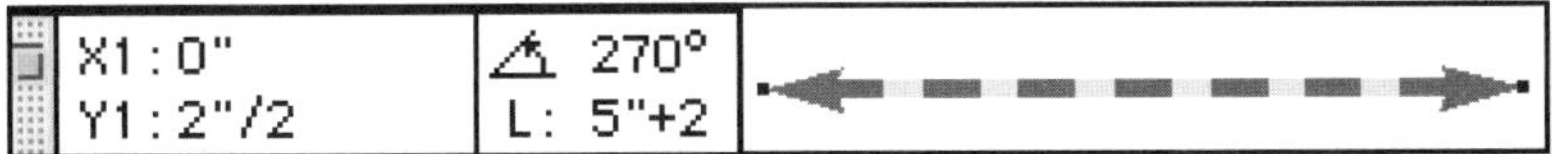

Figure 14.7. Use the division sign (/) to change the line's vertical position and the plus sign to change its length.

6. Use the Mode menu to select Endpoints. The Measurements palette now displays X2 and Y2 values for the line. The X1 and Y1 values still indicate the horizontal and vertical position of the first point. The X2 and Y2 fields indicate the horizontal and vertical position of the last point. Choose Item/Modify and notice that the values in the Measurements palette correspond to the values in the dialog box (Figure 14.8). Click on Cancel.

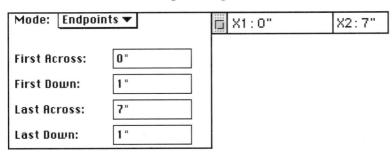

Mode: Endpoints
X1 : 0"
X2 : 7"
First Across: 0"
First Down: 1"
Last Across: 7"
Last Down: 1"

Figure 14.8. The First Across field in the Line Modify dialog box corresponds to the X1 value in the Measurements palette, First Down to the Y1 value, Last Across to the X2 value, and Last Down to the Y2 value.

7. Choose Midpoint from the Mode menu in the Measurements palette and notice that the XC value becomes 3.5, because the center of a line ending at the seven-inch mark is 3.5. The YC value remains at one inch because the center of the line is one inch down from the top margin.

8. Select different modes and make changes in the Measurements palette to see how the right and left points move depending on the values applied to them.

9. Close this file (File/Close) or continue to the next lesson. Don't save your changes.

Macintosh Commands

⌘-W FIle/Close

Windows Commands

Ctrl-F4 File/Close

FYI

Any line can be rotated, regardless of its line mode. However, the Rotate icon in the Measurements palette and the Angle field in the Line Modify dialog box are not available if the line mode is Endpoints.

X2 : 34p1
Y2 : 18p4
Endpoints

Macintosh Commands

⌘-N File/New

Windows Commands

Ctrl-N File/New

FYI

The width of a printed hairline is .25 point wide when printed on an imagesetter. A hairline will print a little wider on a laser printer.

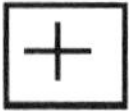

Orthogonal Line tool

The Freehand shape at the bottom of the Shape menu changes a standard-shape line to a Bézier line.

LESSON 5
RESHAPING AND CONVERTING LINES

You can reshape any line using the Shape command from the Item menu as well as by manipulating anchor points and curve handles on Bézier lines. You can also convert any line into a Bézier box and then define the box contents as picture, text, or none.

EXERCISE E

1. Create a new document (File/New/Document) or use the Document Layout palette to add a new page in the document. Use the Orthogonal Line tool to draw a vertical line. Choose First Point from the Mode menu on the Measurements palette and type 5 in the L field. If you are using inches as the unit of measure, the line will measure 5 inches. If you are using picas as the unit of measure, type 5p to create a line that is 5 picas long. Pull down the Style menu and select 12 points from the Width menu. Select a color and style from the Style menu.

2. With the line still selected, choose Item/Shape and drag to select the Freehand line at the bottom of the Shape menu. The line appears the same, but the Resizing pointers at the ends of the line have changed to Bézier points, and the Measurements palette reflects this change (Figure 14.9).

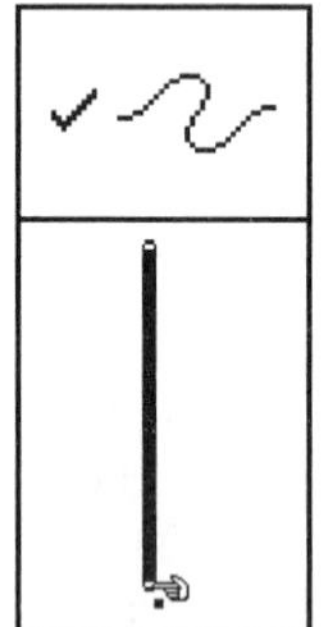

-90° L: 5p	First Point	Orthogonal line values
W: 5p H: p1	-90°	Bézier line values

Figure 14.9. Reshaping the orthogonal line to a freehand line changes the endpoints of the line to Bézier points and measures it in terms of its angle, not its length.

3. Click on any point and reshape the line. Click on a point and press the Control key (Macintosh) or Alt key (Windows) to display the point's direction handles and use these to reshape the line (Figure 14.10).

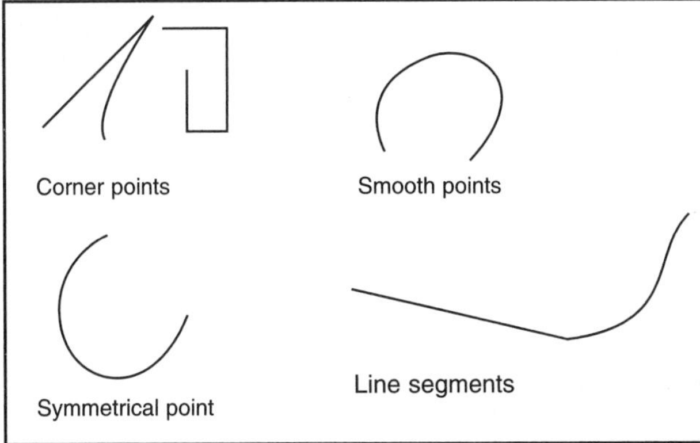

Figure 14.10. Change points and move line segments to reshape a Bézier line.

Macintosh Commands

⌘-W File/Close

Windows Commands

Ctrl-F4 File/Close

4. With the line still selected, choose Item/Shape and select the first box icon in the Shape menu. The line becomes a box with the background color of the original line and contents of None.
5. Choose Item/Content/Text and the box becomes a text box, with the blinking cursor indicating that you can now type inside the box.
6. Close this file or move on to the next lesson.

FYI

You can append dashes and stripes into an active document from another document just as you can append H&Js and style sheets.

LESSON 6 FRAMES

A frame is a stylized border placed around any box. You can select a frame style, width, color, and shade for the frame. If the selected frame is not a solid line, you can also select a color and shade for the gaps, the white areas between the dots or dashes of the frame.

Use the General Document dialog box (Command/Ctrl-Y) to specify whether frames will appear (and print) inside or outside of the box.

FRAME SPECIFICATIONS

When a framed item is selected and you choose Item/Modify, clicking the Frame tab displays the Frame modify dialog box. Here you can select all the specifications for the frame, its width, color, shade, and a gap color if the frame has spaces between the dashes. Choosing the Frame command (Item/Frame) brings up this dialog box automatically.

No frame will display unless a Width value is applied. The Frame Modify dialog box defaults to a frame width of 0, so be sure to select a width from the Width pull-down menu or type a value in the Width field. Many of the frame options will not display properly if the width is too narrow.

Macintosh Commands

⌘-B Item/Frame
⌘-W File/Close

Windows Commands

Ctrl-B Item/Frame
Ctrl-F4 File/Close

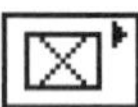

Standard-Shape Rectangle Picture Box tool

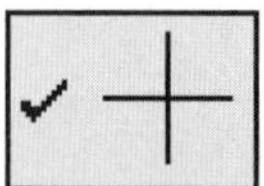

Orthogonal Line shape

A dash (top) is a series of broken line patterns and/or dots. A stripe (bottom) is a pattern made up of straight lines.

EXERCISE F

1. Select the standard-shape Rectangle Picture Box tool and press the Shift key to draw a picture box about 4 inches square.
2. With the box still selected, choose Item/Frame and apply the values displayed in Figure 14.11. Because the selected line style is not a solid line, you can select a color and shade for the gap. Click on OK.

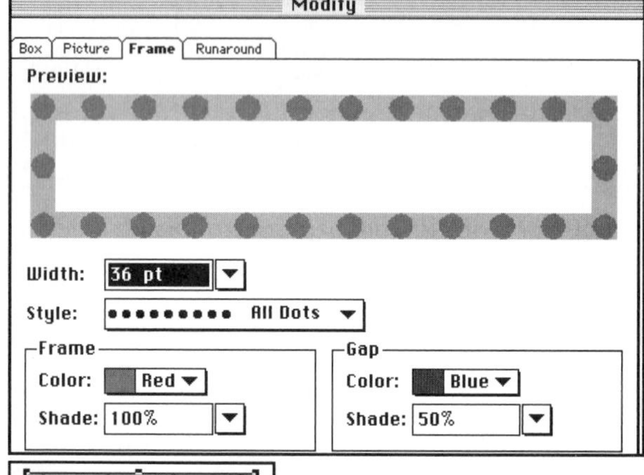

Figure 14.11. Use the Frame Modify dialog box to apply a frame around a box.

3. Click on any of the resizing handles and drag to resize the box. The frame adjusts to the new size.
4. Choose Item/Shape and select the Orthogonal Line shape. The box is converted to an orthogonal line with the characteristics of the selected frame.
5. Choose Item/Shape and select a box shape. The frame disappears and the box contains the background color of the line. The gap color also disappears.
6. Close this file or move on to the next exercise.

LESSON 7
DASHES & STRIPES

Dashes are dotted or broken-line patterns; stripes are solid line patterns. The Dashes & Stripes dialog box is where you create custom line styles that can be applied as frames to boxes, lines, and text paths. Dashes are broken lines, separated by a gap. Stripes are banded line styles. If you create dashes and stripes when no documents are open, those dashes and stripes will appear in the Style menu for selected lines and text paths and in the Frame menu for selected boxes. Otherwise, any dashes and stripes you create in an active document will appear only in the style menus for that document. As with style sheets, you can use the Append command to append dashes and stripes from any saved document to the active document.

Once you create and save a dash or stripe style, you can edit it at a later time and every item to which that dash or stripe was applied will reflect the edited style.

FYI

To remove an arrow from the ruler in any of the Dashes & Stripes dialog boxes, drag it to the right or left off the ruler.

DASHES

Dashes are frame styles that incorporate dashed lines and gaps between those lines. You can use the horizontal ruler in the Edit Dash dialog box to specify the position and shape of the dash as well as the distance (gap) between one dash and another. Both the dash and its gap can be colored from the Frame dialog box.

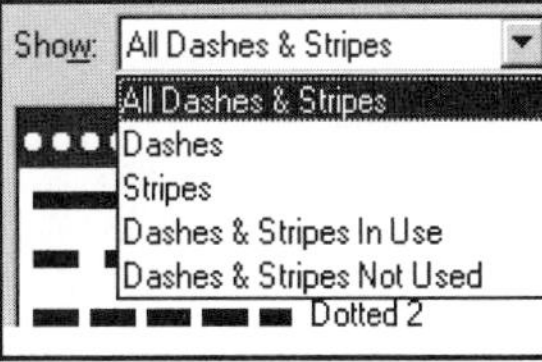

The Show menu in the Dashes & Stripes dialog box lets you specify which dashes and/or stripes are displayed in the dialog box.

EXERCISE G

1. In any document, choose Edit/Dashes and Stripes to display the Dashes & Stripes dialog box.
2. Choose Dashes & Stripes In Use from the Show menu to display only those dashes and stripes used in the current document. Use the Show menu to select All Dashes & Stripes.
3. Use the New pull-down menu to select Dash and display the Edit Dash dialog box. Type *My Dash* in the Name field. The ruler area is where you create the gaps between the dashes. When you click in the ruler area, an arrow is displayed. The arrow indicates the dash part of the line. Click on the 25%, 50%, 75%, and 100% tick marks to create the dash design (Figure 14.12).

Confused?

The easiest way to create dashes and stripes is to click on the ruler and drag arrows to different positions on the ruler, change the values in the Repeat Every field, and use the Preview area until you find a dash you like. This is not brain surgery!

Sorry

Once you assign a frame to a box, you cannot change its position relative to the inside or outside of the box. Any changes you make in the General Document dialog box affect only subsequent frames.

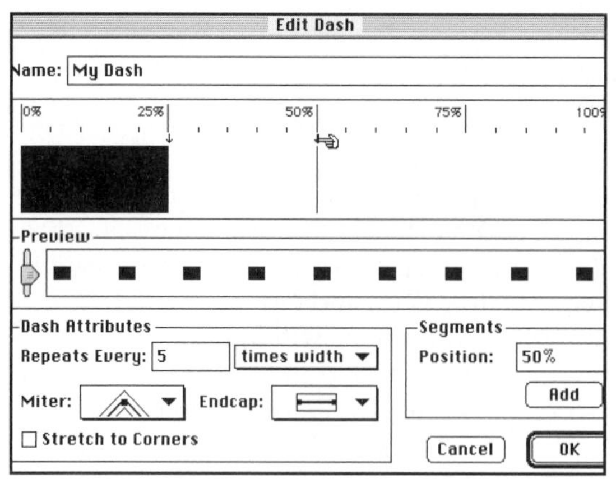

Figure 14.12. Clicking on the ruler creates a dash at that point. The preview area below the ruler displays the current dash design.

4. Click on each arrow and drag it two ticks to the left. Notice how the preview area below the ruler reflects the change in the dash (Figure 14.13).

Frame Editor

This utility which ships with QuarkXPress (Macintosh only), lets you create different bitmap frames. The frames you create in the Dashes & Stripes dialog box, however, are PostScript lines and will print without any "jaggies." However, XPress for Windows can display and print these bitmap frames.

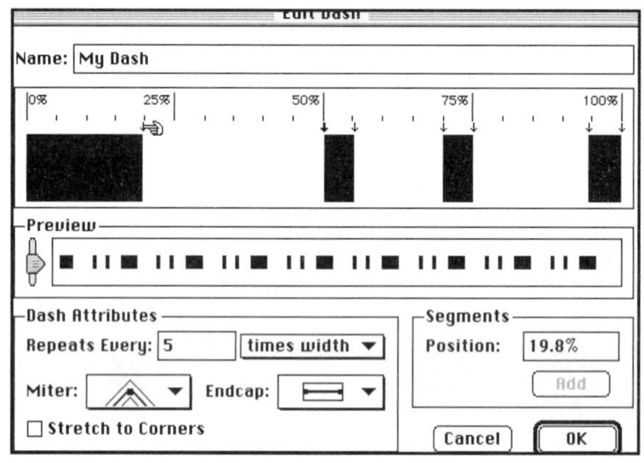

Figure 14.13. Drag the arrows to the right or left to change the dash design.

5. Drag the slider in the Preview area up and down to view the dash at wide and narrow widths (Figure 14.14).

FYI

The dashes and stripes that appear in the Preview window of the dialog boxes are just previews. You must adjust the values and options in the dialog box to change the dash or stripe.

Figure 14.14. Drag the slider in the Preview area to view the dash at different widths.

6. Use the Dash Attributes area to specify how the dashed line style will appear when applied to a line, text path, or box frame. The value in the Repeats Every field (Figure 14.15) specifies whether the length of the dash's repeating pattern will be

proportional to the width of the line or frame it is used with, or whether it is an absolute value. Type 2 in the Repeats Every field and make sure that times width is selected from the pop-up menu. This creates a line that is twice as long as the width of the frame to which it will be applied.

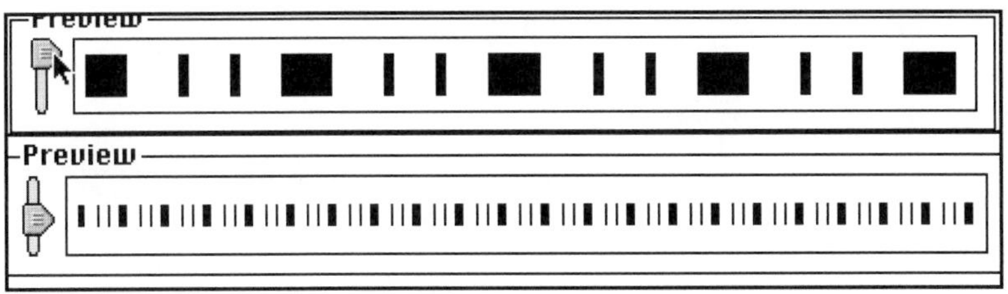

Figure 14.15. A value of 5 in the Repeats Every field, when times width is selected, creates a line that is twice as long as the width of the box or line frame to which it will be applied.

7. Type 20 in the Repeats Every field and choose Points from the pop-up menu to create a dash that measures the repeating pattern in points (Figure 14.16). Click on OK. Click on Save.

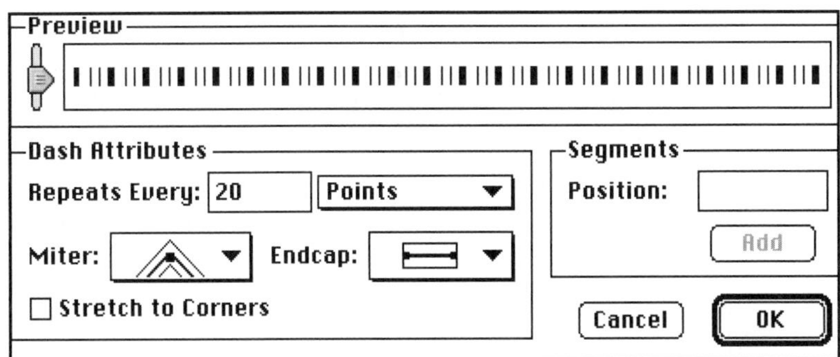

Figure 14.16. Choosing Points from the pop-up menu in the Dash Attributes area creates a dash based on an absolute value instead of on a proportional value.

8. Draw any kind of box on the page. With the box selected, choose Item/Frame. Choose My Dash from the Style pull-down menu. Assign it a width of 12 points. In the Frame field, choose a color and shade. In the Gap field, choose a color and shade for the white areas between the lines of the dash (Figure 14.17). Click on OK to apply the new frame.

Macintosh Commands

⌘-B Item/Frame

Windows Commands

Ctrl-B Item/Frame

Repeats Every

The default setting, times width, makes the dash pattern repeat in increments of the line's width. A wide line with long segments and a small number in this field results in finer dash elements.

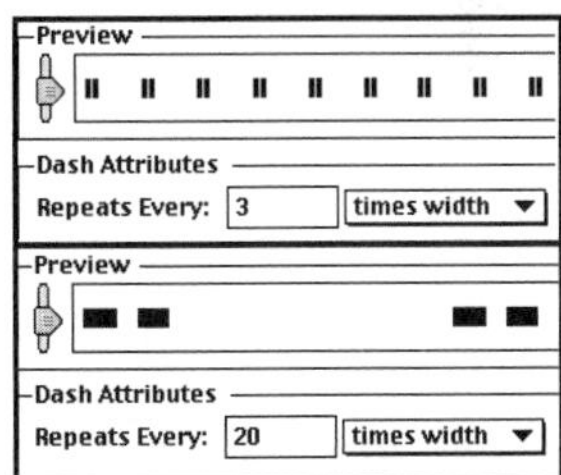

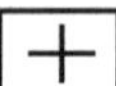

Orthogonal Line tool

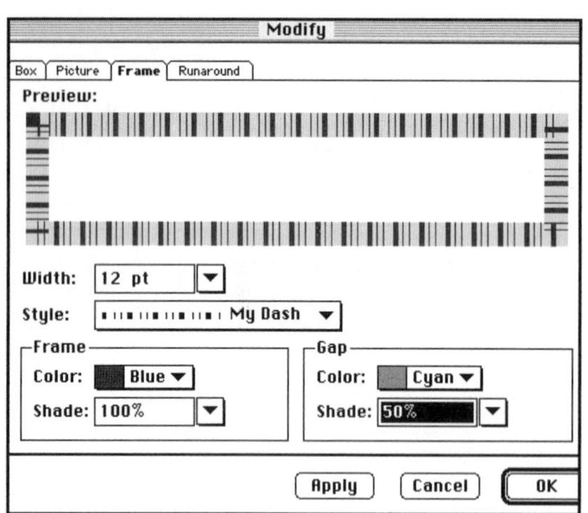

Figure 14.17. Once a new dash is created, it is automatically added to the Style menu in the Frame dialog box.

9. Close this file or keep it open. You can use it for the next exercises. Don't save your changes.

EXERCISE H

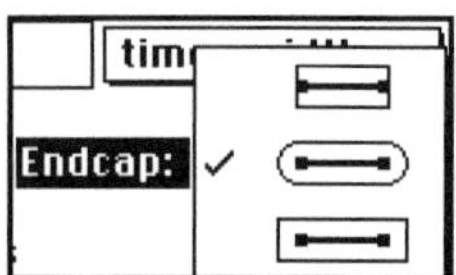

The Endcap field in the Edit Dash dialog box displays options for butt cap, round cap, or projecting square cap.

1. Choose Edit/Dashes & Stripes. Choose Dash from the New pull-down menu to display the Edit Dashes & Stripes dialog box. Type *Round Dash* in the Name field.
2. In the Segments area, type 50 in the Position field and click on the Add button to position an arrow at exactly the 50% mark on the ruler. Once you click Add, you establish a break point in the ruler area.
3. The Miter field lets you decide how the corners will look. Use the Miter pull-down menu to select the Round-Corner icon. Use the Endcap pull-down menu to select the round cap option. Click on the Stretch to Corners box to select it. This makes the dash stretch evenly along a frame so that the corner areas appear symmetrical (Figure 14.18).

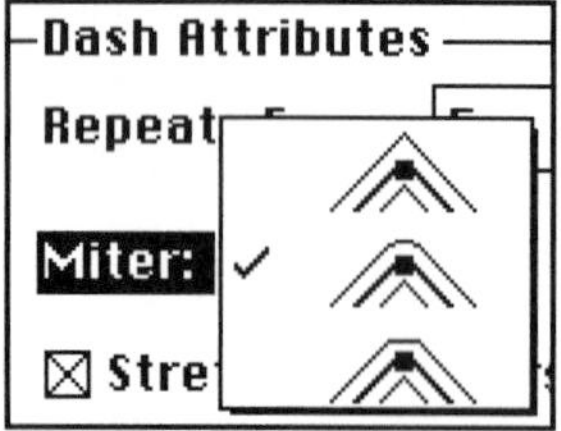

The Miter field displays icons for sharp-corner, round-corner, and beveled-corner attributes for dashes.

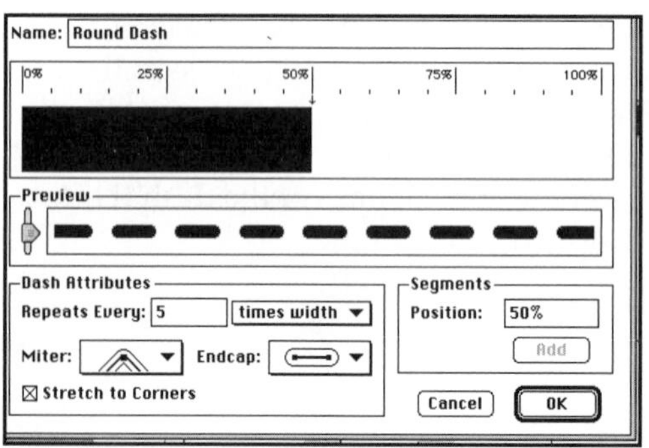

Figure 14.18. Make selections in the Miter and Endcap fields to change the shape of the dashed lines.

4. Click on OK. Click on Save.
5. Draw any kind of box on the page. Choose Item/Frame and select Round Dash from the Style menu. Select 8 from the Width menu. Apply colors to the dashes and to the gaps. Click on OK. The round-cornered dashes appear around the box and in the corners. Click anywhere on the page to deselect the box. Choose View/Hide Guides to see the frame as it will print.
6. Choose Edit Dashes & Stripes again. Choose Dashes & Stripes In Use from the Show pull-down menu. Click on Round Dash and click on Edit.
7. Drag the arrow at the 50% tick on the ruler to the 25% tick. Change the Dash Attributes values for Repeats Every 30 points by selecting Points from the pull-down menu. Use the Miter pull-down menu to select the sharp-corner option (Figure 14.19). Click on OK. Click on Save. The box framed with the original dashed style now reflects the edited changes.

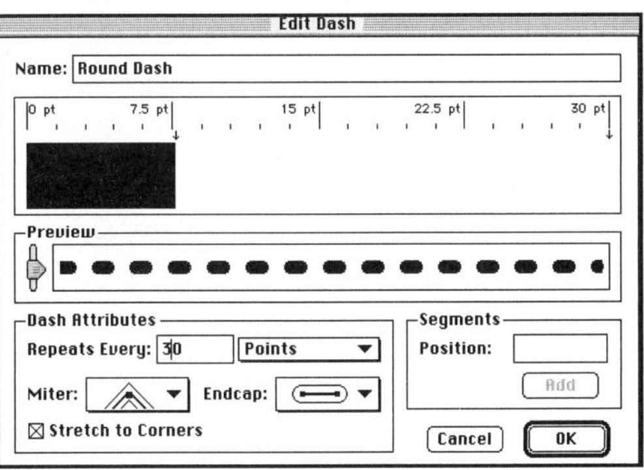

Figure 14.19. When you edit the original Round Dash style, the new changes appear automatically on any item framed with the original dash style.

8. Close this file (File/Close) or go on to the next exercise.

STRIPES

Stripes are solid frames that can be applied to lines and boxes. Like dashes, the area between the stripes is called the gap and can be colored just as the stripe can be colored. By moving the arrows on the vertical ruler, you can adjust the number and width of the stripes.

EXERCISE I

1. Choose Edit/Dashes & Stripes. Use the New menu to select Stripe. In the Edit Stripe dialog box, type *My Stripe* in the Name field. Type 20 in the Position field and click on Add. Type 40 in the Position field and click on Add. Type 60 in the

Macintosh Commands

⌘-B Item/Frame
⌘-W File/Close
F7 View/Show Guides

Windows Commands

Ctrl-B Item/Frame
Ctrl-F4 File/Close
F7 View/Show Guides

FYI

Adding segments to the ruler in the Edit Dash dialog box is like setting tabs. Click to set the position of the segment and drag to increase the segment's width. You can also type a position in the Position field and click on Add to set the dash.

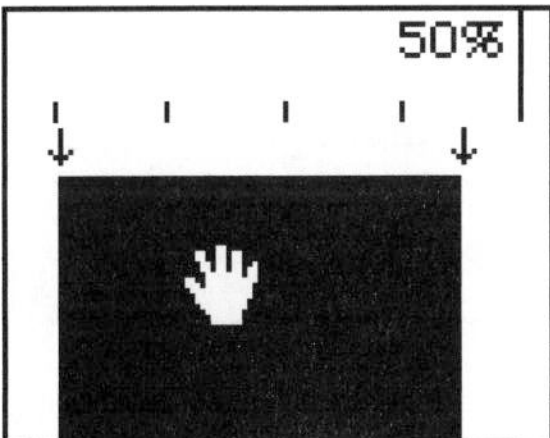

More info

Be sure to click and drag the segment, not the ruler guide, to move the segment. Clicking and dragging on the ruler resizes the segment but does not move it.

Macintosh Commands

⌘-B Item/Frame
⌘-W FIle/Close
F9 View/Show Measurements

Windows Commands

Ctrl-B Item/Frame
Ctrl-F4 File/Close
F9 View/Show Measurements

Position field and click on Add. Type 80 in the Position field and click on Add to create the third stripe.

2. Drag the bottom arrow up and the top arrow down to create two thick stripes and one narrower stripe (Figure 14.20). Click on OK. Click on Save.

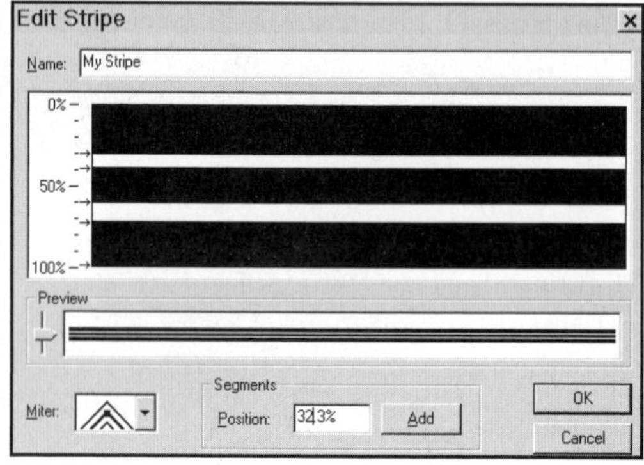

Figure 14.20. Use the arrows on the vertical ruler to adjust the number and width of the stripes.

3. Draw any kind of line on the page. Display the Measurements palette (View/Show Measurements) and use the Style pull-down menu to select My Stripe. Use the W pull-down menu to select 12. The stripe is applied to the line.
4. With the line still selected, choose Edit/Dashes & Stripes. Choose Stripes from the Show menu and double-click on My Stripe. Move the arrows on the upper and lower stripes so that the lines are thinner than the middle stripe. Click on OK. Click on Save. The new stripe is automatically applied to the line.
5. Draw a box anywhere on the page. Choose Item/Frame. Use the Style menu to select My Stripe. Assign it a color from the Frame field, a 24-pt. width from the Width menu, and a color from the Gap field. Click on OK. The box is framed with the My Stripe pattern.
6. Choose Edit Dashes & Stripes. Choose Stripes from the Show menu and double-click on My Stripe. Click on the vertical ruler to add lines to the stripe and move them to make them thicker or thinner. Click on OK. Click on Save. The new stripe replaces the original My Stripe on any line or box to which the original stripe was applied.
7. Close this file. Don't save your changes.

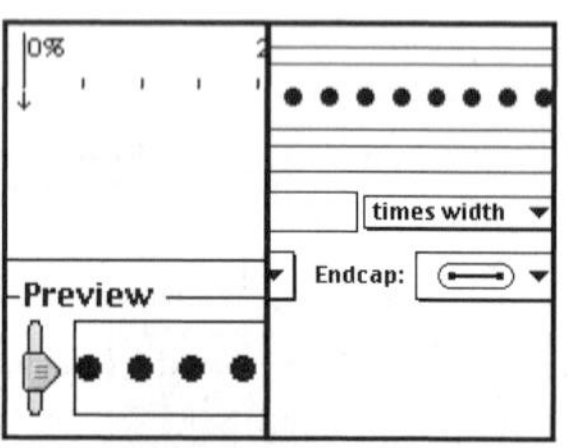

Tip

To create real dots, click at the 0% mark on the ruler and select the rounded endcap option from the Endcaps menu.

DELETING DASHES AND STRIPES

To delete a dash or stripe style, use the Edit Dashes & Stripes dialog box to select the dash or stripe. Click on the Delete button. If you have used that dash or stripe in the document, you will have the opportunity to replace it with another dash or stripe. Make your selection, click on OK, and click on Save to delete an unused dash or stripe or to replace the deleted dash or stripe.

DUPLICATING DASHES AND STRIPES

Sometimes it's easier to create a new dash or stripe from an existing one than from scratch. To do this, choose Edit/Dashes and Stripes, select a dash or stripe, and click on Duplicate. A copy of the selected dash or stripe will appear in the Edit (Dash or Stripe) window, allowing you to give it a new name and to change any of its specifications.

Macintosh Commands

⌘-N File/New/Document
⌘-, (comma) Item/Space/Align

Windows Commands

Ctrl-N File/New/Document
Ctrl-, (comma) Item/Space/Align

LESSON 8 ALIGNING ITEMS

You have already used the X and Y coordinates in the Measurements palette to position items at precise points on a page. However, many times it's easier to use the Space/Align command to position items (lines, boxes, text paths, or groups) in a specific relationship to other items. This command allows you to control the positioning of multiple items simultaneously by distributing them in a horizontal and/or vertical direction. To activate this command, Shift-select two or more items with the Item tool.

FYI

If you apply any values in the Space/Align Items dialog box and change your mind, click the Cancel button. If you click OK, any subsequent Space/Align commands will be based on the previous command.

EXERCISE J

1. Create a new document (File/New/Document) without an automatic text box. Use any of the standard-shape picture box tools to draw three different-sized picture boxes. Display the Colors palette (F12) and click on the Background icon. Select each picture box and click on a color's name in the Colors palette to apply the color to the item. You could also drag the color swatch onto the selected box. Move the three boxes so they are at different positions on the Y (vertical) axis.
2. Select the Item tool and click on the first box. Press the Shift key and select the second and third boxes. With all three boxes selected, choose Item/Space/Align to display the Space/Align Items dialog box.

Macintosh Commands

⌘-, (comma) Item/Space/Align

Windows Commands

Ctrl-, (comma) Item/Space/Align

3. Click the Vertical check box on the right side of the dialog box. Use the Between pull-down menu to select Top Edges (Figure 14.21). Click on OK. The boxes are aligned at the same point on the Y axis. Click anywhere on the page to deselect the three boxes. Display the Measurements palette (F9). Select each box individually and notice that each box displays the same Y value on the left side of the Measurements palette.

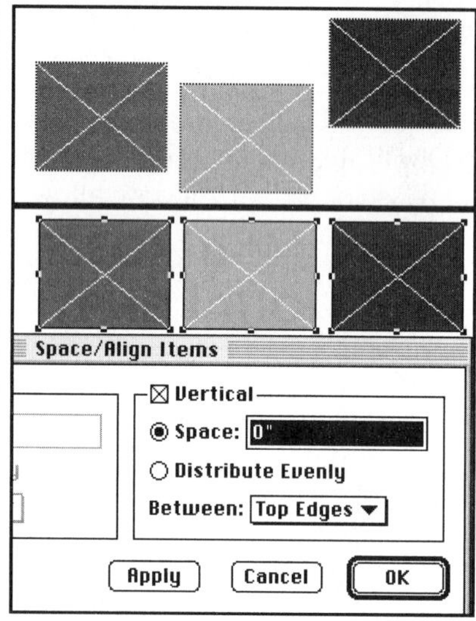

Figure 14.21. Selecting the Vertical and Top Edges options in the Space/Align Items dialog box aligns the selected items at the same point on the Y axis.

FYI

Items are vertically aligned relative to the top-most item. This item does not move; the other selected items move up to its position on the Y axis.

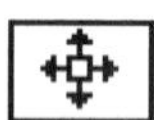

Item tool

4. Use the Item tool to position the boxes one under the other. With the Item tool still selected, drag a selection marquee around the three boxes again. Choose Item/Space Align. Deselect the Vertical option, click in the Horizontal check box, and choose Left Edges from the Between menu. Click on OK. The boxes are aligned at the same point on the X (horizontal) axis. Deselect the boxes. Click on each box and notice that each box is aligned at the same point on the X axis on the Measurements palette (Figure 14.22).

FYI

You must have at least two items selected before the Space/Align command is available.

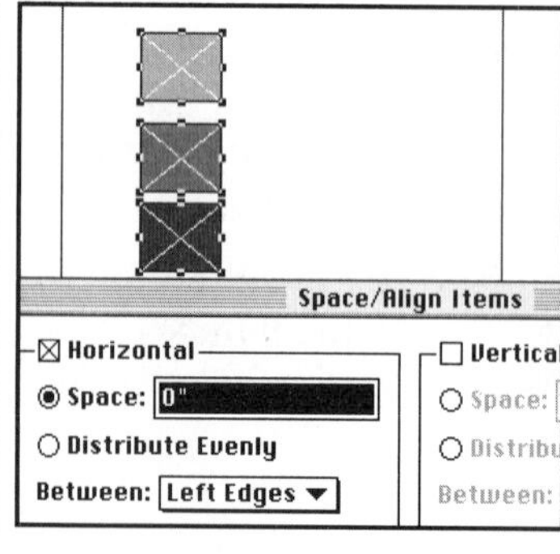

Figure 14.22. Deselect the Vertical option and select Left Edges from the Horizontal alignment option to align the selected objects along their left edges on the X axis.

5. Draw three different-sized squares on the page. Assign each a different color. Use the Item tool to drag the middle-sized square over the largest square. Drag the smallest square so that it overlaps the middle square. With the smallest square selected, choose Item/Bring to Front. Use the Item tool to drag a selection marquee around the three items.
6. Choose Item/Space Align. Select the Horizontal option and choose Centers from the Between menu. Select the Vertical option and select Centers from the Between menu. Make sure that the Distribute Evenly options are not selected in either the Horizontal or Vertical fields. Click on Apply. The squares are aligned by their centers on both the Horizontal and Vertical fields (Figure 14.23).

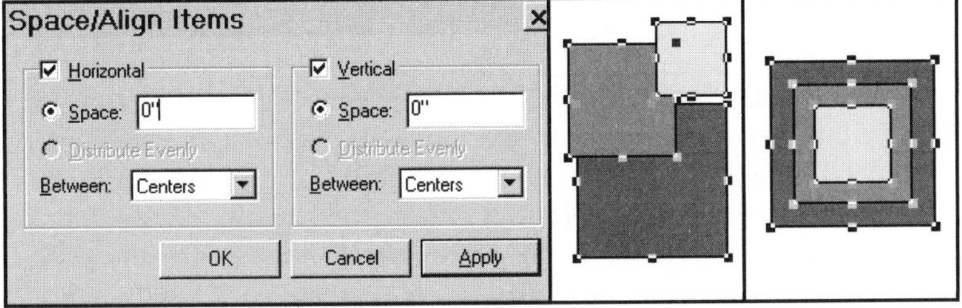

Figure 14.23. Selecting Centers from the Horizontal and Vertical Between menus aligns the selected items on their center points.

7. Close this file (File/Close). Don't save your changes.

Macintosh Commands

⌘-, (comma) Item/Space/Align
⌘-W File/Close

Windows Commands

Ctrl-, (comma) Item/Space/Align
Ctrl-F4 File/Close

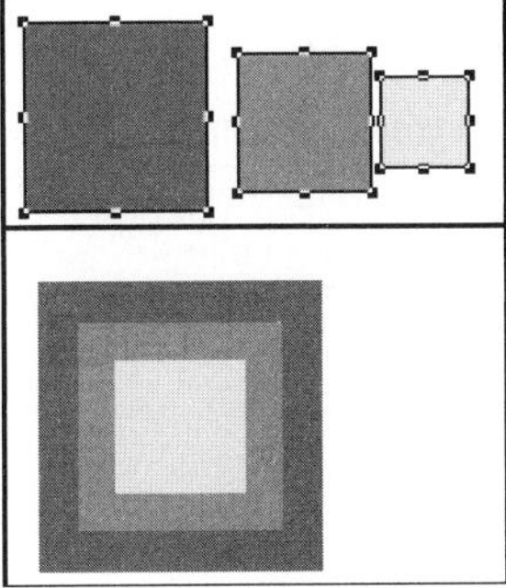

Items don't have to overlap to be horizontally and vertically aligned from their centers.

LESSON 9
COLOR LESSON 3
TOOL COLOR PREFERENCES

There are three ways to apply color and shade to lines: the Line Modify dialog box, the Style/Color menu when a line is selected, and the Colors Palette. To apply color to a frame around any box, specify the color in the Frame dialog box. You can apply either a spot color or a process color to any line or frame.

You have already used the Pantone and CMYK models. The inks in the Pantone colors are standardized and premixed. This gives you greater accuracy in predicting color output, provided of course, that you are using a current PANTONE swatch book for coated or uncoated paper when you specify the color in XPress.

Macintosh Commands

⌘-N File/New/Document
⌘-Y Edit/Preferences/Document

Windows Commands

Ctrl-N File/New/Document
Ctrl-Y Edit/Preferences/Document

Geography lesson

TRUMATCH is used primarily in the United States. FOCOLTONE is used primarily in Europe.

$ info

Because specifying two spot colors in a document results in printing three plates (the two spot color plates and a black plate), you still save the price of a plate by not specifying the two colors as process colors that would require four plates to print.

QuarkXPress 4.0 ships with many other color models, including the TRUMATCH and FOCOLTONE color systems. The TRUMATCH and FOCOLTONE color systems provide predictable color results when printing process colors. Because, unlike other color systems like the Pantone systems, TRUMATCH and FOCOLTONE colors are predefined, if you use a TRUMATCH or FOCOLTONE swatch book when specifying these colors, you can be sure that the printed color will closely match the screen display.

EXERCISE K

1. Create a new document (File/New/Document) without an automatic text box. Use the General Preferences dialog box (Edit/Preferences/Document) to select inches as the unit of measure. Choose Edit/Colors. Click on New and use the Model pull-down menu to select TRUMATCH.
2. Scroll the swatch library to find a warm blue or type 35-a5 in the TRUMATCH field below the swatch library. The number appears in the Name field in the upper left corner of the dialog box. Make sure the Spot Color check box is selected so that this color will print on only one plate (Figure 14.24). Click on OK.

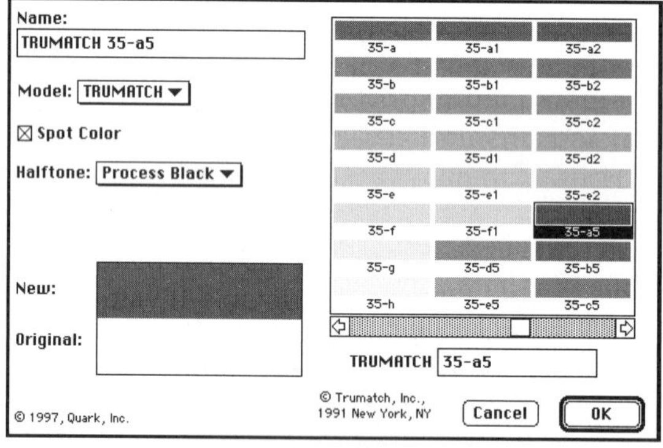

Figure 14.24. Select a color from the TRUMATCH library and select the Spot Color check box to specify the color as a spot color.

3. Click the New button again. Choose Pantone Uncoated from the Model pull-down menu. Type 116 in the Pantone field below the swatch library. Its name appears in the Name field. Select the Spot Color check box to specify this color as a spot color. Click OK.
4. Use the Show pull-down menu to select Spot Colors. It displays the default Red, Green, and Blue (RGB) colors and the two new custom colors. Click on Save.

5. Use the Orthogonal Line tool to draw a vertical line at about the middle of the page. With the line selected, choose Item/Modify to display the Line Modify dialog box. Apply the values displayed in Figure 14.25, using the TRUMATCH spot color for the line and the Pantone spot color for the gap. Click on OK.

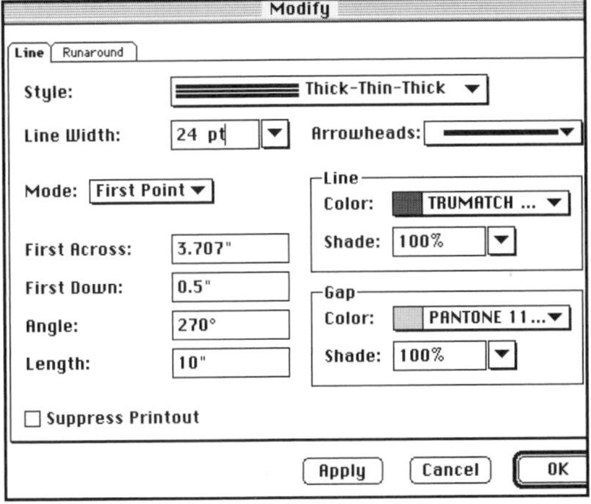

Figure 14.25. Use the spot colors to specify line and gap colors.

6. With the line still selected, choose Item/Step and Repeat. Type 5 in the Repeat Count field to duplicate the selected line 5 times; press the Tab key and type .25 in the Horizontal Offset field to position the duplicates a quarter inch apart. Press the Tab key again and type 0 in the vertical Offset field. Click OK (Figure 14.26).

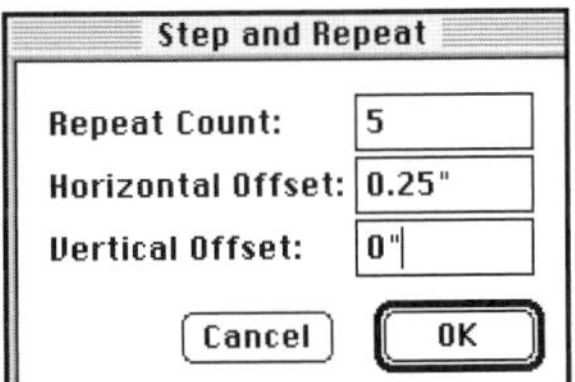

Figure 14.26. Use the Step and Repeat command to create five additional lines positioned right next to each other at the same point on the Y axis.

7. Use the Item tool to drag a selection marquee around the top of all the lines to select them. Choose Item/Group. Use the Item tool to drag the group to the right side of the page where it provides a vertical border for the page (Figure 14.27).

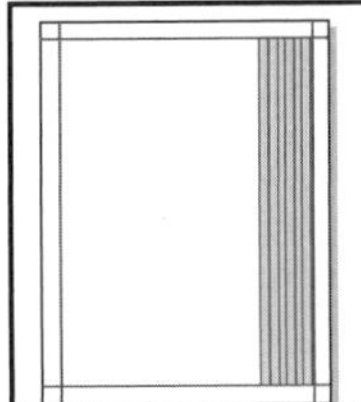

Figure 14.27. The grouped lines are moved to the side of the page to create a vertical border.

Macintosh Commands

⌘-Option-D Item/Step and Repeat
⌘-G Item/Group

Windows Commands

Ctrl-Alt-D Item/Step and Repeat
Ctrl-G Item/Group

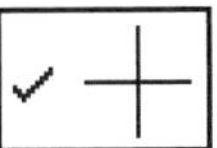

The Orthogonal Line shape in the Shape menu

Oops!

If you make changes in the Line Modify dialog box and get an alert message that "The item cannot be positioned off the pasteboard," click the Cancel button and start over, unless you know which field contains the offending value.

Item tool

Macintosh Commands

⌘-W File/Close

Windows Commands

Ctrl-F4 File/Close

FYI

When you modify a tool, only items created after the modification display the new options. If you make the modification when no document is open, every time you use the modified tool in any document, it will display the modification options. Otherwise, the modifications apply only to the document in which they were made.

Orthogonal Line tool

8. Drag out the Line tool to select the Bézier Line tool. Draw any kind of line on the page. With the line selected, choose Style/Width and drag to select 6 pt.

9. Display the Colors palette (F12). If a line is selected, the Line icon appears highlighted in the top panel of the Colors palette. Click on the Pantone color's name or swatch to apply the color to the selected line. Your screen should resemble Figure 14.28.

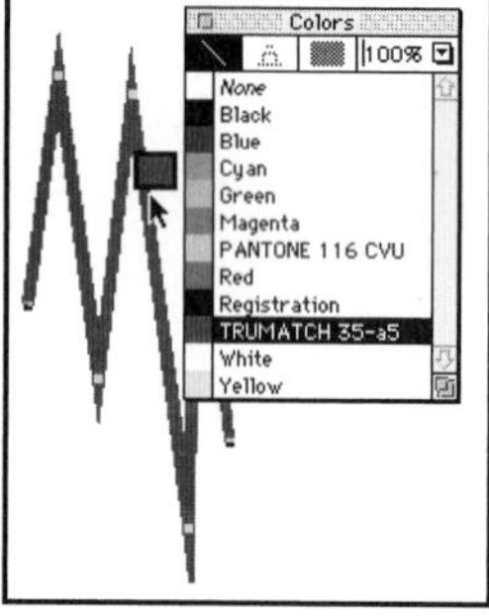

Figure 14.28. With the Line icon selected in the Colors palette, clicking on a color applies that color to the selected line.

10. Double-click on the Orthogonal Line tool to display the Document Preferences for [filename] dialog box. The Orthogonal Line tool is selected. Click Modify to display the Line Modify dialog box. Select the options displayed in Figure 14.29. Click OK twice to return to the document.

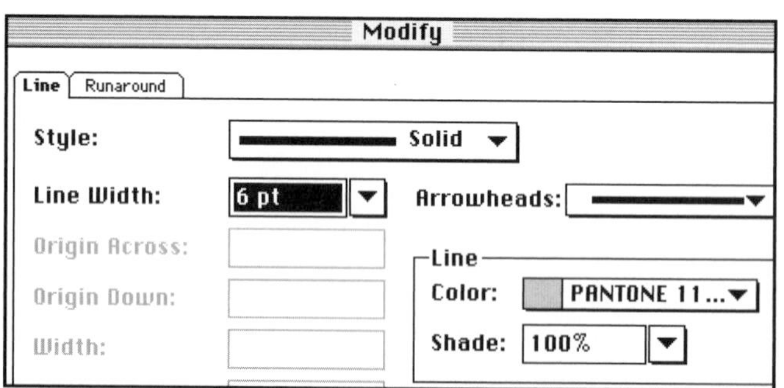

Figure 14.29. Any selections you make in the Line Tool Modify dialog box will apply to every subsequent line you draw in the document. Lines drawn before you made selections in this dialog box are not affected by these values.

11. Use the Orthogonal Line tool to draw horizontal and vertical lines. Every line you draw after modifying the tool will be a solid 6-pt. line in the Pantone color.

12. Close this file (File/Close). Don't save your changes.

UNIT 15

Duplicating, Layering, and Grouping Items

OVERVIEW

In this unit you will learn how to:
Duplicate items
Use the Colors palette
Create a linear blend
Group and ungroup items
Create duplicate items at specific locations

TERMS

blend
bounding box
group
nested group

HOW IT WORKS:

Create and format the text. Select the text box and use the QX-Effects menu to create a new effect. Select Cast Shadow for the contents of the box, in this case the type. Select the Foreground and Background options to merge the type with the background. Choose Grayscale for the color mode and 300 for the dpi if the file is to be printed to an imagesetter with a line screen of 133 lpi. If you are printing to a laser printer at 600 dpi, set the resolution to 200. Make adjustments to the perspective, opacity, and blur options in the the QX-Effects preview box and click on Finish. By giving the X offset value a positive number and the Y offset value a negative number, you will cast the shadow behind the text.

Macintosh Commands

⌘-N File/New/Document
⌘-C Edit/Copy

Windows Commands

Ctrl-N File/New Document
Ctrl-O File/Open

LESSON 1
DUPLICATING ITEMS

There are three ways to duplicate items in QuarkXPress. The simplest way is to select an item like a box or line and use the Duplicate command. This duplicates any selected items. The second way is to use the Copy and Paste commands to copy a single or multiple selection to the Clipboard, and then use the Paste command to paste the copy on the page. The third way is to use the Step and Repeat command, which allows you to specify how many copies you want and where you want them positioned. Once you have created multiple copies of an item, it's a good idea to group them together so they can be moved and transformed as a single unit.

COPY AND PASTE

In QuarkXPress, items are text boxes, picture boxes, text paths, groups, and lines. To duplicate an item, you must first select it with the Item tool. You can duplicate a *selected* item or items by using the Copy and Paste commands. When you select an item with the Item tool and choose Edit/Copy then Edit/Paste, a copy of that item is placed on the Clipboard, a special area of memory that holds anything—items or contents of items—in memory until you choose the Copy command again. Whatever is copied is placed on the Clipboard and overrides anything that was there before.

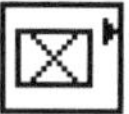

Standard-Shape Rectangle Picture Box tool

When you paste an item using the Paste command (Edit/Paste), that item is positioned on the page according to the specifications in the Step and Repeat dialog box. The Step and Repeat command differs from the Copy and Paste commands in that it copies and pastes items at a specified horizontal and vertical distance from the original and does it a specified number of times.

Item tool

EXERCISE A

1. Create a new non-facing pages document with one-inch margins and without an automatic text box (File/New/Document). Use the standard-shape Rectangle Picture Box tool to draw a rectangle. Select the Item tool and choose Edit/Copy to copy the selected rectangle to the clipboard.
2. Choose Edit/Show Clipboard. The rectangle you copied appears on the Clipboard, indicating that it can be pasted into the document. Click on the Clipboard window's Close box.

3. Choose Edit/Paste to paste the selected rectangle on the page. You now have two rectangles on the page, but only one is selected. Choose Item/Duplicate. Another rectangle appears on the page. Using the Duplicate command saves you the step of copying the item before pasting it.

Macintosh Commands

⌘-V Edit/Paste
⌘-D Item/Duplicate

Windows Commands

Ctrl-V Edit/Paste
Ctrl-D Item/Duplicate

LESSON 2
LAYERING ITEMS

When you draw overlapping items in QuarkXPress, each item is placed on an invisible layer, with the item you created last placed on the frontmost "layer." For example, if you draw a blue box and then draw a yellow circle on top of the blue box, the blue box is considered the backmost item and the yellow circle the frontmost item. If you overlap a line on top of the yellow circle, that line then becomes the frontmost object, with the yellow circle living on the intermediate "layer." You can move these items back and forth, making different items the frontmost and backmost items. It's easier to see how the layering and merging commands work if you apply color to the items, and it's faster to apply colors using the Colors palette instead of the Style menu.

THE COLORS PALETTE

Display the Colors palette by choosing View/Show Colors (F12). This palette has four panels that are used to perform the following tasks:

▲ The top panel contains icons for applying color to a selected box's frame, its text, and its background. When a color is applied, the shade menu on the right side of the panel is available for selecting a percentage (screen) of that color.

▲ The second panel contains a menu for selecting a type of blend or gradient for two colors. It defaults to Solid, which applies solid color instead of graduated color to a selected item.

▲ The third panel is where you select the two colors used in a gradient fill.

▲ The fourth panel lists all the available colors in a document. It defaults to the RGB colors, the four process colors (cyan, magenta, yellow, and black), white, and a registration color.

To apply a color, select an item, select its icon in the top panel of the Colors palette, and click on the color's name or swatch.

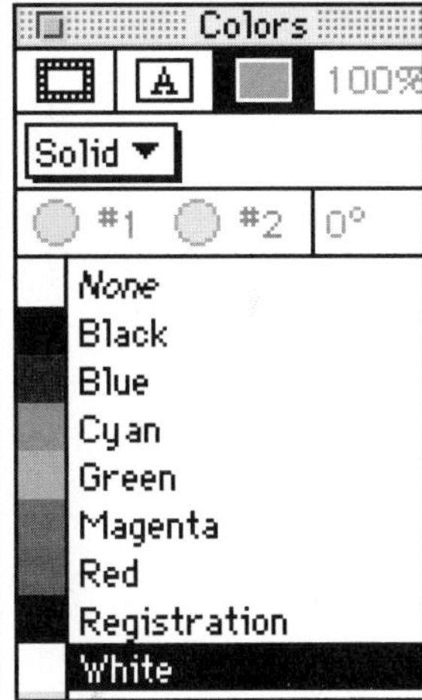

The top panel of the Colors palette displays the Frame, Text, and Background icons. The default Solid menu pulls down to display various gradient options. All the colors available to the current document are displayed in the bottom panel.

FYI

An item or text colored with Registration color appears on every color separation plate that you print. It's a handy tool for creating your own registration and crop marks or for making printing notations.

Macintosh Commands

⌘-N File/New
F12 View/Show Colors

Windows Commands

Ctrl-N File/New
F12 View/Show Colors

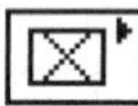

Standard-Shape Rectangle Picture Box tool

Oval Picture Box tool

Rounded-Corner Picture Box tool

Content tool

FYI

Overlapping more than four or five items can significantly slow down screen redraw.

Item tool

EXERCISE B

1. Create a new document without an automatic text box. Choose View/Show Colors (F12) to display the Colors palette.
2. Use the standard-shape Picture Box tool to draw a rectangle about 3 inches long. Click on the Background icon in the Colors palette, and click on the Blue color swatch.
3. Use the Rounded-Corner Picture Box tool to draw another rectangle about 2 inches wide on top of the blue rectangle. Color this rectangle green.
4. Use the Oval Picture Box tool to draw a large oval that overlaps the green and blue rectangles. Color the background of the oval red (Figure 15.1). Right now the red oval is the frontmost object and the blue rectangle is the backmost object.

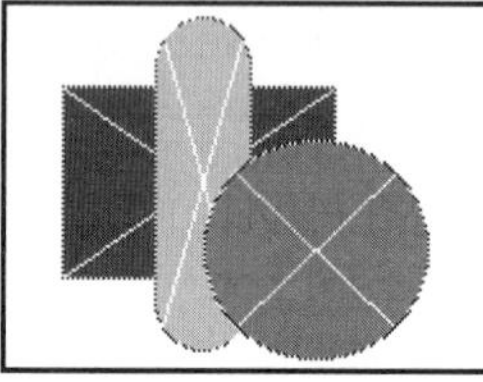

Figure 15.1. Three overlapping objects appear on three distinct "layers."

5. Select the red oval with either the Item tool or the Content tool. Choose Item/Send to Back (Shift F5). The red oval moves behind the blue rectangle, making the green rectangle the frontmost object (Figure 15.2).

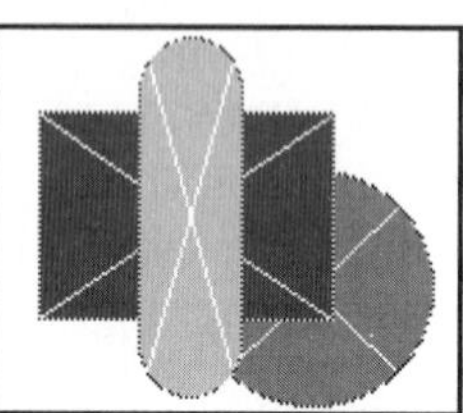

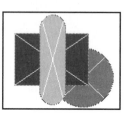

Figure 15.2. When the red oval is sent to the back, it appears behind the other two objects and becomes the backmost object.

6. To move the red oval between the blue and green rectangles, first select it with either the Item tool or the Content tool. Press the Option key (Macintosh) and pull down the Item menu. Notice that the Send to Back and Bring to Front commands are replaced by Send Backward and Bring Forward (Macintosh). In Windows, all four front and back commands appear under the Item menu. Drag to select Bring Forward. The red oval moves forward one "layer" and is positioned between the two rectangles.

7. Click to select the green rectangle, which is currently the front-most item. Press the Alt/Option key and choose Item/Send Backward. This moves the green rectangle one "layer" back behind the red oval.
8. Save this file as *Layers.qxd* in your Projects folder (File/Save as). You will need it for a later exercise.

Macintosh Commands

⌘-Option-S File/Save as
⌘-N File/New/Document
⌘-Y Edit/Preferences/Document

Windows Commands

Ctrl-Alt-S File/Save as
Ctrl-N File/New/Document
Ctrl-Y Edit/Preferences/Document

LESSON 3 GROUPING ITEMS

A group consists of two or more items—boxes, text paths, and/or lines—that can be moved and transformed as a single unit. A text box, for example, with a heavy rule above it can be grouped so that when you move the text box, the rule will move with it. You can also *nest* groups, that is, create one group and then group it with another group. Groups can be moved, resized, rotated, and ungrouped. Color commands applied to a group affect all the items in a group regardless of an item's original color. The important thing to remember about groups is that you use the Item tool to move a group and the Content tool to edit the individual items within a group.

Standard-Shape Rectangle Picture Box tool

MODIFYING GROUPS

The easiest way to make modifications to a group is to select the group and choose Item/Modify. Click on the Group tab to display the Group Modify dialog box. There you can reposition and resize the group as well as change the items' color and shade. Any color you apply in this dialog box, however, applies to the background color of every item in the group. To change the color of an individual item in the group, select that item with the Content tool and make the change.

Tip

Double-click on any item or group with the Item tool to display that item or group's Modify dialog box.

EXERCISE C

Oval Picture Box tool

1. Create a new non-facing pages document (File/New/Document) without an automatic text box. Display the Measurements palette (View/Show Measurements) and use the General Document dialog box (Edit/Preferences/Document) to select inches as the unit of measure.
2. Use the standard-shape Rectangle Picture box tool to draw a small picture box, the Oval Picture Box tool to draw an oval, and the standard-shape Rectangle Text box tool to draw a text box. Type a few words in the text box.

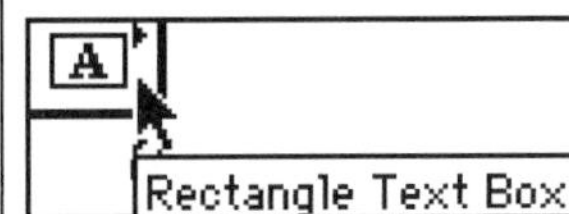

Rectangle Text Box tool

Macintosh Commands

⌘-M Item/Modify
⌘-G Item/Group
⌘-D Item/Duplicate

Windows Commands

Ctrl-M Item/Modify
Ctrl-G Item/Group
Ctrl-D Item/Duplicate

Item tool

Content tool

Important info!

You must first deselect a group before editing its contents with the Content tool.

3. Select each box, choose Item/Modify and in the Box field use the Color pull-down menu to select a different background color for each item. You can also use the Colors palette (F12) to apply the background colors.
4. Select either the Item tool or the Content tool and click on the rectangle picture box to select it. Press the Shift key and click to select the oval and the text box. Don't release the Shift key until all three items are selected.
5. Choose Item/Group. A dashed bounding box appears around the three grouped items, indicating that they constitute a group and can be moved and transformed as one unit (Figure 15.3).

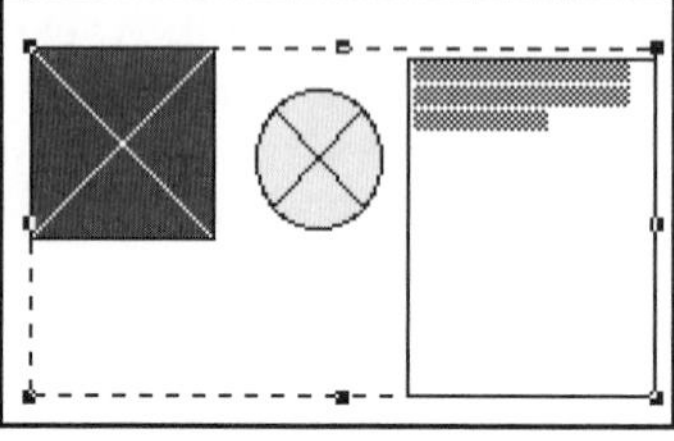

Figure 15.3. A bounding box appears around the three grouped items.

6. With the Item tool still selected, drag the group around the page. Notice that all three items move as one unit.
7. Click anywhere on the page to deselect the group. Select the Content tool and click on the rectangle and oval and resize them. Because you cannot use the Item tool to move an individual item in a group (these three items are still grouped), you must use the temporary Item tool to move the text box. Click on the text box with the Content tool and press the Command/Ctrl key to turn the Content tool into a temporary Item tool. Drag with this temporary Item tool to reposition the text box.
8. Click on the Item tool in the Tool palette and notice that the bounding box again appears around the edited group of items.
9. With the group still selected, choose Item/Duplicate. Move the duplicate to the pasteboard, where it will serve as a reference. Select the original group and choose Item/Modify to display the Group Modify dialog box. Click in the Width field after the inch mark and type /2 to divide the current width by 2. Click in the Height field and type /2 to divide the current height by 2. Click on OK. The group is proportionally reduced 50% in size (Figure 15.4). Deselect this group by clicking anywhere on the page, but don't delete it.

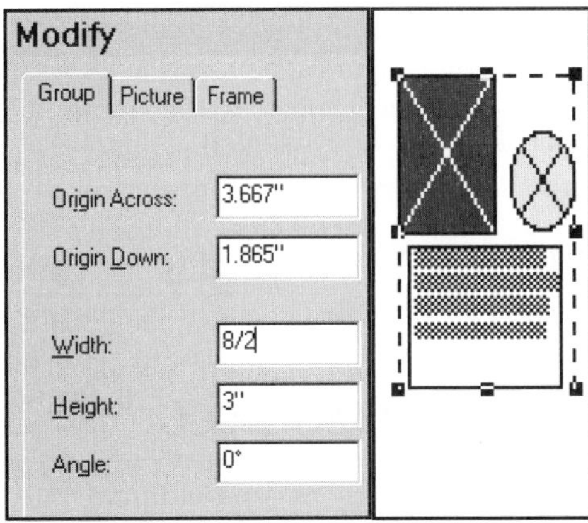

Figure 15.4. You can do math in any XPress dialog box. Here, the selected group is proportionally reduced to half its size because both the width and height were divided by 2.

10. With the Item tool selected, click on the duplicate group you created earlier. Choose Item/Frame. In the Frame dialog box, apply a 4-pt frame. Choose any color from the Color pull-down menu. Click OK. Each item in the group now displays the same frame.

11. With the group still selected, choose Item/Modify to display the Group Modify dialog box. In the Box field, use the Color pull-down menu to select another color. Because you have a group selected, this new color will be applied to every item in the group. Click on the Frame tab and use the pull-down menus to select another frame and point size for the frame. Click on OK. The three items now display the same background color and same frame color and size.

12. With the group still selected, click on the lower right handle and drag to resize the group. All the items are resized, but not proportionally (Figure 15.5).

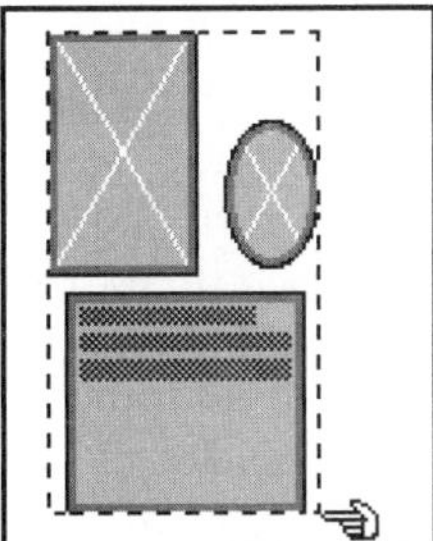

Figure 15.5. Color and frame commands affect each item in a group. When a group is resized manually, it cannot be resized proportionally unless you press the Shift key while dragging.

Macintosh Commands

⌘-B Item/Frame
⌘-M Item/Modify

Windows Commands

Ctrl-B Item/Frame
Ctrl-M Item/Modify

FYI

You can use the Item tool to resize a group. Doing so resizes all the items in the group simultaneously.

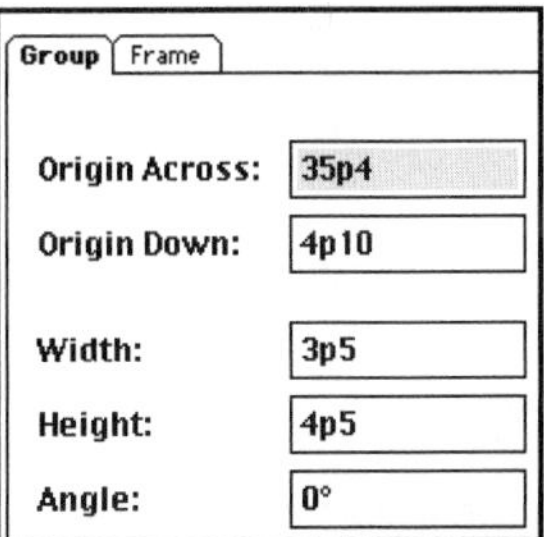

Position, size, and angle of rotation can be specified from the Group Modify dialog box.

Macintosh Commands

⌘-G Item/Group
⌘-W File/Close
⌘-O File/Open
⌘-M Item/Modify

Windows Commands

Ctrl-G Item/Group
Ctrl-F4 File/Close
Ctrl-O File/Open
Ctrl-M Item/Modify

13. Use the Item tool or the Content tool to Shift-select both groups. Choose Item/Group. The bounding box now appears around all six items, grouping the two groups of three items into one larger group. Use the Item tool to move this new group around the page.

14. Close this file (File/Close). Don't save your changes.

LESSON 4
THE GROUP MODIFY DIALOG BOX

Content tool

Once you specify items as part of a group, you can manipulate all the grouped items simultaneously in the Group Modify dialog box. Here you can position, resize, and rotate the group. You can also apply the same solid or blend color to all the items. If you have a large, complex group on a page, you can also suppress the group from printing when you print the page if, for example, you're only proofing text.

EXERCISE D

New feature!

In XPress 4.0 you can Shift-select multiple items with either the Content tool or the Item tool.

1. Open the *Layers.qxd* file you created earlier or open the *Layers.qxd* file in the Unit 15 folder on the CD-ROM. Separate the three overlapping items as you did before. Shift-select the two rectangles and choose Item/Group to display the bounding box around the selected items.

2. With the group still selected, choose Item/Modify to display the Group Modify dialog box (Figure 15.6). Whatever options you select in this dialog box apply to the group, in this case to the two grouped rectangles. Type values in the Origin Across and Origin Down field to position the group on the page. Press the Tab key and type values in the Width, Height, and Angle fields to resize and rotate the group. Click on Apply. Make further changes and click on OK. Notice that only the grouped items are affected by the new values. The red oval remains untouched.

FYI

Type the same values in the Width and Height fields to resize the group proportionally.

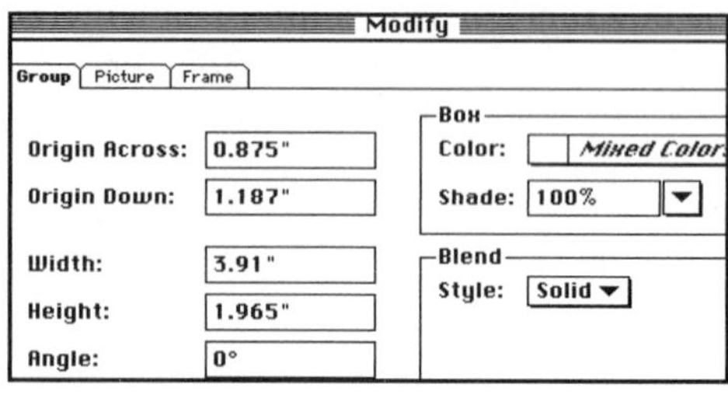

Figure 15.6. The Group Modify dialog box.

3. Choose Edit/Undo to restore the group to its original values. Keep it grouped.

4. With the group still selected (if you deselected, reselect the group with the Item tool), choose Item/Modify again. Right now the group consists of a green item and a blue item, so the Color menu in the Box field displays Mixed Colors. Pull down the Color menu and select Magenta. Click on Apply and notice that both items in the group display the new color. Click on Cancel to restore the rectangles to their original colors.

5. Choose Item/Modify again. This time use the Style pull-down menu in the Blend field to select Linear Blend. Leave the Box field color set at Mixed Colors, but select Yellow from the Color pull-down menu in the Blend field (Figure 15.7). Click on Apply. The color in the blue rectangle blends from blue to yellow and the color in the green rectangle blends from green to yellow. Click on OK.

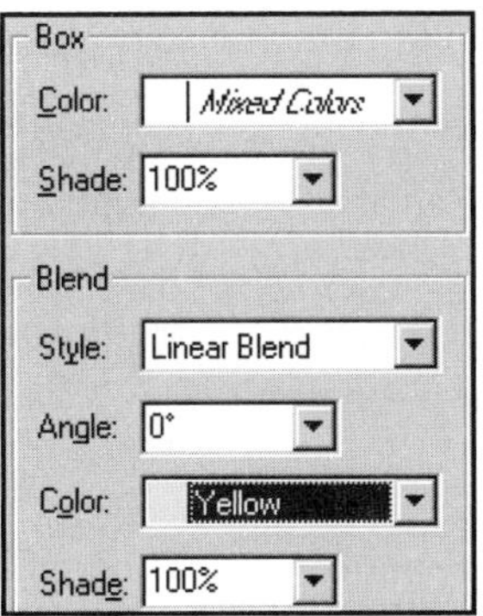

Figure 15.7. Select blend colors for a group in the Blend field of the Group Modify dialog box. The color selected in the Color field will blend with the solid color already applied to the box background.

6. Save this file as *Blend.qxd* in your Projects folder (File/Save as). You will need it for the next exercise.

INDIVIDUAL GROUPED ITEMS

Because the Group Modify dialog box applies values to every item in the group, it's not always the best command to use when you just want to make changes to individual items in a group. To do this, deselect the group and make changes to individual items just as you would do if the item were not part of a group. However, until you apply the Ungroup command, those items remain part of the group and will move with the group.

Macintosh Commands

⌘-Z Edit/Undo
⌘-M Item/Modify
⌘-Option-S File/Save as

Windows Commands

Ctrl-Z Edit/Undo
Ctrl-M Item/Modify
Ctrl-Alt-S File/Save as

FYI

Although you can Shift-select items with either the Content tool or the Item tool before grouping them, you must use the Item tool to select the group itself.

Macintosh Commands

⌘-O FIle/Open
⌘-W File/Close

Windows Commands

Ctrl-O File/Open
Ctrl-F4 File/Close

Content tool

Item tool

Pressing the Command key (Macintosh) or Ctrl key (Windows) changes the arrow cursor (left) temporarily to the Move cursor (right).

EXERCISE E

1. If necessary, open the *Blend.qxd* file you created in the last exercise or open the *Blend.qxd* file in the Unit 15 folder on the CD-ROM (File/Open). Use the Item tool to select the grouped rectangles.
2. Click anywhere on the page to deselect the group.
3. Select the Content tool and click to select the blended green rectangle. Drag the lower handle down to elongate the rectangle.
4. Click with the Content tool on the blue rectangle. Press the Shift key and drag a corner of the rectangle to constrain it to a square.
5. To move the blue rectangle independently of the group, press the Command/Ctrl key to temporarily convert the Content tool cursor to the Item tool cursor. Keeping the modifier key pressed, drag the blue rectangle down on the page. Release the mouse, *then* the modifier key.
6. Select the Item tool and notice that the group bounding box appears. Just because you modified a grouped item does not remove it from the group.
7. Close this file. Don't save your changes. Or choose File/Revert to Saved. You will use the *Blend.qxd* file in the next exercise.

GROUPING AND UNGROUPING GROUPS

Once a group is established, it remains a group until it is ungrouped. You can, however, add items to a group, and you can delete items from a group. When you select more than one group and apply the group command, the individual groups maintain their status as groups. To ungroup Group A from Groups B and C, select Group A and choose Item/Ungroup. Deselect everything, then use the Item tool to select Group A. Its elements remain grouped, but they are independent of Groups B and C.

Remember when working with groups that you must use the Item tool to move the group, but the Content tool to modify a single item in a group.

EXERCISE F

1. Open the *Blend.qxd* file you created in an earlier exercise or open the *Blend.qxd* in the Unit 15 folder on the CD-ROM (File/Open).
2. Select the Item tool and click on the red oval. Choose Item/Duplicate. Use the Item tool to move the duplicate red oval next to the original.
3. With the Item tool active, press the Shift key and click once on the original red oval to select both red ovals. Choose Item/Group. You have created the second group on the page.
4. With the Item tool still active and the red oval group selected, press the Shift key and click on the rectangle group. Both groups' bounding boxes appear.
5. Choose Item/Group to group the two groups. All four items are enclosed in one bounding box (Figure 15.8).

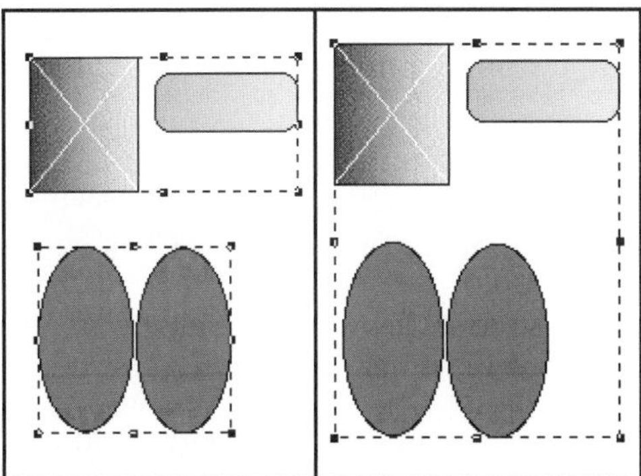

Figure 15.8. Two groups are selected and display the group bounding box around each group (left). When the two groups are grouped, one bounding box appears around both groups (right).

6. With the double-group selected, choose Item/Ungroup. Both groups' bounding boxes appear.
7. Click anywhere on the page to deselect the nested group. Use the Content tool and click on one of the red ovals. Choose Item/Delete to delete it. Because a group must have more than one item, the red oval group is disbanded and the remaining red oval is a single, ungrouped item.
8. Click with the Item tool on the rectangle group. Choose Item/Ungroup. Click anywhere to deselect. The three items on the page are now individual, ungrouped items.

Macintosh Commands

⌘-O FIle/Open
⌘-D Item/Duplicate
⌘-G Item/Group
⌘-U Item/Ungroup

Windows Commands

Ctrl-O File/Open
Ctrl-D Item/Duplicate
Ctrl-G Item/Group
Ctrl-U Item/Ungroup

Content tool

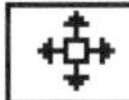

Item tool

Macintosh Commands

⌘-N File/New/Document
⌘-Y Edit/Preferences/Document
⌘-Option-D Item/Step and Repeat
⌘-M Item/Modify

Windows Commands

Ctrl-N File/New/Document
Ctrl-Y Edit/Preferences/Document
Ctrl-Alt-D Item/Step and Repeat
Ctrl-M Item/Modify

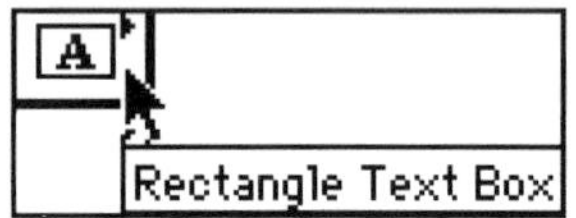

Rectangle Text Box tool

Auto Constrain

If you select Auto Constrain in the General Document dialog box, any box placed on top of an existing box will be constrained when moved or resized to the dimensions of the larger box. You will not be able to move or resize the smaller box beyond the bounds of the larger box.

LESSON 6
STEP AND REPEAT

The Step and Repeat function is a very simple one, yet it is an extremely powerful command. It allows you to create multiple copies of an item offset at a specific horizontal and vertical distance from the original. This can be useful for creating forms or interesting designs on a page.

EXERCISE G

1. Create a new document without an automatic text box (File/New/Document). Choose Edit/Preferences/Document and in the General Preferences dialog box select inches as the unit of measure. Click on OK. Display the Measurements palette (View/Show Measurements).
2. Select the standard-shape Rectangle Text Box tool and draw a text box between the left and right margins. Use the Measurements palette to assign the selected box a W(idth) value of 5.5 and an H(eight) value of .5. Press Return/Enter.
3. With the text box still selected, choose Item/Modify. In the Box Modify dialog box, use the Color pull-down menu to select Black and the Shade pull-down menu to select 30%. Click on OK.
4. With the text box still selected, choose Item/Step and Repeat to display the Step and Repeat dialog box. Type 1 in the Repeat count value, press the Tab key, and type 0 in the Horizontal Offset value. You don't want the copy pasted to the right or left of the original box. Press the Tab key again and type .5 in the Vertical Offset value to paste the copy directly below the original. Click on OK.
5. With the copy still selected, choose Item/Modify; in the Box Modify dialog box, choose 0 from the Shade pull-down menu. You could also select White from the Color pull-down menu. Click on OK. You now have two boxes, one shaded and one white. Use the Item tool, press the Shift key, and select both text boxes.
6. Choose Item/Step and Repeat. Type 3 in the Repeat Count field, and press the Tab key. Type 0 in the Horizontal Offset field because you want the copies placed directly under the originals. Press the Tab key again. Because each box is one-half

inch high, both boxes have a height value of one inch. To paste the copies directly under each other, type 1 in the Vertical Offset field. Click on OK. Your screen should resemble Figure 15.9. You now have shaded and unshaded text boxes that can be used for creating forms.

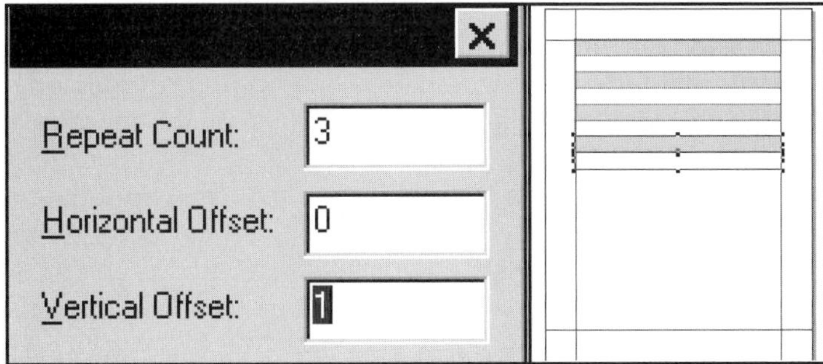

Figure 15.9. Using these values in the Step and Repeat dialog box results in four additional boxes spaced at 1½-inch intervals.

HORIZONTAL AND VERTICAL OFFSETS

The values you assign in the Step and Repeat dialog box can be positive or negative. A positive Horizontal Offset value positions the repeat elements to the right of the original; a positive Vertical Offset value positions them below the original. A negative Horizontal Offset value positions the repeat elements to the left of the original. A negative Vertical Offset value positions them above the original. You can have both positive and negative values in the same dialog box.

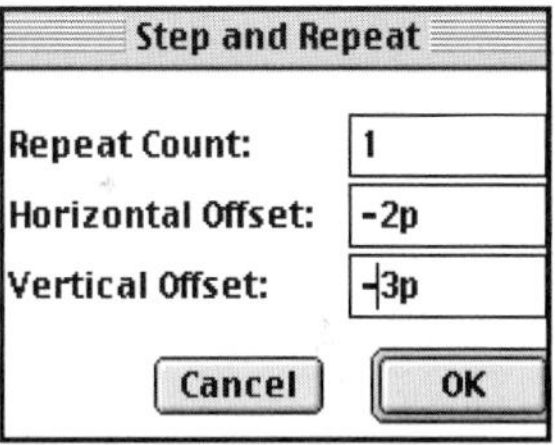

A negative Horizontal Offset value will position the duplicate to the left of the original. A negative Vertical Offset value positions the duplicate above the original.

If you make selections in the Step and Repeat dialog box and get an alert telling you that you can't make duplicates using those offset values, that means that you have too many repeat elements or they are positioned too far apart to all fit on the page. You will then have to change either the number of repeating elements or their distance from the original.

The Step and Repeat command is invaluable in creating repeating elements such as lines and graphics. A simple image, for example, can be duplicated, grouped, and positioned around a central item on the page for an interesting design effect. Lines can be duplicated in exact positions for setting tables and charts.Keep in mind, however, that when you use Step and Repeat with picture boxes, the images inside the boxes are duplicated as well as the boxes, and this can create large file sizes.

Unit 16

Merge and Split Commands

OVERVIEW

In this unit you will learn how to:

Use the Merge commands to combine items

Use the Split commands to split items

Use the Merge and Split commands to create new single items

TERMS

Difference/Reverse Difference Merge
Exclusive Or/Combine Merge
Intersection Merge
Split All Paths
Split Outside Paths
Union Merge

HOW IT WORKS:

The unit text was formatted in a large type size, then selected and converted to a single Bézier box using the Text to Boxes command. This box was then selected and split, using the All Paths option, so that the center of the 6 would be a separate path. That circle was deleted, leaving the center of the 6 transparent against the black background of the text box. The 1 and 6 were merged using the Merge Union command. The resulting single box was then filled with a linear gradient.

Macintosh Commands

⌘-N File/New/Document
⌘-Y Edit/Preferences/Document
F12 View/Show Colors

Windows Commands

Ctrl-N File/New/Document
Ctrl-Y Edit/Preferences/Document
F12 View/Show Colors

Stacking order

In Mac OS, when two items overlap, select the backmost item and choose Item/Bring to Front. Or select the frontmost item and choose Item/Send to Back to change the stacking order. Press the Alt/Option key to select Send Backward or Send Forward to move the selected item only one level forward or back. Windows users have these four commands available from the Item menu.

Standard-Shape Oval Text Box tool

FYI

If nothing is selected on a page, the Measurements palette is blank.

FYI

Alt/Option click on a tool to keep it selected until you choose another tool.

LESSON 1
MERGING AND SPLITTING ITEMS

The Merge and Split commands are advanced graphics techniques that let you create complex geometric shapes from standard-shape and Bézier boxes. The Merge commands affect overlapping boxes, and in some cases non-overlapping boxes. The Split commands are used either to split a merged box into separate boxes, to split a complex box that contains paths within paths into separate boxes, or to split a box that contains a border that crosses over itself, such as a figure eight.

The Merge and Split commands are similar to the Pathfinder filters in Adobe Illustrator, and like those filters let you create entirely new objects from existing items. When working with the Merge and Split commands, keep in mind that items' stacking order affects the way the commands work. When Items are merged, the front and back items (items on top and behind) are merged to create a new item, based on which items are in front and which are in back.

INTERSECTION MERGE COMMAND

The Intersection command keeps only the overlapping areas of the selected items. If different colors are applied to the items, the resulting intersected item has the color of the backmost item.

EXERCISE A

1. Create a new document without an automatic text box. Choose Edit/Preferences/Document and in the General dialog box choose inches as the unit of measure. Display the Measurements palette (F9). Alt/Option click on the standard-shape Oval Text Box tool and draw a circle about two inches in diameter. Draw another smaller circle and position it on the top half of the first circle.
2. Display the Colors palette (F12). Click the Background icon in the Colors palette. Select the lower circle and fill it with Magenta. Select the upper circle and fill it with green.
3. Click inside the top circle and type a few words. Click inside the bottom circle and type a few different words. Use the Item tool to drag a selection marquee around the two circles or Shift-select the two circles. Choose Item/Merge/Intersection. An alert appears telling you that the text in the green circle will be deleted. Click OK. Only the areas of the circle that over-

lapped remain and the circle shape is replaced by the shape of the overlap that contains the color and text of the backmost object, the magenta circle (Figure 16.1).

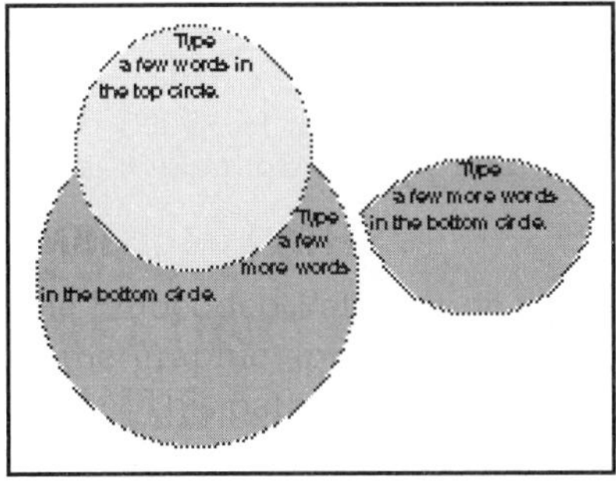

Figure 16.1. The Merge Intersection command removes all the items except the area that overlaps and applies the color of the underlying item to it

4. Close this file or keep it open for use in the next exercise.

Macintosh Commands

⌘-Y Edit/Preferences/Document
⌘-Option-D Item/Step and Repeat
⌘-W File/Close

Windows Commands

Ctrl-Y Edit/Preferences/Document
Ctrl-Alt-D Item/Step and Repeat
Ctrl-F4 File/Close

LESSON 2
UNION MERGE COMMAND

The Union merge combines all of the selected items into one box, keeping *both* the overlapping and non-overlapping areas. As with the Intersection command, the color of the backmost object is applied to the new single item. Use this command to create an outline shape of all the selected shapes.

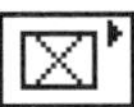

Standard-Shape Rectangle Picture Box tool

Standard-Shape Oval Picture Box tool

EXERCISE B

1. In the current document, choose Page/Insert and click OK to insert a new page after the current page. Or, create a new document without an automatic text box. Choose Edit/Preferences/Document and in the General dialog box choose inches as the unit of measure. Display the Measurements palette (F9). Use the standard-shape Rectangle Picture Box tool to draw a one-inch box.
2. Use the standard-shape Oval Picture Box tool to draw a circle with a diameter of one inch. Use the Item tool to position the circle over the top half of the square.
3. Drag a selection marquee around the two boxes and choose Item/Step and Repeat. Type 3 in the Repeat Count field, 1 in the Horizontal Offset field to place the three new items 1 inch from the original, and type 0 in the Vertical Offset field to keep

Tip

Press the Shift key while drawing any box to constrain the box to a square or circle—depending on the tool you're using.

the three new items at the same vertical position (Y axis) as the original. Click on OK. Your screen should resemble Figure 16.2.

Tip

To create a duplicate positioned precisely on top of the original, apply Horizontal and Vertical Offset values of 0 [zero].

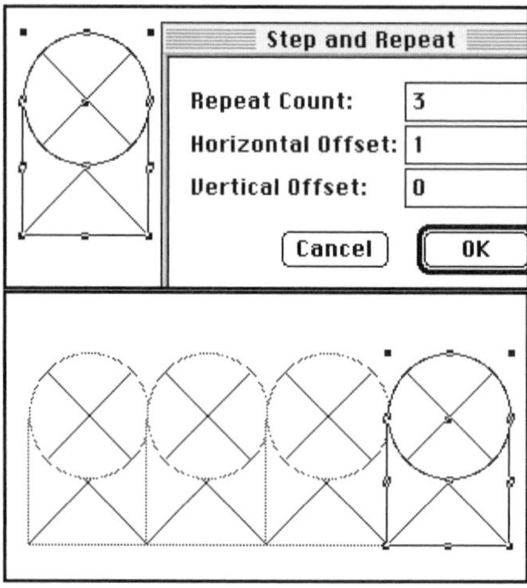

Figure 16.2. The two original items are duplicated to create four items.

Multiple-select

To select multiple items with one keystroke, use the Content tool or Item tool to drag a selection marquee around the items.

4. Display the Colors palette (F12). Shift-select the four circles and click the Background icon on the Colors palette. Click on the yellow swatch to fill the circles with yellow. Shift-select the four squares and fill them with red.
5. Marquee all eight items and choose Item/Frame. Choose 2 from the Width menu and Cyan from the Color menu in the Frame field. Click on OK.
6. With all eight items still selected, choose Item/Merge/Union. The eight standard-shape picture boxes are merged into one Bézier picture box with the background color of the backmost item, the original square (Figure 16.3). Even if the square or circle had been a standard-shape text box instead of a picture box, the result of the Merge command would still be a Bézier picture box. You can now manipulate this box just as you would any other Bézier item.
7. Close this file or keep it open. to use with the next exercise.

FYI

Whenever you use the Duplicate command, the duplicate is positioned using the values you last typed in the Step and Repeat dialog box.

The Reshape pointer indicates that a Bézier point is selected.

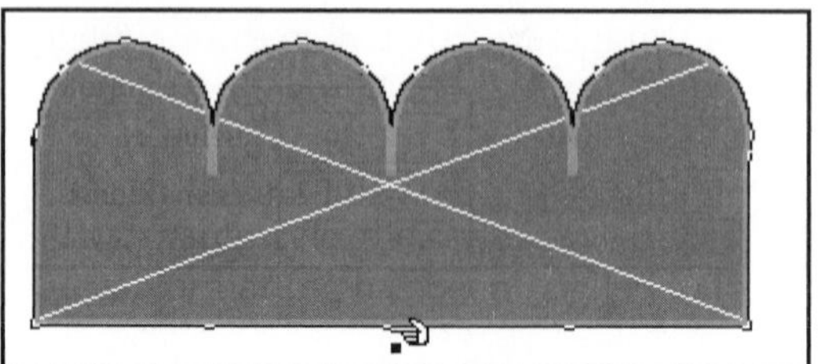

Figure 16.3. The Merge Union command combines all the selected standard-shape items into one Bézier box.

LESSON 3
DIFFERENCE AND REVERSE DIFFERENCE MERGE COMMANDS

The Difference Merge command strips the frontmost items from the selected items and leaves only the overlapping areas, giving you a jigsaw puzzle effect. The Reverse Difference Merge command strips the backmost item from the selected items and leaves only the overlapping areas.

Macintosh Commands

⌘-R View/Show Rulers

Windows Commands

Ctrl-R View/Show Rulers

EXERCISE C

1. On a new document page, use Master Page icon or a Blank Page icon on the Document Layout palette (View/Show Document Layout) to drag a new page icon down onto the document page panel. Display the Measurements palette (F9).
2. Use the standard-shape Rectangle Picture Box tool to draw a rectangle and the Measurements palette to assign it a width of 3 inches and height of 6 inches. Remember to press Return/Enter to execute the size commands.
3. Make sure that the rulers are displayed (View/Show Rulers). Drag the Zero Point over the top left corner of the rectangle. The ruler changes to reflect the upper left corner of the rectangle at the zero point on the ruler. Drag a horizontal ruler guide down onto the top of the rectangle. The X and Y values in the Measurements palette should read 0″. Drag a vertical ruler guide out to the left side of the rectangle. Again, the X and Y values on the Measurements palette should read 0″.
4. Use the Oval Picture Box tool to draw a circle. Assign it a W and H value of 1″ in the Measurements palette. Drag the circle over the top left corner of the rectangle so that the center of the circle sits on the corner. Because a circle and square are measured from the top left resizing handle, and because this circle is one inch in diameter, type -0.5 in the X and Y fields of the Measurements palette. Press Return/Enter to position the center of the circle precisely on the corner of the rectangle (Figure 16.4).

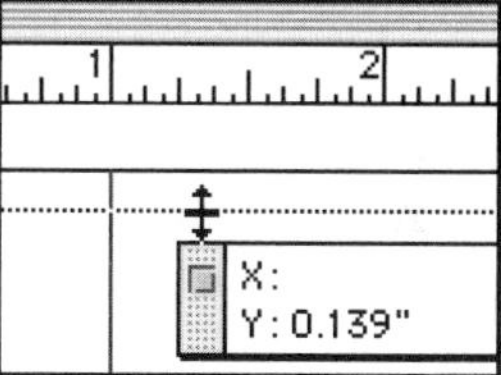

When you drag a horizontal ruler guide down from the ruler, its position is displayed in the Measurements palette.

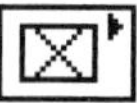

Standard-Shape Rectangle Picture Box tool

Standard-Shape Oval Picture Box tool

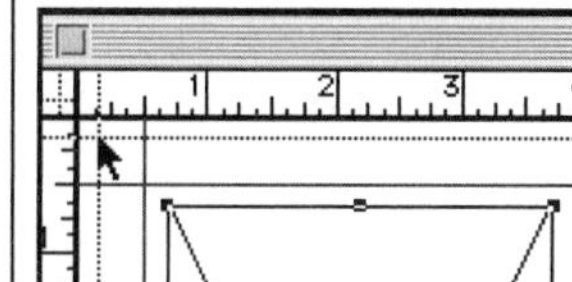

Drag the Zero Point to create a new zero point on the ruler at the intersection of the box's corner.

Macintosh Commands

⌘-Option-D Item/Step and Repeat
⌘-Option-S File/Save as

Windows Commands

Ctrl-Alt-D Item/Step and Repeat
Ctrl-Alt-S File/Save as

FYI

Once you name and save a file, choosing File/Save (Command-S, Macintosh or Ctrl-S, Windows) saves the file by overriding the original file of the same name.

FYI

When the first six commands under the Merge menu are applied to lines, the lines are converted to Bézier boxes.

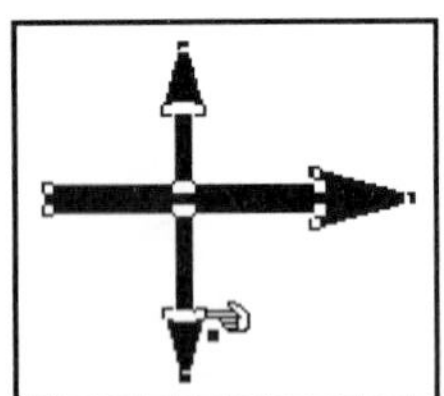

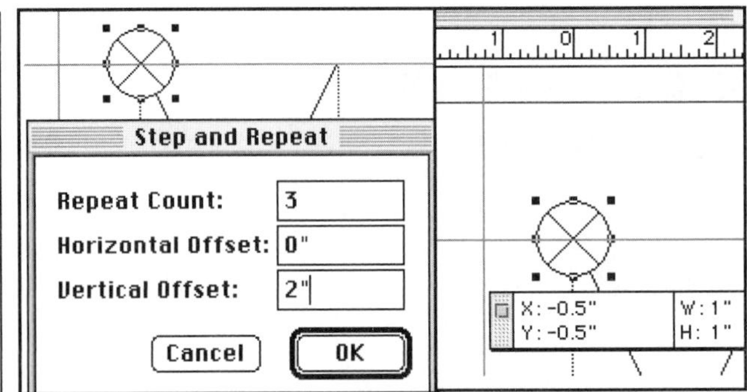

Figure 16.4. Typing -0.5 in the X and Y fields of the Measurements palette places the center of the selected circle exactly at the zero point of the ruler.

5. Choose File/Save. Save the file as *Merge.qxd* in your Projects folder.
6. With the circle still selected, choose Item/Step and Repeat. Type 3 in the Repeat Count field to create three new items; type 0 in the Horizontal Offset field because you don't want the new items moved from the original horizontal position. Type 2 in the Vertical Offset field to position the three new items exactly two inches down from each other. Click on OK. Your screen should resemble Figure 16.5.

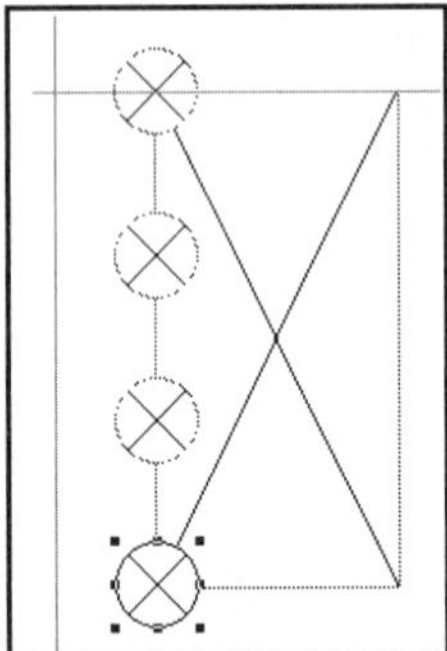

Figure 16.5. Because the rectangle is 6 inches long and the one-inch circles are offset 2 inches apart, the bottom circle falls directly on the lower left corner.

7. Shift select the three other circles. When all four circles are selected, choose Item/Step and Repeat. Type 1 in the Repeat Count field, type 3 in the Horizontal Offset field to move the four circles precisely 3 inches from the -0.5 position, and type 0 in the Vertical Offset position. Click on OK. Your screen should resemble Figure 16.6. Save the file (File/Save).

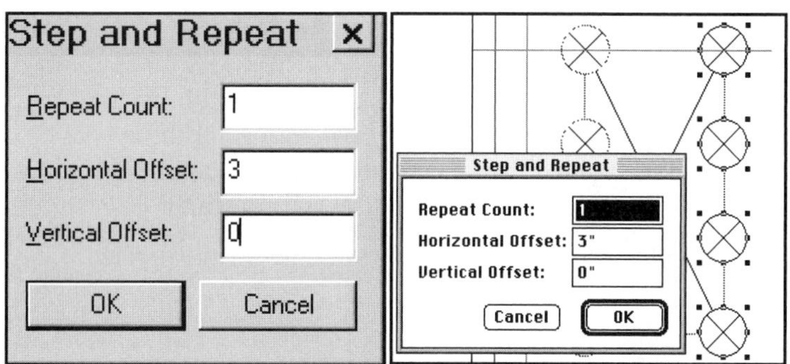

Figure 16.6. The four selected circles are offset exactly 3 inches from the original -0.5 position, placing the top and bottom circles precisely on the corners of the rectangle.

8. Display the Colors palette (F12) and click the Background icon. Shift-select the eight circles and click on the red swatch in the Colors palette. Select the rectangle and click on the blue swatch in the Colors palette.

9. Drag a selection marquee around all nine items, or Shift-select the eight circles and the rectangle and choose Item/Duplicate. Use the Item tool to drag the duplicate (all nine items should still be selected) to the pasteboard. Drag a selection marquee around the original nine items and choose Item/Merge/Difference. Because the circles were the frontmost objects, they were entirely deleted, leaving only the outline of where they overlapped the rectangle. The standard-shape picture boxes are now merged into one Bézier picture box (Figure 16.7).

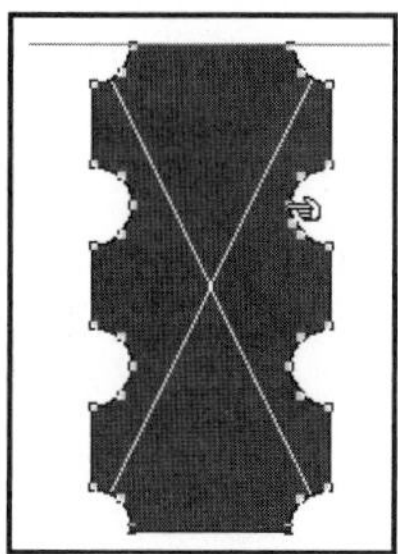

Figure 16.7. The Merge Difference command removes all the frontmost objects (circles), leaving only the outline of where they overlapped the backmost object (rectangle). This new item is now a Bézier picture box.

10. With either the Item tool or the Content tool selected, press the Alt/Option key to change the cursor into the Grabber Hand. Keep the modifier key pressed while clicking and dragging the page until the duplicate items are centered on the screen. Click on the rectangle to select it; choose Item/Frame and in the Frame dialog box choose 2 from the Width field. Click on OK to apply a 2-point black frame to the rectangle.

Macintosh Commands

⌘-D Item/Duplicate
⌘-B Item/Frame

Windows Commands

Ctrl-D Item/Duplicate
Ctrl-B Item/Frame

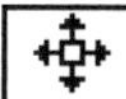

Item tool

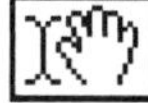

Content tool

11. Drag a selection marquee around the duplicate nine items, and choose Item/Merge/Reverse Difference. The backmost item is deleted (rectangle), leaving only those areas of the circles that did not overlap the rectangle. Also, the frame and blue background color, applied only to the rectangle, are now applied to the frontmost items, the circle wedges (Figure 16.8).
12. Close this file or keep it open to use for the next exercise.

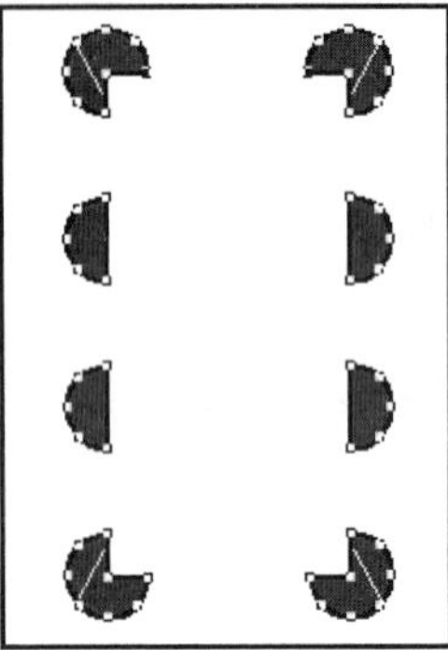

Figure 16.8. The Merge/Reverse Difference command deletes the backmost item (rectangle) and applies the background color and frame specifications to the non-overlapping areas.

Can you read the text in the box through the hole created

Use the Exclusive Or Merge command to create a peek-a-boo effect.

LESSON 4 EXCLUSIVE OR AND COMBINE MERGE COMMANDS

The Exclusive Or Merge command leaves all the shapes in their original form, but cuts out any overlapping areas. It also creates two Bézier points at every location where two lines originally crossed. This is the command used to create a see-through effect with overlapping items.

The Combine Merge command is much like the Exclusive Or command except that no points are added where lines intersected in the original overlap.

JOIN ENDPOINTS

This command is available only when overlapping lines and curves are selected. To use this command, select the two endpoints and use the Merge/Join Endpoints command. This is useful when you have created a drawing with the Freehand Line tool and want to connect the separate lines in the drawing.

EXERCISE D

1. Insert a new page in the document (Page/Insert) or create a new document. Display the Measurements palette (F9) and the Colors palette (F12). Use any of the picture box tools to draw a rectangle. Give it a background color of red. Use the standard-shape Oval Picture Box tool to draw a circle. Use the Item tool to drag the circle onto the lower left corner of the square.
2. Drag a selection marquee around both items and choose Item/Duplicate. Use the Item tool to drag the duplicate next to the original.
3. Shift-select the two items in the original group and choose Item/Merge/Exclusive Or. The overlapping area is cut out and makes that area transparent against the white page. Click on a Bézier point where the items overlap and notice that the Corner Point icon is highlighted in the Measurements palette.
4. Shift-select the two smaller boxes in the duplicate group of boxes. Choose Item/Merge/Combine. The overlapping area is cut out, the area is transparent against the page, but no corner points are created where the items overlaps in Figure 16.9. (There must be hundreds of uses for this command!)

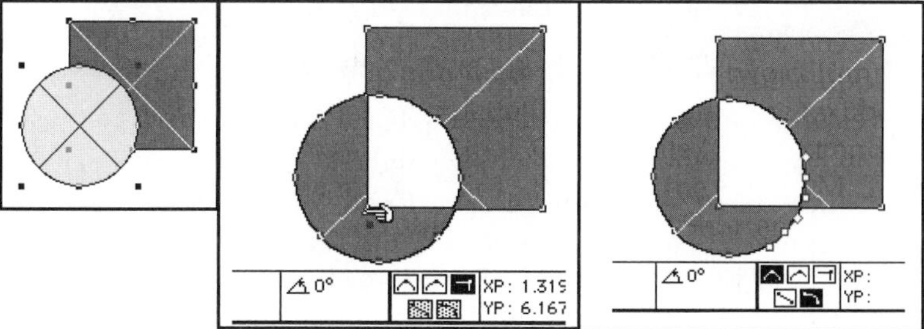

Figure 16.9. When the Merge Exclusive Or command is applied to two selected overlapping images (left), the original item shape remains, but when it is cut out, it makes the cutout area transparent and corner points are created where the items overlap (center). When the Merge Combine command is applied, the area is cutout and transparent against the page, but no corner points are created.

Macintosh Commands

F12 View/Show Colors

Windows Commands

F12 View/Show Colors

Oval Picture Box tool

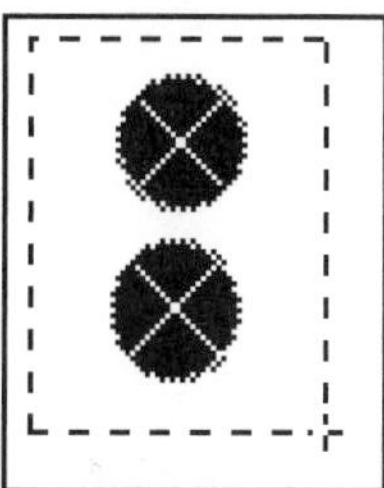

Click and drag with either the Item tool or the Content tool to draw a selection marquee around multiple items (above). Be careful not to include the automatic text box if there is one. Should you include any item you don't want, press the Shift key once you've drawn the marquee and click on the item you want to deselect (below).

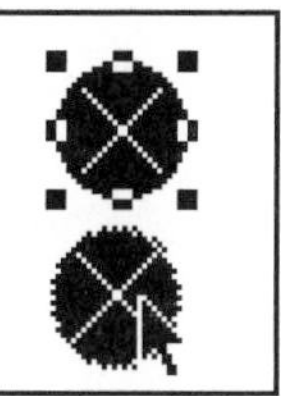

When the bow (top) was split using the Outside Paths command, only two new boxes were created, one for each side of the bow.

When the bow (top) was split using the All Paths command, four separate boxes were created, two for the black ribbon areas of the bow and two for the gray, inner, blank areas of the bow.

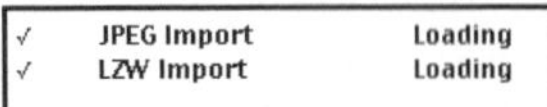

These XTensions must be active to import a JPEG image saved with LZW compression.

Concave-Corner Picture Box tool

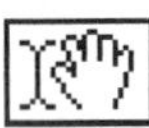

Content tool

LESSON 5
SPLIT COMMANDS

The Split command is used to split merged boxes that contain nonoverlapping shapes, to split boxes that contain shapes within shapes, or to split boxes that contain a border that crosses over itself, such as a figure eight.

SPLIT OUTSIDE PATHS

The Outside Paths option from the Split command splits a box that consists of two or more closed paths and that are separated by a space. If, for example, you use the Bézier Freehand tool to draw a bow that consists of an inside (blank area) and outside (ribbon area), when you select that item and apply the Split/Outside Paths command, the result is two separate boxes. The interior or blank area of each side of the bow is not split into separate boxes.

SPLIT ALL PATHS

The Split All Paths command splits all the closed paths in the selected item and creates separate boxes for those closed paths. This command works for Bézier boxes shaped like a donut. The Split All Paths command will create four boxes, two for the outside shape and two for the holes.

EXERCISE E

1. Before beginning this exercise, make sure the JPEG and LZW XTensions are active. On a new page in the document, use the Concave-Corner Picture Box tool to draw two picture boxes. Assign them each a different background color from the Colors palette (F12). Make sure the boxes are close to each other but not overlapping (Figure 16.10).
2. Shift-select both boxes and choose Item/Merge/Union. The two boxes appear to be separate, but they have been joined into one Bézier box that displays the color of the first box you created (Figure 16.10).
3. With the new box selected, choose File/Get Picture. Navigate to the Unit 16 folder on the CD-ROM and import the *Firemen* file (a TIFF image) into the box. Select the Content tool and click inside the box. Use the Picture Mover pointer to position the image so that part of it appears in each box (Figure 16.10).

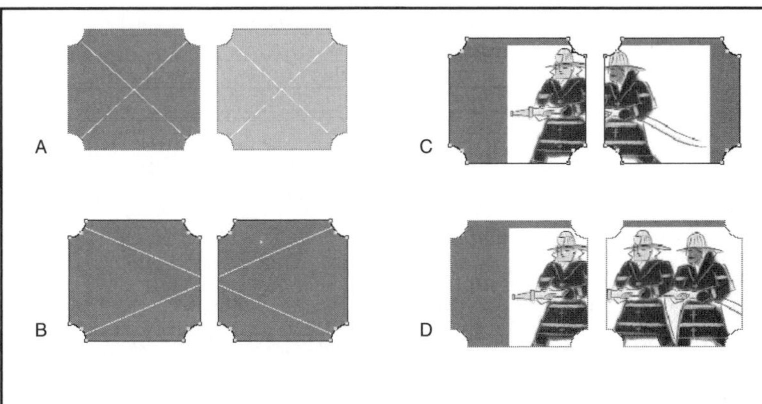

Figure 16.10. Two separate picture boxes (A) are merged using the Union command making them one picture box (B), into which a graphic is imported (C). That same box is split, using the Outside Paths option, into two boxes that can be moved independently of each other (D).

4. Use the Item tool to select the original Bézier box and choose Item/Split/Outside Paths. Choosing Outside Paths keeps all the outside path information and divides any nonoverlapping outside paths into separate boxes. In this case, the Split command will split the single Bézier box into two separate Bézier boxes with a separate image in each box.
5. Use the Item tool to select one of the picture boxes and delete it (Item/Delete). Select the remaining picture box and drag its Bézier points to the center to create a new shape (Figure 16.11). Make sure some areas of the box overlap other areas, otherwise the Split command won't be available.

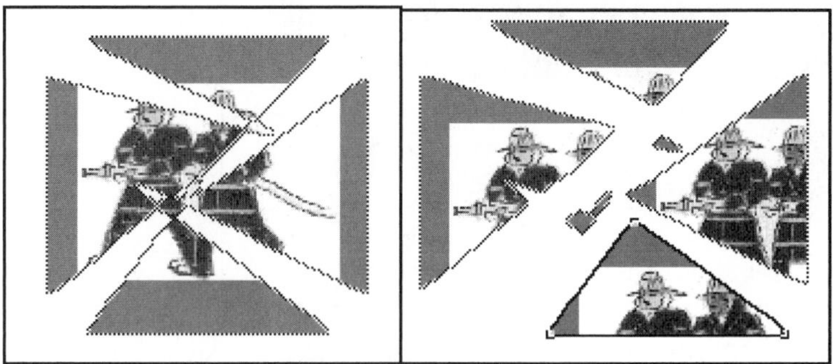

Figure 16.11. Drag the Bézier points to reshape the picture box (left). When you choose the Split/All Paths command, any non-overlapping areas will be split off as separate shapes(right).

Macintosh Commands

⌘-K Item/Delete

Windows Commands

Ctrl-K Item/Delete

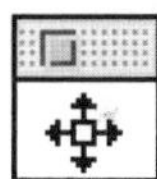

Item tool

Image info

The *Firemen* file is from *Metropolis* by Rob Porazinski, for Artville.

6. With the box still selected, choose Item/Split/All Paths to create separate boxes from every shape within the original box (Figure 16.11). Use the Item tool to move the smaller boxes around on the page.
7. On a new page in the document create a large text box. Type *Go, Going, Gone!* Press Return/Enter. Format the type in a bold type face and large type size. Make sure all the type is on the same line.
8. Select the type and choose Edit/Copy. Click below the line of type and choose Edit/Paste to create a second line of type.
9. Select the first line of type with the Content tool and choose Style/Text to Box to convert the text characters to a single Bézier box. With the Bézier box selected, select a background color from the Colors palette. Then choose Item/Split/Outside Paths. Notice that the interior of the box "characters" are transparent because the whole "character" is one path.
10. Select the second line of type and choose Style/Text to Box. Fill the Bézier box with a background color. With the box still selected, choose Item/Split All Paths. Click on the center of the *o* in Gone and choose a contrasting background color from the Colors palette. Because the center of the box is a separate path, it can be manipulated separately from the rest of the "character" and different colors can be applied to the separate paths. You can also delete unwanted paths (Figure 16.12).
11. Close this file (File/Close) Don't save your changes.

Figure 16.12. When the Split All Paths command is applied to Bézier boxes, any interior paths are also split and can be manipulated separately from the other boxes. When a frame is applied to the selected outlines, the interior paths are not framed.

Macintosh Commands

F12 View/Show Colors
⌘-W File/Close

Windows Commands

F12 View/Show Colors
Ctrl-F4 File/Close

When Split/Outside Paths is selected, no interior paths are created. Framing the boxes creates a frame around the entire box outline.

TEXT TO GRAPHICS

OVERVIEW

In this unit you will learn how to:

Convert standard-shape boxes to Bézier boxes
Convert lines to text paths
Convert text to graphics
Reshape boxes
Split boxes

TERMS

Content
Contentless box

HOW IT WORKS:

Begin by formatting the text and converting it to boxes. Import a graphic that has been sized to fit the height and width of the single Bézier picture box. (Because the boxes are not split, one graphic will fill what is a single Bézier picture box). Once the graphic has been imported, select the single Bézier box and choose the Split Outside command to split the single picture box into multiple boxes. Use the Item tool to move the boxes closer together. Select all the boxes with the Item tool and add a frame for emphasis. The most efficient way of creating this effect is to split the boxes and import individual images that have been sized in Photoshop to fit the "text" character picture boxes.

Macintosh Commands

⌘-N File/New

Windows Commands

Ctrl-N File/New

Orientation: 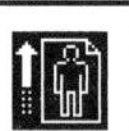 

Selecting the Landscape icon creates a page wider than it is high.

Color options

Once text is converted to a box, it can be filled with a gradient from the Modify dialog box or from the Colors palette.

LESSON 1
CONVERTING TEXT TO GRAPHICS

Whether you import text into a QuarkXPress text box or type it in directly from the keyboard, you are working with text, not graphics. You can only apply text formatting attributes to the text. For example, to resize text, select it and choose another point size from either the Style menu or from the Measurements palette. You can change the type's horizontal or vertical scale and its position on the baseline, but you can't manipulate it as you would an item consisting of Bézier segments unless you first convert the individual text characters to picture boxes.

When a text character is converted to a picture box, it no longer exists as text, but as a Bézier picture box. This means that you can import a picture into the item and manipulate the image just as you would in any picture box you create with the picture box tools. And because the picture box has Bézier points and handles, you can reshape the item any way you wish. You can then convert the picture box to a text box by selecting an option from the Item/Content menu. Just remember that once you convert text characters to boxes, you are no longer working with text, so you can't apply any of the text formatting commands to the Bézier items.

EXERCISE A

1. Create a new document with half-inch margins and an automatic text box. Select the Landscape icon in the Orientation field to create an 11 X 8.5 page. Type *HARD* in the text box, double-click to select it, and format it in any typeface at about 200 points.
2. With the word still selected, choose Style/Text to Box. The four text characters are duplicated as a single picture box (Figure 17.1).

Figure 17.1. The Text to Box command converts the four text characters to a single Bézier picture box.

3. Select the Item tool and click on the new box. Move it around the page and notice that all four text characters now form one picture box.
4. With the picture box still selected, choose File/Get Picture. Navigate to the Unit 17 folder on the CD-ROM and double-click on the *Stone1* file (a TIFF image) to open it. The graphic fills almost the whole box.
5. Select the Content tool and use the Picture Mover pointer to drag the image around the box. Position the graphic so that the bottom part of the box is empty. Keep the box selected.
6. Display the Colors palette (F12), click on the Background icon, and select a color from the palette. It fills the remaining part of the box.
7. With the box still selected, click on a color swatch in the Colors palette and drag it onto the picture box. The new color replaces the original background color.
8. Choose File/Save and save this file in your Projects folder as *Boxes.qxd*. You will need it for the next exercise.

Macintosh Commands

⌘-Y File/Get Text/Picture
F12 View/Show Colors
⌘-S FIle/Save

Windows Commands

Ctrl-Y File/Get Text/Picture
F12 View/Show Colors
Ctrl-S FIle/Save

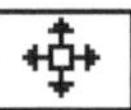

Item tool

Content tool

LESSON 2
SPLITTING BOXES

When you first convert text to a box, all the selected text converts to one picture box. The outline of that picture box follows the contours of the original text, but the box behaves as one item. This means that you can import only one graphic into the box. To import a different graphic into each converted text character, you must split the large picture box into individual picture boxes.

SPLIT OUTSIDE PATHS

The Split Outside Paths command creates single boxes shaped to the outside path specifications of the type. For example, this command splits a text character such as *O* into one box, not into a box for the outer character and another one for the center of the character.

SPLIT ALL PATHS

The Split All Paths command creates boxes from every shape in a character. If this command is applied to a box converted from the *P* character, two boxes would result—one for the outline of the *P* and one for the interior bowl of the *P*, called the counter.

The original type (top) is converted to a box that is split using Outside Paths (center), which results in only three paths, and split using All Paths (bottom), which results in five paths.

Macintosh Commands

⌘-O File/Open
⌘-W File/Close
F12 View/Show Colors

Windows Commands

Ctrl-F Edit/Find Change
Ctrl-F4 File/Close
F12 View/Show Colors

Don't move an item until the Item tool icon appears; otherwise, you'll reshape the item instead of moving it.

Tip

It's sometimes easier to select a Bézier item with the temporary Item tool than with the Item tool itself. Press the Command/Ctrl key to convert most tools to the temporary Item tool.

Item tool

Content tool

EXERCISE B

1. If necessary, open the *Boxes.qxd* file you created in the last exercise or open the *Boxes.qxd* file in the Unit 17 folder on the CD-ROM. Select the large automatic text box. Display the Colors palette (F12), click the Background icon, and click the Cyan color. Drag the Percent menu down to 60. This gives you a soft background color for the box so that when you split the boxes, you'll see exactly what becomes transparent against the cyan background.
2. Use the Item tool to select the large picture box, and choose Item/Split/Outside Paths. This creates an individual Bézier box out of each "text character."
3. The first box, the *H* box, is selected. Use the Content tool to drag the graphic around inside the box. Then click with the Content tool on the other three boxes that also contain the entire graphic, and drag the graphic around the box. Where the graphic is moved beyond the boundary of the box, the background color appears. Your screen should resemble Figure 17.2.

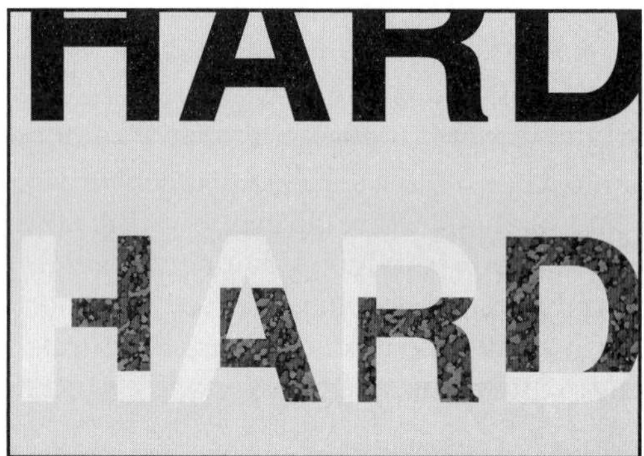

Figure 17.2. The four boxes contain four copies of the original graphic that can be moved independently of each other.

4. Use the Item tool to select each box and move it around the page. Because the boxes are each individual picture boxes, they can be moved independently of one another.
5. Close this file (File/Close). Don't save your changes.

LESSON 3
CONVERTING BOXES

Any picture box created in version 4.0 can be converted to a text box and any text box can be converted to a picture box. You can also specify a box to be neither a picture box nor a text box, just an item. When you convert a box from one type or another, an alert displays telling you that the contents of the box will be lost if you make the conversion, so be sure you have saved the graphics and/or text before you convert boxes.

Macintosh Commands

⌘-O File/Open
⌘-W File/Close

Windows Commands

Ctrl-O File/Open
Ctrl-F4 File/Close

Item tool

EXERCISE C

1. Open the *Boxes.qxd* file you created earlier or open the *Boxes.qxd* file in the Unit 17 folder on the CD-ROM. Select the Item tool and click on the HARD picture box below the text. Choose Item/Split/Outside Paths.
2. Select the Item tool and click on the *A*. Choose Item/Content/Text. Picture is currently selected, indicating that this box is a picture box. Click OK at the alert. The graphic is stripped from the picture box, leaving only the background color for the new text box.
3. Click on the Content tool and type a few words in the new text box. Your screen should resemble Figure 17.3.

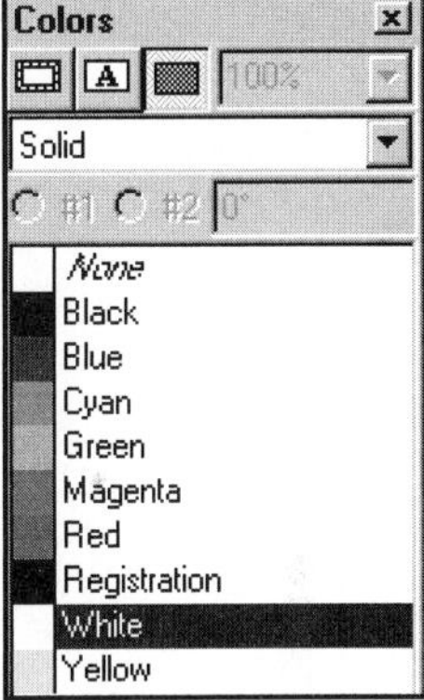

Click to select the Background icon to change the background color of any box. Click on a color's name to apply the color, or drag a color swatch on to the selected box to change its background color.

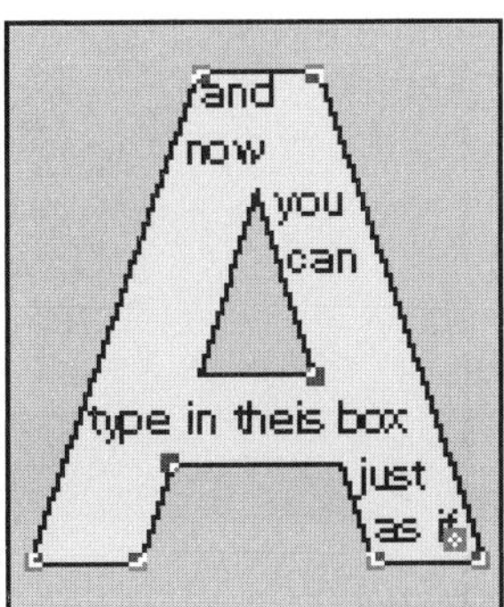

Figure 17.3. When a picture box is converted to a text box, you can type inside the box just as if you had created the box as a multi-sided text box.

4. Click on the *H* box and choose Item/Content/None. Click OK at the alert. If you choose File/Get Text or File/Get Picture, you will get a beep, indicating that this box can no longer hold text or display graphics, only a background color.
5. Close this file (File/Close). Don't save your changes.

FYI

A box with contents of None is called a *Contentless box.*

Macintosh Commands

⌘-O File/Open

Windows Commands

Ctrl-O File/Open

Item tool

Content tool

Sorry

You can convert only one line of text to a box at one time. To convert more than one line of text, select each line and use the Text to Box command each time.

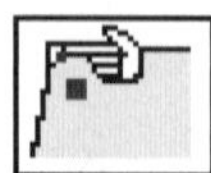

When you move the cursor over a point on a selected Bézier item, the Point pointer (black square) appears, indicating that you are on or have selected a Bézier point.

LESSON 4
RESHAPING BOXES

Once you convert text to Bézier picture boxes, those boxes can be reshaped just like any Bézier box by dragging the anchor points around the box. You can also convert the anchor points, just as you did with Bézier boxes created with any of the Bézier picture box tools.

EXERCISE D

1. Choose File/Open and open the *Boxes.qxd* file in your Projects folder or in the Unit 17 folder on the CD-ROM. Display the Measurements palette (View/Show Measurements).
2. Use the Item tool to select the large picture box and choose Item/Split/Outside Paths. Select the Item tool and click on the *H* box to select it. Press the Delete/Backspace key. Delete the *R* and *D* boxes. Use the Content tool to select the word *HARD* and delete it. This leaves only the *A* picture box on the page.
3. Use the Zoom tool to magnify the lower part of the *A* box. Click on the corner point to select it. Press the Shift key while clicking on the opposite corner point to select it also. Release the Shift key and drag the selected points downward to reshape the box (Figure 17.4).

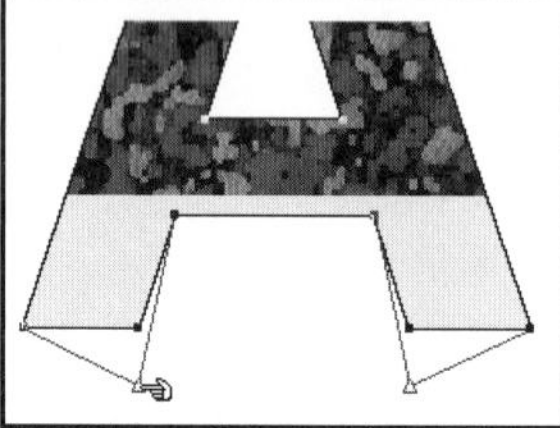

Figure 17.4. The two corner points were Shift-selected and dragged together to reshape both sides of the box.

4. Shift-select the two points at the top of the A (Figure 17.5). Click on the Symmetrical icon in the Measurements palette (the middle icon) to convert the corner points to symmetrical smooth points. Use the direction handles to expand the width of the box (Figure 17.6). Continue to reshape the box until it is large enough to display a graphic.

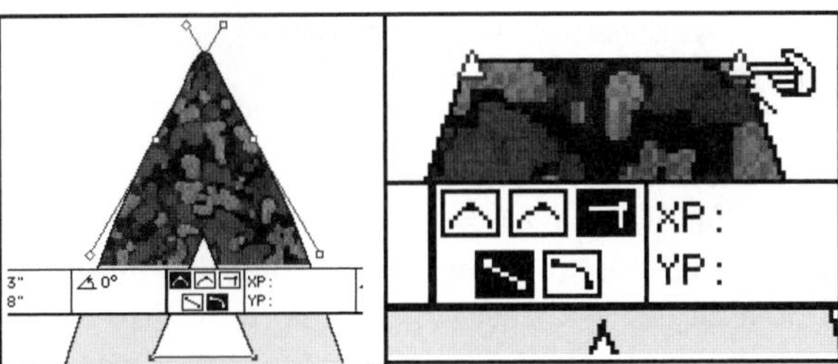

Figure 17.5. Shift-selecting the two corner points at the top of the A box, and clicking the Symmetrical icon in the Measurements palette, converts the corner points to smooth points with direction handles equidistant from the selected points.

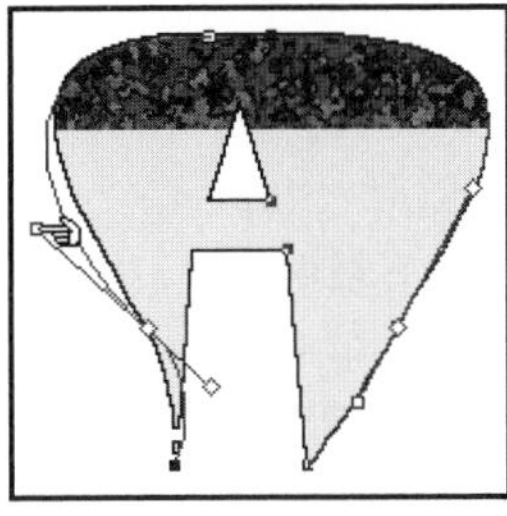

Figure 17.6. Moving the direction handles instead of the anchor points widens the box.

5. With the box still selected, choose File/Get Picture. Navigate to the Images folder on the CD-ROM and import a picture into the box. Use the Content tool to move the picture around the box. Press the Command-Option-Shift < or > keys (Macintosh) or Ctrl-Alt-Shift < or > keys (Windows) to proportionally reduce or enlarge the graphic in the box.
6. Close this file. Don't save your changes.

LESSON 5
CONVERTING LINES TO TEXT PATHS

Any conventional line can be converted to a Bézier text path using the commands under the Item menu. Once a line created with either the Orthogonal Line tool or the Line tool is converted to a Bézier line, the Content (Item/Content) of that line can be changed from None to Text, making the line a text path.

Once a line has been converted to a Bézier text path, the Shape menu can be used to convert it back to a conventional line. Although the conventional line will still display the text, it no longer has Bézier points. Instead, it displays only one resizing handle at each end of the line.

Macintosh Commands

⌘-E File/Get Text/Picture
⌘-Option-Shift </> Enlarges or reduces a picture in 5% increments
⌘-W File/Close

Windows Commands

Ctrl-E File/Get Text/Picture
Ctrl-Alt-Shift </> Enlarges or reduces a picture in 5% increments
Ctrl-F4 File/Close

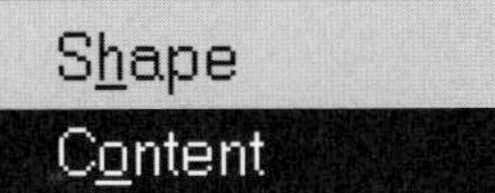

The Content menu (Item/Content) displays a check mark next to the the current contents of a selected box.

Macintosh Commands

⌘-N File/New/Document
⌘-W File/Close

Windows Commands

Ctrl-N File/New/Document
Ctrl-F4 File/Close

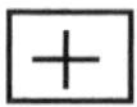

Orthogonal Line tool

The Bézier Line icon is selected under the Shape menu.

FYI

Select the Bézier line option from the Shape menu to convert a conventional line to a Bézier path.

Shape up

The Shape option must be selected under the Item/Edit menu before you can reshape and convert a line.

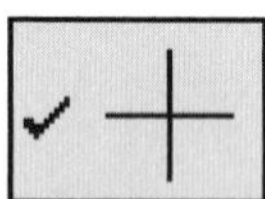

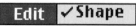

The Orthogonal Line icon is selected under the Shape menu.

EXERCISE E

1. Create a new document (File/New/Document) without an automatic text box. Display the Measurements palette (F9). Use the Orthogonal Line tool to draw a horizontal line about 4 inches long. Choose Style/Width/6 pt. Choose Item/Edit and make sure that Shape is selected.
2. With the line still selected, choose Item/Shape and drag to select the Bézier line icon, the last option in the menu. The line now has Bézier points and can be reshaped. Click on each of the endpoints and reshape the line. Press the Control key (Macintosh) or Ctrl-Shift (Windows) while clicking on a point to display its direction handles, and use the handles to reshape the line.
3. With the line still selected, choose Item/Content/Text. This converts the Bézier line to a Bézier text path. The I-beam cursor appears at the beginning of the path. Type *SMILE!* on the path. Double-click on the word and use the Measurements palette to change its font, type size, and alignment. With the word still selected, use the tracking arrows to add space between the characters. Your screen should resemble Figure 17.7.

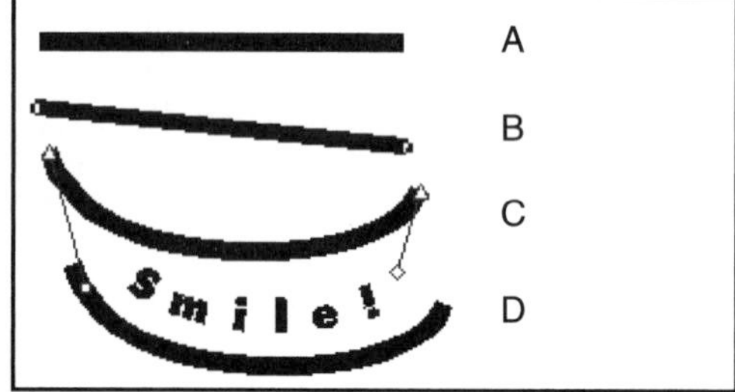

Figure 17.7. The top line (A) was created with the Orthogonal Line tool. It was then converted to a Bézier line (B) and its endpoints were reshaped (3). The Contents were changed to Text, making the original conventional line a Bézier text path (C). Text was added and styled using the Baseline Shift command (D).

4. With the path still selected, choose Item/Shape and select the Orthogonal Line icon to convert the Bézier path to a conventional line. Click on the resizing handle at one end of the line and notice that you can no longer reshape the line, only resize it.
5. Close this file. Don't save your changes.

UNIT 18
Anchored Items and Rules

OVERVIEW

In this unit you will learn how to:
Anchor items to text
Anchor rules to text

TERMS

anchored item
anchored rule
rule

HOW IT WORKS:

The Rule Below command applied an 18-point rule to the Anchored Items paragraph. Pressing Return/Enter twice created two new paragraph returns (¶), to which rules were applied. The first rule was assigned a width of 12 points, indented 6 picas from the right, and shaded at 60% black. The second rule was assigned a width of 6 points at 30% black. The line style alternated between thick and thin lines.

LESSON 1
WHY ANCHOR?

There are several ways an item can dance with text in QuarkXPress 4.0. It can intrude on the text, it can repel the text, and it can have the text run around the item. In all these instances, if you reflow or edit the text, its relation to the item changes, and you may have to reposition or resize the graphic to keep the effect you want to create. However, if you anchor that graphic (such as an initial cap) to the text, then no matter how you edit the text, add or delete characters, resize or realign the text, that graphic item will remain anchored to its original position in the paragraph.

You can anchor any item to a paragraph, whether it's a standard-shape or Bézier picture box, text box, text path, or line. You can even convert text to a Bézier box and anchor that Bézier box anywhere in the paragraph. Like all anchored boxes, anchored Bézier boxes can be reshaped after they have been anchored.

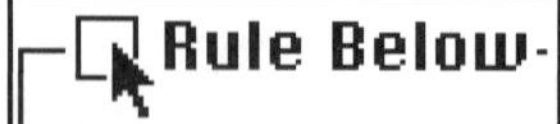

Very important info!

Each time you press the Return/Enter key after a paragraph with an anchored rule, the rule information attaches to the paragraph return (¶). To remove the rule, select the paragraph mark, choose Style/ Rules, and deselect the Rule Above or Rule Below check box.

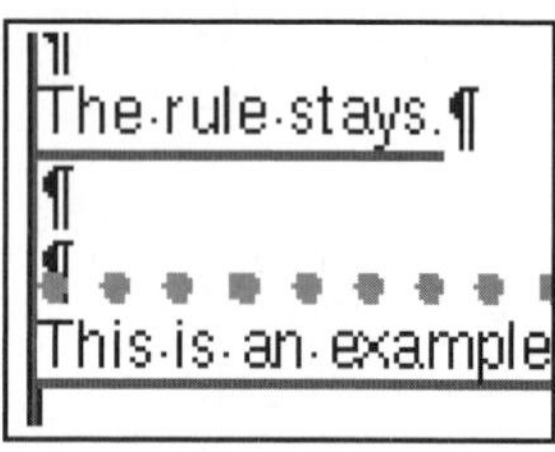

ANCHORED ITEMS

Anchoring items is a two-step/two-tool process. First, select the box, text path, or line with the Item tool and choose Edit/Cut. Then select the Content tool, click anywhere in a paragraph, and choose Edit/Paste. The cut item is pasted at the selected position and remains anchored to the paragraph at that position regardless of how the paragraph flows as you edit the text. To remove an anchored item, use the Content tool and click immediately after the anchored item, then press the Delete/Backspace key. Or select the anchored item with the Item tool and choose Edit/Cut.

ANCHORED RULES

A line attached to a paragraph is called a *rule*. Anchored rules are used above and below text as design elements to set off the information in a particular paragraph. It is absolutely critical that a line associated with a paragraph move with the paragraph, and the only way to do this is to use the anchored rule command.

The Rules tab in the Formats dialog box is used to specify the kind of rule that will be anchored to a paragraph and its distance above and/or below the selected paragraph. Although this dialog box looks complicated, it's really easy to use. Once a rule is anchored to a paragraph, it cannot be removed from that paragraph unless you use the Rules dialog box and deselect the Rule Above and/or the Rule Below check box. Like most elements in XPress, a rule can be edited and incorporated into a paragraph style sheet.

EXERCISE A

1. Create a new file (File/New/Document) with an automatic text box. Choose view/Show Invisibles. Type *This is an example of a rule below a paragraph.* Press the Return/Enter key to generate a paragraph return. Click anywhere inside the paragraph to select it.

2. Choose Style/Rules to display the Paragraph Attributes dialog box. The Rules tab is active. Click on the Rule Below check box to activate the function. Use the Length pull-down menu to select Text. Type 30% in the Offset field to position the rule 30% of the distance from the baseline of the last line of the paragraph. Type 2 in the Width field and choose blue from the Color menu. Click on OK. Your screen should resemble Figure 18.1.

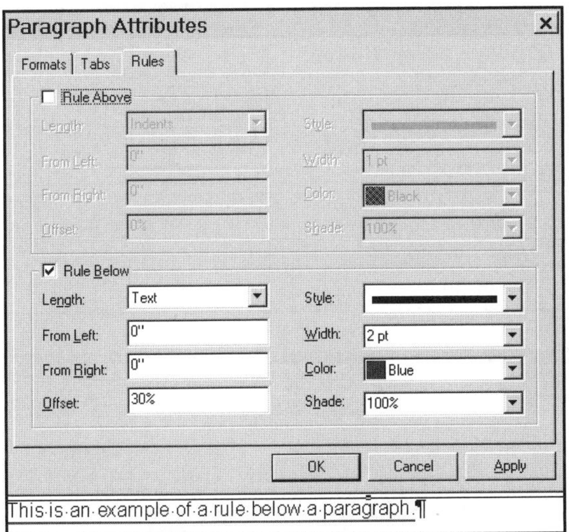

Figure 18.1. A 2-pt. blue rule is applied to the paragraph. It will run only the length of the last line of the text in the paragraph and is positioned 30% of the distance from the baseline of the text.

3. Click before the first letter in the paragraph and press the Return/Enter key a few times. Notice that the rule remains anchored to the paragraph.

4. Click anywhere in the paragraph to select it. Choose Style/Rules again. Click the Rule Above check box to activate the function. Choose Indents from the Length menu. Press the Tab key twice and type 1 in the From Right field to offset the rule 1 inch from the right margin. Press the Tab key once and type 1p in the Offset field to offset the rule 1 pica from the top of the first line in the paragraph.

Macintosh Commands

⌘-N File/New/Document
⌘-I View/Show Invisibles
⌘-Shift-N Style/Rules

Windows Commands

Ctrl-N File/New/Document
Ctrl-I View/Show Invisibles
Ctrl-Shift-N Style/Rules

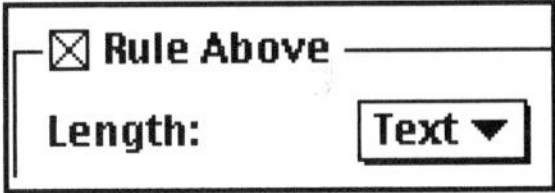

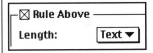

FYI

Selecting Text from the Length pull-down menu runs the rule only the length of the last word in the paragraph.

Macintosh Commands

⌘-Shift-N Style/Rules
⌘-W File/Close

Windows Commands

Ctrl-Shift-N Style/Rules
Ctrl-F4 File/Close

FYI

A rule is a paragraph format and you must select the paragraph before applying the rule. To remove a rule select the paragraph, or the paragraph return mark if it's an empty ruled line (¶), and use the Rules dialog box to deselect the rule option.

5. Choose All Dots from the Style menu, 6 from the Width menu, and red from the Color menu. Click on OK. Your screen should resemble Figure 18.2.

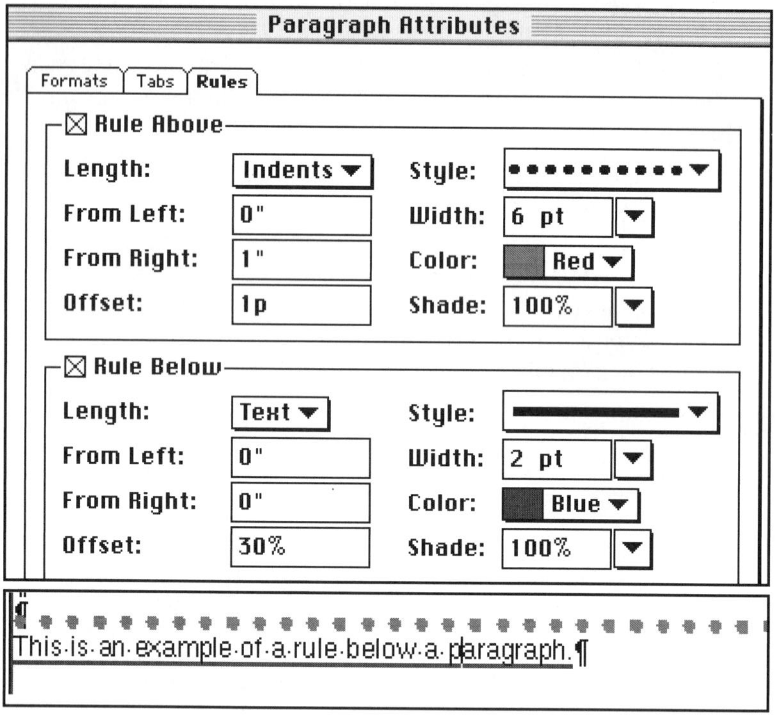

Paragraph Attributes

Formats | Tabs | Rules

☒ Rule Above

Length:	Indents	Style:	•••••••••••
From Left:	0"	Width:	6 pt
From Right:	1"	Color:	Red
Offset:	1p	Shade:	100%

☒ Rule Below

Length:	Text	Style:	———
From Left:	0"	Width:	2 pt
From Right:	0"	Color:	Blue
Offset:	30%	Shade:	100%

This is an example of a rule below a paragraph.¶

Figure 18.2. A paragraph can have an anchored rule above and below the paragraph.

6. With the paragraph still selected, choose Style/Rules. Deselect the Rule Below check box to remove the blue rule. Click OK. Only the red rule above the paragraph remains.
7. Close this file. Don't save your changes.

LESSON 2 ANCHORED BOXES

You can anchor a box or line to a paragraph so that when the paragraph moves, the box or line moves with it. In other words, anchored boxes and lines are treated like text characters, in that they are part of the paragraph just as any text character is.

EXERCISE B

1. Create a new file with an automatic text box (File/New/Document). Type the following sentence: *Men won't ask for directions on the information highway either.* Press the Return/Enter key.
2. Open the *Anchor Library* (File/Open) in the Unit 18 folder on the CD-ROM. It displays several images. Use the Item tool to drag the *M* image out of the library and onto the page. With the *M* box still selected, choose Edit/Cut.
3. Select the Content tool and click before the *M* in the sentence. Choose Item/Paste. The image is anchored to the paragraph. Delete the original capital *M* in the sentence. You have created an initial cap anchored to the paragraph. Click before the anchored image and press the Return/Enter key a few times. Notice that the image moves with the paragraph (Figure 18.3).

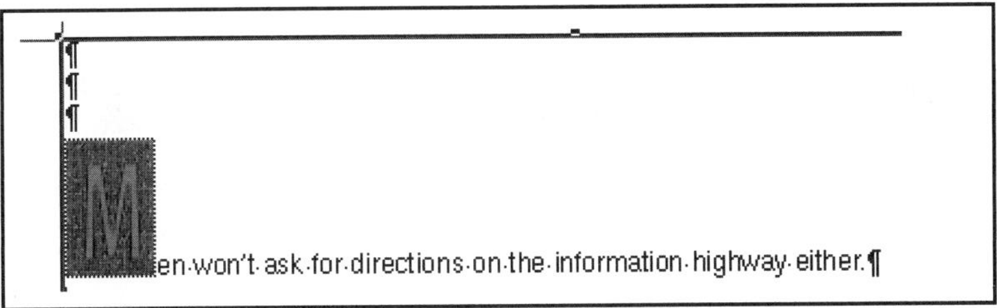

Figure 18.3. The TIFF image was imported into an XPress picture box, stored in a library, and anchored to the paragraph.

4. Display the Measurements palette (F9). Click on the anchored box and click on the top Alignment icon at the extreme left of the Measurements palette to align the anchored box with the ascent of the top line. Click on the bottom Alignment icon to align the anchored box with the baseline of the text.
5. Select the anchored box with the Content tool. Resize the box using the Resizing pointer, and use the X% and Y% values in the Measurements palette to resize the image.
6. Select the anchored box with the Content tool and choose File/Get Picture. Navigate to the Images folder on the CD-ROM and import any of the images in the folder. Resize the anchored picture box to accommodate the graphic.

Macintosh Commands

⌘-N File/New/Document
⌘-X Edit/Cut
⌘-V Edit/Paste
⌘-E File/Get Text/Picture

Windows Commands

Ctrl-N File/New/Document
Ctrl-X Edit/Cut
Ctrl-V Edit/Paste
Ctrl-E File/Get Text/Picture

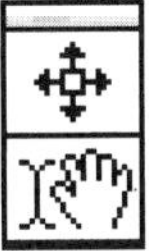

Item tool (above) and Content tool (below)

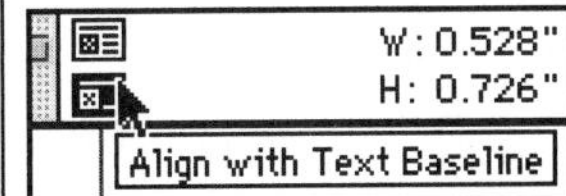

When an anchored item is selected, click on this icon to align the anchored item with the ascent of the first line in the paragraph.

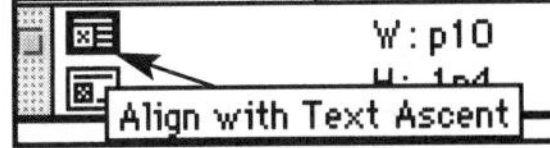

When an anchored item is selected, click on this icon to align the anchored item with the baseline of the first line in the paragraph.

Macintosh Commands

⌘-N File/New/Document
⌘-X Edit/Cut
⌘-V Edit/Paste
⌘-W File/Close

Windows Commands

Ctrl-N File/New/Document
Ctrl-X Edit/Cut
Ctrl-V Edit/Paste
Ctrl F4 File/Close

7. To delete an anchored box, click on the item to select it, click with the Content tool to the right of the box, in front of the *e* in *en* and press the Delete/Backspace key. Or, select the anchored item with the Item tool and choose Edit/Cut. You can then use the Content tool to paste the item somewhere else in that paragraph or in another paragraph.
8. Close this file (File/Close). Don't save your changes.

LESSON 3
ANCHORED LINES

Both Bézier and conventional lines can be anchored to a paragraph in the same way a text box or a picture box is anchored to a paragraph. Anchoring lines lets you create interesting design effects without worrying about keeping the line with the paragraph when you flow text before or after the paragraph.

EXERCISE C

Item tool

1. Create a new file with an automatic text box (File/New/Document). Type any name and press the Return/Enter key. Repeat until you have a list of five names.
2. Use any of the line tools to draw any kind of line below the list of names. Select the line with the Item tool and choose Edit/Cut.
3. Click before the first character in the first line and choose Edit/Paste. Repeat for the four other paragraphs.
4. Click on any line and resize it or reshape it, or, if it's a Bézier line, reshape it.
5. Close this file (File/Close). Don't save your changes.

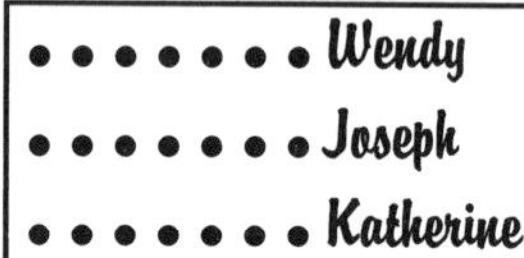

Use any line style to indent names with an anchored line.

UNIT 19
Color

Image from *Roundhead Executives*
by Barton Stabler, for Artville

OVERVIEW

In this unit you will learn how to:
Specify, apply, edit, and delete colors
Use different color models
Create gradients
Specify trapping values

TERMS

choke
color models
gradient
Hexachrome Color System
knockout
misregistration
multi-ink color system
overprint
spot color
spread
trapping

HOW IT WORKS:

This image from Artville started life as an EPS color image. Because only a smaller grayscale version was needed, the image was opened in Illustrator, resized, and saved as an Illustrator EPS file. A new Photoshop document was created in Grayscale mode with a resolution of 300 pixels per inch. The EPS file was placed (not opened) in the Photoshop file, where it was automatically converted to grayscale. It was then saved as a Photoshop EPS file and imported into an XPress picture box. The image could also have been converted to grayscale automatically when imported into the picture box. Pressing the Command/Ctrl key when clicking on Open in the Get Picture dialog box automatically converts a color image to grayscale.

LESSON 1
COLOR PRINCIPLES

You have been creating and editing color in several earlier units, so by now you should be familiar with some of the basic principles that apply to color. You know that you should always specify color from the swatch book that matches the color system you have selected. You know that colors must be created in the Edit/Colors dialog box and added to a document's color list before they can be accessed from any of the menus, dialog boxes, or the Colors palette. You know that selecting the Spot Color check box in the Edit Color dialog box will print that color on a separate plate; deselecting the Spot Color check box will separate the color onto four plates. And perhaps by now you also know that there's a lot of voodoo in color work. The type of press, the pressperson's skill, the weight and coating of the paper, the quality of the inks—all these contribute to producing print documents that, hopefully, resemble what we call "living color."

Colorizing TIFF files

Color can be applied to 1-bit and grayscale TIFF images, not to color TIFFs.

CMS XTension

QuarkXPress 4.0 ships with CMS, a color management XTension. This XTension checks the colors in the source image against the colors displayed by the monitor profile you select and against the printer profile you select. If your monitor or printer can't support a color specified in the document, Quark CMS changes the offending color to the closest matching color. To use Quark CMS, the XTension must be loaded via the XTensions Manager and the Color Management Active check box must be selected in the Color Management Preferences dialog box.

ADDING AND EDITING COLORS

QuarkXPress 4.0 ships with many color libraries, including the popular PANTONE and TRUMATCH systems as well as the new Multi-Ink and Hexachrome color systems. However, before you can apply a color to an item, a frame, text, Bézier paths, or certain graphic files, that color must be selected and named in the Edit Color dialog box. Once that is done, the color becomes part of that document's color list and is available for you to apply from either the Style menu, the Colors palette, or several dialog boxes. If you select and name a color when no documents are open, that custom color becomes part of the QuarkXPress color list and you can access it from any document. You can always delete a custom color.

HIGH-END COLOR MODELS

QuarkXPress 4.0 ships with two high-end color models, Multi-Ink and Hexachrome Uncoated and Hexachrome Coated. The Multi-Ink model lets you create a single ink color based on screen percentages of existing process tints and/or spot color inks. The Hexachrome models, sometimes called "HiFi color," are color matching systems developed by Pantone, Inc., that consist of process colors printed with six plates instead of the traditional four plates. By adding orange and green to the four CMYK plates, you can create brighter colors and increase the range of reproducible colors. Before specifying either of these colors, check with your printer, as these colors have special press requirements and are expensive to print.

EDITING COLORS

There are several ways to edit a color that has been added to the document's color list. You can change the color model, for example, from Pantone Coated to CMYK. You can then edit the CMYK color, by increasing or decreasing the percentages of any or all of the four process colors, cyan, magenta, yellow, and black. You can also change a color from spot color to process color or visa versa. The only thing you should not edit is a color's name/number if the color was selected from a color model like Pantone or TRUMATCH. A color's name/number in the QuarkXPress library is the same name/number for that library in Adobe Photoshop, Adobe Illustrator, and many other graphics applications. If you change the number, other applications will not be able to apply it when you move text and images across applications and across computer platforms.

EXERCISE A

1. Create a new document without an automatic text box (File/New/Document). Choose Edit/Colors and click on New. Choose Pantone Process from the Model pull-down menu.
2. Scroll to locate color 111-1 or type 111-1 in the PANTONE field beneath the swatch library. A warm red appears in the New field on the left side of the dialog box. Be sure that the Spot Color check box is deselected, because this color will be separated and printed on four plates. Click OK. Pantone S-111-1 appears in the color list for the active document. Click on Save.
3. Use any of the picture box tools to draw a picture box. Display the Colors palette (F12). The new color appears in the Colors palette, indicating that it is available for use. With the picture box still selected and the Background icon selected on the Colors palette, click on the name of the Pantone color or drag the swatch for PANTONE S-111-1 onto the selected picture box to fill it with the background color.
4. Command/Ctrl-click on the Pantone color in the Colors palette to display the Colors for [filename] dialog box. Click on Edit. Choose CMYK from the Model pull-down menu. The Pantone color's name appears in the Name field (Figure 19.1) and the New/Original fields on the left side of the dialog box display the original color (Pantone Process) and the new color (CMYK).

Macintosh Commands

⌘-N File/New/Document
F12 View/Show Colors
Shift-F12 Edit/Colors

Windows Commands

Ctrl-N File/New/Document
F12 View/Show Colors
Shift-F12 Edit/Colors

Easy access

Command/Ctrl-click on any color in the Colors palette to display the color selected in the Colors dialog box for the document.

☐ Spot Color

Deselect this option in the Edit Colors dialog box to print the selected color as a process color.

FYI

Any color added to the document's color list appears automatically in the document's Colors palette.

Macintosh Commands

⌘-Option-S File/Save as
Shift-F12 Edit/Colors

Windows Commands

Ctrl-Alt-S File/Save as
Shift-F12 Edit/Colors

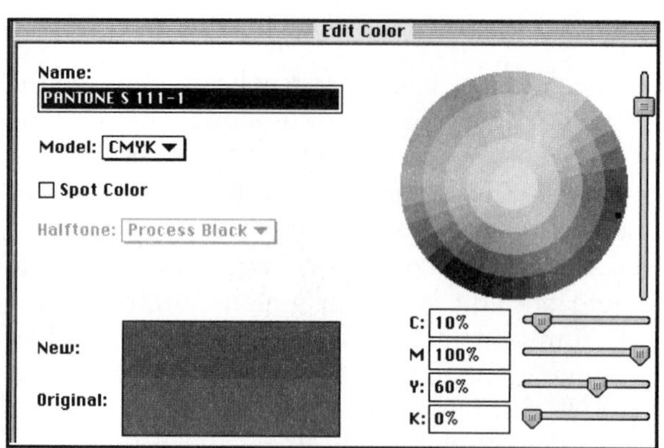

Figure 19.1. When you change a color model, the new color appears in the New field above the original color.

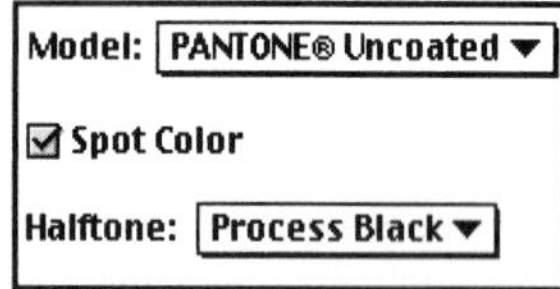

Select the Spot Color check box to specify a color that prints on only one plate.

5. Type CMYK Red in the Name field and move the CMYK sliders to change the color to a different color red. The new color appears in the New field in the dialog box. Click on OK and notice that CMYK Red replaces the original PANTONE color in the list of colors for the document (Figure 19.2). Click on Save. CMYK Red appears in the Colors palette instead of PANTONE S 111-1 and replaces the Pantone color in the picture box.

Figure 19.2. When a color is edited, its new name appears in the document's color palette.

Printing RGB colors

XPress automatically converts RGB colors to CMYK, which can make them appear murky. The best way to avoid this problem when printing to a color printer is to convert the colors to CMYK in an image editing program such as Photoshop.

You can also load the CMS (Color Management System) XTension and configure it to the appropriate device profile for your color printer. Choose Edit/Preferences/Color Management.

6. Choose Edit/Colors (Shift-F12). Use the Show menu to display Process Colors. Click on CMYK Red to select it and click on Edit. Click to select the Spot Color option so that this color will print as a spot color on one plate instead of as a process color on four plates. Click on OK. Click on Save.
7. Save the file as *Color.qxd* in your Projects folder. You will need it for the next exercise.

LESSON 2
DELETING COLORS

You can always delete any color from the document's color list. If you have applied that color to text or to an item, an alert will appear, giving you the opportunity to substitute another color for the color you are deleting. The Delete Color command is an easy way to globally substitute one color for another in a document without selecting items and text and reapplying the color.

EXERCISE B

1. If necessary, open the *Color.qxd* file or open the *Color.qxd* file in the Unit 19 folder on the CD-ROM. Display the Colors palette (F12). Choose Edit/Colors (Shift F12).
2. Click on New and select Pantone Uncoated from the Model pull-down menu. Select Pantone 166 from the swatch library or type 166 in the Pantone field below the library. Make sure the Spot Color check box is selected so the color will print on only one plate instead of on four plates. Click on OK. Click on Save to add the new color to the document's color list and to the Colors palette.
3. Choose Edit/Colors (Shift F12). Select Spot Colors from the Show menu. Both CMYK Red and Pantone 166 appear along with the default RGB colors. The Colors palette should also display CMYK Red and PANTONE 166 along with the default process and spot colors.
4. Click on CMYK Red to select it and click on Delete. An alert appears asking you what color you want to use as a replacement for CMYK Red. Use the pull-down menu to select Pantone 166 (Figure 19.3). Click on OK. Click on Save. CMYK Red is removed from the document's color list and Colors palette, and the background color of the picture box changes to Pantone 166.
5. Close this file. Don't save your changes.

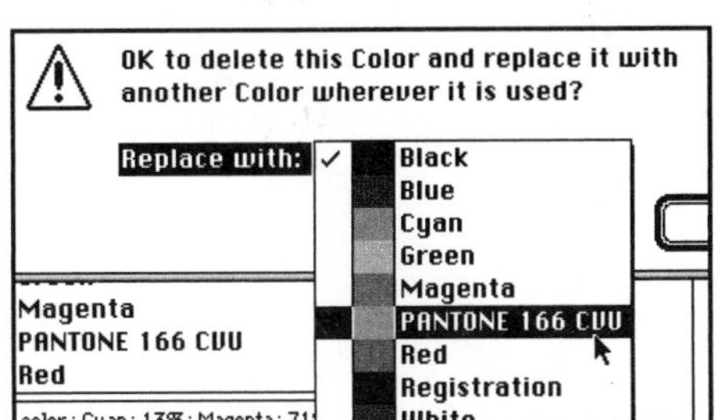

Figure 19.3. When a color that has been used in the document is deleted, you must choose a replacement color for the deleted color.

Macintosh Commands

⌘-O File/Open
⌘-W File/Close

Windows Commands

Ctrl-O File/Open
Ctrl-F4 File/Close

Quark color on the Web

QuarkXPress does not ship with a color-safe palette for use with documents converted to HTML pages or for use in QuarkImmedia projects.

Model: PANTONE® Uncoated

Printing on paper

The kind of paper you use affects color output. Use the Pantone Uncoated color model when printing with genuine Pantone inks on (less expensive) uncoated paper; use the Pantone Process color model when printing color separations with Pantone inks. The Pantone ProSim model is used when printing color separations with inks not manufactured by Pantone, Inc.

Macintosh Commands

⌘-N File/New/Document
⌘-O File/Open
Shift-F12 Edit/Colors

Windows Commands

Ctrl-N File/New/Document
Ctrl-O File/Open
Shift-F12 Edit/Colors

LESSON 3
DUPLICATING AND APPENDING COLORS

If you don't want to bother creating new colors, you can duplicate an existing color and edit the copy, or you can append one or all of any spot or process colors you created previously from any other XPress document. Just remember that when you duplicate and append colors, the spot color or process color designation stays with the color. If you have three or more spot colors in a document, you should convert all the spot colors to process colors so that you won't print more than four plates.

EXERCISE C

1. Create a new document (File/New/Document). Choose Edit/Colors (Shift-F12) and click on New. Choose Pantone Uncoated and select a color. Specify it as a spot color by selecting the Spot Color check box in the Edit Color dialog box. Click on OK.
2. Click on New again and create another Pantone Uncoated spot color. Click on OK. Use the Show menu to display Spot Colors. Your two new colors should appear along with the default RGB colors. Click on Save. Save the file as *Color1.qxd* in your Projects folder.
3. Open the *Color.qxd* file in the Unit 19 folder on the CD-ROM. Choose Edit/Colors (Shift-F12). Click on Append. Navigate to the *Color1.qxd* file in your Projects folder and click on Open.
4. In the Append Colors to [filename] dialog box, click on the first Pantone color in the Available panel and click on the black forward arrow to add it to the Including panel. Repeat for the second Pantone color. Click on OK. Click on Save. The two new colors are added to the Colors palette for the *Color.qxd* document (Figure 19.4).
5. In the *Color.qxd* file, choose Edit/Colors. Choose Spot Colors from the Show menu. Click on CMYK Red. Click on the Duplicate button to display the Edit Color dialog box. CMYK Red copy appears in the name field.

FYI

You can Shift-select multiple colors in the Available panel, then click the forward arrow once to include the colors.

FYI

A file must first be saved before anything—colors, style sheets, etc.—can be appended from it.

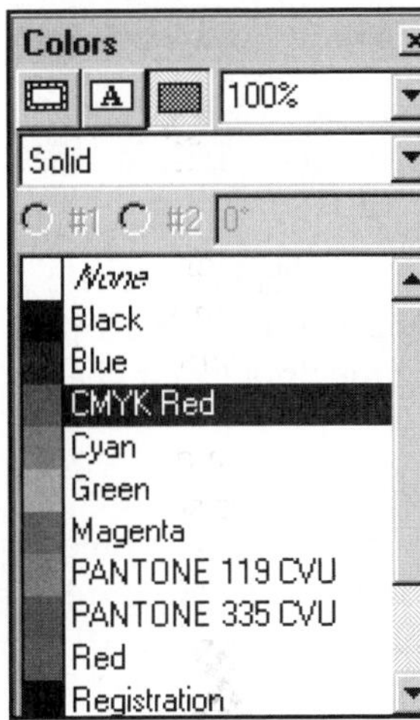

Figure 19.4. The two Pantone colors are appended to the Colors palette of the *Color.qxd* file.

6. Move the CMYK sliders to change the color, type a new name for the new color, and click on OK. Click on Save. CMYK Red copy is replaced by the new color.
7. Close this file. Don't save your changes.

LESSON 4 CREATING GRADIENTS

A blend, or as it is more properly called, a graduated fill or gradient, is comprised of two colors from the document's color list. You can create a blend in the Colors palette or in the Box Modify dialog box. QuarkXPress ships many different styles of blends, giving you unlimited design opportunities. Remember, however, that you must have created the colors you want to blend before you can create the blend. Never use any of the RGB colors for a blend in a print document. If you want to use any of the four process colors, select them from one of the libraries in the Edit Color dialog box. You'll get much better printing results.

To create anything but a linear blend, the Cool Blends XTension must be loaded before launching QuarkXPress. If the Cool Blends XTension is not in your XTension folder in the QuarkXPress folder, drag it out of the XTensions Disabled folder and into the XTension folder. Then relaunch QuarkXPress. Without the Cool Blends XTension active, only Linear and Solid are available options in the Colors palette.

Macintosh Commands

⌘-W File/Close

Windows Commands

Ctrl-F4 File/Close

The Cool Blends XTension must be in the XTensions folder in the QuarkXPress 4.0 folder in order to access all but the default gradient.

☑ Accurate Blends

Accurate Blends

Selecting Accurate Blends in the General Document Preferences dialog box will slow down screen redraw on pages with blends. Use this option only if your monitor is set to display 256 colors. Otherwise, you don't need it.

Macintosh Commands

⌘-N File/New/Document
⌘-M Item/Modify
F12 View/Show Colors
Shift-F12 Edit/Colors

Windows Commands

Ctrl-N File/New/Document
Ctrl-M Item/Modify
F12 View/Show Colors
Shift-F12 Edit/Colors

Color and Gray TIFFs

Set Color TIFFs to 8-bit and Grayscale TIFFs to 16 levels to speed up screen redraw. These options affect only screen display, not printed output.

EXERCISE D

1. Create a new document without an automatic text box. Use any of the picture box tools to draw a picture box. Display the Colors palette (F12).
2. Choose Edit/Colors (Shift-F12), click on New, and create two Pantone Uncoated colors, Pantone 396 and Pantone 2602. Specify both colors as spot colors by selecting the Spot Color check box in the Edit Color dialog box.
3. Select the picture box and click the Background icon in the Colors palette. Use the Blend pull-down menu to select Linear Blend. Click on button #1 and click on Pantone 2602 (Figure 19.5).The box is filled with the purple color .

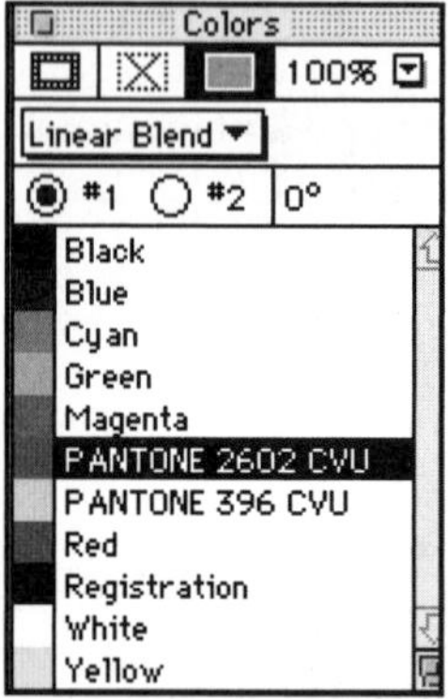

Figure 19.5. Use the Blend menu to select Linear Blend.

4. Click on button #2 and click on Pantone 396. The box is filled with a linear blend of the two Pantone colors. With the box still selected, use the Blend pull-down menu to select another blend style.
5. With the box still selected, choose Item/Modify to display the Box Modify dialog box. Use the Color pull-down menu in the Box field to select Pantone 396 as the first color. Use the Color menu in the Blend field to select Pantone 2602. Choose Full Circular Blend from the Style menu. Change the angle of the second color to 45 degrees (Figure 19.6). Click on OK to apply the new blend style.

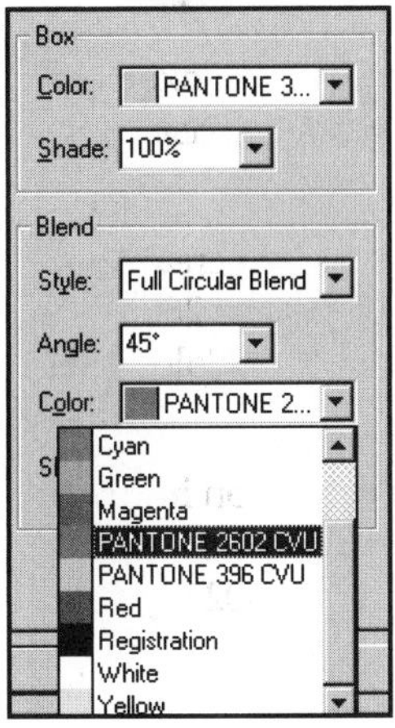

Figure 19.6. Use the Box Modify dialog box to apply blends from any two available colors.

6. Close this file or leave it open to use with the next exercise.

LESSON 5
COLOR TRANSPARENCY

A frequently used design technique is to overlay text on top of a graphic. If you want the graphic to show through the text box, you must make the text box transparent. To make any box transparent, choose a background color of None.

EXERCISE E

1. Create a new document without an automatic text box (File/New/Document). Display the Measurements palette (F9).
2. Use the Rectangle Picture Box tool to draw a picture box about 7 inches wide and 2 inches high. Choose File/Get Picture and navigate to the Unit 19 folder on the CD-ROM. Open the *Pencil* file (an EPS image). Press Command-Option-Shift-F (Macintosh) or Ctrl-Alt-Shift-F (Windows) to fit the pencil in the box.
3. Draw a text box over the yellow area of the pencil. Type *No. 2* and use the Measurements palette to align the type to the right side of the box.
4. With the text box still selected, choose Item/Modify. Use the Color pull-down menu in the Box field to select None (Figure 19.7).

Macintosh Commands

⌘-W File/Close
⌘-N File/New/Document
⌘-M Item/Modify

Windows Commands

Ctrl-F4 File/Close
Ctrl-N File/New/Document
Ctrl-M Item/Modify

Standard-Shape Rectangle Picture Box tool

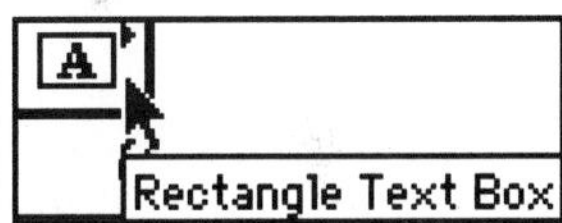

Rectangle Text Box tool

Right Align icon is highlighted in the Measurements palette.

Macintosh Commands

⌘-W File/Close

Windows Commands

Ctrl-F4 File/Close

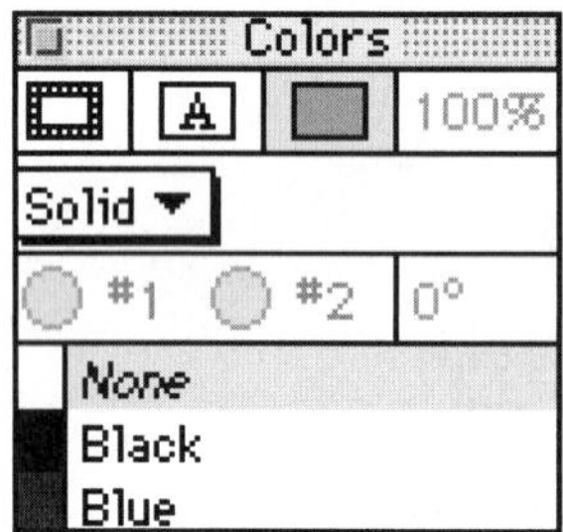

Click on the Background icon in the Colors palette and select None from the Colors list to make a box transparent.

Not your problem

If you're printing to a low-resolution printer like an ink jet, color laser, or dye-sublimation printer, you don't have to deal with trapping issues.

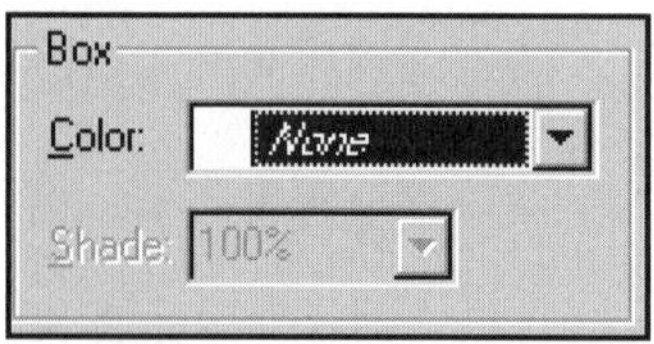

Figure 19.7. Select None in the Color field of the Box Modify dialog box to make the box transparent against any background.

5. Click on the Text tab and use the Type Menu in the Vertical Alignment field to select Centered (Figure 19.8).

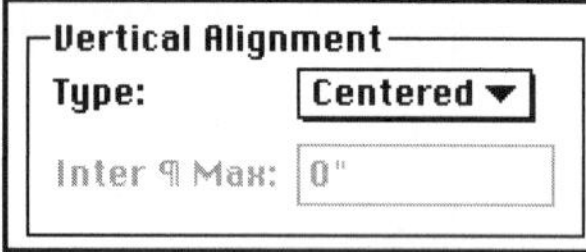

Figure 19.8. Center the text vertically in the text box by choosing Centered from the Vertical Alignment pull-down menu in the Text Modify dialog box.

6. Click on OK. Deselect the box by clicking on an empty area of the page. Press F7 to hide the guides. The text is centered next to the eraser directly on the pencil because the text box is transparent against it (Figure 19.9).

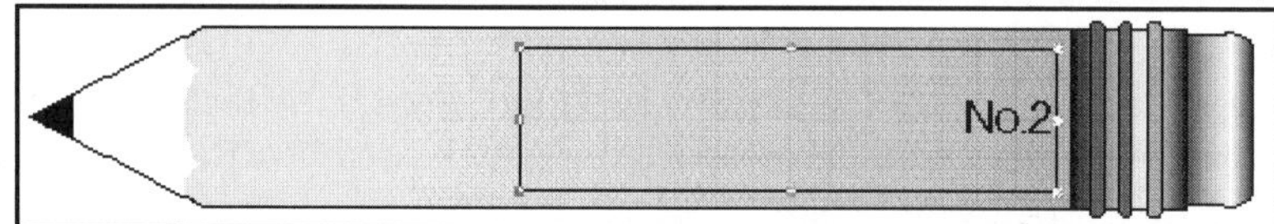

Figure 19.9. The text appears directly on the background because the text box has a background color of None.

7. Close this file. Don't save your changes.

LESSON 6
TRAPPING

Each time a sheet of paper slip-slides under a different printing plate in a multi-colored job, it shimmies just a fraction of a decimal of an inch. This causes tiny shifts of color to appear between the cyan, magenta, yellow, or black plates. If the job calls for printing a spot color, the white paper shows beneath the single color. This shift is called misregistration, and the problem is solved by trapping the colors (Figure 19.10). QuarkXPress provides sophisticated trapping controls, although it is always better to trap in a dedicated trapping program, an application most printers and imagesetters use.

Figure 19.10. The white area between the colored foreground object and the background color (made larger than normal for emphasis) is the "peek" and results when the paper misregisters on the press.

SPREAD

Trapping compensates for these unwanted displays of color (misregistration) by extending the lighter colors very slightly over the darker ones in a process called spreading. If you have a light object on a dark background, expand the lighter object to create a spread. The spread traps or overlaps the darker background and prevents the darker color from "peeking" through the gap left by the paper shift (Figure 19.11).

Figure 19.11. A spread (dark line made darker for emphasis) prevents the "peek" from showing when a lighter object overlaps a darker background.

CHOKE

If you have a dark object overlapping a lighter background object, the darker color is choked, that is, the knockout area beneath the darker object is reduced, thus avoiding the "peek-a-boo" effect. (Figure 19.12).

Figure 19.12. The light background is choked to allow the darker foreground object to overlap the knockout when the paper misregisters on the press.

FYI

For trapping purposes, the foreground item is called the *object*; the backmost item is called the *background*. You trap the object against the background. Below, the lighter circle is the object that traps against the darker background, the square.

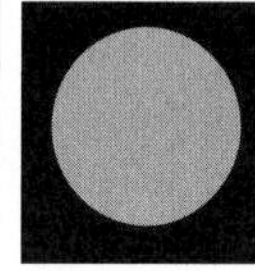

Spread or choke?

A general rule when trapping objects is to spread the lighter foreground object against a darker background. You should also choke a dark object against a lighter background.

OVERPRINT

If you specify that the object overprint the background, there is no knockout area and nothing is erased. There is no spreading or choking. Color A is printed directly on color B. Unless Color A is black, or unless the overlapping colors contain percentages of the same process color, pray that the two colors don't bleed at the edges.

Knockout

Knockout is the default trapping value in XPress. Unless you specify otherwise, foreground objects will cut out (knockout) any overlapping area.

KNOCKOUT

Knockout works like a cookie cutter. When a foreground object knocks out the background object, it leaves a space for the foreground object to "fit." When misregistration occurs because of the paper shifting, the foreground object doesn't always fit perfectly into the knockout area and "peeks" can occur.

HOW MUCH TRAPPING?

Let's be very clear about this. Creating color traps is complicated, technical work best done by professional color strippers. No matter how sophisticated the computer program, trapping is still difficult and should be left to a professional or to dedicated trapping programs used by the imagesetter or printer. If you are doing your own trapping in XPress, ask your printer how much trapping you should apply. QuarkXPress defaults to .144 pt of trapping. which is a very conservative amount. Most printers will recommend .25 pt of trapping, but always ask before applying traps.

TRAPPING TYPE

Try to use black or other dark colors for text and specify that they overprint the lighter backgrounds. Text characters, with their serifs and specialized shapes, are very difficult to trap and rarely do so successfully.

Color gamut

Different printers can reproduce different ranges of color. For example, you can get more colors from a dye sublimation printer than from an ink jet printer. The range of colors that a device such as a printer can reproduce is called its *color gamut.*

LESSON 7 DEFAULT TRAPPING

QuarkXPress 4.0 provides a default trap. You set the value in the Trapping Preferences dialog box and whenever XPress feels you need to trap, it applies that default value.

TRAPPING METHOD

The Trapping Preferences dialog box provides three kinds of default trapping: Absolute, Proportional, and Knockout All (Figure 19.13). Absolute trapping uses the values in the Auto Amount and Indeterminate fields in the Trapping dialog box. The default value is 0.144, but you can change that value to whatever your printer tells you should be the trap value. The Proportional option compares luminance and decides what should be trapped based on how light or dark the background and foreground objects are. Proportional trapping multiplies the value in the Auto Amount field by the difference between the luminance of the object color and background color. Use the Knockout All option to turn off all trapping in the document. No chokes or spreads are applied; all foreground objects have a trap value of 0. Knockout All is your best option when printing a color composite or when printing to a laser printer, as traps are only visible on color separations.

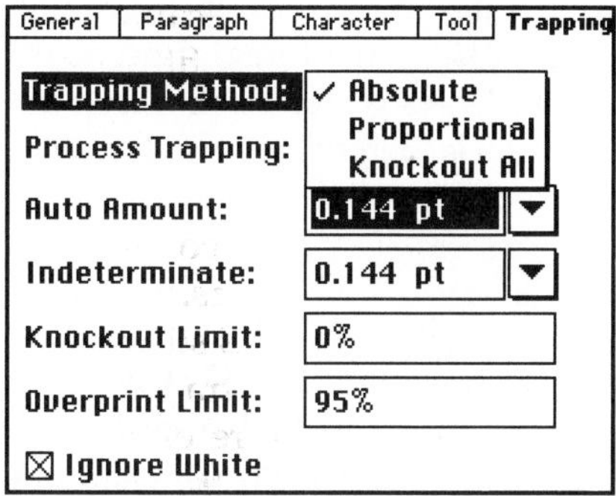

Figure 19.13. The Trapping Preferences dialog box.

PROCESS TRAPPING

If you turn Process Trapping on, XPress will trap each process separation plate individually if a document page contains process colors that overlap. If you are using trapping values in a document, turn Process Trapping on.

AUTO AMOUNT

Auto Amount is the value XPress will use when choking and spreading objects. This value is dictated by the printer and should be the first question you ask before you apply any traps. Choose Overprint to cause any object and background colors trapped with the Auto Amount value in the Trapping Preferences dialog box or with an Auto Amount (+) or (-) value in the Trapping palette to overprint (Figure 19.14).

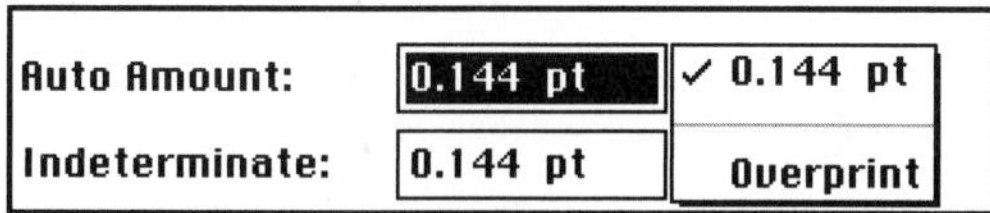

Figure 19.14. Specify the amount of spreading and choking XPress applies when it traps objects. Choose the Overprint option to automatically overprint objects instead of choking or spreading them.

Auto Amount: 0.144 pt

Trapping Method

This menu in the Trapping Preferences dialog box defaults to Absolute trapping, which means that XPress traps objects against their backgrounds using the trapping values specified in the Auto Amount field.

Overprint Limit: 95%

A 95% Overprint Limit value tells XPress to overprint any color that is (1) specified to Overprint in any trapping dialog box, and (2) with a shade value of 95% or greater.

Overprint

Selecting Overprint from the Auto Amount pull-down menu specifies that the foreground object prints directly on top of the background as long as the (foreground) object is darker than the value specified in the Overprint Limit.

Indeterminate

An object positioned on top of a continuous tone image such as a photograph reads that background as indeterminate.

INDETERMINATE

Sometimes an object must be trapped against a background with multiple colors, such as a gradient fill. The Indeterminate value specifies how much trapping should be applied when there are conflicting color relationships. You can also choose Overprint to override the trapping and print the foreground object directly on top of the multiple-color background.

KNOCKOUT LIMIT

The Knockout Limit value is a percentage of the darkness of the foreground object compared with the darkness of the background. If you leave this value at the default 0%, then a foreground object with a shade less than 0%—which is always white—will knock out the background. This lets the user set a percentage so that very light colors don't trap to dark colors; instead, they knock out the darker colors.

OVERPRINT LIMIT

The Overprint Limit value determines how dark an object to which you have applied the Overprint command must be before it overprints. If you specify 95% in the Overprint Limit field, for example, a foreground object that is shaded 80% and set to overprint will not overprint because its 80% shade is less than the Overprint Limit value. Instead, it will trap according to the value in the Auto Amount field.

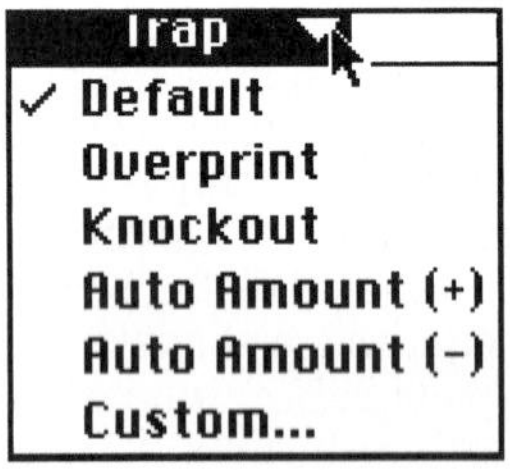

Trap
✓ Default
Overprint
Knockout
Auto Amount (+)
Auto Amount (-)
Custom...

When a background color is selected, the Trap pull-down menu in the Trap Specifications dialog box allows you to select the type of trap you want applied.

IGNORE WHITE

Check the Ignore White option to specify that a foreground object on a multicolored background that includes white does not factor in that white in the background when trapping. As with this and all of these options, check with your printer before specifying values and applying traps.

LESSON 7
COLOR-SPECIFIC TRAPPING

In QuarkXPress you can use the Trap Information palette to override the default trapping specifications in the Trapping Preferences dialog box. This lets you apply the same trapping values to any foreground color relative to any background color.

EXERCISE F

1. Create a new document without an automatic text box (File/New/Document). Display the Colors palette (F12).
2. Choose Edit/Colors (Shift-F12) to display the Edit Colors dialog box. The first thing you should do when working with color for a print document is delete the three RGB colors because they are never used in print work. Click on Red and click Delete. Repeat for the Blue and Green colors.
3. Now click on New. Choose Pantone Process from the Model pull-down menu. Type 186-1 in the Pantone S field below the swatch library. Make sure the Spot Color check box is deselected, because this color is being defined as a process color. Click on OK to add the dark purple color to the document's color list.
4. Click on New again and repeat to add Pantone Process color S1-6, a light yellow, to the document's color list. Click on OK. Click on Save. Your Colors palette should resemble Figure 19.15.

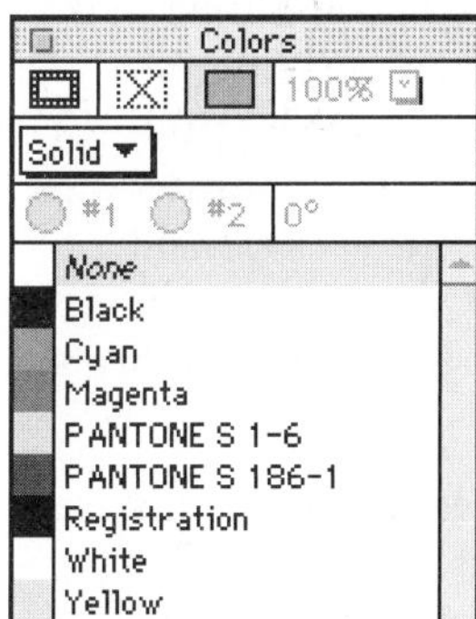

Figure 19.15. The three RGB colors have been deleted from the Colors palette and two Pantone process colors have been added.

5. Use any picture box tool to draw a picture box. Make sure the Background icon is selected in the Colors palette and click on the Pantone 186-1 name or color swatch in the Colors palette to

Macintosh Commands

⌘-N File/New/Document
Shift-F12 Edit/Colors

Windows Commands

Ctrl-N File/New/Document
Shift-F12 Edit/Colors

Standard-Shape Rectangle Picture Box tool

Bézier Picture Box tool

apply the purple to the background of the picture box.

6. Use the oval picture box tool to draw a circle on top of the purple box. Fill its background with Pantone S1-6.

7. Choose Edit/Preferences/Document and click on the Trapping tab. Enter the values in Figure 19.13, choosing Absolute as the trapping method. Click on OK.

8. Choose Edit/Colors and choose Process Colors from the Show Menu. Only the four default process colors (cyan, magenta, yellow, and black) and the two Pantone colors are listed. Click on Pantone S1-6, the foreground object color, and click on the

Trap Specifications for PANTONE S 1-6

Background Color	Trap	←?→	Reverse
Indeterminate	0.144 pt		
Black	0.144 pt	←⊓→	Overprint
Cyan	0.144 pt	←⊓→	-0.144 pt
Magenta	0.144 pt	←⊓→	-0.144 pt
PANTONE S 186-1	0.144 pt	←⊓→	-0.144 pt
Yellow	-0.144 pt	←⊓→	0.144 pt

Figure 19.16. Selecting a color and clicking Edit Trap displays the Trap Specifications dialog box for that color.

Edit Trap button. The Trap Specifications dialog box for Pantone S1-6 appears (Figure 19.16).

9. Click on the background color, Pantone 186-1, the dark purple color, to select it. Use the Trap pull-down menu to select Default. This tells XPress to decide which color will choke or which color will spread according to the value specified in the Auto-Amount field of the Trapping Preferences dialog box. But, to have more control over the trap, use the Trap pull-down menu to select Auto Amount (+). This takes the decision away from XPress and specifies that the yellow circle will spread over the purple background using the value in the Auto Amount field. The asterisk after the 0.144 value indicates that Auto Amount (+) has been selected.

10. In the Dependent/Independent column, leave the current trapping relationship between the yellow and purple set to Dependent. This option deals with inversing two colors and tells XPress to reverse the trap. Unless you know what you're doing, leave this set to Dependent. Click OK. Click Save.

11. Save this file as *Trap.qxd.* in your Projects folder. You will need it for the next exercise.

Macintosh Commands

⌘-Y Edit/Preferences/Document
Shift-F12 Edit/Colors
⌘-Option-S File/Save as

Windows Commands

Ctrl-Y Edit/Preferences/Document
Shift-F12 Edit/Colors
Ctrl-Alt-S File/Save as

Oval Picture Box tool

FYI

An object's color is always trapped against a background color. In Figure 19.16, Pantone S1-6 can be trapped against any one of the six background colors in the Trap Specifications dialog box.

LESSON 8
ITEM-SPECIFIC TRAPPING

Even when you specify automatic trapping in the Trapping Preferences dialog box, there may be times when you want to customize the trapping specifications for a particular object. You do this in the Trap Information palette. You can use this palette to set trapping values for text, pictures, lines, and frames as well as for the backgrounds of boxes.

EXERCISE G

1. If necessary, open the *Trap.qxd* file you created in the last exercise or open the *Trap.qxd* file in the Unit 19 folder on the CD-ROM. Choose View/Show Trap Information to display the Trap Information palette. Click the yellow circle to select it. The Trap Information palette displays Default as the current trapping specification. Click the Question icon on the right side of the palette to display the current trapping values (Figure 19.17).

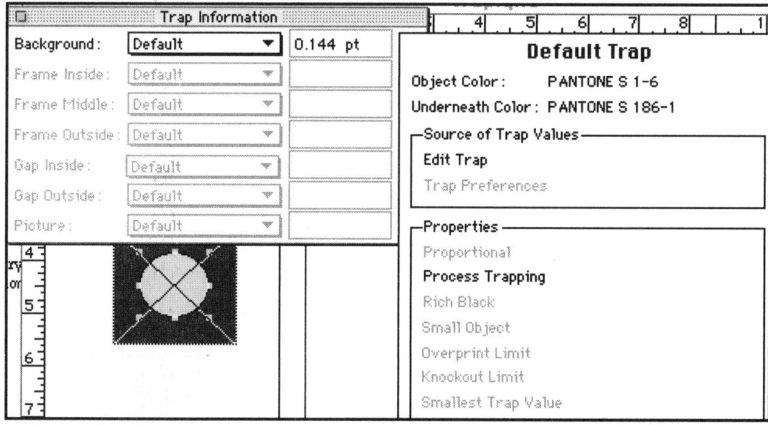

Figure 19.17. Clicking on the Question icon in the Trap Information palette gives you information about the trapping specifications for the selected object.

2. With the circle still selected, choose Item/Frame. Apply a 6-pt. cyan frame. Choose Dotted from the Style menu. Choose yellow for the Gap color. Click OK to apply the frame. Now the Trap Information palette allows you to specify trapping values for the frame and the gap (Figure 19.18).

FYI

Any options that are grayed out in the Trap Information palette do not relate to the selected object you are trapping.

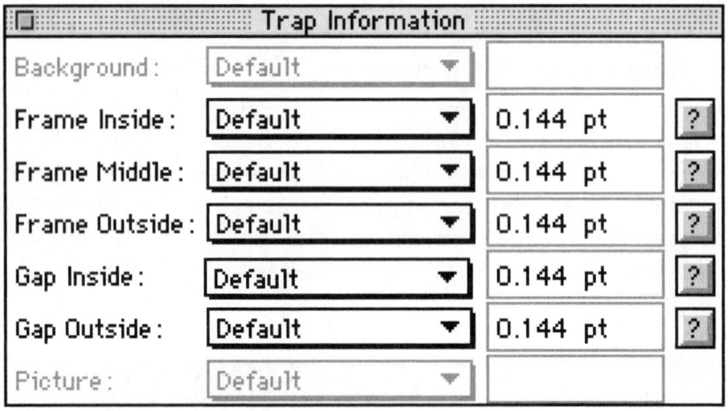

Trap Information

Background:	Default	
Frame Inside:	Default	0.144 pt
Frame Middle:	Default	0.144 pt
Frame Outside:	Default	0.144 pt
Gap Inside:	Default	0.144 pt
Gap Outside:	Default	0.144 pt
Picture:	Default	

Figure 19.18. When a framed object is selected, trapping values can be modified in the Trap Information palette.

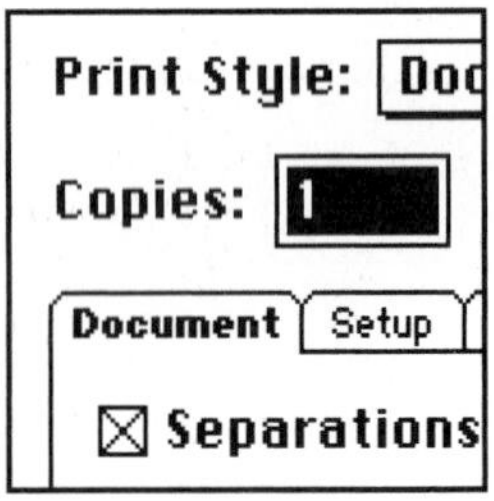

Print Style: Doc
Copies: 1
Document Setup
☒ Separations

Always check the Separations check box when printing an EPS image that you have trapped to a colored background in XPress.

3. The Frame Inside value traps the innermost color of a frame (cyan) to where it overlaps the box it's framing (Pantone S1-6). The Frame Outside value traps the outermost color of a frame to the background color (Pantone 186-1) that it's overlapping. The Frame Middle value specifies trapping to the color of the frame itself (cyan). The same applies for the gap color within the frame.
4. Use the Frame Inside and Gap Inside pull-down menus to select Overprint.
5. Close this file. Don't save your changes.

WARNING!

Don't scale a stroked EPS image in XPress— XPress scales the strokes as well as the image and this stroke scaling throws off the trapping values.

LESSON 9 TRAPPING AND EPS IMAGES

If you are planning to trap an EPS image with strokes to a background color in XPress, you must first create those strokes in a graphics program such as Illustrator or Photoshop, not in XPress. Make the width of the strokes twice the width of the trapping value you will specify in XPress. For example, if you are using a .25-pt. trapping value in XPress, make the stroke in the graphic program .5 pt. Then set all the strokes to overprint, because XPress uses the image's overprint settings that are saved with the image to trap the image against a colored background. Finally, when you print an EPS image you have trapped against a colored background in XPress, always click the Separations check box in the Document tab of the Print dialog box.

Sorry

You can't trap an EPS image to a TIFF image in XPress. This shouldn't be a problem, but check your match print to see what the final output will look like.

UNIT 20

OVERVIEW

In this unit you will learn how to:
Create, display, and edit a List
Use the Book palette to synchronize documents

TERMS

Book
Chapter
List
Master Chapter
synchronize

HOW IT WORKS:

Format the type in a bold typeface at a large type size. Give the text box a background of None. Select the text and apply a vertical scale value of 300% from the Style menu (Style/Horizontal/Vertical Scale). Select the text box and use the Step and Repeat command with a 0 [zero] Horizontal Offset value to create the duplicate boxes.

LESSON 1
LONG DOCUMENT COMPONENTS

Very often a long document like a book or magazine will be comprised of several QuarkXPress files. Hopefully, each file will use the same style sheets, the same H&J values, the same dashes and stripes, and the same lists, but frequently each file reflects a subtle change in these attributes. You may have changed the Heading 3 style, for example, in one file and not changed it in all the other files for the same project. This omission can cause serious problems at the print level or when the book is published and your client/boss fires you. To avoid these synchronization errors, use the Book command in QuarkXPress 4.0.

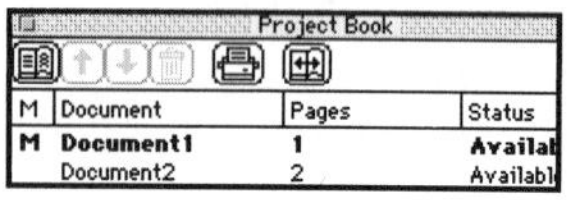

Project Book

M	Document	Pages	Status
M	**Document1**	**1**	**Availal**
	Document2	2	Availabl

The Book palette displays two documents to be compiled in a Book.

The Book command begins by creating a Book. A Book is simply a collection of XPress documents related to one project. There are almost thirty separate QuarkXPress files for the book you're reading now. This *collection of files related to a single project* is called a *Book*. The document files—the separate QuarkXPress files that constitute the longer Book—are called *Chapters*. In creating a Book, one Chapter is designated as a Master Chapter, and its specifications are used to override any differing specifications in the other Chapters in the Book. So, if the Heading 3 style calls for yellow type reversed on a blue rule in the Master Chapter, once the Book is synchronized, the Heading 3 style in every Chapter in the Book will display yellow type reversed on a blue rule.

Styles in List:

Name	Level	Numbering	Format As
¶ Body	1	Text... Page#	¶ Head
¶ Command	2	Text... Page#	¶ Body

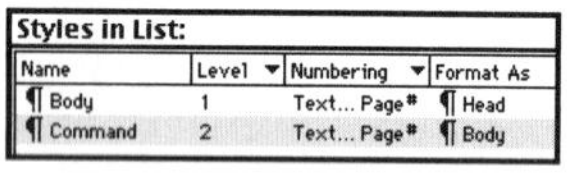

The Lists dialog box is where paragraphs with different styles are compiled to be updated in the List palette.

LISTS

Before you begin creating Books, you have to understand what a List is in XPress. A list is a group of one or more paragraph style sheets specified by the user and imported into the Lists palette to gather the text in those paragraphs for a particular purpose. For example, all the chapter titles, lesson titles, and lesson subheads in this book were tagged in the Lists palette and then assembled to create the table of contents for the book you're reading.

Creating a List is a three-step process. First, create the List in the Lists dialog box; second, generate (update) the list in the Lists palette; and third, flow (build) the list into a selected text box. Because you do not usually need all the styles in a document's Style Sheets palette for a List, you have the opportunity to select which paragraph styles, and hence which paragraphs, will be part of your List.

EXERCISE A

1. Open the *List1.qxd* file and the *List2.qxd* files in the Unit 20 folder on the CD-ROM. Click on the *List1.qxd* file to activate it. If you get an alert telling you that these files use fonts not installed in your system, click OK at the alert.

2. Choose Edit/Lists to display the Edit List dialog box. Click New. Type *TOC List* in the Name field. You don't need the Body style in the table of contents, so ignore the Body style, but click on the Chapter # style below it, and click on the forward black arrow to add that style to the Styles in List panel (Figure 20.1). If you make a mistake, click on the style in the Styles in List panel, and click on the backward black arrow to remove it from the List.

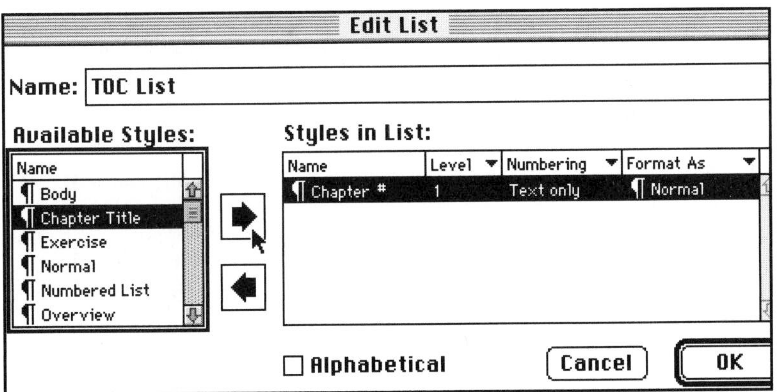

Figure 20.1. Select a paragraph style and click the black arrow to add that style to the List.

3. Repeat to add the Chapter Title and Subhead styles to the Styles in List panel (Figure 20.2). Click on OK and click on Save. Choose File/Save as and save the file with its current name in your Projects folder.

Figure 20.2. The three styles necessary to create the table of contents are added to the Styles in List panel.

Macintosh Commands

⌘-O File/Open
⌘-Option-S File/Save as

Windows Commands

Ctrl-O File/Open
Ctrl-Alt-S File/Save as

☐ **Alphabetical**

Select this check box in the Lists dialog box to arrange a list in alphabetical order.

4. Choose Edit/Lists, highlight the TOC List, and click on Edit. You must now specify a Level, or the order in which these styles will appear in the table of contents. Because the chapter number is the first paragraph that should appear, leave its Level at 1. Click on Chapter Title in the Name field to select it. Use the Level pull-down menu to select 2, thus making all the paragraphs tagged with the Chapter Title style appear under the paragraphs tagged with the Chapter # style (Figure 20.3).

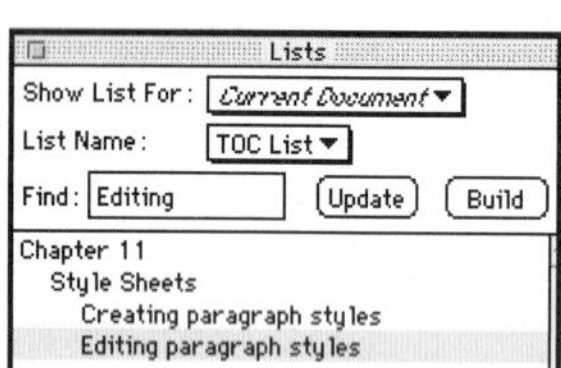

Type a word in the Find field to highlight that word in the row of list entries. This Find command does not find words in the document, only in the list displayed in the List Name field.

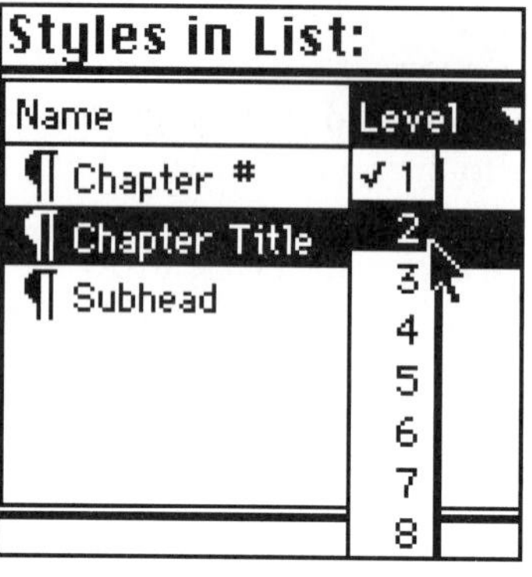

Figure 20.3. Use the Level menu to specify that the Chapter Title style will be the second level in the List and appear under the Chapter # style in the table of contents.

5. Click on the Subhead style to select it and assign it Level 3.

6. The Numbering pull-down menu lets you specify how the text appears in reference to the page number. In a list of people's names, you might not want a page number to appear next to the name, so you would choose the Text only option. But because this is a table of contents, you want the page number to appear. Select the Chapter # style, press the Shift key, and click on the Chapter Title and Subhead styles to select all three styles. Use the Numbering pull-down menu to choose the Text…Page# option for all three styles (Figure 20.4). Click on an empty area of the palette to deselect all the styles.

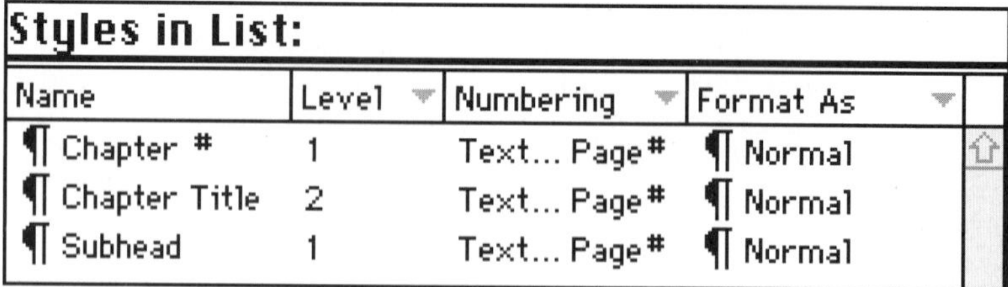

Figure 20.4. Shift-select all the paragraph styles and use the Numbering pull-down menu to specify that page number will appear to the right of the text.

7. The last formatting task is to apply a paragraph style to each Name [of style] in the list. Click on the Chapter # style to select it. Use the Format As pull-down menu to select the Chapter # paragraph style. You could, of course, apply any paragraph style listed in the Style Sheets palette, like a special style you created just for the table of contents.

8. Select Chapter Title in the Name field and choose Chapter Title from the Format As menu. Select Subhead in the Name field and choose Subhead from the Format As menu (Figure 20.5).

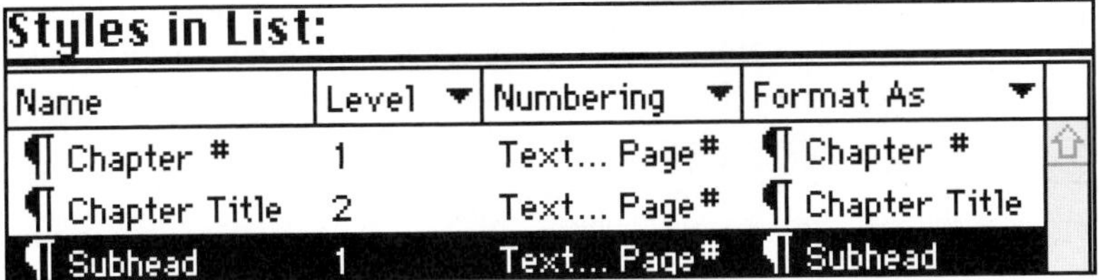

Figure 20.5. Select a paragraph style for each item in the List from the Format As pull-down menu.

9. Click OK. Click Save. You have completed Step 1 of the three-step List-generation process.

10. Now that the List options are specified, you can build the List. Choose View/Show Lists to display the Lists palette. Choose Current Document from the Show List pull-down menu. Choose TOC List from the List Name pull-down menu. Click the Update button to add the paragraphs styled with the selections you made earlier in the Lists dialog box (Figure 20.6). You have completed the second step in generating a list.

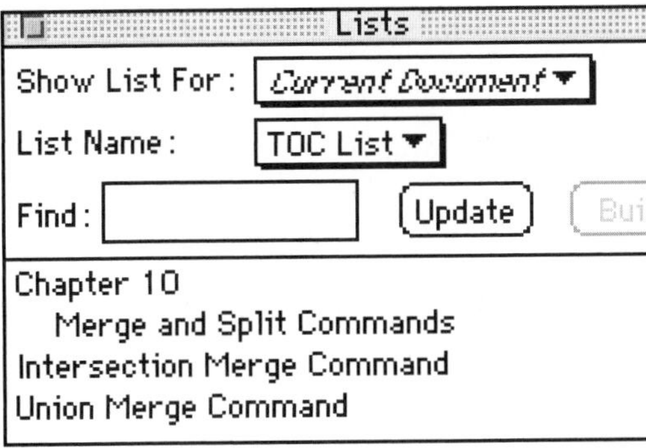

Figure 20.6. The Lists palette displays the list elements for the List selected in the List Name field.

Macintosh Commands

Option-F11 View/Show/Lists

Windows Commands

Ctrl-F11 View/Show/Lists

Update info

Update frequently if you are making any changes to the text.

Macintosh Commands

⌘-Option-S File/Save as
⌘-W File/Close
⌘-Option-A File/Append
⌘-W File/Close

Windows Commands

Ctrl-Alt-S File/Save as
Ctrl-F4 File/Close
Ctrl-Alt-A File/Append
Ctrl-F4 File/Close

11. Press the Alt/Option key and use the Grabber Hand to drag the page to the right or left so that the pasteboard appears. Use the Rectangle Text Box tool to draw a text box a few inches long. Don't worry about the size of the text box; you can resize it later. For the third and final step, you will generate the list.

Rectangle Text Box tool

12. With the text box selected, click on the Build button in the Lists palette. The table of contents (List) appears in the selected text box (Figure 20.7). Choose File/Save as. Navigate to your Projects folder. In the Save as dialog box, click on the New [folder] button to create a new folder. Type *Book Files* in the Name field and click on Create. Click on Save to save the *List1.qxd* file with its List in the new Book Files folder. Close the file (File/Close).

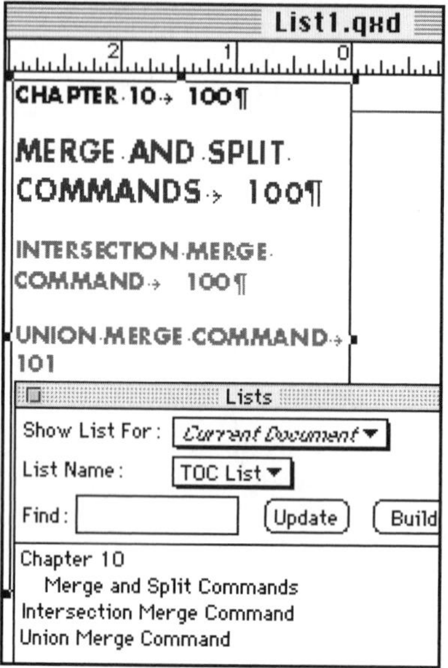

Figure 20.7. Select a text box and click the Build button to generate the table of contents.

Click on the New button in the Save As dialog box to create a new folder.

13. Click on the *List2.qxd* file to activate it. Choose File/Append. Highlight the *List1.qxd* file in the Unit 20 folder on the CD-ROM. Click on Open. In the Append dialog box, click the Chapter # style and click on the forward arrow to append it to the *List2.qxd* file. Repeat for the Chapter Title and Subhead styles (Figure 20.8). Click on OK. Click on OK at the alert.

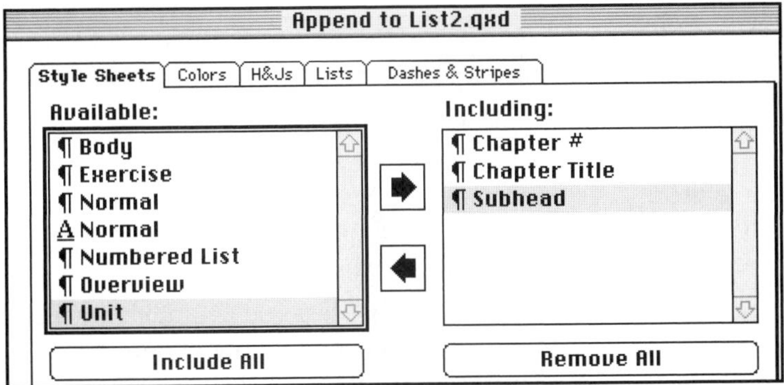

Figure 20.8. Select the paragraph styles and click the forward arrow to append that style in the *List1.qxd* file to the *List2.qxd* file.

14. Once you have appended the style sheets, you can append the List that you created in the *List1.qxd* file. Still in the *List2.qxd* file, choose Edit/Lists. Click on the Append button. Navigate to the *List1.qxd* file in the Book Files folder on the CD-ROM, highlight it, and click on Open.
15. The Append Lists dialog box tells you that only one List exists for the *List1.qxd* file, the TOC list. Click to select it and click the forward arrow to add it to the Including panel. Click OK twice and click on Save. The TOC List is now added to the *List2.qxd* file.
16. Choose View/Show Lists. Click the Update button in the Lists palette to display the List. Draw a text box on the pasteboard and, with the text box selected, click the Build button on the Lists palette to flow the list. Close the Lists palette by clicking on its Close box.
17. Choose File/Save as. Navigate to the *Books Files* folder in your Projects folder and click on Open. Click on Save to save the *List2.qxd* file with its List in the *Book Files* folder. Close the file (File/Close).

LESSON 2
CREATING A BOOK

A Book is a collection of documents called Chapters, with one document designated as the Master Chapter. It is the specifications of this Master Chapter that determine the styles, lists, H&Js, and dashes and stripes in every Chapter of the Book. The Chapters are compiled and synchronized in the Book palette.

Macintosh Commands

Option-F11 View/Show Lists
⌘-W File/Close

Windows Commands

Ctrl-F11 View/Show Lists
Ctrl-F4 File/Close

Lists palette Close box

The Close box is in the upper left corner of the palette (Macintosh) and in the upper right corner (Windows).

EXERCISE B

1. Choose File/New/Book. Navigate to the Book Files folder you created in the last exercise and type *My First Book* in the Book Name field. Click on Create. The Book palette appears and displays the name of the Book, My First Book. Notice that no document is open, just the Book palette.
2. Because Books are made up of Chapters and Chapters are just QuarkXPress documents, you must open those documents in the Books palette. Click the Add Chapter icon on the Book palette. Navigate to the *Book Files* folder you created in the last exercise and click on the *List1.qxd* file to select it. Click the Add button to import it into the Book palette (Figure 20.9).

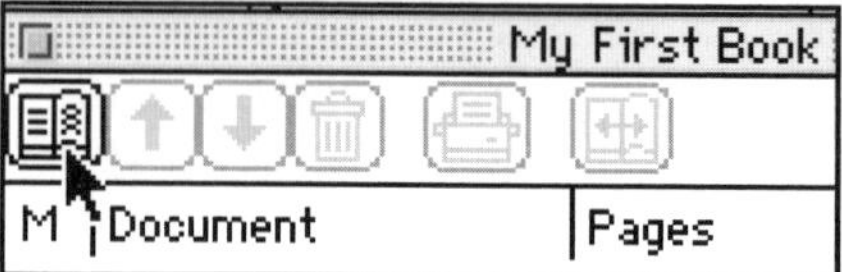

Figure 20.9. Click on the Add Chapter icon to add a document as a Chapter in the Book.

3. Click on the Add Chapter icon again and add the *List2.qxd* file in the *Book Files* folder. Your screen should resemble Figure 20.10.

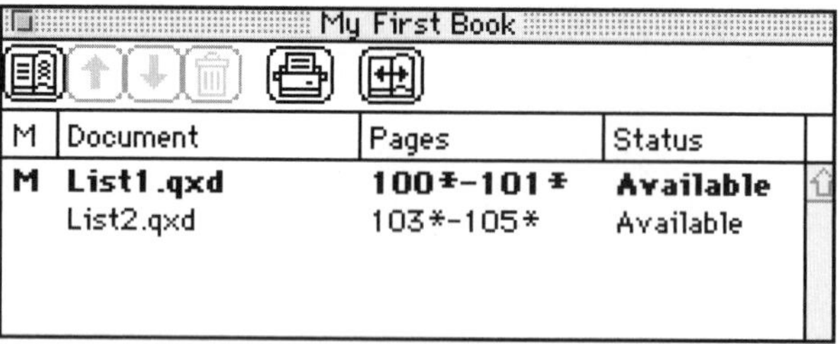

Figure 20.10. Chapters appear in the order in which they are opened in the Book palette.

Click the Reorder arrows to move a selected file up and down in the Book palette. The Chapter with an M to the left of its name is the Master Chapter.

4. By default, the first file you open in the Book palette appears in boldface because it is the Master Chapter. You can select any file and click the up or down Reorder arrows to move the file to a new position in the palette. However, the first file in the palette is always the Master Chapter and displays an M to the left of its name. To specify another Chapter as the Master Chapter, click on the Chapter to select it and use the Reorder arrows in the Book palette to move it to the first position in the palette. Then click on M at the left side of the palette.
5. The Pages column in the Book palette displays the page sequence of each Chapter. In this Book, both Chapters display an asterisk before and after each page number, indicating that these page numbers were created using the Section command.

If these Chapters did not have sectioned pages, XPress would create a "Chapter Start" page number. To override this (and keep control of the page numbering sequence), override the automatic page numbering by using the Section command. Choose File/Open and open the *List1.qxd* file in the Book Files folder in your Projects folder. Display the Page Layout palette (F10/Macintosh; F4/Windows).

6. In the *List1.qxd* file, double-click on the Page 1 icon in the Document Layout palette to display that page. Choose Page/Section to display the Section dialog box. In the Number field, type 90 to change the start of the section from page 100 to page 90. Click on OK (Figure 20.11).

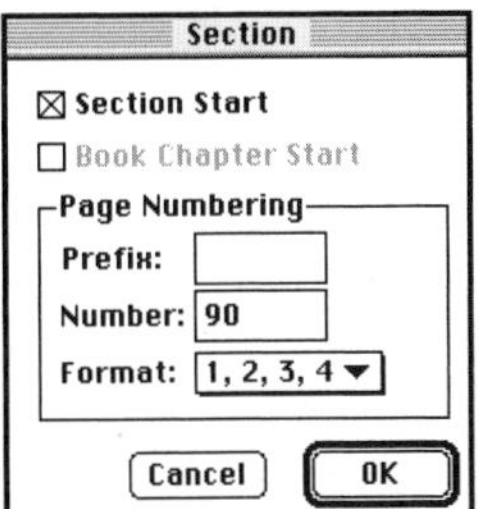

Figure 20.11. Use the Section command to change a file's page numbering sequence.

7. When you do this, two things happen in the Book palette. The page sequence for the *List1.qxd* file displays 90*-91* and the status for that file changes from Available to Open (Figure 20.12). Choose File/Close, save the changes, and notice that the Status line for the *List1.qxd* file changes from Open to Available.

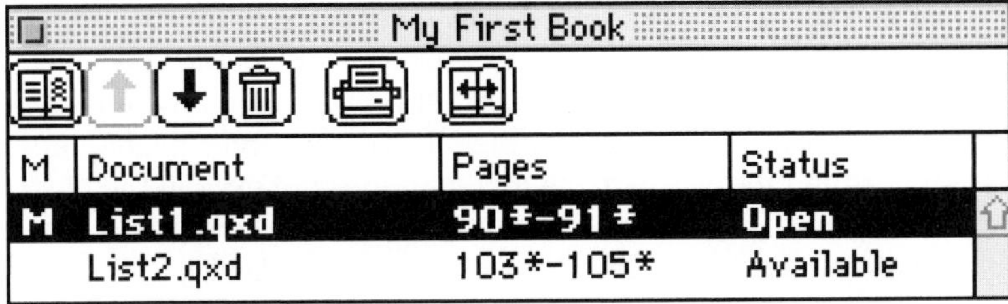

Figure 20.12. Changing a page numbering sequence in the Section dialog box causes the Book palette to update and reflect that change.

8. Leave the Book palette open for use in the next exercise.

Macintosh Commands

⌘-O File/Open
⌘-W File/Close
F10 View/Show Document Layout

Windows Commands

Ctrl-O File/Open
Ctrl-F4 File/Close
F4 View/Show Document Layout

Macintosh Commands

⌘-W File/Close
F11 View/Show Style Sheets

Windows Commands

Ctrl-F4 File/Close
F11 View/Show Style Sheets

FYI

One of the advantages of the synchronization command is that it allows you to make global changes to any of the styles in a Book. For example, if you decide to change the width of a rule or the size of a paragraph's text characters in all the chapters, you can change the specification in the Master Chapter, then synchronize the Book again.

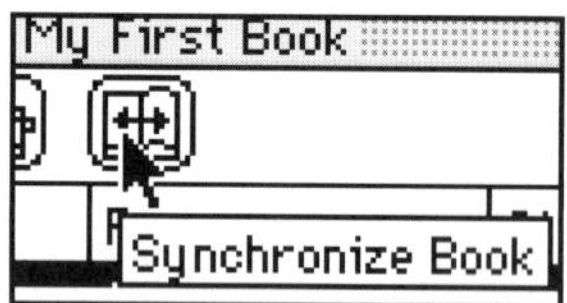

Synchronize Book icon on the Book palette

SYNCHRONIZING CHAPTERS

The process of synchronizing the Chapters in a Book takes place in the Book palette. This ensures that all the styles, H&Js, Lists, and dashes and stripes are consistent across all the Chapters (files) in the Book (long document). Once you have specified a Chapter as a Master Chapter, all the other Chapters in the book will display the specifications of that Master Chapter.

EXERCISE C

1. Open the *List2.qxd* file in the Books Files folder you created earlier. Display the Style Sheets palette (F11). Click in the text box, Control-click (Macintosh) or Right-click (Windows) on the Chapter Title style in the Style Sheets palette, and drag to select Edit Chapter Title. Click on the Formats tab and change the Alignment from Left to Centered. Click on OK. Save the File (File/Save) and close the file (File/Close).
2. If necessary, open the *My First Book* Book. Make sure that the *List1.qxd* file is the Master file. Also make sure that the Status line for both files reads Available. If a Chapter is not available, it cannot be synchronized.
3. Click the Synchronize Book icon on the Book palette. Click OK at the alert. When you do this, three things happen: First, any style sheets with the same name in every Chapter are checked against the same style in the Master Chapter. If there are any differences, all those styles are edited to match the attributes of the styles with the same name in the Master Chapter. Second, any style in the Master Chapter that is missing in any other Chapter is added to that Chapter; Third, any style in Chapters (other than the Master Chapter) that does not exist in the Master Chapter is left untouched. In the case of this Book, the center alignment of the Chapter Title style in the *List2.qxd* Chapter is changed to left aligned to match the Chapter Title style in the Master Chapter.
4. The *List2.qxd* Chapter briefly displays Open on the Status line while XPress changes its alignment from centered to left aligned. Choose File/Open and open the *List2.qxd* file in the Book Files folder. Notice that the paragraph tagged with the Chapter Title style is now left aligned. Both Chapters are synchronized and the project is consistently formatted.
5. Close the file (File/Close). Don't save your changes.

UNIT 21

Generating an Index

OVERVIEW

In this unit you will learn how to:
Compile an index of terms in one document
Compile an index of terms over multiple documents

TERMS

run-in index
nested index

HOW IT WORKS:

Create the text in a large typeface. Choose Drop Shadow/Soft Shadow from the QX-Effects menu. Click the Back box to get to the Effect Attributes dialog box and type the correct value in the dpi box. Because this file was printed to an imagesetter with a 133 lpi (line screen), a a value of 300 dpi was applied. QX-Effects then creates a TIFF file called *Shadow 1* in the same folder as the XPress document. The high-resolution shadow appears in a picture box directly behind the text. Group both boxes to preserve the positioning of the shadow. This high-resolution file must be available to the printer to print the shadow at the correct resolution.

LESSON 1
TYPES OF INDEXES

Creating an index is a tedious, time-consuming process. In most cases the author will provide an index or a professional indexer will be engaged to create an alphabetical listing of every relevant term in the book with its corresponding page number. Unless the book is a "bodice-ripper" or other work of fiction, it will need an index to guide the reader to the appropriate pages.

The Index XTension in QuarkXPress 4.0 lets you create two kinds of indexes, a run-in index and a nested index. A run-in index might read

QuarkXPress 4.0, Style sheets, 76.

This is a two-level index with the first level (*QuarkXPress 4.0*) arranged alphabetically and *Style sheets, 76* as the second level appearing immediately after the first level.

The other kind of index is a nested index. A nested index can have up to four levels and might read

QuarkXPress 4.0 (First Level entry)
  Style sheets, 66 (Second Level entry)
    Character styles, 77–82 (Third Level entry)
    Paragraph styles 66–76
      deleting, 70 (Fourth Level entry)
      editing 69, 73

Sorry

The tedium of tagging the words is still going to be part of the indexing process. No microchip currently available knows that *Love* is the First Level index entry and *at first sight* is the Second Level entry.

You can create a cross-referenced index, one that lets the reader refer to other topics listed in the index. For example, in the chapter on QuarkXPress 4.0, you might list as a cross-reference *See compatibility with version 3.3*. The cross-reference can be to an existing index entry, or you can add a new entry such as *Compatibility with version 3.3* specifically for the cross-reference.

Other indexing options include specifying whether an index entry will cover a word, a number of paragraphs, a text selection, or all of the text until the index encounters another style sheet. There are many formatting options for the index, and by using master pages and style sheets, you can build an index quickly and efficiently. No matter how you design your index, generating an index is a two-step process: First, *tag* the entries in the Index palette; and second, *build* the index from the Build Index command under the Utilities menu.

LESSON 2
INDEX PREPARATION

Before you generate the index, you must set your preferences for the way the index entries will appear when you build the index. You should also create any style sheets you want applied to the different levels in the index. This makes the styles available from the Index palette, which means you don't have to format each entry in the index separately. You should also make sure that you have a linked automatic text box on the master page of your document.

FYI

You must have the Index palette open to activate the Build Index command from the Utilities menu.

INDEX PREFERENCES

Choose Edit/Preferences/Index (Figure 21.1) to display the Index Preferences dialog box. Specify the character you want to appear following an entry (usually a comma) in the Following Entry field. To do this, press the Spacebar after that comma to create a space between the comma and the page number. Unless you delete or change any of the separation characters, a comma will appear between the page numbers, an en-dash will appear between a range of pages like 64–67, and a period will appear before a cross-reference such as *QuarkXPress. See also QuarkImmedia.* Click on OK to exit the dialog box and save your preferences.

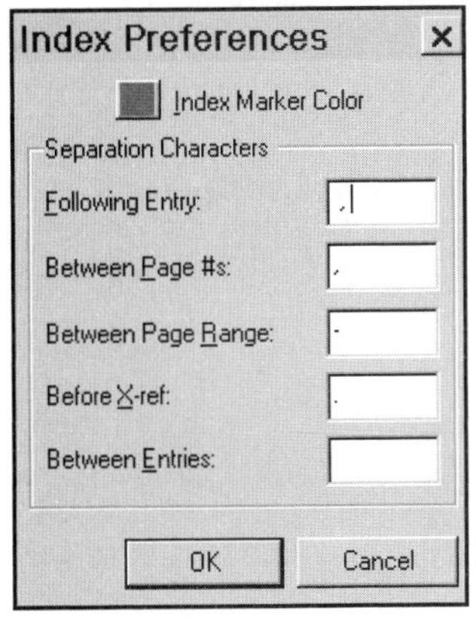

Figure 21.1. The Index Preferences dialog box is where you specify which characters will appear between entries and page numbers. A space was inserted after the comma in the Following Entry field.

INDEX STYLES

You can apply one style sheet to the index entry and another style to the page number following the entry. Format the index entries in any paragraph style available in the current document, and format the page numbers in any character style available in the current document. You can also specify that the page numbers display the same style as the entry style. Because this can get complicated, especially if you don't want all the formatting connected with a

The Intact Chain icon on the master page indicates that the document was created with an automatic text box.

paragraph style to be attached to the index entry, it's a good idea to create a new index entry style, and then either apply that same entry style to the page numbers or create a separate character style for the page numbers.

LINKED MASTER PAGES

It's unlikely that you would create an index in a document or for a Book (synchronized Chapters in the Book palette) that did not contain an automatic text box. If you create a new document with the Automatic Text Box option selected, that text box appears on every document page based on Master Page A because the Automatic Text Box option creates a text box on Master Page A and on every document page based on that master page. If for some reason that automatic text box has been unlinked, then when you go to build the index, an alert appears.

FYI

The Intact Chain icon in the upper left corner of the master page on the left indicates that this document contains a linked master page. The Broken Chain icon for the master page on the right indicates that either there is no automatic text box on the master page or that the automatic text box has been unlinked.

It's always a good idea to check your master page before building the document and make sure the automatic text box is linked to the Intact Chain icon (Figure 21.2). To establish a linked text box on the master page, go to the master page. If there is no automatic text box on the page, use any text box tool to draw a text box on the master page. Click the Linking tool in the Tool palette to select it. Then click once on the Broken Chain icon in the upper left corner of the master page and click inside the text box you just created. An arrow will appear connecting the icon to the text box and the Broken Chain icon will be replaced by the Intact Chain icon (Figure 21.3).

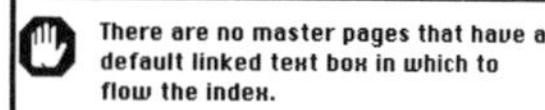

If your document does not have a linked text box on the master page, this alert appears.

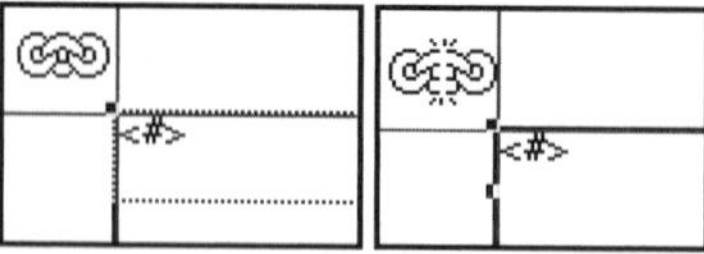

Figure 21.2 displays the Intact Chain icon in the upper left corner of the master page (left) and the Broken Chain icon (right).

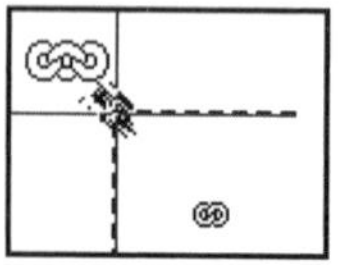

Figure 21.3. Select the Linking tool; click on the Broken Chain icon to change it to the Intact Chain icon and create a linked text box on the master page.

Enable	Name
✓	Cool Blends
	CPSI Fixer
	Font Creator
	FRÆMZ PS XT
✓	Index
✓	JPEG Import

Click in the Enable field to make an XTension active the next time you launch QuarkXPress.

LESSON 3 THE INDEX PALETTE

The Index palette is available only when the Index XTension is loaded. To load the Index XTension, make sure the Index XTension is in the XTensions folder in the QuarkXPress 4.0 folder. Choose XTensions Manager from the Utilities menu to display the XTensions Manager dialog box. Use the Set pull-down menu to select a set or just click in front of Index in the Enable column. You have to quit QuarkXPress and then relaunch the application for any newly enabled XTension to load.

EXERCISE A

1. Open the QuarkXPress 4.0 folder on your hard drive. Open the XTension folder and make sure the Index XTension is in that folder. If it isn't, (1) open the XTensions disabled folder and drag the Index XTension into the XTension folder. (2) Quit and relaunch QuarkXPress.
2. Open the *Ch01.qxd* file in the Unit 21 folder on the CD-ROM. Display the Document Layout palette (F10/Macintosh; F4/Windows). Double-click on the Master Page A icon to get to that master page. Click on the Linking tool in the Tool palette to select it. Click on the Intact Chain icon in the upper left corner of the left master page and notice the arrow going from the icon to the automatic text box. Scroll to the right master page and click on its Intact Chain icon. The linking arrow appears. Both master pages in this facing pages document were created with an automatic text box. Click on the Content tool.
3. Double-click on document page 1 to get to that page. Choose Edit/Style Sheets (Shift-F11). Use the New pull-down menu to select Paragraph. Type *First Level index* in the Name field. Click on the Edit button in the Character Attributes field and assign it any typeface in size 14 points. Assign the type a color. Click OK.
4. Click on the Formats tab and select the Keep with next ¶ check box so the First Level entry will always be followed by any Second Level entry. Click on OK.
5. Choose Paragraph from the New menu and type *Second Level index* in the Name field. Click on the Edit in the Character Attributes field. Assign the style a typeface, 12 points from the Size menu, and another color from the Color pull-down menu. Click on OK. Click on the Formats tab and type 1p in the First Line field to indent the entry one pica from the page margin. Click on OK.
6. In the Style Sheets dialog box, choose Character from the New pull-down menu. Type *Page number style* in the Name field and choose any typeface at 9 points for the Second Level style. Click on OK. Click on Save. Display the Style Sheets palette (F11). It should resemble Figure 21.4.

Macintosh Commands

⌘-O File/Open
F11 View/Style Sheets
Shift-F11 Edit/Styles

Windows Commands

Ctrl-O File/Open
F11 View/Style Sheets
Shift-F11 Edit/Styles

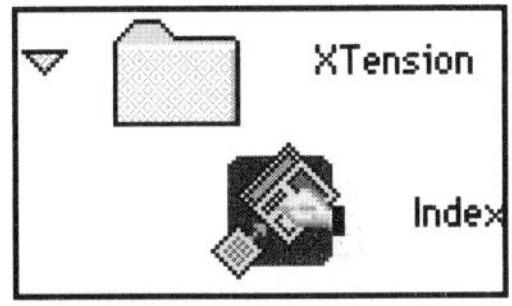

The Index XTension in the XTension folder. The XTension folder must be in the QuarkXPress 4.0 folder or XTensions will not load.

Linking tool

Content tool

Locked out?

If an alert tells you that a file is locked and that you can't save changes, click OK to open the file and then just save it under a different name.

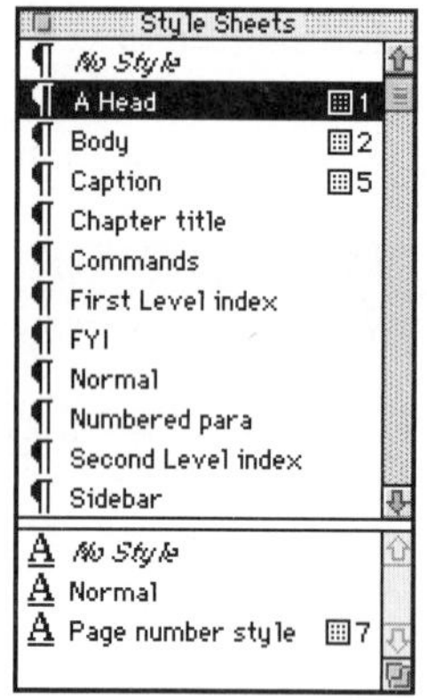

Figure 21.4. Two new paragraph styles, First Level index and Second Level index, and one character style, Page number style, were created.

ABC

When you add a First Level entry to the Index palette, it is listed alphabetically with the other First Level headings. You can only use the arrow to specify a location for a secondary (Second, Third, and Fourth Levels) heading, not for a First Level heading.

7. Choose Edit/Preferences/Index. In the Following Entry field, type a comma and press the Spacebar. Click on OK.
8. Now that the index preparation is complete, choose View/Show Index to display the Index palette. Make sure you are on document page 1, the Introduction page. Double-click on *Introduction* and notice that it appears in the Entry area on the Index palette in the Text field.
9. Use the Level pull-down menu to select First Level, because this is the primary index entry.
10. In the Reference area, use the Style pull-down menu to select the character style sheet, Page number style. This will format only the page numbers in the Page number style.
11. Use the Scope pull-down menu to select Selection Text. This will create the index entry from the selected text.
12. Click the Add button in the lower panel to add the contents of the Text field to the list of entries. The entry appears followed by the number of times it has been tagged in the document under the Occurrences menu. Notice that *Introduction* in the document is surrounded by two red brackets, indicating that it has been tagged as an index entry. Your Index palette should resemble Figure 21.5.

Once a selection has been tagged as an index entry, brackets appear before and after the selection. These brackets are visible only when the Index palette is open. Closing the Index palette does not remove the brackets, only hides them.

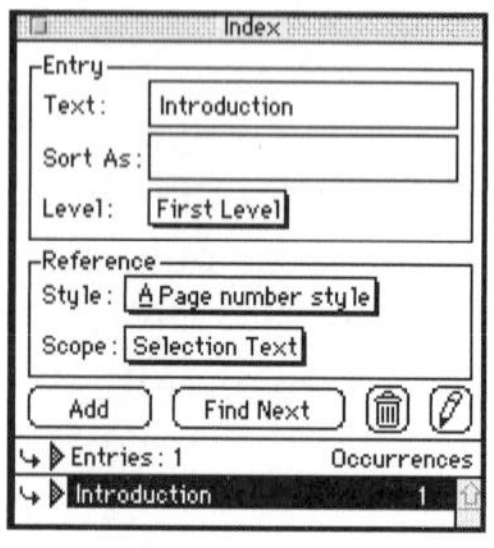

Figure 21.5. Click the Add button to add the contents of the Text field to the Entries column. The number 1 in the Occurrences column is not the page number; it's the number of times the word Introduction has been flagged for the index.

13. Click the Find Next button in the lower panel to move from the current Text Insertion bar (invisible on the selected text) to the next occurrence of the word *Introduction* in the Index palette. Because this word does not appear again *in the Index palette,* the alert beeps. Save the file as *Index1.qxd* in your Projects folder.

14. Click the Edit button (the Pencil icon) on the right side of the lower panel The pencil changes color, indicating that you are in Edit mode. The text in the Text field is highlighted and ready for editing. Type *Introduction to This Book* and notice that the new text appears in the Entries column in the lower panel of the Index palette (Figure 21.6). When you complete the editing, click on the Edit button to leave the Edit mode.

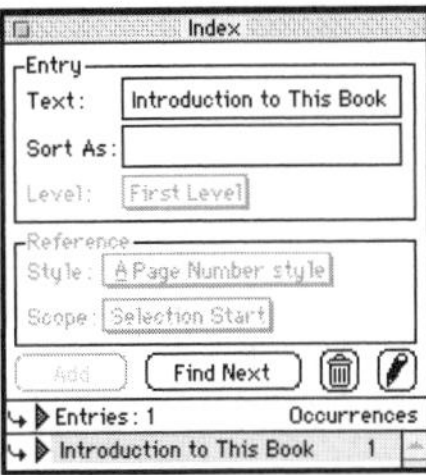

Figure 21.6. Click the Edit button (Pencil icon) to enter the Edit mode. The pencil changes color and the Text field is highlighted, allowing you to edit the index entry. Any changes to the Text field are reflected in the Entries field.

15. Click on the single entry in the Entries column to select it and click on the Trash icon (Macintosh) or ✗ button (Windows) to delete the entry (Figure 21.7). Click OK at the alert. The entry is deleted from the palette and the brackets are removed from the selection in the document.

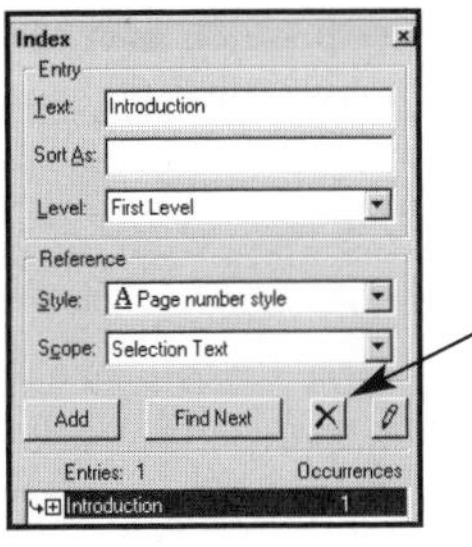

Figure 21.7. Click on an entry and click on the Trash icon (Macintosh) or ✗ icon (Windows) to delete the entry.

16. Double-click on *Introduction* again on document page 1. Specify it again as a First Level entry, Selection Text, and with Page number style sheet selected in the Reference field. Click on Add to add it to the list of entries in the lower panel of the Index palette.

Macintosh Commands

Option-F11 View/Lists
⌘-W File/Close

Windows Commands

Ctrl-F11 View/Show Lists
Ctrl-F4 File/Close

FYI

The Find Next button in the Index palette does not locate occurrences of the entry in the document, only in the Index palette. To locate other occurrences of the entry in the document, use the Find/Change command.

In Windows, click the ✗ icon next to the Pencil button on the Index palette to delete an entry.

✓ Selection Start
Selection Text
To Style:
Specified # of ¶s:
To End Of:
Suppress Page #
X-Ref:

Selection Start from the Scope menu will list only the page number of the page that contains the index marker's open bracket. **Selection Text,** in contrast, will list the page number from the index marker's open bracket to its closed bracket.

Sort

The Sort As field lets you override the alphabetical sorting of an entry in the text field. For example, if you had selected 10 Worst Dressed Men and wanted to change the number 10 in the Entry field to the word Ten, you would type Ten Worst Dressed Men in the Sort As field.

FYI

Click the triangle (Macintosh) or +/- icons (Windows) before a heading in the Index palette to display the page number on which that index entry occurs.

17. Double-click on document page 2 in the Document Layout palette. Drag to select only *QuarkImmedia Palette* at the top of the page. You don't want the word *the* alphabetized in the index. Leave the other options for a First Level entry as they are in the Index palette and click the Add button to add the selection to the list of Entries in the lower panel (Figure 21.8). Save the file.

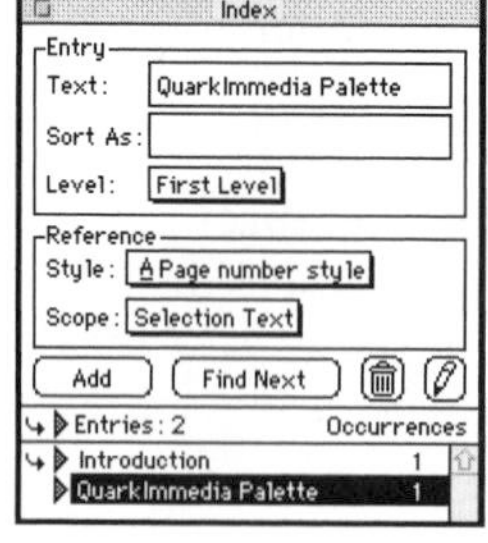

Figure 21.8. A second First Level entry is added to the Index palette. The Windows Index palette displays a + or - sign instead of a triangle.

18. Scroll down to the caption for Figure 1.1 under the screenshot at the bottom of the page. Double-click the word *tabs* to select it. It appears in the Text field of the Index palette. Choose Second Level from the Level pull-down menu. Leave the Style and Scope options set as they were for the First Level entries.

19. Before you add tabs to the Entries list, make sure that it will appear under its proper heading, *QuarkImmedia Palette.* To do this, click to the far left of *QuarkImmedia Palette* in the Entries field. If you click on the triangle (Macintosh) or +/- (Windows) directly to the left of the entry, the entry expands to reveal the document page number for that entry. Instead, click to the left of the triangle (Macintosh) or +/- sign (Windows) to the left of *QuarkImmedia Palette* and specify it as the primary heading (Figure 21.9).

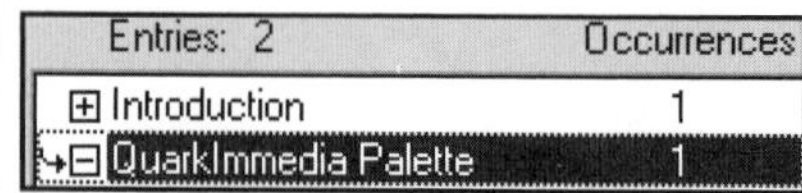

Figure 21.9. Select a heading and click to its far left (not on the triangle (Macintosh) or +/- (Windows) to specify it as the level under which the next level will be added. Clicking on the triangle (Macintosh) or + icon (Windows) displays the page number for the selected entry.

20. With *QuarkImmedia Palette* specified as the active level and *tabs* displayed in the Text field, click the Add button to add *tabs* to the list of entries. Click the triangle (Macintosh) or the +/- icons (Windows) to the left of the *tabs* entry and notice that it displays 2 as the document page number for this entry.

21. Double-click on the page 3 icon in the Document Layout palette. Select *Book Conventions* at the top of the page and specify it as a First Level heading, just as you did with the other First Level headings. Click the Add button and the Book Conventions First Level heading is listed alphabetically in the Entries column. Save the file.

22. Repeat to specify *QuarkXPress vs. QuarkImmedia* and *Saving Files* as First Level headings, and click the Add button to add them to the list of index entries (Figure 21.10).

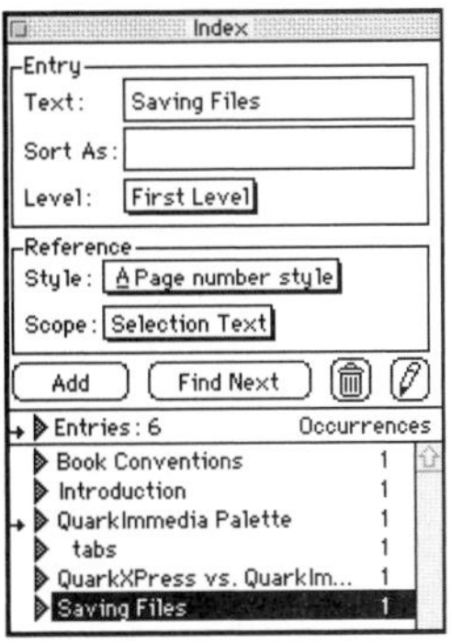

Figure 21.10. First Level headings are listed in alphabetical order in the Entries column of the Index palette. First level headings are not indented.

23. Double-click on the page 4 icon on the Document Layout palette. Select *Unit of Measure* and specify it as a First Level heading. Click the Add button to add it to the Index palette.

24. Click to the far left of the Unit of Measure heading to move the arrow to that entry. Double-click on *points* in the Unit of Measure paragraph in the document. It appears in the Text field of the Index palette. Specify it as a Second Level heading and click the Add button to add it as a Second Level entry under the Unit of Measure First Level entry (Figure 21.11).

Figure 21.11. A Second Level entry appears indented under the First Level entry marked with the arrow.

Macintosh Commands

⌘-O File/Open

Windows Commands

Ctrl-O File/Open

FYI

The Suppress Page # option under the Scope menu is useful when the index entry is a First level heading and should not display a page number, because the entries below it will display the page numbers for that reference.

Macintosh Commands

⌘-O File/Open
⌘-Option-S File/Save as

Windows Commands

Ctrl-O File/Open
Ctrl-Alt-S File/Save as

Click the Edit button to highlight text in the Text field and enter the Edit mode.

25. Select *Troubleshooting* on page 4, specify it as a First Level entry, and click on Add. Make sure the arrow appears to the left of *Troubleshooting* in the Entries column. Select *execute functions* in the second paragraph under *Troubleshooting* and specify it as a Second Level entry under Troubleshooting. Repeat for *Click in check boxes* in the third paragraph under *Troubleshooting* on page four. Your Index palette should resemble Figure 21.12.

Figure 21.12. First Level entries are followed by indented Second Level entries.

26. To edit the entries before building the index, click on the *Click in check boxes* entry to select it. Click the Edit button to enter the Edit mode. Change the uppercase C in *Click* to lowercase. Click the Edit button to exit the Edit mode.

27. Save this file with all the changes. Don't close it. You will need it for the next exercise.

LESSON 4
BUILDING THE INDEX

Now that you've done all the work in tagging the index entries and selecting all the options, it's time for Quark to go to work. Before you build your index, save your file and back it up. You should be doing this all along, but it's especially critical when you're subjecting your document to a command as extensive as the Index command, which searches and acts on the entire document. Remember, you can always build the index more than once for any document, and if you've made any changes to the document after building the index, you should build it again.

EXERCISE B

1. If necessary, open the *Index1.qxd* file you created earlier or open the *Index1.qxd* file in the Unit 21 folder on the CD-ROM. Save the file under another name (File/Save as)—just in case! Display the Document Layout palette (F10/Macintosh; F4/Windows) and the Index palette (View/Show Index).

2. Double-click on document page 4 to get to that page. Select the automatic text box on page 4. Choose Utilities/Build Index to display the Build Index dialog box (Figure 21.13). Click the Nested button to build a nested index. Click the Replace Existing Index check box, and click the Add Letter Headings check box to add the letters before each entry. Use the Style pull-down menu to select a paragraph style for those letters.

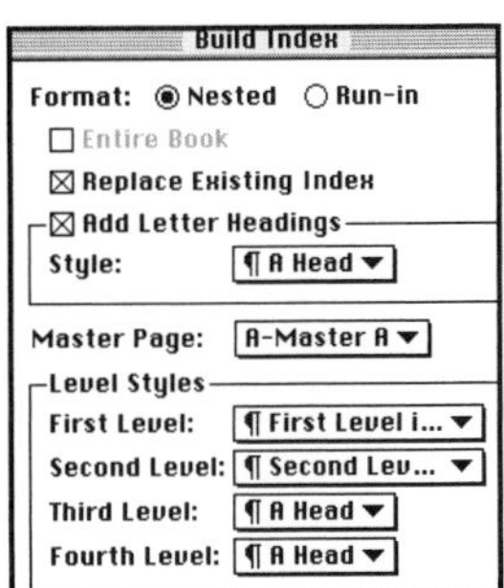

Figure 21.13. The type of index and styles for index levels are specified in the Build Index dialog box.

3. Leave the Master Page set to Master Page A. Under the Level Styles, choose First Level index for the First Level entry and Second Level index for the Second Level entry. Because you don't have any Third or Fourth Level entries, the other options won't affect the index. Click OK. In a few seconds, the index is created and appears on a new document page, page 5 (Figure 21.14 in sidebar).

4. You can edit the index just as you would any text or paragraph by changing the style or by applying local formatting. Close this file. Don't save your changes.

Deleting index entries

To delete an index entry

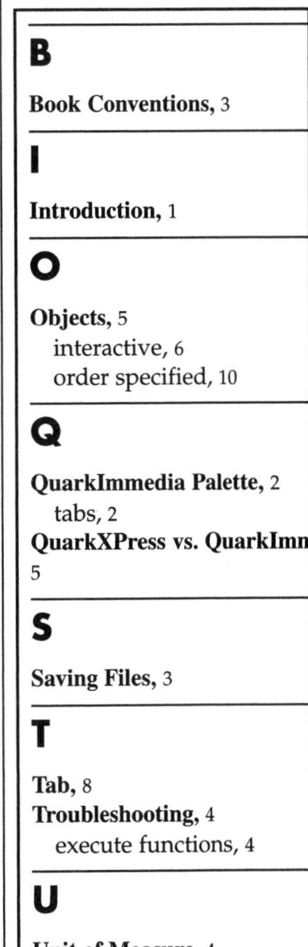

B

Book Conventions, 3

I

Introduction, 1

O

Objects, 5
interactive, 6
order specified, 10

Q

QuarkImmedia Palette, 2
tabs, 2
QuarkXPress vs. QuarkImm
5

S

Saving Files, 3

T

Tab, 8
Troubleshooting, 4
execute functions, 4

U

Unit of Measure, 4
click in check boxes, 4
points, 4

Figure 21.14. The index is generated and all entries display the assigned styles and formats. You can then edit the entries.

Macintosh Commands

⌘-Option-A File/Append

Windows Commands

Ctrl-Alt-A File/Append

LESSON 5
INDEXING AND THE BOOK COMMAND

The index you generated in the last exercise compiles entries from only one document. In a long document project like a book, a convention program, or a journal, for example, you need to compile the index from all the documents that comprise the project. To do this, use the Book command.

EXERCISE C

1. Open the *Ch02.qxd* file in the Unit 21 folder on the CD-ROM. Display the Document Layout palette (F10/Macintosh; F4/Windows) and the Index palette (View/Show Index).
2. Choose File/Append. Open the *Index1.qxd* file in the Unit 21 folder on the CD-ROM. In the Append dialog box, select the First Level index, Page number style, and Second Level index. Click the forward black arrow to copy each of those styles to the Including field (Figure 21.15). This saves you the trouble of recreating the styles for the Chapter 2 document. Click OK twice.

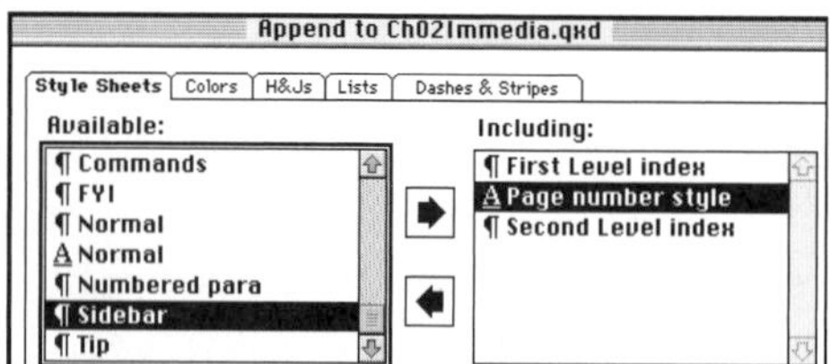

Figure 21.15. Append the index styles to the new document.

Screen Space

Close the Document Layout palette when working with both the Find/Change and Index palettes to give yourself more screen space.

3. Double-click on document page 1, and double-click on *Objects* in the first heading. Specify it as a First Level entry, with the Selection Text option from the Scope menu. Choose Page number style from the Style menu in the Reference field. Click on Add. Red brackets appear around *Objects* in the document, indicating it has been tagged as an index entry. Deselect the word.
4. To find the next occurrence of *Objects* in the document, use the Find/Change command. Choose Edit/Find/Change. Type *objects* in the Find What field, and select the Document, Whole Word, Ignore Case, and Ignore Attributes check boxes. Alt/Option-click on Find Next to change it to Find First. The word you just added to the Index palette is highlighted. Click Find Next. Ignore any instances of *Objects* found in the running header at the top of the page. You want *objects* in the first paragraph on page 2.

5. When *objects* in the first paragraph on page 2 is highlighted, notice the word is used in reference to interactive objects. Double-click on *objects* in the Text field of the Index palette and type *interactive*. Specify it as a Second Level entry and apply the Page number style from the Style field. Click on Add (Figure 21.16). The red brackets appear around *objects* in the document, indicating that it has been tagged as an index entry and *interactive* appears as a Second Level entry in the Index palette.

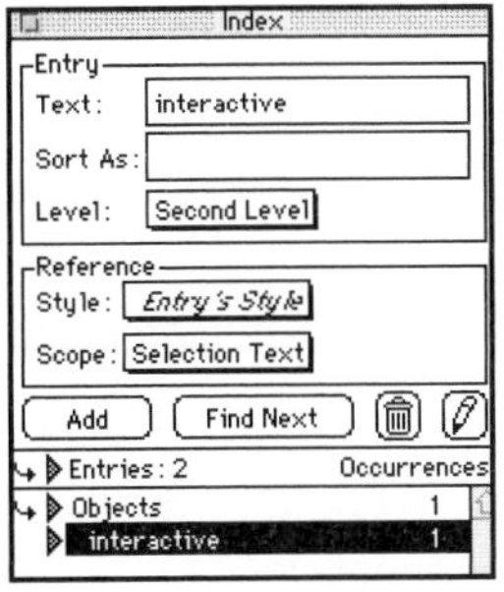

Figure 21.16. The word *objects* was selected and *interactive* typed in the Text field. *Interactive* was then specified as a Second Level entry before clicking the Add button.

6. Continue to click on Find Next, ignoring all instances of *objects* in the running headers until *objects* in the sidebar on page 6 is highlighted.

7. When *objects* in the sidebar on page 6 is selected, notice that the word is used in reference to the order of naming objects. Double-click to select *objects* in the Text field of the Index palette and enter the Edit mode. Type *order specified*. Select the same options as for the Second Level entry and click on Add to add interactive objects as a Second Level entry under *Objects* and to exit the Edit mode. The Index palette displays one First Level entry, *Objects*, and two Second Level entries under *Objects*, *interactive* and *order specified*.

8. Click on Find Next again in the Find/Change palette. Ignore the selections until the beep alerts you to the fact that there are no more instances of *objects* in the file. Click the arrow at the bottom of the document page in the page number field to display the page icons and drag to select page 3 (Figure 21.17).

FYI

Double-clicking on the text in the Text field of the Index palette *before* clicking on Add is the same thing as clicking once on the entry in the Entries column and clicking the Edit button. Double-clicking text in the Text field automatically takes you into Edit mode. You don't have to click the Edit button to exit the Edit mode. Clicking Add automatically exits the Edit mode.

FYI

Brackets indicating that a word or phrase has been tagged as an index entry appear only when the Index palette is open. They are non-printing markers and can be customized in the Edit/Preferences/Index dialog box.

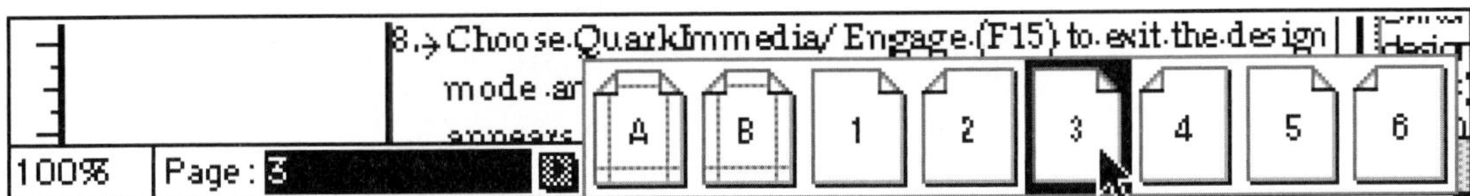

Figure 21.17. Use the page icons to navigate the document when several palettes are open.

9. Scroll to find the *Page Panel* head at the bottom of page 3. Drag to select *Page Panel*. Specify it as a First Level head in the Index palette and click the Add button. Make sure the arrow appears to the left of the Page Panel entry. If necessary, open the Find/Change palette and type *Page Panel* in the Find What field.Click on Find Next until the words are highlighted in the sidebar under the screenshot on page 4 (Figure 21.18).

WARNING!

When clicking in the left column next to an entry, be careful not to highlight the entry itself. Doing this will replace the Text field in the Index palette with the entry.

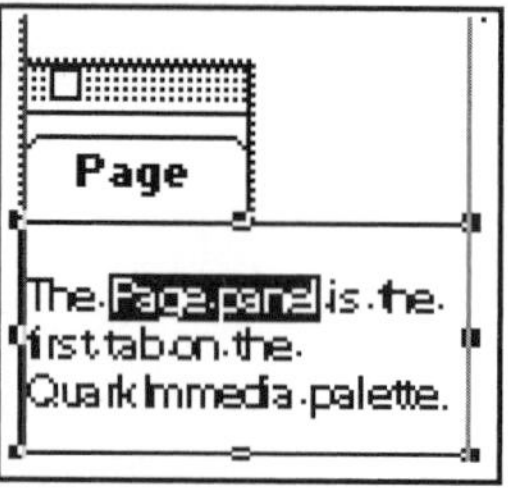

Figure 21.18. Page panel is highlighted in the sidebar.

10. The two words (Page panel) appear in the Text field of the Index palette. Because the Page Panel *tab* is what needs to be indexed as a Second Level entry, double-click on Page panel in the Index palette to enter Edit mode and drag to select both words. Type *tab;* select Second Level from the Level menu and Page Number style in the Reference field. Click on Add to add *tab* as a Second Level entry under Page Panel and to exit the Edit mode.

The Edit button changes color when you are in Edit mode. Click the button to toggle between Edit and Non-Edit mode.

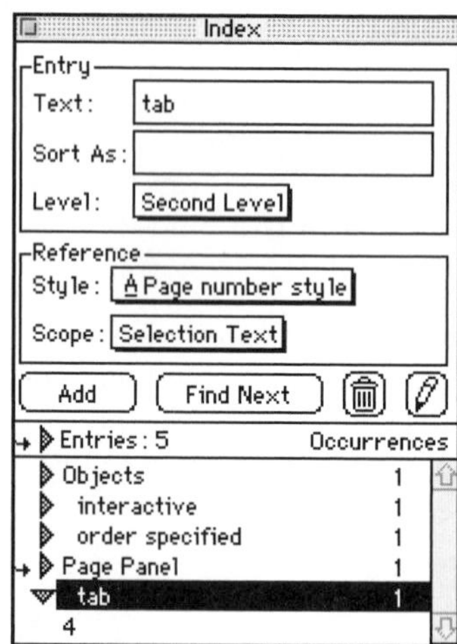

Figure 21.19. The Index palette displays two First Level entries and three Second Level entries. Clicking the triangle (Macintosh) or +/- icons (Windows) displays the document page on which that entry appears.

11. Choose Utilities/Build Index. Choose Nested Index; select the Replace Existing Index and Add Letter Headings check boxes. Select the appropriate styles for the First Level and Second Level entries. Click on OK. The index flows on page 7. Save this file as *Index2.qxd* in your Projects folder (File/Save as). Keep it open, however.
12. Choose File/Save as again. Click on the New Folder icon on the right side of the dialog box. Type *Indexed Files* in the Name field and click Create. Click on Save to save the *Index2.qxd* file in the newly created Indexed Files folder.
13. Choose File/Open and open the *Index1.qxd* file. Choose File/Save as and save it in the Indexed Files folder. Both the *Index1.qxd* and *Index2.qxd* files should now be in the Indexed Files folder.
14. Choose File/New/Book. Type *Indexed Book* in the Book Name field. Navigate to the Indexed Files folder and click on Open. Click on Create to create and save the Indexed Book palette in the Indexed Files folder.
15. Click the Add Chapter icon, the first icon, in the Indexed Book palette. Navigate to the *Index1.qxd* file in the Indexed Files folder. Click on Add. The file is displayed in the Book palette. Notice that it is boldfaced and displays an M to its left, indicating that it is currently the Master Chapter, the one on which all the styles and attributes will be based.
16. Click the Add Chapter icon again. Navigate to the *Index2.qxd* file in the Indexed Files folder. Click on Add. Both Chapters are displayed in the Indexed Book palette, with *Index1.qxd* in boldface indicating that it is the Master Chapter (Figure 21.20).

Indexed Book

M	Document	Pages	Status
M	**Index1.qxd**	**1-5**	**Open**
	Index2.qxd	7-12	Open

Figure 21.20. Two files (Chapters) are added to the Indexed Book palette. The *Index1.qxd* file is boldfaced and displays an M in the M(aster) column, indicating that it is the Master Chapter on which the attributes of the other Chapters in the Book will be based.

Macintosh Commands

⌘-Option-S File/Save as

Windows Commands

Ctrl-Alt-S File/Save as

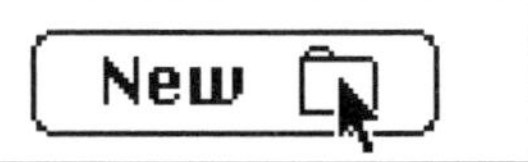

Click on the New Folder icon in the Save as dialog box to create a new folder.

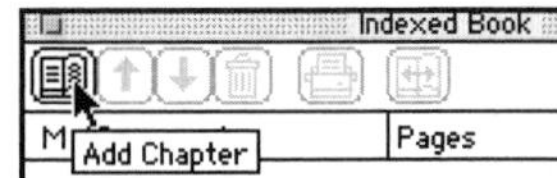

Click the Add Chapter icon to add a document (Chapter) to the Book.

17. Click the Synchronize Book icon in the Indexed Book palette. Click OK to synchronize.

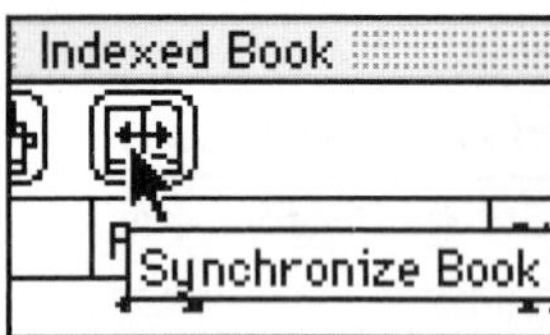

Clicking the Synchronize Book icon synchronizes all the Chapters in a Book.

18. Display the Index palette (View/Show Index). With both the Indexed Book palette and Index palettes open, choose Utilities/Build Index. Click to select the Entire Book check box in the Build Index dialog box (Figure 21.21). Make sure the appropriate styles are applied for the Levels, make any other necessary selections, and click on OK. The index of both documents (Chapters) appears on a new page at the end of the active document.

19. Close these files. Don't save your changes.

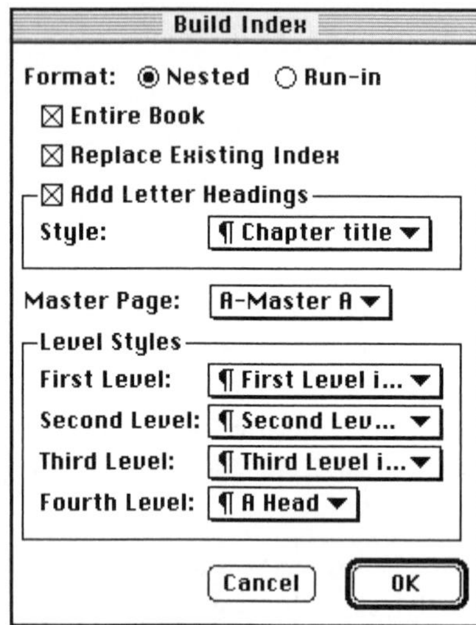

Figure 21.21. Click to select the Entire Book option to build an index based on all the entries in the individual documents (Chapters) in a synchronized Book.

APPENDIX

QUARKXPRESS ON THE INTERNET

If you are planning to repurpose your QuarkXPress print documents for Internet distribution, you have several different options depending on whether you want to include multimedia elements in the Internet project. Regardless of the option you select, you might have to use some HTML code to tweak the project, but in most cases the result will be beautifully formatted Web pages that keep the graphic and typographical elements of your XPress document's page design.

QUARKIMMEDIA

The easiest way to create multimedia projects for Internet and CD-ROM distribution is to use QuarkImmedia. QuarkImmedia, from Quark, Inc. is a two-part tool, the design tool and the viewing tool. Using the QuarkImmedia XTension, you start with a QuarkXPress document, change XPress items like boxes, lines, and text paths to QuarkImmedia objects, and assign those objects events like moving, playing movies and animations, or generating sounds. All of this is done via the QuarkImmedia palette, where English commands like "Play Movie" and "Go to page 5" make it easy to create complex projects. Once you've finished assigning events to objects, you then export the project to create an interactive multimedia project created directly from a static print document (Figure A.1).

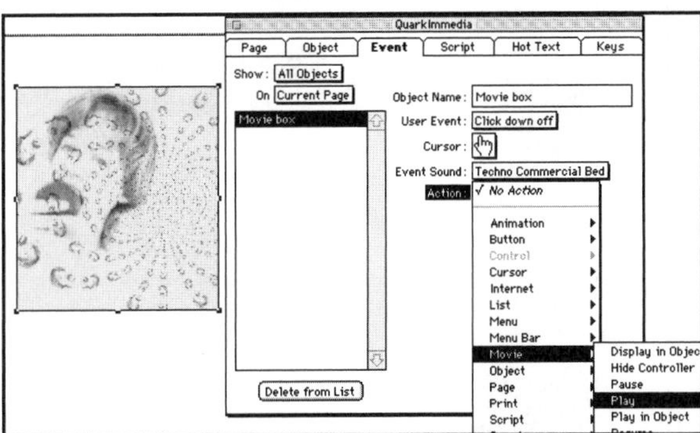

Figure A.1. A movie imported into a QuarkXPress picture box will play when the user clicks on it. The picture box was specified as a QuarkImmedia object and named Movie box.

Design options let users specify either a unique 256-color palette for each page in the document or thousands or millions of colors for the entire project. This means that viewers with monitors capable of displaying more than the standard 256 colors can take advantage of enhanced color when viewing projects. Richer visual interest is also available from the opacity and drop shadow options.

The QuarkImmedia Viewer lets your viewers interact with the project on a CD or over the Internet. You can embed both the Macintosh and/or Windows Viewers into your project if it is being prepared for a CD-ROM, or you can distribute the viewers (royalty-free) to users via the Internet. The advantage of using QuarkImmedia is that you don't have to learn HTML, because QuarkImmedia doesn't use HTML code to create its projects. All you have to do is use your design skills in QuarkXPress to create exciting, interactive pages that sing and dance!

BEYONDPRESS 3.0

Another powerful QuarkXPress-to-Web XTension is BeyondPress 3.0 from Extensis. Unlike QuarkImmedia, BeyondPress converts QuarkXPress documents to HTML-formatted Web pages. Version 3.0 also lets you create Web pages directly from a new QuarkXPress document using the program's authoring tools. In Document Conversion mode, the program lets you add text chains and graphic elements from your QuarkXPress document to the Document Content palette. You can then drag these elements into any order, and apply your own HTML style tags to link elements in your document to other URLs. (See why you need to tweak in HTML?) An Elements palette lets you add QuickTime movies, Java applets, and Shockwave animations by dragging them onto the QuarkXPress page. Because your exported projects are in HTML code, you can upload them directly to the Web without a viewer. Once you export a project, BeyondPress creates all the HTML tags and previews the page in your browser so you can see how it will look on the Internet (Figure A.2).

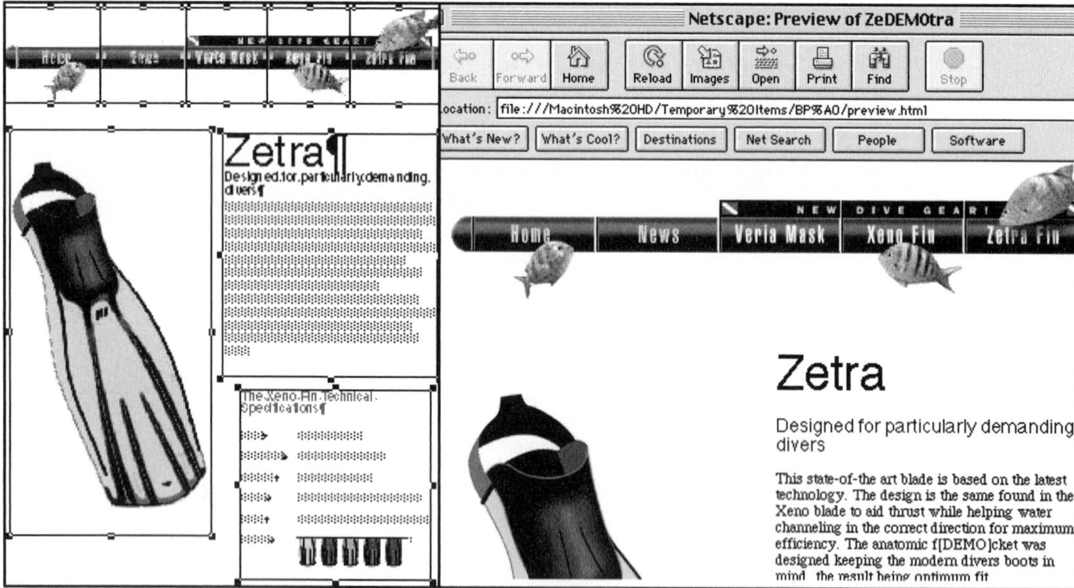

Figure A.2. The original page in XPress contains text and pictures. Each image in the bar at the top of the page is specified as an image map with links to different HTML pages. The Export command adds the HTML links and displays the page in your browser's window.

FINDING QUARK ON THE INTERNET

The first place to find Quark on the Internet is Quark's home page. From there, you can link to other sites or explore some of the ones listed below.

Quark, Inc.
http://www.quark.com

Extensis, developers of QX-Effects, QX-Tools, Preflight Pro, and Preflight Designer.
http://www.extensis.com

Message board for Quark users.
http://desktop publishing.com/quark/quarktalk.html

Frank Romano's Quark tips.
http://www.rit.edu/~spmswww/frank/qxtips.htm

Digital Directions, an electronic magazine guide to new design technology with Photoshop and Quark XPress tips.
http://www.iglou.com/eblawler/directions/directions.html

GetInfo Newsletter provides the latest in DTP/Internet tips and tricks, covering Quark, Illustrator, Photoshop, and FreeHand.
http://getinfo.asap.net/

WHAT'S ON THE CD-ROM?

EXTENSIS DEMOS

If you plan to use QuarkXPress like a grownup, you *must* use XTensions from Extensis. These powerful XTensions let you customize QuarkXPress for the way you work, and at the same time extend the capabilities of XPress to meet specific design and production needs. Although all the demos are currently available only for the Macintosh platforms, Extensis distributes other XTension products for Windows.

QX-EFFECTS 3.0

This XTension helps you create high-quality effects right in QuarkXPress that you used to have to create in Photoshop. Many of the chapter openers in this book display effects created with QX-Effects, and a description of how each effect was achieved appears on that page. Install the QX-Effects demo from the CD-ROM, and create these (and different) effects yourself. Glows, shadows, bevels, embosses, and perspective shadows can be applied with a single keystroke to text and to QuarkXPress items. Each effect displays an interactive Effect Guide preview, letting you see exactly how the effect will be applied. Who said QuarkXPress wasn't fun?

QX-TOOLS 2.0

The most powerful and useful suite of XTensions is QX-Tools. This is a collection of fifteen XTensions designed to increase the productivity of QuarkXPress. It contains a wide variety of time-saving features, including scaling multiple objects, using layers, customizable toolbars, navigation tools, and a powerful search and replace utility.

PREFLIGHT PRO 1.0 AND PREFLIGHT DESIGNER 1.0

This is a powerful combination of preflighting software tools designed to save time, materials, and money by tracking down and solving prepress problems before it's too late. It lets you easily inspect your documents and take corrective action before output, and collect screen and printer fonts and graphics to deliver complete, accurate files to the imagesetter and printer.

Extensis Corp.
1800 SW First Avenue
Suite 500
Portland, OR 97201
503-274-2020
http://www.extensis.com

IMAGES

Most of the images in the lesson folders are from Artville. These files are fine art images, drum-scanned and color corrected to the most rigorous demands. Artville gives you the quality of commissioned work and the value, convenience, and flexibility of royalty-free art. The Artville images in the lessons folders are provided for use with this text only. If you want to use them in production work, you must purchase them from Artville.

Several of these images have been copied to a folder named *Images* on the CD-ROM. Access this folder for graphics when you need to import a picture into a picture box that is not connected to an exercise, or if you want to work with any of the Extensis demos.

Artville
3210 Darwin Road
Madison, WI 53704-3108
800-631-7808
http://www.artville.com

QUARKXPRESS 4.0 DEMO

The demo versions of QuarkXPress 4.0 for Macintosh and Windows will let you get started with learning how to use this powerful new upgrade. You cannot save files in the demo version and printing options are limited, but otherwise all of the program's features and functions are available.

REVIEW QUESTIONS AND REVIEW EXERCISES

The review projects on the CD-ROM will give you practice in creating projects by combining many commands and functions that you learned in separate chapters. By doing the review exercises and substituting your own text, graphics, and other specifications, you will soon become comfortable working with QuarkXPress projects.

GLOSSARY

Absolute leading is an assigned leading value that remains constant regardless of the point size of any character in the paragraph. The term "12 on 14" specifies 14 points as absolute leading.

Absolute page number is a page's position relative to the first page of the document regardless of the actual **folio** (page) number. For example, the third page in the document has an absolute page number of 3 even though its folio number is 64.

Anchored item is a box, line, or text path pasted in a paragraph that moves with the paragraph.

Anchored rule is a line set above or below a paragraph that moves with that paragraph.

Append command is used to add to the current document the colors, style sheets, or **H&J** specifications from other documents.

Aspect ratio is the ratio or proportion of an item's width and height. Maintaining aspect ratio when resizing the item does not distort the item.

Auto Image Runaround value specifies how far from the picture (not the picture box) the text should wrap.

Auto leading sets the leading value as a percentage (usually 20 percent greater than the font size) of the largest font size on any given line in a paragraph. If the largest font size in the paragraph is 12 points, auto leading sets the distance between baselines in that paragraph to 14.4 points.

Auto Page Insertion option (General Document dialog box) specifies whether, and if so, where, new pages will be inserted in the document when text overflows the automatic text chain.

Auto Picture Import determines whether QuarkXPress will automatically update pictures that have been modified since the document was last opened.

Automatic text box automatically appears on the **master page** and on its corresponding document pages when you select the option in the New Document dialog box.

Auxiliary dictionary is a dictionary of user-defined words used in conjunction with the main QuarkXPress dictionary.

Baseline is the invisible horizontal line upon which characters "sit."

Baseline grid is the non-printing horizontal guide based on the **leading** value on which text is set. Baseline grid is especially important in multi-column documents

Baseline Shift command is applied to selected characters to raise or lower the text relative to their normal baseline position.

Bézier line, named after Pierre Bézier, is a mathematically defined line that uses two handles (called points in QuarkXPress) to determine where the line segment begins and ends.

Bézier point can be a corner point, smooth point, or symmetrical point. A corner point connects two straight lines, a straight line and a curved line, or two noncontinuous curved lines. A smooth point connects two curved lines to form a continuous curve. The curve handles attached to a smooth point revolve together so that they always rest on a straight line through the point, but can still be distanced independently of each other. A symmetrical point connects two curved lines to form a continuous curve. Although the curve handles move together so that they always rest on a straight line through the point, they are always equidistant from the point.

Bézier text path is created with the Bézier Text-Path tool or with the Freehand Text-Path tool and contains Bézier points that can be manipulated to reshape the path.

Bitmap images, or raster images, are graphics created by a pattern of pixels in a bitmap application like Photoshop.

Blend is a color applied to a box background created by a gradual transition between two colors. Also called a **gradient**.

Book is a file displayed as a palette where you group multiple QuarkXPress documents called **Chapters**. These Chapters then all assume the specifications of a **Master Chapter** using the **Synchronize** command.

Bounding box is a non-printing box that appears around all the items in a group, allowing you to move the grouped items as a single unit.

Chapter is a QuarkXPress file opened in the Book palette.

Character style sheet is a saved set of character attributes applied to selected text in a paragraph. See **paragraph style sheet**.

Choke is a color-trapping command in which the **knockout** area of the background color is slightly reduced, thus allowing the foreground object to slightly overlap that area.

Clear command deletes selected text without putting it on the Clipboard. The Delete command under the Item menu deletes an item without putting it on the **Clipboard**.

Clipboard is an area of memory used to store text and items until they are replaced by other text or items via the Cut, Copy, or Delete commands.

Clipping path is a Bézier path that outlines areas of an image. The area inside the clipping path is opaque; the area outside the clipping path is transparent. Clipping paths can be embedded in Photoshop images and exported with the image.

Collect for Output command creates a text file listing all the properties of a QuarkXPress file in preparation for printing.

Color models such as PANTONE, TRUMATCH, and others define color using on-screen color swatches from that model.

Combine Merge command. See Exclusive/Or.

Consecutive page number symbol (<#>) indicates that pages in the automatic text chain are to be numbered consecutively.

Content command from the Item menu refers to the contents of a text box (text) or a picture box (graphic). The Content tool is used to manipulate the contents of an item. See **contentless box.**

Contentless box is neither a text box nor a picture box. Only a background color can be applied to it.

Copy is to copy the selected text or item to the **Clipboard**.

Corner Point is a Bézier point that connects two straight lines.

Cut is to delete text or an item and place it on the **Clipboard**.

Dash is a user-created broken line style that can be applied to lines, text paths, and box frames. See **stripe**.

Default setting is a predetermined setting that can be changed by the user. For example, the unit of measure defaults to inches, but can be changed to another unit of measure such as picas. Changing default settings when no documents are open makes the new setting the default setting for all subsequent documents.

Difference/Reverse Difference Merge command that removes all the selected item shapes except for the backmost shape (Difference) or keeps all the shapes except for the backmost shape (Reverse Difference).

Direction handles appear with Bézier points and are used to reshape the segment, especially its slope, attached to those points.

Document Layout palette is used to create, duplicate, and delete master pages. It is also used to move document pages, create multipage spreads, and apply a new master page format to document pages.

Drop cap is an initial text character or characters positioned below the first line in a paragraph that extends (drops) vertically more than one line into the paragraph.

Em dash (—) is a dash the width of two zeros. Create an em dash by pressing Option-Shift-hyphen (Macintosh) or Ctrl-Shift-= (Windows).

Embedded path is a Bézier path around part of an image embedded in the image and exported with that image from a program such as Photoshop. QuarkXPress can create a **clipping path** from that embedded path.

Endpoints mode defines a line by the position of its left (start) and right (end) points.

Entry label is used to catalog an entry in the **Library palette**.

EPS (Encapsulated PostScript) file can be imported into a QuarkXPress picture box and resized without affecting its output resolution (image detail).

Exclusive Or/Combine Merge commands keep all the selected item shapes and cut out any overlapping areas, creating one item. No points are added where two lines cross (**Combine**); where two lines cross, points are added (**Exclusive Or**).

Facing pages are alternating left and right pages. This option is always selected in the New Document dialog box when documents are being printed on both sides of the paper. Facing pages icons display turned-down corners at the top of the icon.

Filters are XTensions that allow you to import text and graphic files into QuarkXPress.

Find Attributes option in the Find/Change dialog box lets you find and replace text, style sheets, fonts, font sizes, and type styles.

Find First finds the first instance in the document of the contents of the Find What field in the Find/Change dialog box. Display Find First by Alt/Option clicking on the **Find Next** button.

Find Next finds the next instance in the document of the contents of the Find What field in the Find/Change dialog box. If the Document check box is not selected, Find Next locates the Find What text from the insertion point.

First Point is the tip of the line that starts a line drawn with either the Line tool or the Orthogonal Line tool.

Folio is the actual page number of a document page as generated by the Consecutive Page Number symbol or by the Section command. The folio number has no relation to the page's numerical position in the document.

Font Usage dialog box lists all the fonts in a document. Missing fonts display a minus sign.

Frame is a border around a box. You can apply the frames supplied with QuarkXPress or create your own in the Dashes & Stripes dialog box.

Gamut is the range of colors that a device, such as a printer or a monitor, is capable of reproducing or displaying.

Global formatting is character and paragraph styling as specified in a character style sheet or a paragraph style sheet. Any change to these specifications is called **local formatting**.

Gradient is a box background color created by the gradual transition of two colors; in QuarkXPress, it is called a **blend**.

Greek(ed) pictures and text are displayed as gray bars for faster screen redraw. Greeking does not affect output, only display.

Group is two or more selected items surrounded by a bounding box and moved and manipulated as one item.

Guides are non-printing lines used to position text and items. Drag horizontal and vertical guides down and out from the rulers.

Hexachrome Color System, a new matching color system from Pantone, adds orange and green to the CMYK plates to create more intense colors and thus increase the range (**gamut**) of reproducible colors.

Hyphenation and Justification (H&Js) command specifies if and how words hyphenate and the way words and characters are spaced in justified and non-justified text.

Image resolution is the degree of detail in a bitmap graphic, usually measured in pixels per inch.

Image runaround value determines the distance between a graphic and the text that wraps around the image.

Increment value in the Baseline Grid area of the General Document preferences determines the amount of space between the grid's baselines. The Increment value should equal the paragraph's leading value when locking text to the baseline.

Intersection Merge command keeps any areas that overlap the shape in the back and cuts out the rest of the shape. This command results in one box from the two or more selected items.

Invisibles are non-printing characters, such as Tab, Space, and Enter characters, that display on the screen when Show/Invisibles is selected from the View menu.

Item runaround value determines the distance between an item (box, line, or text path) and the text that wraps around the item.

Jump lines are references to page numbers where a text chain is continued on a page other than the one on which it began. Jump line commands are usually preceded by "Continued on page" or "Continued from page."

Keep Changes/Delete Changes apply to keeping or deleting modified master page items when a new master page is applied or when the same master page is reapplied to a document page based on any master page.

Kerning is adding or deleting space between two characters using the Kerning dialog box under the Style menu or by clicking on the Kerning arrows in the Measurements palette. A positive value increases space; a negative value reduces space.

Knockout is created in color work when an object is placed in front of a background area. The background area "knocked out" by the foreground object is not printed on the color separation plate.

Last point is the tip of the line that ends a line drawn with either the Orthogonal Line tool or Line tool.

Leading is the amount of space between baselines. In QuarkXPress, the leading value includes the font size plus the space between the lines.

Library is an XPress file where items are stored.

Library palette is a file containing items that have been drag-copied from a document page. Drag-copy items out of the Library palette onto a document page.

Link or join text boxes so text will automatically flow from one linked box to another.

Linked image establishes a path from the low-resolution image imported into a QuarkXPress picture box to the high-resolution image at a specific location on the hard drive or external disk. The linked image, with all its modifications, must be able to follow that path in order to print the modified high-resolution image.

List is a group of one or more paragraph style sheets selected by the user for the purpose of copying and assembling the text tagged by those style sheets. A List can be created, for example, to generate a table of contents.

Local formatting is any change made to text tagged with character styles or paragraph styles. See **global formatting**.

Master Chapter is the first chapter in a Book, whose styles, colors, and H&Js are applied to every other **Chapter** in the Book.

Master page is a non-printing page used to automatically format document pages. Any item created on a master page appears on all document pages based on that master page.

Master page items include text boxes, lines, picture boxes, and groups created on the master page and applied to every document page based on that master page. Master page items can be modified and deleted. See **Keep Changes/ Delete Changes.**

Midpoint describes the position, angle, and length of an active line relative to its center.

Misregistration occurs when the movement of paper through the printing press causes colors to be printed inaccurately. **Trapping** is used to correct for misregistration.

Multi-ink color system is a special color model in QuarkXPress that lets you create a multi-ink document using screen percentages of existing process color inks and/or spot colors.

Nested group is one set of grouped items grouped with another group.

Nested index contains up to four levels of entries separated by paragraph returns and different style sheets. See **run-In index**.

New Line Marker appears when you press Shift/Return after any line in a paragraph. This command creates a new line in the same paragraph without ending the paragraph and applies the paragraph formatting to that new line and to subsequent lines.

No Style, when applied to a paragraph, strips it of any style sheet attributes while leaving **local formatting** intact. When a new style sheet is applied to that paragraph, the local formatting will be overridden.

Noise is any discernible part of the image eliminated by a closed path. To tighten a closed path in the Clipping dialog box, choose a higher Noise value.

Non-facing pages are pages designed to be printed on only one side of the paper.

None runaround allows an item to sit directly on top of text, obscuring it.

Normal style is the default style for text applied to every paragraph and text character in a document, unless you modify the Normal style or apply another paragraph or character style.

Offset Across/Offset Down fields in the Picture Modify dialog box specify a picture's distance relative to the left and top sides of the picture box.

Open command displays the Open dialog box from which you can select a drive or external disk and a document on that drive or disk to open.

Orientation icons for the printed page in the New Document and Page Setup dialog boxes refer to the vertical (Portrait) or horizontal (Landscape) position of the paper.

Orphan is the first line of a paragraph that falls at the bottom of a column. See **widow**.

Output resolution is the greatest level of detail produced by the imagesetter or printer and is usually measured in dots per inch.

Overflow Indicator, a small box with an x in the middle, appears in the lower right corner of a text box when more text than can fit into that text box is either typed in or imported into the box.

Overprint indicates that a colored object is not knocked out of the background's color separation plate, but instead prints over the background color. See **knockout**.

Page Number Box in the lower left corner of the Document Layout palette displays the current page. Highlight the number, type a new page number, and press Return/Enter to navigate to that page. If you have sectioned your document, the Page Number box displays the actual page number (folio), not the absolute page number.

Paragraph alignment specifies the position of text relative to the left and right sides of the text box—standard-shape or Bézier. Paragraphs can be left, right, center, justified, and force justified aligned. See **vertical alignment**.

Paragraph style sheet is a saved set of text and paragraph format commands applied to an entire paragraph. See **Character style sheet**.

Paste command places the contents of the **Clipboard** at the insertion point on the page.

Preview option in the Save and Save as dialog boxes (Macintosh only) displays a thumbnail of a document's first page when that document is selected in the Open [document] dialog box.

Process colors (4-color process) are cyan, magenta, yellow, and black. A process color is a single color composed of percentages of cyan, magenta, yellow, and black. Each of these four colors is printed on a separate separation plate. Overlaying these four plates in the printing process creates process color (4-color) art and text.

Reverse Difference. See **Difference/Reverse Difference**.

Revert to Saved command closes the current document without saving any changes and opens the most recently saved version of that document.

Rule is a line anchored to a paragraph and that moves with that paragraph.

Run-in index has two levels of entries in the same paragraph. See **nested index.**

Save command saves a previously named and saved document under the name it was assigned when it was first saved and at the same location.

Save as command displays the Save as dialog box, and allows you to name or rename a document and save it at another location.

Scale Across/Scale Down values specify the size of the graphic relative to 100%. A value less than 100% reduces the horizontal (Scale Across) or vertical (Scale Down) size of the image; a value greater than 100% enlarges the image.

Section dialog box is where you specify a new section with new page numbers.

Smooth point connects two curved lines to form a continuous curve.

Smoothness field in the Clipping Modify tab lets you determine how accurate the clipping path is. The lower the value in the Smoothness field, the more accurate—but complex—the **clipping path**.

Split All Paths command splits all the closed paths in the selected item, including any paths contained within other paths, such as the inside path in a donut shape.

Split Outside Paths command splits a box that consists of two or more closed paths separated by space. This command does not split closed paths contained within these paths, such as the inside of a donut shape.

Spot color is a color printed with one ink; it produces a single separation plate for that color.

Spread (pages) is comprised of two or more adjacent horizontal pages. In color trapping, applying a spread means to enlarge the color of the foreground object.

Story is text in a linked chain of text boxes. Each time you import a text file or word processing file into a text box, that text becomes a story.

Stripe is a user-defined style for lines and box frames made of solid stacked bars with white or colored gaps between those bars. See **Dash**.

Symmetrical point connects two curved lines to form a continuous curve. Its curve handles are equidistant from the point.

Synchronize is to apply the style sheets, colors, dashes and stripes, and H&J specifications of a **Master Chapter** to every **Chapter** in a **Book**.

Text path is a straight or curved line created with any of the Text-Path tools and which contains text. See **Bézier text path**.

Threshold value in the Runaround Modify dialog box specifies how black an alpha channel must be to fall inside the initial clipping path. Only pixels darker than the Threshold value are included inside the runaround path.

Thumbnails view displays a miniature view of document pages and allows you to drag-copy pages between documents and to move pages within a document.

TIFF (Tagged Image File Format) images are bitmapped black-and-white line art, grayscale, or color images created in programs such as Adobe Photoshop or Fractal Design Painter.

Tracking is adding or deleting space between selected characters and words from either the Tracking command under the Style menu or by clicking the Tracking arrows on the Measurements palette. A positive value adds space; a negative value reduces space.

Trapping is compensating for printing misregistration by increasing the foreground object (**spread**) or reducing the background color (**choke**).

Undo command (available for most functions) cancels the last executed command.

Union Merge command combines all the selected objects into one shape outlined by their non-overlapping areas.

Unit of measure defines the measurements for all values in a document as in picas, inches, etc.

Unlink command breaks links between text boxes. Shift-click with the Unlinking tool on a linked text box to remove the text box from the chain and force it into the next linked text box in the chain.

Vector images, also called object-oriented graphics, use X and Y coordinates to describe objects such as lines, curves, type, and objects. Because vector images are based on mathematical coordinates, they can be resized and reshaped without losing detail.

Vertical alignment specifies the position of text relative to the top and bottom sides of the text box. Text can be top, bottom, center, and justified aligned. See **paragraph alignment**.

Widow is the last line in a paragraph that falls at the top of a column or at the top of the next text box. See **orphan**.

Index

D

N

O

P

Q

R

S

T

U

V

W

X, Y, Z

License Agreement for Delmar Publishers
an International Thomson Publishing company

Educational Software/Data

You the customer, and Delmar incur certain benefits, rights, and obligations to each other when you open this package and use the software/data it contains.
Be sure you read the license agreement carefully, since by using the software/data you indicate you have read, understood, and accepted the terms of this agreement.

Your rights:

1. You enjoy a non-exclusive license to use the enclosed software/data on a single microcomputer that is not part of a network or multi-machine system in consideration for payment of the required license fee, (which may be included in the purchase price of an accompanying print component), or receipt of this software/data, and your acceptance of the terms and conditions of this agreement.

2. You own the media on which the software/data is recorded, but you acknowledge that you do not own the software/data recorded on them. You also acknowledge that the software/data is furnished as is, and contains copyrighted and/or proprietary and confidential information of Delmar Publishers or its licensers.

3. If you do not accept the terms of this license agreement you may return the media within 30 days. However, you may not use the software during this period.

There are limitations on your rights:

1. You may **not** copy or print the software/data for any reason whatsoever, except to install it on a hard drive on a single microcomputer and to make one archival copy, unless copying or printing is expressly permitted in writing or statements recorded on the diskette(s).

2. You may **not** revise, translate, convert, disassemble or otherwise reverse engineer the software data except that you may add to or rearrange any data recorded on the media as part of the normal use of the software/data.

3. You may **not** sell, license, lease, rent, loan, or otherwise distribute or network the software/data except that you may give the software/data to a student or and instructor for use at school or, temporarily at home.

Should you fail to abide by the Copyright Law of the United States as it applies to this software/data your license to use it will become invalid. You agree to erase or otherwise destroy the software/data immediately after receiving note of Delmar Publisher's termination of this agreement for violation of its provisions.

Delmar gives you a **limited warranty** covering the enclosed software/data. The **limited warranty** can be found in this package and/or the instructor's manual that accompanies it.

This license is the entire agreement between you and Delmar Publishers interpreted and enforced under New York law.

Limited Warranty

Delmar Publishers warrants to the original licensee/purchaser of this copy of microcomputer software/data and the media on which it is recorded that the media will be free from defects in material and workmanship for ninety (90) days from the date of original purchase. All implied warranties are limited in duration to this ninety (90) day period. THEREAFTER, ANY IMPLIED WARRANTIES, INCLUDING IMPLIED WARRANTIES OF MERCHANTABILITY AND FITNESS FOR A PARTICULAR PURPOSE ARE EXCLUDED. THIS WARRANTY IS IN LIEU OF ALL OTHER WARRANTIES, WHETHER ORAL OR WRITTEN, EXPRESSED OR IMPLIED.

If you believe the media is defective, please return it during the ninety day period to the address shown below. A defective diskette will be replaced without charge provided that it has not been subjected to misuse or damage.

This warranty does not extend to the software or information recorded on the media. The software and information are provided "AS IS." Any statements made about the utility of the software or information are not to be considered as express or implied warranties. Delmar will not be liable for incidental or consequential damages of any kind incurred by you, the consumer, or any other user.

Some states do not allow the exclusion or limitation of incidental or consequential damages, or limitations on the duration of implied warranties, so the above limitation or exclusion may not apply to you. This warranty gives you specific legal rights, and you may also have other rights which vary from state to state.

Address all correspondence to:

Delmar Publishers
3 Columbia Circle
P. O. Box 15015
Albany, NY 12212-5015

System Requirements

Macintosh

CPU Type and Speed: Macintosh computer with a 68030 or greater processor (Power Macintosh® recommended)

Operating System: Apple ® System Software version 7.1 or later (7.1.2 or later for Power Macintosh)

Memory: 16 MB of RAM (32 MB recommended)

Hard Drive Space: 20 MB

Graphics: 8-bit (256 colors) or greater display adapter

CD-ROM Speed: 2x or better CD-ROM drive

Windows

CPU Type and Speed: Intel 486 ™, Windows NT (version 3.5.1 or later)

Memory: 16 MB of RAM (32 MB recommended)

Hard Drive Space: 25 MB

Graphics: 8-bit (256-color) or greater display adapter

CD-ROM Speed: 2x or better CD-ROM drive